CONVERGENCE OR DIVERSITY?

To the 'spirit' of the Center for European Studies,
Henrietta Grant-Peterkin

Convergence or Diversity?

Internationalization and Economic Policy Response

Edited by
BRIGITTE UNGER
Department of Economics,
Vienna University of Economics and Business Administration,
Austria

FRANS VAN WAARDEN
Department of General Social Science and
Centre for Policy and Management,
Utrecht University,
The Netherlands

Avebury
Aldershot • Brookfield USA • Hong Kong • Singapore • Sydney

© Brigitte Unger and Frans van Waarden 1995

Published by
Avebury
Ashgate Publishing Limited
Gower House
Croft Road
Aldershot
Hants GU11 3HR
England

Ashgate Publishing Company
Old Post Road
Brookfield
Vermont 05036
USA

British Library Cataloguing in Publication Data

Convergence or Diversity?
   I. Unger, Brigitte II. Waarden, Frans van
   337

   ISBN 1 85628 925 7
   JK
Library of Congress Catalog Card Number: 95-78191

Printed and bound by Athenæum Press Ltd., Gateshead, Tyne & Wear.

Contents

v

vi

Tables

BK Title:

Preface

NA

The market of Europe has become gradually more and more extensive'.
Adam Smith 'Wealth of Nations' (1776: 307).

Smith's quote could also have been a newspaper heading anno 1992. Economic internationalization is apparently not from today or yesterday. But it certainly has accelerated in recent years.

Does internationalization produce convergence? That is the research question of this book. We try to answer it here for economic policies. But it most certainly holds for academia. Increased internationalization brings together researchers from different countries, and in the process different disciplines as well. Across nations, we read each other's work and criticize it, we do joint research projects, and as a result there is a certain convergence of questions studied, of theoretical perspectives applied, and of concepts used. This book is a manifestation of such convergence between nations. Authors from six countries contribute to it: Germany, Britain, Austria, the Netherlands, Switzerland, and the USA. And they are economists, sociologists, and political scientists. They do have converged on their leading research questions, however they report on a diversity of countries and policy fields, and come to a diversity of answers and results. In the introductory chapter we have tried to summarize these findings.

The idea for the book was born at the Center for European Studies at Stanford University. In this inspiring environment the book was also completed. We are grateful to the directors, subsequently Philippe Schmitter, Hans Weiler, and Tim Josling, and in particular also to Henrietta Grant-Peterkin, the heart of the Center, for extending hospitality time and again. A first version of some of the papers was presented at the Conference of the Society for the Advancement of Socio-Economics

(SASE) at the New School for Social Research in New York in 1993. We would like to thank the participants of the three SASE-panels on convergence for their presence and comments. Thanks go also to Dan Kelemen, who revised the style of some of the papers quite substantially and who had many critical remarks. Without Henrietta Grant-Peterkin's support and patience the tables of this book would most likely still not have been printed out. In the 'Vienna phase' of the book production, Michaela Schmutzer helped us to read some of the 'illegible' computer files, with similar admirable patience. The invisible hand and tail of Daniel Eckert and Edmund Mufferl kept new relevant literature appearing on our desks. Philippe Schmitter gave sparkling comments on earlier versions, wherever he appeared on the globe. Tim Josling discussed an earlier version of this book at an Eurolunch talk at Stanford, and generously gave access to his office for its final revision. Last but not least, one of us wants to thank her sponsors, who made the joint interdisciplinary work across nations possible: the Austrian National Bank and in particular its former president Dr. Maria Schaumayer, for the fellowship which bears her name.

Our endeavor would have almost been a 'convergence to the bottom', when the infection with ideas, through our international exchanges across cyberspace, became also a real virus infection. Luckily, Christian Ragacs, always smiling, always calm, even in the face of dramatic events, helped us to salvage the final manuscript from annihilation by a hungry and malicious computer formula.

1 Introduction:
An interdisciplinary approach
to convergence

Brigitte Unger and Frans van Waarden

Policy diversity and international interdependence

Public policies differ between nations, in their goals, instruments, and styles. Some nations give high priority to social security for all, others place a higher value on personal freedom and choice, at the cost of social equality. Some nations have strict air and water pollution standards, while others are less concerned about the environment. In some countries, civil servants have large discretionary authority in policy implementation, in others they have only very limited room for maneuver. Many comparative policy studies have investigated these differences and their causes and effects. To mention just a few: full-employment policies have been compared by Schmidt 1982 and Scharpf 1984; health and health insurance policies by Döhler 1990 and Immergut 1992; and social security arrangements by Alber 1982 and Esping-Andersen 1990. Differences in implementation styles have been studied by Richardson 1982 and Vogel 1986.

Policy outcomes vary as well. Countries have different unemployment and inflation rates, crime rates, average life expectancies, traffic death rates, statutory minimum wages, and literacy and education rates.

There are many reasons for this rich diversity: geographic and demographic differences, culinary traditions, consumer preferences, culture, political ideas, political movements, voting systems, state executive decisionmaking, and authority of the courts. In general, policies and policy outcomes are the result of successive different combinations of ideas, interests, and institutions, whereby each combination prestructures new combinations at a later point of this nation's history in a path dependent way. This is what makes each nation have its specific history. Because much of policy substance, form, and outcome is linked to national cultures and institutions which are strongly rooted in history, they will be rather persistent over time. Some policies will

1

change easier than others. Those that touch the 'core' of a nation's belief system (Sabatier and Jenkins 1991) will be the most difficult to change, such as the belief that welfare state programmes are indispensable to a civilized solidaristic society.

Will this diversity in policy goals, instruments, and outcomes persist or even increase as history unfolds? Even if countries experience similar problems and contingencies, will not cultural and institutional differences make each country select its own specific policy solutions, resulting in different outcomes? Or will nation-states and their policies become more similar? Will policies converge?

One is tempted to think so, in an age of increasing economic, social, cultural, political, and legal interdependence. Technological innovations allow for much easier communications and travel across the globe, thus facilitating information exchange and joint cultural experiences. Television connects worldwide audiences, and digital traffic on the cybersuperhighway is thousands of times denser than traffic on the Los Angeles Freeways. Shared information and experiences may provide for similar consumer tastes, and multinational companies will try to enhance this through world-wide advertising. Eight hundred million people from all over the world watch the Super Bowl game at one point in time. In between they are confronted with the same commercials, and a large percentage of them will munch Italian pizza during the game and flush it down with American coke.

Modern technology has increased political interdependence with often economic consequences. A political coup in Nigeria broadcasted worldwide may send oil prices on the Rotterdam spot market up and prices on the Tokyo stock exchange down. Improved means of transportation and communication have also increased international trade and the mobility of factors of production, thus intensifying international economic competition. This is further amplified by the reduction of trade barriers through such political agreements as GATT, EU and NAFTA. The increasing importance of multinational companies provides for organizational bridges between nations, across which not only capital flows, but also labour, information, and technological know-how and patents. While worldwide information exchange *allows* for voluntary mutual learning and imitation between nations, people and their organizations and governments, worldwide competition may *force* different nations to adopt similar policies. Regulations and agreements by supranational organizations such as the UN, the IMF, the EU, and specialized agencies such as the international postal congress or the IATA do both. They facilitate voluntary learning but also compel nations to incorporate and adopt uniform international regulations.

Increased interdependence confronts nations with similar developments and problems, whether they are of a technological (e.g. more sophisticated health technology), demographic (aging, migration), economic (rising costs of the

2

welfare state), political (popularity of neo-liberalism), environmental (acid rain) or value (importance of equity) nature. Policy solutions adopted by one nation will have consequences for other ones. Hence, such increased interdependence is likely to exert pressures for convergence of national policies and their outcomes. How much these pressures will be able to influence national policies depends on how solidly national institutions and cultural preferences are ingrained in the various societies. How much do national systems of law resist incorporation of international agreements or how much do they modify them in the process of adaptation and reception? How strong are non-tariff trade barriers? How well-established are national consumer preferences, political traditions, and bureaucratic routines? Will Frenchmen ever leave their camembert for cheddar and will Japanese ever be taken to eat cheese at all? Will Germans lessen their fear of inflation?

How much convergence is there in national policies and policy outcomes under the pressure of increased international interdependence? That is the question addressed in this book. In order to keep the research problem somewhat manageable, we restrict ourselves to the field of economic policies and economic variables.

The convergence debates

Convergence has been defined in social sciences as 'the tendency of societies to grow more alike, to develop similarities in structures, processes, and performances' (Kerr 1983: 3). The term refers to a long term process, not a state. Convergence means that two variables approach each other as time elapses by either one approaching the other (weak convergence) or by both moving towards each other (strong convergence). There must be movement over time towards more similarity. This is important to stress, because the term is often used erroneously to merely indicate a state of differences and similarities rather than changes towards a common point (see e.g. Brickman, Jasanoff and Ilgen 1985).

The topic of convergence has recently gained in popularity, following the Maastricht agreement among EU Member States that some of their macroeconomic indicators should 'converge', in order for the European Monetary Union to become reality. This has increased the interest in 'convergence' in the economic literature. European integration has also influenced the comparative policy literature. The latter was originally mainly interested in studying differences and similarities between national state policies. However, economic and political integration has produced an interest in changes in these policies over time. At a more general level, the so-called globalization debate on the question whether the world is becoming one single society, has enhanced the interest in convergence as well. Furthermore, the end of the

Cold War has inspired such popular historical works as Fukuyama's (1992) 'End of History', which sees all societies converging upon the democratic-capitalist model.

However, the question of convergence of nations and their structures, policies and performances, is an old one. It keeps reappearing in politics and science, as if following some invisible cycle. The issue has been central to theory formation in most social sciences, in sociology, in economics, in political science, in policy analysis, and in law.

The various convergence debates have basically addressed three questions:

1   *What* converges? What is the substance or topic under investigation? Is there convergence, and how much and how quick do the specified variables move towards a common point or interval?

2   *Why* does or should something converge? What are the causes of convergence?

3   *How* does convergence work, what are the mechanisms or channels of convergence?

As the various disciplines study different subjects, the various disciplinary convergence debates can be distinguished by the answers they give to the first question. The subject of convergence can be:

a   a complete social system (in sociology);

b   only one segment of society, such as the economy, the political structure, or the legal system (in the respective disciplines)

c   policies of social actors, in particular state agencies (the subject of the policy sciences).

In this section we will discuss the various convergence debates. In the following one, the causes of convergence, the answer to the 'why' question, are discussed. The subsequent fourth section has as its topic the third question, the channels or mechanisms of convergence.

System convergence

The term 'convergence' has been used often to refer to 'system convergence', the growing together of whole societies, the developed and developing, the industrialized and industrializing, the democratic and totalitarian, the capitalist

4

and socialist. It has been the topic of the overarching non-specialized social science, sociology. The classics of sociology, writing at a time when most European societies experienced industrialization, urbanization, secularization, state formation, and imperialism, all had implicit or explicit theories of convergence as part of their theories of modernization. Toennies perceived a change from 'Gemeinschaft' to 'Gesellschaft'. Durkheim saw an increase in the societal division of labour and feared the replacement of organic by mechanical solidarity, resulting in anomia. Marx predicted increasing tensions between the forces and relations of production, a gradual lowering in profit rates and eventually the end of capitalism. Weber observed a general rationalization and bureaucratization of state and society, and Spengler predicted the *Untergang des Abendlandes*. The classic authors also identified causes and mechanisms of convergence. Marx saw these in the innate dialectical logic of capitalist development, which spurred the development of the forces of production (that is, technology). Spencer's theory of social darwinism stressed the importance of the forces of competition and selection, leading to a survival of the fittest, the 'one best way' in institutions, policies, and performance.

Theories of system convergence were not only popular among sociologists but among economists as well. Marx has already been mentioned. The Austrians had a 'right' prediction for any turn of history. Schumpeter forecasted like Marx the 'end to capitalism', while his compatriot Hayek predicted the 'impossibility of socialism'. This thesis is again en vogue as demonstrated by Fukuyama's work.

The Postwar period saw a revival of convergence theories. Fukuyama's thesis is a somewhat modified version of the modernization theories of the 1960s and 1970s. Then, authors such as Tinbergen (1959), Bell (1960), Aron (1962, 1968), Ellul (1964), Kerr, Dunlop, Harbison and Myers (1960, 1973), Kerr (1983), Galbraith (1971), and Inkeles (1981) predicted the 'end of ideology', as Fukuyama prophesies now the 'end of history'. These authors argued that the ideological and structural distinctions between communism and capitalism would gradually disappear. Countries in east and west would develop into more or less similar 'industrial societies'. The global spread of technology, industrialization and economic growth would confront all countries with similar imperatives. Technology and investments would require more and longer term private and public planning by 'technostructures' (Galbraith 1971). Market failures in capitalism would require capitalist states to intervene more and more in society and to develop welfare states. State failures in communism would require such states to allow for more market and more democracy in their systems. There might be differences in timing, some nations being ahead in this development towards 'industrial society', others following later. However, all would go sooner or later through a similar set of 'stages of economic growth' (Rostow 1968). The uniform

5

imperatives of growth and technology would make ideological distinctions irrelevant and class differences would disappear. The convergence proponents strongly believed in harmony and in technological determinism.

However, such perspectives have been more popular in certain periods than in others. The 1960s, with attention for similarities and convergence, were followed by the 1970s and 1980s with more attention for international differences and divergence. Goldthorpe (1984) attacked the stratification studies of the earlier modernization theories and argued that class differences still matter in capitalism, making convergence with socialism less likely. Fordism was no longer seen as the dominant industrial model for west as well as east. Kern and Schumann (1976) demonstrated empirically that technology did not have the unifying effect it has often been presumed to have. First of all, technological development tended to increase the level of required skills for higher level jobs, but to decrease them for lower level ones, resulting in a divergence in skill requirements, working conditions, and workers' consciousness. Secondly, such effects of technology differed by sector. Implicit here was the further argument that, as different societies have different sectoral portfolios, technology would affect various societies differently, thus leading to divergence, rather than convergence.

Several other studies in the volume edited by Goldthorpe pertain to the political organization of classes and emphasized the differences between corporatist and pluralist systems, thus at least complicating the simple dichotomy of capitalism and socialism in the earlier convergence theories.

In the 1990s, the convergence thesis has again gained in popularity, owing to the perceived globalization, the end of the Cold War, and the political integration in supranational organizations as the EU and GATT. European integration has become a field in itself, in which economic and policy convergence plays an even more important role than system convergence. As this book deals with economic policy, we will outline shortly the economic and policy convergence debates.

Economic convergence

Convergence in economics refers to convergence of economic variables, such as interest rates, inflation or unemployment, indicators which can also be seen as economic policy outcomes. There has been considerable disagreement as to convergence in the various theories. For every convergence theory there is an opposing divergence theory.

Three mechanisms for convergence can be identified in various approaches in economics: technology, competition, and political enforcement (see the section on mechanisms of convergence). Neoclassical growth theory expects convergence of living standards and productivity between poor and rich countries through the diffusion of similar technology. International Trade

6

Theory stresses the convergence of factor prices (wages, interest rates) and good prices as a result of trade. The latest newcomer in the convergence debate is 'Maastricht convergence'. The Maastricht Treaty sets criteria for inflation rates, nominal interest rates, budget deficits, and public debts, to which Member States are supposed to converge in order for them to be allowed to join the planned European Monetary Union. If convergence should take place, it will be partly the result of this political enforcement.

Neoclassical growth theory expects convergence through the channel of imitation. Poor countries will imitate the technology and know how of rich countries. Modern technology will diffuse worldwide. By taking advantage of Kuznets' 'transnationally available stock of useful knowledge' and by replacing their entire capital stock with the latest high tech capital stock of developed countries, poor countries should eventually 'catch-up'.

Abramovitz (1986) showed that 'falling behind and forging ahead' instead of 'catching up' of income and growth will occur, if poor countries are unable to use the foreign technology due to 'social inabilities'. Poor countries will *not* catch up, if they cannot implement the technology of the rich countries on a one to one basis, e.g. because labour skills differ. Kuznets' 'stock of knowledge' can then simply not be extracted by the poor. Thus the convergence theory of growth rates found its divergence counterpart.

While growth theory sees convergence by means of imitation of technological progress, International Trade Theory expects convergence through market forces, trade, and competition. The neoclassical factor price equalization theorem states that interest rates, profit rates, wages, prices, and income will converge due to the mobility of factors of production and the mobility of goods and services. Instantaneous, perfectly flexible reactions of market participants will guarantee arbitrage in all fields. Financial capital goes to the highest interest rates. Physical capital goes to the highest profits. Thus resulting in a convergence of interest rates and profit rates. Labour goes to the highest wages and entrepreneurs to the lowest wages. Their claims meet at the international market clearing wage rate. If wages are below the equilibrium rate, labour would go abroad, if wages are above the equilibrium rate, capital would abandon the high-wage country. As a consequence, wages will converge due to market forces. If factors of production are somehow prohibited from smoothly flowing across borders, than the mobility of goods will bring about convergence. Consumers buy from the cheapest offer of goods. Goods prices across countries will thus converge. And since labour and technology are incorporated in goods, wages and profit rates will converge as a consequence of trade in goods.

A consequence of this overall mobility of factors and goods is that economic policies are constrained by exogenously internationally given prices, wages and interest rates. Thus policies are either impotent or forced to be the same across countries. They have to converge. The convergence hypothesis proclaims a smooth, automatic adjustment of economic outcomes and as a consequence also of economic policies.

For every convergence hypothesis there is one of divergence. It usually stresses some imperfections and frictions. International Trade Theory of factor price equalization and income adjustment was criticized most prominently by Krugman (see Dehesa and Krugman 1992). He showed that convergence by means of trade depends on two crucial assumptions: the same efficiency in production among countries, and constant returns to scale. Differences in efficiency may prevent physical capital from flowing from the rich to the poor countries. If capital flows to the rich, this would widen the gap of income differentials. Falling behind and forging ahead instead of catching up and convergence would be the outcome, due to differences in efficiency in production.

Economies of scale tend to promote agglomerations. Firms tend to cluster, to be close to markets. Reduced barriers to trade make it also profitable for firms to concentrate production in a few locations to achieve economies of scale. It has been indicated that seen from an airplane, Europe at night looks like a 'blue banana', with blue lights stretching from Milan to Copenhagen, rather than being evenly spread over Europe as in the shape of a grape (Dehesa and Krugman 1992). Thus regional disparities seem to become greater, rather than smaller, as trade theory would predict.

Financial capital does not behave well either. According to neoclassical theory, capital will go to the highest interest rates, provided that exchange rate risks are subtracted. Arbitrage will lead to a convergence of interest rates. Differences in interest rates only account for the risk. Due to diminishing returns, poor countries have higher returns than rich countries. Capital should thus flow from the rich to the poor. But capital flows systematically from the poor to the rich countries. Financial capital follows expectations and primarily creates speculative waves instead of intertemporal smooth adjustment. Political risk and inefficient production in many poor countries make it unattractive for investors to place their capital there, even though interest rates are exorbitantly high and put poor countries in financial and economic crisis.

Labour mobility neither satisfies the assumption of international trade theory. Convergence of wages is to be expected, if labour mobility is high. But labour mobility is very limited due to linguistic, cultural, and social barriers. Sassen in this volume casts doubt upon economists' assumption of a clear causal relationship between labour mobility and convergence of economic outcomes. If labour mobility is not exogenous but is itself dependent on capital mobility, if higher profits and not higher wages induce higher labour mobility, if migration policies increase migration instead of stopping it, divergence of wages and incomes is to be expected.

8

Even if factors are immobile, the Stolper-Samuelson theorem would claim that convergence would, nevertheless, be the outcome. Prices would converge as a consequence of trade (all sorts of transportation and other transaction costs would still allow for differences in prices). Wages and incomes would also converge, since (immobile) capital and labour are incorporated in mobile goods. Immobile factors cross borders in their transformed version as commodities. However, critics would stress that trade does not take place by means of free and unlimited competition on markets. As Bellak shows in this volume, only one-third of worldwide trade is really free trade. The rest is managed trade and trade by the hierarchies of multinational firms. That is, non-market institutions determine trade.

Economic convergence theories usually refer to the real outcome of economic policy, to the convergence of real variables (physical measurable variables), like real income distribution or growth of real GDP. Convergence of nominal variables was never an economic issue, since poverty, structural inequalities, or disparities of income were the long term economic concerns. Only recently, since the planned Monetary Union of Maastricht, did the convergence of nominal variables (inflation rates, nominal interest rates) become an issue. We will refer to these as 'Maastricht convergence'. The problem with this is that a theory, explaining why convergence of such variables should take place and through which mechanisms this should occur, is (still) lacking. As indicated, real convergence is mainly an issue in two fields of economics: in growth theory, and in international trade theory. In the latter the openness of the economy, barriers to trade, mobility of goods and factors explain convergence or divergence. In both theories convergence is the outcome of increased interdependence and market forces and not a prerequisite for integration to take place.

Maastricht convergence, which imposes convergence criteria on countries wanting to join the currency club, addresses a third channel of convergence. Here convergence is not the result of imitation of technology or of market forces, but the result of political norms and political enforcement. This form of convergence is of course not new, as throughout history states have invaded other states and imposed their culture, religion, or language on the conquered. In economics, however, this concept is new. For the first time in economics, convergence of economic outcomes should be realized through policy and enforcement, rather than through imitation or market forces.

'Maastricht convergence' has a much shorter time horizon (1997 or 1999) than real convergence. It, furthermore, does not have an explicit theory. The Maastricht criteria are quite arbitrary. The fiscal norms, for example, were set according to the status quo of the year they were decided in, and turned out to be unfeasible in the years of crisis that followed. By 1994 no country fulfilled the Maastricht criteria anymore (see Buiter 1992, who heavily criticizes them).

9

The idea behind 'Maastricht convergence' is that a monetary union should be a low-inflation union. Therefore, countries should be forced by means of nominal variable convergence to keep inflation low. The price a high inflation country has to pay in order to bring inflation down can be many years of recession, high unemployment and real dispersion. Maastricht convergence can thus lead to divergence of real variables and to increased inequalities in welfare, since the price, which countries have to pay for it, differs. The trade-off between different variables is a concern in the convergence debate. If nominal variables are forced to converge, real variables will have to bear the full burden of adjustment. Is seems as if Delors himself does not believe in economic convergence by means of competition and had to enforce it by means of Maastricht criteria. This shows, that the planned currency union is inherently unstable. Europe is no optimal currency area (Eichengreen 1991). Free riding of countries joining the currency club is obviously feared by those in favour of convergence criteria (Unger in this volume). Thus problems of collective action seem more important than traditional economic causes for the convergence of such economic policies and policy outcomes.

Policy convergence

Whereas sociologists have studied the convergence of nation states, and economists the convergence of macroeconomic indicators, policy analysts have analyzed the policies with which policymakers try to affect society and economy. The macroeconomic indicators with which economists have been concerned, can be considered not only 'outcomes' of economic processes, but also 'outcomes of public policy'.

Comparative policy analysis has originally been much more interested in cross-national comparisons than in cross-temporal ones. Hence, the question of convergence has figured less prominently in this literature. Policy analysts have typically taken a single universal problem, and then analyzed how different nations have reacted to them. Such problems have been the demand for welfare provisions, the fiscal crisis of the state making such provisions more problematic, rising unemployment, the arms race, the new poverty, increase in crime, or in air and water pollution. They have found that nations react differently, in policy goals, instruments, and styles. On the basis of these findings, various policy typologies have been made. Sometimes, such cross-national comparisons at one point in time have been used to make inferences as to convergence. Thus some authors have mistakenly interpreted differences between national policies as an indication of divergence.

There are however also a number of studies which have traced the development of policies of different states over time. Dye has compared policies of the fifty American states over time and has found some convergence. Waltman and Studlar (1987) investigated whether the entry of neo-conservative governments produced a convergence of policies in the US and Britain. Döhler (1990) did the same for the neo-conservative health policies of Britain and Germany, and Grande (1989) for French and German telecommunication policies. Vogel (1986) studied convergence of US and British environmental policy, O'Connor (1988) studied welfare policies of OECD countries over time, and Bennett (1988) data protection policies. The overall results have been somewhat inconclusive. Convergence here, divergence there. The neo-conservative 'change' in politics of the early 1980s however did not produce the convergence, expected by the authors.

Comparative policy analysis stresses the importance of the distinction between policies and their outcomes. Outcomes and policy goals and instruments may be only loosely related. They do not all have to converge. It is very well conceivable that governments share similar goals, but choose different instruments, and produce different outcomes. Actually, policy goals are often indeed similar, at least at a relative general level. Many governments try to stimulate economic growth, reduce unemployment, keep inflation low, fight pollution and drug abuse, and minimize teenage pregnancies. Of course, the relative importance of such goals may differ, especially since there are trade-offs between some of these goals. Low inflation can increase real wages and produce high unemployment, low unemployment can lead to higher wage claims and consecutively higher inflation, high growth can go at the cost of a clean environment, etc.

Goals such as 'increasing the welfare of the nation' shared by all governments at a general level, can turn out to be quite different when a concrete policy choice has to be made. Especially when it comes to choosing instruments, policies can be quite different. Political and administrative cultures may exclude certain policy options. Some European governments may fight teenage pregnancies by making abortion and/or birth control information readily available, even at school. American culture does not allow for this. Instead, some economic advisors in the US even urge the government to reduce welfare benefits to unwed mothers. Their underlying assumption is that teenage girls make a free rational choice between getting pregnant (and cash in on welfare benefits) and not getting pregnant. If the costs of raising a child exceed welfare benefits, their cost-benefit analysis would restrain teenagers from getting pregnant. This measure of 'birth control' by cutting welfare expenditures in turn would be unacceptable in Europe.

Such different measures produce different outcomes. Teenage pregnancies are much more common in the US than in most European countries. However, it is also imaginable that different instruments produce nevertheless similar results. Conversely, similar instruments may produce different results. Some countries may be more successful with comparable instruments than others. Thus unemployment rates may still differ substantially, although different governments try to reduce it by the same budget measures.

Policy analyses have shown that convergence can be different regarding policy and their output. Vogel (1986) argued that although British and American governments chose quite different instruments and followed different styles in environmental policy, nevertheless the outcome in terms of reduction of pollution was more or less the same. Waltman and Studlar (1987) found a convergence on policy goals, but differences on policy content for a variety of industrial, social, and health policy areas. Bennett (1988) demonstrated a convergence on content (basic principles) of data protection policy, but a divergence in chosen policy instruments. In our study, Thomasberger shows that monetary policies of European countries converge, but that, nevertheless, policy outcomes in terms of interest and inflation rates differ substantially. Heritier, by contrast, demonstrates that environmental policies of Britain and Germany differ but converge towards higher levels of environmental protection outcome.

The pressures of internationalization

Policies do not change easily, as policy preferences are often rooted in systems of institutions. The more policy substances, procedures or intended outcomes affect the core of such institutions and cultural values, the stronger the resistance to change will be. For the very basic policy preferences, major shocks are often required to induce change, such as war, revolution, or major economic depressions, may be required to induce change (Crozier 1964, Lehmbruch 1987).

Although not a sudden event, such as war or revolution, the ongoing and increasing economic and political internationalization could be just such a force to elicit policy change and possibly policy convergence. That it will have effects seems certain. This begs further questions: On what policies and policy choices will it have effects? How much? Towards convergence or further diversity?

And does internationalization *force* convergence? Is it a deterministic contingency? Or does it leave room for choice regarding change? Will nations that do not adapt their policies loose out in international competition and perform poorer? Is it a matter of survival of the fittest? Of adaptation or dying? These questions have a rich tradition in social science. The dichotomy between determinism and voluntarism or choice has been a major dividing line between theoretical schools, between functionalism and marxism on the one hand and symbolic interactionism and phenomenology on the other. Social darwinism was one of the early approaches in sociology, it is the dominant paradigm in economics, and it has recently reemerged in population ecology in organizational sociology. In their generality these basic questions cannot really be answered.

The answers depend among others on what is meant by internationalization. The concept is often used as synonymous with several others, notably interdependence, globalization, and integration. These represent however different phenomena, which will affect policy diversity in different ways. It will be useful to disentangle them here.

Internationalization is a *process* that refers to the increase of contact between nations, to the transcending of national borders. If it concerns nations all over the globe, one speaks of globalization. However, this term is also used metaphorically, to indicate a worldwide orientation of individuals - global man - or of cities - global cities. This contact can be economic, political, scientific, technological, social, or cultural. Economic internationalization means more economic contact between countries, that is, greater cross-border flows of information, financial capital, physical capital (production plants), labour, goods and services. Political internationalization implies more political contact between nations, political ideas cross borders, politicians look over the border, etc. Countries link their political and military fate to that of others, and, adjust their policies to those of their neighbors. Internationalization, which is a process, may result from and increase interdependence, which is a *state of being*.

Interdependence does not necessarily require or produce similarity. On the contrary. Man and woman are interdependent, as are employer and employee, precisely because they are dissimilar. Interdependence between nations may even produce greater differences, as nations specialize in a worldwide division of labour. However, interdependence may also enhance competition between nations in similar fields, and this competition may force them to act similarly or become more alike.

Integration is somewhat different from internationalization. Integration refers, given the latin term from which it stems (latin: integrare, produce a unity), to *a process* that aims at producing a unit. If this unit is a supranational one, nation-states partake in it. If it is a nation, regions partake in it. It can be an economic unit, such as a customs union, a common market, or a common currency area. An economic unit which is worldwide is a global unit. The supranational unit can also be political, then we speak of political integration (and most economic units have the form of a political and legal unit). Countries can agree, in formal treaties, to establish supra-national political units, such as the NATO or the EU, in which they partake and to which they may surrender part of their sovereignty. The process of integration usually has a planned beginning, but the outcome may be uncertain, go its own way. As Philippe Schmitter once put it in a talk, 'integration is like a bicycle, once you have started, you cannot stop it anymore. To stop it would be similar to trying to stand still on a bicycle'.

13

Integration can enhance differences, as Member States of the larger unit could develop a division of labour among themselves. It can however also produce similarities, as the members agree to certain common regulations with which they have to comply and to which they have to adjust their specific policies.

Economic pressures on national policies: internationalization and economic integration

Economic pressures on national policies stem from increased economic internationalization, and from more advanced economic integration.

Economic internationalization is increasing, due to the higher mobility of factors of production and goods. The breakdown of barriers to mobility, such as national regulations, allows financial capital to cross borders at an almost unlimited speed. The mere push of a button on a computer can transfer financial capital all over the globe. Physical capital is less mobile, as it is more tied to sales markets, proximity to raw materials markets, and the availability of qualified labour and transport facilities. Nevertheless, the number of multinational and transnational enterprises and the speed with which firms change their location has also increased over the time. Bellak's contribution shows that Foreign Direct Investment - an indicator of physical capital mobility - has increased dramatically since the 1980s.

Labour mobility - the amount and speed with which workers move across national borders - has also increased, though to a still lesser degree. It certainly is much lower than capital mobility. Furthermore, labour mobility is not a homogenous flow across countries. It is institutionally, historically and culturally embedded. Whatever there is in terms of labour mobility follows specific patterns. Sassen's contribution shows that labour mobility takes place within specific segments of the labour market, is restricted to specific historical phases, and occurs typically between a limited set of countries and thus affects some countries more than others. That is, it creates divergence. Furthermore, migration streams between countries are often created by transnational and multinational corporations (MNCs). They create networks. People in the host country come to know the culture and opportunities of the MNCs country of origin and come to consider it as a potential migration country. Bridges between the two countries are built. Interestingly enough, immigrants originate from countries which receive foreign aid, investment, and exports of consumer goods. Measures commonly thought to deter immigration seem to have had precisely the opposite effect.

Trade of goods and services between countries has also increased very much. As Bellak shows in this volume, international trade currently amounts to 4.5 trillion USD. However, about two-thirds of world trade is managed trade and intrafirm trade by multinational and transnational enterprises.

14

Beside economic internationalization *economic integration*, that is, the cooperation of nation-states in larger units, may put pressure on national economic policies. Economic integration facilitates internationalization processes and can occur to various degrees. A rather limited form is a free trade area, such as the EFTA, where trade restrictions and tariffs are removed only within the union. A customs union goes further, establishing a common unique tariff for countries outside the union. Step three is a common market with a common competition policy. A still higher level of integration is an economic union which demolishes borders for labour, capital, goods, and services and establishes a common economic policy at a supranational level. The highest stage of integration is the planned monetary union, step three of the Delors-plan. This entails the abandoning of national currencies. It is explicitly made conditional upon the convergence of budget deficits, debt-output ratios, interest rates and inflation rates, the so-called Maastricht criteria. Here convergence becomes a precondition for integration, a reverse of the normal pattern. However, the fixing of these criteria produces political pressure to realize such convergence through policy measures.

Economic pressures and state competition

Will these common pressures of economic internationalization and integration lead to more similar economic policies and policy outcomes? Most countries undergo the pressures of these increases in flows of capital, labour, and goods. Through these flows they come more in contact with each other and have to compete for the same pool of production factors, goods, and markets. They are under pressure to attract or keep capital, labour, and markets for their goods and services. As a large share of international trade takes place within multinational companies, countries are also under pressure to compete for the location of such enterprises. Their competitive position in the world economy will depend in large part on their economic policies and policy outcomes. Do they have a secure currency, low inflation, a good infrastructure of transport and communications, pleasant living conditions, low costs of living, high wages (to attract labour) or low wages (to attract capital), qualified labour, educational institutions, research and development facilities, attractive tax regimes, few regulations that bother industry, and whatever else goes in the making of the competitive position of nations? As international competition increases, so will the pressure to compete with other nation-states. Nations will have to adjust their economic policies and the chance is great that these policies will become more similar, especially in their substance. Countries may try to offer similar infrastructures, tax regimes, inflation rates, wage levels, and regulations. Economics predicts that

15

increased factor mobility should bring about a levelling of economic indicators, such as prices, inflation, unemployment, and profit rates.

Insofar as convergence could take place, there are contrasting hypotheses as to at what level this will happen. First there is the *thesis* that internationalization will produce a *'race to the bottom'*, i.e. a convergence at a low level of regulation. A competing one is that of convergence at a high level of protective regulation, a *'race to the top'*. It will be discussed in the next section.

The more well-known thesis of the 'race to the bottom' implies that countries will try to surpass each other with lower wage levels, lower costs of social security, and less regulatory restrictions to business. Conservatives saw this as the great attraction of the European Common Market. Former British prime-minister Thatcher called it the 'greatest deregulation operation in history'. The financial speaker of the social democrats in the Austrian parliament, Ewald Nowotny, concurred: 'Obviously, this is a race to the bottom. And obviously the one wins this race who is more mobile, better informed or also more ruthless. Hence it is likely that this will be capital (notably financial capital) rather than labour, the large enterprise rather than the small, and actors with low social and ecological morals rather than responsible businessmen.' (translated from Nowotny in *Der Standard*, November 1994)

There are however a number of qualifications to this theory of social dumping. First a specific one, as to economic integration. Formal integration as in the European Union, does not immediately become economic reality. That what exists de jure, does not immediately also exist de facto. The legal establishment of the 'four freedoms' does not automatically create high factor and product mobility across borders.

Mobility is in many cases still limited. Capital may flow relatively easy, when regulatory restrictions are removed. But mobility of goods has limits. Some products are more mobile than others. For construction products, perishable goods, and human services it is often difficult to separate the location of production from the location of consumption. This seriously restricts the mobility of these goods and services.

A study by the Dutch Social Economic Council (SER-COB 1994) found that physical capital mobility was even low in official European border regions (Euregio's) between Germany and the Netherlands, where the state authorities cooperate across borders and try to stimulate similar cooperation in private business. The survey showed that Dutch businessmen look hardly over the border for business (Van Houtum en Van Kerkhoff 1994, Corvers and Dankbaar 1994). Problems with language, legal regimes, differences in mentality and product preference - coupled with product specialization of firms - seem to limit mobility.

16

Still more limited is the mobility of labour, except for some very specific, very high and very low skilled jobs. Even in the United States, with a more homogeneous working population, which speaks basically the same language, labour mobility is not unlimited. Wage and unemployment rates still differ significantly and do not automatically trigger 'compensating' flows of labour (Dye 1991). Unemployment rates by state varied in 1991 between 10.5 per cent in West Virginia and 2.7 per cent in Nebraska. In Europe, the barriers to migration are much higher. Labour mobility in Europe is about one-third of the US. Unemployment rates in the European Union differ between 23.8 per cent for Spain and 6.0 per cent for Portugal (OECD 1993). Another indication is the low intercountry mobility of self-employed craftsmen, in principle some of the more mobile workers. Between 1966 and 1987, 807,275 craft businesses were founded in Germany, but only 2,754 of them were by artisans from other Member States, that is less than 0.5 per cent of all new establishments (Grote 1992: 162). Most of these were temporary businesses by artisans from across the border. Of the 495 artisans from other Member States registered with the Handwerk Chambers in 1991, 86 per cent came from the neighboring countries Denmark and the Netherlands, and 91 per cent of the permissions concerned building trades, where mobility is relatively high, but often also temporary (Heck 1993: 14). The number of authorizations has been rather stable over the last twenty-seven years (Heck 1993: 14).

A second qualification to the theory of a race to the bottom is that not all countries are equally affected by the pressures of internationalization. As indicated, labour mobility occurs typically between specific supplying and receiving countries. Furthermore, the dependence of the various nation-states on foreign trade varies. The degree of openness of the economy to world markets varies between ten per cent of exports to GDP for the US, to about sixty percent for some European countries like the Netherlands. Hence countries are not all affected to the same degree. This could also vary the pressure for convergence.

Thirdly, wage levels, regulations and state expenditures are not as malleable as presumed. They serve specific purposes and interests, such as labour and environmental protection, which cannot be neglected for electoral reasons. What is more, they are often also in the interest of business. It is not quite so clear what makes up a good competitive position in world markets. There is often a trade-off between facilities. Lower wages may attract foreign enterprises, however, the resultant lower qualification levels of personnel may keep them away. There is a similar trade-off between lower taxes and less infrastructural facilities, or between less environmental regulation and a worse image with consumers. As the contribution by Mosley empirically shows, if all aspects that are favourable for business are taken into account, it is not so clear anymore, which country is the most attractive for business' locations.

17

Legal and political integration

Internationalization goes very often hand in hand with political and legal integration. The breakdown of barriers to trade and factor mobility between countries is mostly the result of political intervention: the conclusion of international treaties, such as the GATT, the NAFTA and the EU. These treaties, and their later elaborations and additions, also contain a number of rules of the game for international economic relations. First of all to steer and facilitate free international trade, such as anti-cartel, anti-trust, and anti-dumping provisions. Secondly, more and more they will also contain compensations - in the form of supranational regulations - for the breakdown of non-tariff trade barriers. This is in particular the case in the European Union. European law has and is striking down national regulations which are considered to function as non-tariff barriers to trade. As more and more national regulations get invalidated, pressure has been mounting in the Member States to replace such national regulations with supranational ones. This has led to a veritable flood of regulations and directives from the European Commission. Political conflict is over the level of protection of this legislation. Should it be high or low? Countries which themselves have high levels of protection press for adoption of their norms by the EU. Such political integration - and political competition between Member States within this supranational unit - could fuel a counterhypothesis, that of a 'race to the top', rather than to the bottom, i.e. to a convergence at a high level of protective regulation.

The effects of political integration may still go further. In the case of the European Union, integration entails the creation or emergence of new supranational state institutions, a legal system, a High Court, a system of government, administrative structures and traditions, and so on. This is likely to induce considerable institutional change at the national level. Member States loose part of their sovereignty. They become subject to EU-law and to Decisions of the Court and the Commission. Countries which never before knew judicial review (the assessment of the constitutionality of legislation by a constitutional court), like Britain and the Netherlands, are being confronted with it now. Vertical policy integration and cooperation becomes a necessity as EU-executive agencies have to work closely together with national agencies. The latter have to implement directives from Brussels. State formation has always been closely linked with institution building. Most national state institutions date back to the orginal phases of state formation. Something similar could happen now with supranational state building. And that may also affect national policies in substance, form, and outcomes.

European integration is in particular legal integration. It has considerable consequences for national legal systems. European law gives nation-states much to do. More than seventy per cent of all laws that passed the Dutch

18

parliament in 1992 were implementations of EU regulations and directives. Nevertheless, even legal integration does not affect all Member States equally. As Bogdandy (1993: 55) points out, numerous requirements of the Single European Act of 1986 and of the Treaty on European Union (Maastricht Treaty) of 1992 allow for differentiated integration in many subfields. A 'Europe of several speeds' could be the outcome, according to Bogdandy. Thus there may turn out to be political, economic, and social constraints to legal integration. That makes it more uncertain what the effects regarding convergence will be.

Given the competing hypotheses as to the effects of economic internationalization on national policies, these should be subject to investigation. That is what the authors in this volume do. Will there be a 'race to the bottom' or not? Or will there be a 'race to the top'?

Mechanisms of convergence

The third question related to convergence, mentioned in section 2, is the 'how' question. If internationalization does lead to policy convergence, how does this happen? How is the relation between these variables mediated? What are the processes, mechanisms or channels by which convergence takes place?

International competition and supranational law are forces that exert pressure on policies. But these forces do not unambiguously dictate what policy goals and instruments should be chosen. There is no simple determinism here. Perceptions and choices of policymakers are in between. Policymakers have to perceive that they are in competition with other nations, they have to estimate the seriousness of this threat. They have to perceive what the competitive advantages of their competitors are. Less regulations? But which ones specifically? Which are considered by international business to be such a serious hindrance that it would prevent them from investing in this country? Policymakers furthermore have to identify their own competitive advantages, how strong they are, and whether, why, and in which direction they have to be changed. Where supranational regulations are concerned, interpretations of these may vary, a.o. because the wording may mean different things to policymakers socialized in different legal systems and different administrative and political environments. Differences in interpretation may not only concern the substance of the regulation, but also the importance, the pressing nature of it. Furthermore, standards of what effective implementation of such supranational regulations is, may differ. Policymakers also have to appraise the possibilities for such change, whether the institutioanl surroundings allow for that, how much opposition there will be to such change. They will have to acquire knowledge about how the policy goals, e.g. lower inflation or less crime, can best be realized, what the causal relations between goals, instruments, and outcomes are. There are usually significant uncertainties involved here or there is disagreement in politics and/or in science about what the most effective and efficient means are to realize the policy goals.

All these perceptions, estimations, ambiguities, and limited knowledge produce uncertainties and room for choice. The pressures for convergence do not automatically dictate the policies. The perceptions and choices are guided by a variety of factors: ideological preferences of policymakers, research and information facilities they may have at their disposal, the structure of decisionmaking, e.g. monocratic or collegiate, etc. As far as pressures of internationalization are concerned, the international environment may also influence the choices, such as examples from abroad, the clearness of success of competing nations, or information acquired from foreign policymakers.

Bennett (1991) distinguished four mechanisms by which policymakers from different nations may influence each other: emulation, elite networking or policy communities, harmonization, and penetration. Harmonization is not really a channel through which information and pressures pass. It is more or less the same as the creation of European law, what we consider a 'force' for convergence, rather than a channel. The other three are useful distinctions.

With *emulation* Bennett means imitation.

> The central characteristic of emulation is the utilization of evidence about a programme or programmes from overseas and a drawing of lessons from that experience. ... In the emulation of policy goals, the policy of another country is employed as an exemplar or model which is then adapted and, one would hope, improved upon. (1991: 221).

Such emulation takes place through contact between policymakers of different nations. Political integration will certainly facilitate such contacts, as civil servants from different nations are often involved in the preparation of policy at the supranational level. *Elite networking* involves 'a transnational group of actors sharing motivation, expertise, and information about a common problem', whose members 'then go forth to "spread the word" to their respective societies and governments' (1991: 224-5). While emulation, imitation, learning, and elite networking are voluntary and cooperative processes, Bennett's last category, *penetration*, involves force by external actors. Multinational companies may function - like transnational elites of policymakers - as bridges for information and expertise, but may in addition put pressure upon national governments to adjust their national policies to that of others. They may want similar technical and safety standards for their products, or they may challenge protectionist measures of other or their own states in court. These external actors may even 'participate in the selection of goals, the allocation of costs, and the mobilization of resources and capabilities in the domestic policy process' (Siegel and Weinberg 1977: 67, quoted in Bennett 1991: 227).

Bennett's (1991) typology seems interesting for further research. We do think however that emulation should be more clearly distinguished from learning (one can learn also from another's mistakes and do the opposite of imitating) and that harmonization is not a proper channel. Since most papers of this volume do not provide sufficient information on Bennett's channels, we distinguish for the sake of comparison not between such channels but between the following mechanisms of convergence: (a) market force, (b) imitation, and (c) enforcement. Countries may be mutually influenced through exchange, trade, mobility of production factors, i.e. market forces. Alternatively, they may imitate each other. Thirdly, policy change may be the result of coercion, a variety on Bennett's concept of penetration, but including also coercion by other nation-states. This not infrequently practiced process is somewhat different from enforcement by third actors such as multinationals.

Differences in convergence by policy fields

The balance of forces pro and contra convergence is likely to differ between policy fields. Just as the degree of policy diversity may differ between fields, so will their susceptibility to change. Some policy fields will be more affected by international competition or by supranational regulation than others. The resistance to change will also vary. Policy fields differ in their degree of institutionalization. And one may hypothesize that the stronger the institutionalization, the more persistent policy styles and networks should be. In 'old' policy fields, e.g. agriculture, with long standing regulations, well fixed in law, with old administrative traditions, and established organized interests, change will be more difficult, than in 'newer' ones, such as environmental policy, where regulations are still more flexible, policy networks more open, and state agencies more open to learning (Naßmacher 1991: 205 ff). Because of such expected differences between policy fields we have selected a variety of policy fields in this study, to investigate the effects of internationalization.

There are many typologies of policy fields, such as Lowi's (1964) famous distinction between distributive, redistributive, and regulatory policies. This is somewhat similar to the older, and for economic policy more useful typology of Musgrave (1959), who distinguishes between policies for allocation/regulation, distribution, and stabilization. These correspond to the three main functions, Musgrave attributed to the public sector: allocation, distribution, and stabilization.

The allocative or regulatory function refers to the correction of market failures. The state attempts to correct the market allocation of factors and goods, either indirectly, by influencing relative prices (e.g. through subsidies) or directly, through administrative regulations, such as price controls or quality standards. Where public goods and positive externalities would not be supplied by the market at all or not in sufficient amounts, the state reallocates resources into their production. Where markets would produce negative externalities, such as those affecting the environment, the state reallocates resources into the avoidance of their production. Every allocative correction of market results has, as a 'by-product', also distributional effects, but they are not the main concern of regulatory state intervention. Chapters dealing with the allocative function of the state are those by Bellak on industrial policy, Sassen on migration policy, Keller on labour relations, Eichener on workplace safety and health regulations, and Heritier and Kelemen on environmental policy.

The second role of the state is distribution. Even if market allocation produces optimal results, the outcome can be inacceptable from a moral or social point of view. Poverty and great social inequalities may be the result. The state tries to influence income distribution first of all through the budget, i.e. taxes and government expenditures. Wage bargaining policy is not only an allocative but also an important distributional instrument (since it determines the distribution of income between labour and capital), as is social security policy. The latter determines among others the distribution between the younger and the older generation. Kitzmantel and Moser deal with tax policy, Mosley, and Hemerijck and Bakker discuss welfare state policies, and Engbersen anti-poverty regimes.

The allocative function of the state - though highly contested in degree - has been recognized as long as there is economic theory. Adam Smith listed already a long set of allocative state tasks. Distribution became an issue only in the nineteenth century, notably in the work of Karl Marx. Recognition of a role of the state in stabilizing the economy is a more recent phenomenon. Keynes was the first to claim for systematic state intervention to dampen business cycles and to prevent unemployment. (Though mercantilist state spending policy was certainly in line with some of his suggestions.) The primary means of intervention should be fiscal and monetary policy. During boom periods the state should be restrictive, by tightening the budget and increasing interest rates. During recession it should increase budget deficits and lower interest rates to stimulate the economy. Thomasberger on monetary policy and Unger on budget policy analyze the state's role in stabilizing the economy.

One would expect that internationalization affects these three types of economic policy differently. An increase in factor mobility should reduce the options of those policies that are dependent on the most mobile factor - capital - more than the options of other policy fields. Thus, stabilization policy should be more affected by pressures of internationalization and, therefore, should show some convergence among countries. By contrast, distributive and allocative policies are less directly affected by this most mobile factor and more embedded in national culture, law and public administration. However, regulatory policies are more affected by European regulations, which aim at unifying non-tariff trade barriers such as technical norms and standards. Economic and legal forces should thus affect different policy areas to different degrees.

Main findings of the articles

The book starts with the pressures of capital mobility and the policy fields most sensitive to economic internationalization, stabilization policies. Thomasberger deals with monetary policy, whose options suffer most drastically from the liberalization of financial markets. He shows that increased capital mobility does indeed tie the hands of central banks who are now kept busy with stabilizing the exchange rate in the light of increased speculative flows. There is no room for maneuver left for stabilizing the domestic economy. But surprisingly enough, and unlike what is usually predicted by mainstream economics, this does not lead to a convergence of inflation and interest rates, as is summarized in Table 1.1. The reason for this is that monetary variables are no longer determined by (converging) monetary policies, but by fiscal and incomes policy, which differ substantially between countries. High budget deficits and high wages can push prices up, while the central bank cannot follow an anti-inflationary domestic policy any more.

The liberalization of capital markets in Europe puts pressure not only on monetary policies but also on fiscal policies, the topic of chapter three. In the European Monetary System (EMS) high and increasing budget deficits would be 'punished' by the threat of devaluation of the currency by exchange rate markets. In a Currency Union, where devaluation cannot occur anymore because there is a single currency, these deficits would be 'punished' by higher interest rates charged by capital markets. As a consequence, budget deficits would become more similar across nations. This convergence could be countered by some countries trying to free ride in the Currency Union by expanding their deficit in the hope that the Union will 'bail them out' in spite of the politically declared 'no bail out clause'. Some room for maneuver for fiscal policy will thus be left. There will be definitely more room than for monetary policy. But even if budget deficits and fiscal policies become more similar (converge), institutional differences in wage bargaining will persist. Setting different wages and influencing productivity and competitiveness through institutional settings will partly replace the stabilizing role of fiscal policy for the economy. Given the Maastricht criteria, this can result in a convergence of monetary variables and a divergence of real variables like productivity, employment and output. Thus Unger, who discusses fiscal policy, argues that both tendencies of convergence and divergence occur at the same time.

It seems that, although internationalization restricts stabilization policy, other policy areas, such as incomes policy, become more important for the outcome. Thus possible trends towards convergence are offset by country specific, divergent reactions.

Bellak and Sassen analyze the threats of physical capital mobility to national policies and discuss the effects on the two types of allocative policies that directly affect the main factors of production. Bellak's topic is industrial policy, which affects the allocation and mobility of physical capital, Sassen discusses migration policy, which affects labour.

Bellak stresses the importance of multinational enterprises for the mobility of financial and physical capital, as well as for trade. Two-thirds of international trade is trade managed by and within multinationals. Furthermore, Foreign Direct Investment carried out by multinational enterprises has increased more than international trade. The increased importance of multinational and transnational firms reduces the room for maneuver of national governments in their industrial policies. National industrial policies cover less of the nation's firms, since a large share of their activities occur abroad. Conversely, national policies also affect foreign firms. Hence they are constrained by other countries' industrial policies influencing these firms' behaviour. Furthermore multinational enterprises could also lobby for the optimum conditions they experience in one of the countries, thus using the relocation threat to force national policies to converge. The competition between national governments for the location of such multinational firms could produce a convergence of industrial policies. However, Bellak sees divergence of national industrial policies as a more likely outcome. Multinational enterprises do not have homogenous interests, governments may compete for the location of enterprises by means of specialization, by creating a unique environment for specific industries, necessitating different industrial policy measures, etc. Hence industrial policy will continue to differ, despite increases in physical capital mobility.

Sassen also analyzes multinational companies but as 'information channels' for migration flows. She shows that their activity produces labour migration and influences its patterns. Her contribution gives further support to the imbalance between capital and labour mobility, also mentioned by Thomasberger and Unger. She argues that there is convergence in removing borders for flows of capital, information and goods, and a convergence in maintaining borders to flows of immigrants (and refugees). On the one hand, labour mobility is socially produced by transnational enterprises and thus not a migration influx suffered by the labour receiving country. On the other hand, labour mobility is also politically steered. The globalization process leads to converging anti-migration policies across nations and gives labour and capital an uneven chance to 'cross the globe'.

The second part of the book deals with distributive policies. Kitzmantel and Moser argue that tax policy - a major economic instrument of redistribution - is substantially influenced by EU legal harmonization as well as by the high mobility of financial capital, which enhances tax competition between nations. Convergence is hence most apparent regarding this most mobile and most price-sensitive resource, financial capital. Thus in most countries foreign operators are typically exempted from income taxation whilst domestic operators are not. Tax competition has been more important than joint action. Concerted measures have been mainly limited to harmonizing indirect taxes (VAT, excise duties), whereas direct taxation (company taxes, personal income taxes) has remained largely a subject of national initiatives. Notwithstanding some tendencies towards convergence, the authors do not expect a convergence to the bottom, to very low tax rates, since nations have financing needs that will prevent them from lowering taxes so far. Furthermore, considerable discrepancies between national tax systems still exist, both with respect to tax rates and tax exemptions. Since the mobile factors cannot be taxed further due to international tax competition, the tax burden will be shifted more and more towards the immobile factor, in particular labour.

All of the papers, so far, focus on the impact of financial market liberalization and the increasing importance of international business. Economic policies - which depend on the mobile factors financial and physical capital - loose room for maneuver. This development goes at the cost of the most immobile factor - labour. Sassen shows, that labour is prevented to cross borders while capital can move freely, Kitzmantel and Moser argue that labour is taxed higher, while capital can escape taxation to a large extent. Thomasberger and Unger maintain that due to financial market liberalization, monetary and fiscal authorities cannot control the internal economy anymore and that this can lead to increased unemployment. The threat of firms to relocate their business, puts governments under pressure. Nevertheless, these common contingencies are accompanied by quite different developments in different countries. The principle of subsidiarity within the EU gives some room for maneuver back to Member States. In the area of tax policies, company taxes and personal income taxes are delegated to the Member States by the EU. The tax structure is and will thus be quite different in EU member countries. The outcome of these policies will depend highly on institutional settings, differing among countries.

Kitzmantel and Moser draw quite a dark picture of the future of welfare states. Internationalization is likely to produce a 'convergence to the worse', though not a 'race to the bottom'. Hemerijck and Bakker give some theoretical support to the empirical analysis of Kitzmantel and Moser. Internationalization does not only affect economic variables but also the way in which people think and perceive the future. Thus there has been an international debate on the practice and prospects of the welfare state, which has influenced policymakers in the various countries. The emphasis in the debate has varied over time, including the perception among theoreticians and politicians as to the convergence or divergence of welfare states. For a while, convergence was expected, and such authors have focussed on determining variables such as internationalization and technical determinism. More recently, divergence has been stressed, and causes identified in different historical paths and institutional differences among countries.

Engbersen elaborates on the concept of welfare states in his study of poverty regimes in Europe. He shows that poverty regimes in Britain, France, and the Netherlands differ, and so do their outcomes, the 'life chances' of the European poor. The 'residual welfare state' in Britain produces material deprivation including lack of food and clothing, which would be unthinkable in the Dutch welfare state. In this well-developed welfare state, poverty means not so much financial deprivation as well as social isolation, structural exclusion, alienation of the poor from central societal institutions, and permanent dependence on the welfare state. The author expects and fears convergence towards a 'residual welfare state'. A continuation of the actual trend of lowering welfare benefits could bring about greater social inequality and social problems, such as anomie, in many European nations.

Mosley analyzes national regimes of workers' protection in Europe and argues that economic and political integration is unlikely to result in 'social dumping', but neither in 'upward' convergence through high standards of social protection of a European authority. While some EU countries have the competitive advantage of low labour costs (the periphery), others have the competitive advantage of higher welfare facilities (the core). Welfare state arrangements are not always a burden, but can create competitive advantages due to e.g. better training and health of workers. Regulations and welfare programmes differ among European countries, but 'any hierarchy in the overall "burden" on enterprises is difficult to discern'. Nevertheless, center-core problems related to wage differentials could become important in certain sectors, such as labour intensive industries. Even though social dumping does not occur, social benefits are on the defensive in many EU-countries. Mosley attributes this 'convergence towards the worse' to ideological trends and not to internationalization and European integration. Some convergence could emerge in the core countries, while divergence may appear in the core-periphery relation.

In summary, social policies, in casu welfare policy in general (Hemerijck and Bakker), protection of workers (Mosley), and poverty regimes (Engbersen) do not converge either. Convergence and divergence occur simultaneously in distribution policies as well.

26

Regulatory or allocative policies are the subject of the third part of the book. Keller analyzes labour regulation policies. He finds some convergence to the bottom, towards minimal standards, but also differentiation at the firm, sectoral and national level. He agrees with Engbersen in that he neither expects a well-developed European welfare state. He argues that a European social policy - especially in the field of labour relations - is unlikely. A Europeanization of labour relations is not to be expected, given the divergent interests and different organizational structures of trade unions. Furthermore, the strengthening of the position of employers makes bargaining above the company level less attractive to them. Interest representation and participation at the company and factory level in transnational enterprises - though rare and difficult - is nevertheless easier to imagine than a centralized European system of collective bargaining.

Eichener studies workplace health and safety standards and neither perceives a convergence to the bottom. He argues that the fear of some countries that their high levels of protection would be undercut by social and ecological dumping is unjustified. Such expectations were based on political integration theories which analyzed European policymaking primarily as intergovernmental bargaining, which would only lead to lowest common denominator agreements. European occupational health and safety regulation, however, provides a surprisingly high level of protection and develops even innovative approaches. This is because it is the outcome of interactions among complex configurations of actors, including not only national governments (as in intergovernmental bargaining theories) but also national interest groups and European actors, particularly the European Commission. The latter's institutional self-interest is an important factor explaining the innovativeness of health and safety regulation.

Héritier analyzes clean air policies in Europe. Air pollution is a policy problem which ideal-typically represents 'international interdependence'. Firstly, as atmospheric pollution transgresses national boundaries, it cannot effectively be dealt with within the territorial boundaries of one state. States which suffer from pollution (and from international treaties, designed to reduce the problem) will exert pressure on other states. Secondly, since emission regulation affects the competitive position of the regulated industries in an integrated market, harmonization is a prime concern especially of the high-level regulation countries. Therefore, environmental policymaking has become increasingly a matter for European authorities, and for mutual influence between national and European agencies. As Mosley and Eichener, Héritier neither finds a race to the bottom. But whereas Eichener stresses the role of the European Commission in maintaining or creating a high level of protection, Héritier finds the cause in policy competition between Member States. Countries try to stay ahead of EU-regulations and regulatory intentions in their national policies. They try to assume a leadership role to save on costs of harmonizing national legislation with EU-legislation. But once they have installed new regulations they tend to stick to them and become 'laggards' instead of 'leaders'. Upwards convergence takes thus place in a kind of catching up and forging ahead process. Nevertheless, policy differences persist, because of different geographic and geopolitical conditions which influence the concern with air pollution, of different political structures which give environmental groups and issues varying access to the political arena, of different administrative structures and traditions, which influence motives, concerns, and priorities of politicians and civil servants, and of different legal systems which prefer either voluntary self-regulation or detailed, mandatory regulations. These differences produce different perceptions and approaches to the problem of air pollution, which seem to be remarkably persistent.

Kelemen does not find a 'race to the bottom' for environmental policy either, but is more pessimistic about a race to the top, since EU-countries with low environmental standards get delays for adjustments. He takes as his point of departure the potential conflicts between European competition and environmental policy. This gives the European Court of Justice leeway in deciding which should prevail over which. Kelemen shows that Decisions of the Court and the Commission have tended to advance environmental protection but that the Council, where intergovernmental bargaining between high and low standard countries takes place, tends to retard the development of EU environmental policy. The Treaties agreed upon by the Member States can hence be read as steps backward, which should correct for steps forward, made by the Court.

Van Waarden does not write about a specific policy field. While the other authors discuss policy content or substance, he focusses on national policy style, which should be found in different policy fields within one nation. He argues that countries differ in their dominant styles of policy formation and implementation and describes the typical styles of the US, Britain, France, Germany, and the Netherlands. Furthermore he emphasizes that these differences are not incidental nor accidental, but structural, in that they are strongly rooted in national state institutions, such as legal systems and structures and traditions of the public administration. This makes these policy styles rather resistant to change, whether change towards convergence or further divergence. Even the pressures of internationalization will be resisted, which is not to say that change could not take place of course. However, as long as implementation styles are different between Member States, this will also affect the degree of real integration. The differences in national styles imply that European policy may be implemented differently - and unequally - in different countries - as long as EU-policies are implemented by national state agencies.

Conclusion

Most of our chapters find tendencies towards convergence as well as divergence. The majority expect net divergence, perhaps a disappointing conclusion for proponents of convergence theory. In sofar as authors find some convergence, it is not necessarily convergence towards the bottom. Authors such as Eichener and Héritier give hope that convergence in environmental regulation and the regulation of product safety standards might be for the better.

Forces towards convergence and towards divergence work at the same time. Sometimes the ones are stronger, sometimes the others. Phases of convergence are followed by periods of divergence. Peace follows war, the Post-fordist period of specialization and selective tastes follows the Fordist period of mass production and homogenous tastes. Convergence wins over divergence and vice versa like a pendulum swing in history.

Economic policies which depend on the most mobile factors financial and physical capital loose room for maneuver due to internationalization. Nevertheless, we observe even in monetary and fiscal policy different policies and policy outcomes between countries. The more so in policies less dependent on capital mobility. Asymmetries of factor mobilities (by nature, or politically and socially produced) and institutional differences make for persistence of policy differences.

Financial market liberalization, multinational firm's threat of relocation, the spread of political ideologies, and EU-harmonization laws are the main factors of internationalization affecting national economic policies. Of these, state competition for the location of firms seems to be more important for convergence than enforcement of EU-harmonization laws. And imitation of political ideology seems more important than market forces. Market forces are main channels for convergence only in monetary and migration policy. They may after all be less important that often thought. And, as some papers demonstrate, internationalization or globalization does not necessarily imply that market forces become more important. Globalization may also mean that 'hierarchies' (such as multinationals), or niches, or agglomerations gain in importance. And these factors work partly against convergence.

29

Table 1.1

Internationalization, convergence mechanisms and outcomes by policy fields

Policy field and author	Main pressures of internationalization affecting policy field	Mechanisms of convergence	Mechanisms of divergence	Net outcome
MONETARY POLICY (Stabilization) *Thomasberger*	Financial market liberalization (E)	Market forces, tying central banks' hands	Asymmetries of power between key currency countries and other countries, and between monetary and fiscal policy makers	Convergence to policy impotence but divergence in outcomes (interest rates and inflation)
FISCAL POLICY (Stabilization) *Unger*	Political ideology and Maastricht convergence criteria (PL)	Imitation of political ideology, legal enforcement of Maastricht	Problems of collective action-free riding, institutional differences of state spending	Range of options, convergence not likely
INDUSTRIAL POLICY (Allocation) *Bellak*	Multinational firms (E)	State competition of industrial policy for the location of multinational firms	Political choice of actors for selective industrial policy, creation of niches by using comparative advantage over other countries	Divergence of industrial policy strategies more likely
MIGRATION POLICY (Allocation) *Sassen*	Multinational firms (E)	Market forces and trade	Historical paths, culture and networks, politically-induced unequal chances for labour and capital to cross borders	Convergence and divergence
TAX POLICY (Distribution) *Kitzmantel and Moser*	Financial market liberalization and multinational firms (E)	State competition of tax policies in order to attract capital	Institutional differences of tax systems, disparities in the mobility of capital and labour	Convergence towards the worse, some didifferences remain
WELFARE POLICY (Distribution) *Hemerijck and Bakker*	Diffusion of technology, global interdependence of risks (E)	Imitation of technology evolutionary enlightenment of actors	Path dependence of institutions, strategic options of actors	Both convergence and divergence

Policy field and author	Main pressures of internationalization affecting policy field	Mechanisms of convergence	Mechanisms of divergence	Net outcome
SOCIAL PROTECTION POLICY (Distribution) *Mosley*	Political ideology (PL)	Imitation of ideas	Institutional differences, center-periphery problems	No social dumping, center-periphery divergence
ANTIPOVERTY POLICY (Distribution) *Engbersen*	Political ideology, financial problems of the welfare state (PL)	Imitation of ideas	Institutional differences in welfare state regimes	Convergence to deprivation and anomia
HEALTH AND SAFETY POLICY (Allocation) *Eichener*	EU harmonization laws (PL)	Legal enforcement	Institutional differences in implementation	No race to the bottom, convergence to better standards
LABOUR RELATIONS (Allocation) *Keller*	Organizational structures of capital and labour (PL)	National interests and organizational structures	Divergent national interests and disparities in the organization of capital and labour	At best, persistence of status quo due to different interests and organization
CLEAN AIR POLICY (Allocation) *Héritier*	International law and political pressure (PL)	Political pressures	National interests being more or less receptive to environmental problems	Convergence and divergence, importance of international pressures
ENVIRONMENTAL POLICY (Allocation) *Kelemen*	EU law and Court decisions (PL)	Legal enforcement	Different opinions between Council and Commission, unclear priority of competition and environmental law	Convergence towards the worse or divergence due to different interests of Court, Commission and Council
REGULATORY STYLES (Policy implementation) *Van Waarden*	EU harmonization (PL)	Legal enforcement	Institutional embeddedness of public administration, routinized behaviour	Persistence of differences due to history and institutions

Note:
PL: Political and/or legal pressure. E: Economic pressure

31

References

Abramovitz, Moses A. (1986), 'Catching up, forging ahead, and falling behind', *Journal of Economic History*, vol. XLVI, no. 2, June.

Alber, Jens (1982), *Vom Armenhaus zum Wohlfahrtsstaat. Analysen zur Entwicklung der Sozialversicherung in Westeuropa*, Campus, Frankfurt am Main.

Anderson, Kym, and Richard Blackhurst (eds) (1993), *Regional Integration and the Global Trading System*, Harvester Wheatsheaf, New York.

Aron, Raymond (1962), *The Opium of Intellectuals*, Norton, New York.

Aron, Raymond (1968), *Democracy and Totalitarianism*, Praeger, New York.

Bell, Daniel (1960), *The End of Ideology*, Free Press, New York.

Bennett, Colin J. (1988), 'Different processes, one result: the convergence of data protection policy in Europe and the United States', *Governance*, vol. 1.

Bennett, Colin J. (1991), 'Review article: what is policy convergence and what causes it?', *British Journal of Political Science*, vol. 21.

Bogdandy, Armin von (1993), 'Konturen des integrierten Europa, Stand und Perspektiven der europäischen Integration', *Europa Archiv*, no. 2.

Brickman, Ronald, Sheila Jasanoff, and Thomas Ilgen (1985), *Controlling Chemicals: The Politics of Regulation in Europe and the United States*, Cornell University Press, Ithaca.

Buiter, Willem (1992), 'Should we worry about the fiscal numerology of Maastricht?', *CEPR Discussion Paper*, no. 668, June, Center for European Policy Research, London.

Corvers, F., and B. Dankbaar (1994), 'Bedrijven in Euregio Maas-Rijn kijken amper over de grens', *Geografie*, no. 3.

Crozier, Michel (1964), *The Bureaucratic Phenomenon*, University of Chicago Press, Chicago.

Dallago, Bruno, Horst Brezinski, and Wladimir Andreff (1993), *Convergence and System Change. The Convergence Hypothesis in the Light of Transitions in Eastern Europe*, Dartmouth, Aldershot.

Dehesa, Guillermo de la, and Paul Krugman (1992), 'EMU and the regions, Group of Thirty', *Occasional Papers*, no. 39, Washington DC.

Döhler, Marian (1990), *Gesundheitspolitik nach der 'Wende'. Policy-Netzwerke und ordnungspolitischer Strategiewechsel in Großbritannien, den USA und der Bundesrepublik Deutschland*, Sigma Bohn, Berlin.

Dore, Ronald (1983), 'Goodwill and the spirit of market capitalism', *The British Journal of Sociology*, vol. 34.

Dore, Ronald (1986), *Flexible Rigidities. Industrial Policy and Structural Adjustment in the Japanese Economy, 1970 - 1980*, Athlene Press, London.

Dye, Thomas R. (1991), *Politics in States and Communities*, Prentice Hall, Englewood Cliffs, New Jersey.

Eichengreen, Barry (1991), 'Is Europe an optimum currency area?', *NBER Working Paper*, no. 3579, January, National Bureau of Economic Research, Cambridge, Mass.

Ellman, M. (1984), *Collectivization, Convergence and Capitalism*, Academic Press, London and Orlando.

Ellul, Jacques (1964), *The Technological Society*, Vintage Books, New York.

Esping-Andersen, Gosta (1990) *The Three Worlds of Welfare Capitalism*, Princeton University Press, Princeton.

Fukuyama, Francis (1992), *The End of History and the Last Man*, Free Press, New York.

Galbraith, John K. (1971), *The New Industrial State*, Houghton Mifflin, Boston, Mass.

Garrett, Geoffrey (1992), 'International cooperation and institutional choice', *International Organization*, vol. 46.

Goldthorpe, John H. (1964), 'Social stratification in industrial society', *The Sociological Review Monograph*, no. 8.

Goldthorpe, John H. (1984), 'The end of convergence: Corporatist and dualist tendencies in modern western societies', in Goldthorpe, John H. (ed), *Order and Conflict in Contemporary Capitalism*, Oxford University Press, Oxford.

Grande, Edgar (1989), *Vom Monopol zum Wettbewerb? Die neokonservative Reform der Telekommunikation in Großbritannien und der Bundesrepublik Deutschland - eine vergleichende Analyse ökonomisch-politischer Konfiguration*, Deutscher Universitäts Verlag, Wiesbaden.

Granovetter, Mark (1985), 'Economic action and social structure: The problem of embeddedness', *American Journal of Sociology*, vol. 91.

Grote, Jürgen R. (1992), 'Small firms in the European Community: modes of production, governance and territorial interest representation in Italy and Germany', in Greenwood, Justin, Jürgen R. Grote, and Karsten Ronit (eds), *Organized Interests and the European Community*, Sage, London and Newbury Park.

Hall, S.G., D. Robertson, and M.R. Wickens (1992), 'Measuring convergence of the EC Economies', *The Manchester School*, vol. LX, supplement, June.

Heck, Hans-Joachim (1993), 'EWG-Handwerks-Verordnung. Keine Benachteiligung für deutsche Staatsbürger', *Deutsches Handwerksblatt* 15-16/93.

Hemerijck, Anton C. (1993), *The Historical Contingencies of Dutch Corporatism*, D.Phil., Balliol College, Oxford.

Hollingsworth, J. Rogers, Philippe C. Schmitter, and Wolfgang Streeck (eds) (1994), *Governing Capitalist Economies. Performance and Control of Economic Sectors*, Oxford University Press, Oxford.

Houtum, H. van, and R. van Kerkhoff (1994), 'Grenzenloze economie binnen Europese Unie nog ver weg: het euregionale beleid', *Geografie*, no. 3.

Hudson, Michael (1992), *Trade, Development, and Foreign Debt. A History of Theories of Polarization and Convergence in the International Economy*, 2 volumes, Pluto Press, London.

Immergut, Ellen (1992), *Health Politics, Interests and Institutions in Western Europe*, Cambridge University Press, Cambridge, Mass.

Inkeles, Alex (1981), 'Convergence and divergence in industrial societies', in Attir, Mustafa O., Burkart Holzner, and Zdenek Suda (eds), *Directions of Change: Modernization Theory. Research and Reality*, Westview Press, Boulder, Colo.

Kelman, Steven (1981), *Regulating America, Regulating Sweden: A Comparative Study of Occupational Safety and Health Policy*, MIT Press, Cambridge, Mass.

Kern, Horst, and Michael Schumann (1976), *Industriearbeit und Arbeiterbewustsein*, Europaeische Verlagsanstalt, Frankfurt am Main.

Kerr, C., J.T. Dunlop, H. Harbison, and C. Myers (1960), *Industrialism and Industrial Man*, Harvard University Press, Cambridge, Mass.

Kerr, Clark (1983), *The Future of Industrial Societies: Convergence or Continuing Diversity?*, Harvard University Press, Cambridge, Mass.

Lehmbruch, Gerhard (1987), 'Administrative Interessenvermittlung', in Adrienne Windhoff-Héritier (ed.), *Verwaltung und ihre Umwelt. Festschrift für Thomas Ellwein*, Opladen.

Lowi, Theodore (1964), 'American business, public policy, case studies, and political theory', in *World Politics*, vol. 16, no. 4.

Musgrave, Richard (1959), *The Theory of Public Finance*, McGraw Hill, New York.

Nader Ralph, and 16 others (1993), *The Case Against 'Free Trade'. GATT, NAFTA, and the Globalization of Corporate Power*, Earth Island Press, San Francisco.

Naßmacher, Hiltrud (1991), *Vergleichende Politikforschung. Eine Einführung in Probleme und Methoden,* Westdeutscher Verlag, Opladen.

O'Connor, Julia S. (1988), 'Convergence or divergence? Change in welfare effort in OECD countries 1960-1980', *European Journal of Political Research*, vol. 16.

Pfeil, Susanne (1993), *Die Konvergenz der wirtschaftlichen Entwicklung in den Staaten der Europäischen Gemeinschaft*, dissertation, Universität Erlangen-Nürnberg.

Richardson, Jeremy (ed.) (1982), *Policy Styles in Western Europe*, Allen & Unwin, London.

Rostow, Walt (1968), *The Stages of Economic Growth*, Cambridge University Press, Cambridge, Mass.

Sabatier, Paul A., and Hank C. Jenkins-Smith (1991), *Policy Change and Learning: An Advocacy Coalition Approach*, Westview, Boulder.

Scharpf, Fritz W. (1984), 'Economic and institutional constraints of full-employment strategies: Sweden, Austria, and West Germany', in Goldthorpe, John (ed.), *Order and Conflict in Contemporary Capitalism. Studies in the Political Economy of Western European Nations*, Oxford University Press, Oxford.

Schmidt, Manfred G. (1982), *Wohlfahrtsstaatliche Politik unter bürgerlichen und sozial-demokratischen Regierungen. Ein internationaler Vergleich*, Campus, Frankfurt am Main.

SER-COB (1994) *Nieuwe kansen voor bedrijven in de grensregio's*, Staatsuitgeverij, The Hague.

Siegel, Richard L., and Leonard B. Weinberg (1977), *Comparing Public Policies: United States, Soviet Union and Europe*, Dorsey Press, Homewood, Ill.

Tinbergen, Jan (1959), *The Theory of the Optimum Regime*, North Holland, Amsterdam.

Tinbergen, Jan (1961), 'Do communist free economies show a converging pattern?', *Soviet Studies*, vol. XII, no. 4.

Vogel, David (1986), *National Styles of Regulation. Environmental Policy in Great Britain and the United States*, Cornell University Press, Ithaca and London.

Vogel, David (1992), 'Protective regulation and protectionism in the European Community: The creation of a Common Market for food and beverages', *Minda da Ginzburg Center for European Studies, Harvard University Working Paper*, no. 37, Cambridge, Mass.

Waltman, Jerold L., and Donley T. Studlar (eds) (1987), *Political Economy: Public Policies in the United States and Britain*, University Press of Mississippi, Jackson, Miss.

Part 1
PRESSURES OF ECONOMIC INTERNATIONALIZATION AND DIRECTLY AFFECTED POLICY FIELDS

2 Financial market liberalization and monetary policy

Claus Thomasberger

EU
F33
F36
F52
E58

> *The freedom of money was, paradoxically enough, a result of restrictions of trade. ... In contrast to men and goods, money was free from all hampering measures and continued to develop its capacity to transact business at any distance and time. The more difficult it became to shift actual objects, the easier it became to transmit claims to them. While trade in commodities and services was slowed down and its balance swayed precariously, the balance of payments was almost automatically kept liquid with the help of short term loans that fitted over the globe, and funding operations that only faintly took note of visible trade. (Polanyi, regarding the period after 1879)*

Summary

Capital market integration at the European as well as at the global level alters the socioeconomic context of monetary policy. Starting from an analysis of the budget constraints on monetary and fiscal authorities, the paper discusses the consequences of the recent liberalization strategies. The resultant restrictions on national monetary independence have an asymmetric and limited impact on the monetary authorities of different countries. This constitutes a particular structure of international relations, a key-currency system. The paper examines why a key-currency system, like the European Monetary System, ties the hands of the central bank of the key-currency country, and cannot ensure the convergence of economic and monetary variables in different countries. I argue that today capital market integration has become - as paradoxical as it may sound - a threat to the transition to a European economic and monetary union. A laissez-faire strategy that sees capital markets as the starting point of integration in Europe, therefore, runs the risk of coming to a deadlock.

Introduction

In many respects, European monetary integration at the end of the 1980s constitutes no more than a rerun of the initiatives of the 1970s. One need only think of the goal of monetary union, the three stages to complete it, or the significance attached to exchange rate stability. However, the integration at the end of the 1980s was marked by one radical change: while the 1970 Werner Report envisioned capital market integration as the *result* of progress toward economic and monetary convergence, the 1989 Delors Report (and, proceeding from it, the Maastricht Treaty) placed the liberalization of capital markets at the *beginning* of the process. This is all the more astonishing as in Europe restrictions on the movement of capital have traditionally played a major role in maintaining room for monetary maneuver at the national level. Nor can, as is suggested by the formula 'completion of the single market', the priority attached to capital market integration in the 1980s simply be interpreted as a supplement to the liberalization of commodity markets. Eichengreen (1990) rightly points out that capital market integration is not necessary to obtain the benefits stemming from integration of commodity markets. Efficiency gains resulting from capital market integration can be explained theoretically only if special conditions such as market imperfections, external effects, etc. are assumed. Indeed, as the discussions organized by the Commission (1988) show the key factor responsible for the strategic change was less concern regarding efficiency and the benefits of integration than considerations of political economy: capital market integration as an instrument of strengthening economic cohesion, stabilizing integration, and harmonizing monetary performance between the Member States of the European Monetary System (EMS).

One of the essential conditions for realizing capital market integration at the level of the European Community was a fundamental change in the valuation of national monetary independence. True, the awareness that integration of capital markets at fixed exchange rates constituted a restraint on national independence was not a new insight: all approaches making reference to the Mundell-Flemming model (e.g. Padoa-Schioppa 1987, Wyplosz 1988) were based on the idea that commodity and capital market integration, fixed exchange rates, and national monetary independence represent, in the global economic context, an 'inconsistent tertiate' and cannot be achieved simultaneously. But the view that a loss of national monetary independence need no longer be weighed against other benefits (such as a lowering of transaction costs), but must itself be seen as a benefit, marked a fundamental turning point in the discussion. Just as the 'advantage of tying one's hands' (thus the title of the landmark study by Giavazzi and Pagano 1988) was being evoked at the theoretical level, political economy considerations focused on the autonomy of monetary against fiscal policy and the subordination of the latter to the exigencies of the capital markets. (As always, precursors can be found here as well: for instance, the positive aspects of the 'discipline of a free international system of payments' was emphasized in the German ordoliberal discussion at the end of the 1950s on the implications of achieving convertibility of the Western European currencies (see, e.g., Röpke 1959).

The turbulence of the EMS in 1992-93, the withdrawal of the lira and sterling from the Exchange Rate Mechanism, and the expansion of the bands of fluctuation permitted within the EMS represented a first practical critique of the integration strategy adopted in the 1980s. This raises the question of theoretical foundation. The paper will focus on some theoretical questions concerning the relation of capital market integration, national monetary independence, and efforts to overcome the divergence of monetary performance. The discussion on European capital market integration will - even when not explicitly emphasized - form the background of the analysis.

As will become clear in the course of the paper, monetary and fiscal policy must be discussed in different terms. The following considerations focus mainly on the implications of capital market integration for monetary policy. The consequences for fiscal policy will be addressed briefly in the second part of the study.

Budget constraint and national monetary independence in the international context

The space in which economic subjects shape their decisions is limited by budget constraints. In a modern monetary economy where - as Clower puts it - 'money buys goods and goods by money, but goods do not buy goods' this means that demand is limited by the economic actor's disposal of money. This applies not only to individual economic agents but - as the mercantilists were already aware - to entire nations as well: the volume of foreign exchange at a country's disposal constitutes that country's budget constraint. The approach chosen in this paper differs methodologically from the conventional neoclassical reasoning in that it does not assume that a country's budget constraint - which is basically a monetary constraint (its liquidity in foreign exchange, i.e. the money the authorities of the country concerned are unable to create) - can be reduced to natural resources, real capital, and labour at its disposal in the long run. Exporting resources and goods may increase the supply of foreign exchange, but - as the evidence of multiplying foreign trade deficits during the last decades (not only of the USA) clearly demonstrates - a country's external budget is limited not at all by the volume of export trade. The volume of foreign exchange at a country's disposal depends at least as much on international movements of short and long term capital (i.e. the confidence of international banks and other asset holders in that currency) as it depends on the exports of goods and services.

The advantage of this approach is twofold. First, it makes it possible to overcome both the naturalism dominating the traditional theory of international trade on the one hand and the constructivism that characterizes international monetary economics on the other hand. It enables us to discuss the economic relations between different countries as *social* relations, as relations that express the specific social organization of international economic affairs and that - being manmade - can be changed. If money 'is merely a token of purchasing power which, as a rule, is not produced at all, but comes into being through the mechanism of banking or state finance' (Polanyi 1944: 72), money has to be designed neither as a commodity nor as a medium of exchange, but as a social institution. Second, it provides the basis for an understanding of the key role that international capital markets have played not only in the last decades but also in the nineteenth century for the development of global markets.

Foreign exchange liquidity - in its function as budget constraint - is not identical in meaning with restrictions on a country's monetary policy independence. Every country has a number of different instruments that it can employ to build up, or prevent the loss of, foreign exchange. A country can encourage exports and restrain imports. It can consider more or less selective trade restrictions, export promotion, devaluation or undervaluation of its own currency, and similar instruments. Foreign exchange inflows would in this case be a reflex of balance of payments surpluses. Or the country's economic policy may seek to gain influence on capital transactions, prevent capital exports and/or encourage the import of capital with the aid of administrative or fiscal measures.

Only if laissez faire strategies dominate, i.e. if international relations are designed as an economic system controlled and regulated by markets alone and no measure or policy is endorsed that would direct the action of markets, does interest rate policy have to take on the role of influencing the relative attractiveness of both investments denominated in domestic currency and the currency itself. In such a constellation, short term interest rates fulfill the function of giving expression, vis-à-vis the individual economic subjects, to the budget constraint represented by a country's foreign exchange holdings. If monetary policy is assigned the role of maintaining a country's foreign exchange liquidity, national monetary independence is forfeited because monetary policy loses its capacity to influence internal developments by means of the discount, lombard and other short term interest rates. Monetary policy cannot at the same time

42

seek to maintain a country's liquidity in foreign exchange and, for instance, to regulate domestic price level. When international capital markets are integrated, monetary policy has no choice. Losses of foreign exchange become a sanction mechanism: any such losses force monetary policy to recognize the primacy of external stabilization.

Normally countries will make use of all the instruments at their disposal - albeit in different combinations - to protect themselves against any loss (or even excessive inflow) of foreign exchange reserves. Even today only a small minority of countries are prepared to dispense with the use of administrative controls on money and capital. Of the 152 members of the International Monetary Fund (IMF), the currencies of only fifty-two countries met the criterion of 'convertibility of current transactions', and the currencies of a mere thirty of these matched the criterion of 'unrestricted convertibility'. In Europe it was only in recent decades, particularly the 1980s, that the way was cleared for the integration of capital markets. The removal of administrative controls forced monetary policy to maintain liquidity in foreign exchange above all via interest rate policy - that is, recognition of the primacy of external stabilization. From this point of view, capital market integration is merely another expression for the removal of direct regulations on the movement of capital and the reciprocal development of appropriate market institutions. I assume an extreme degree of capital market integration when economic policy dispenses entirely with administrative measures, forcing monetary policy to fulfill the function of signaling shortages of foreign exchange to the private sector.

At this point it is already clear that national monetary independence in the global economic context is a relative concept, one which may be achieved in various degrees. A country's monetary independence is greater, the more the country is able to encounter the budget constraint with a multiplicity of instruments. A country's monetary independence is diminished, the more - at given transaction costs - monetary policy is assigned the task of maintaining the country's liquidity in foreign exchange. Complete loss of national monetary independence in the global economic context is no more than a (negative) utopia. Different periods can be distinguished in terms of the degree to which their monetary autonomy was restricted. The classical period of the gold-Sterling standard on the one hand and the 1980s on the other may stand as examples for highly integrated capital markets and a low level of monetary autonomy, while the 1930s, 1940s, and 1950s may be seen as examples for periods with a high level of monetary autonomy.

But even in the case of integrated capital markets the restriction of national monetary independence is asymmetric. The loss of foreign exchange represents a hard budget constraint, an inflow of reserves does not restrict the room for maneuver in the same way. Integrated capital markets set disproportionately higher bounds on expansive than on restrictive monetary policy. In many cases - and Germany within the EMS is the best example - central banks succeed in sterilizing great quantities of foreign exchange inflows. This is why France under Mitterand's first presidency - to recall only the most prominent example - felt the international constraint much stronger than Germany in the wake of the unification. The on the whole restrictive bias marking Europe's development during the 1980s and the growing unemployment figures are at least in part a consequence of these asymmetries.

As mentioned above, conventional neoclassical theory tries to reduce the monetary budget constraint that the disposal over foreign exchange represents for every country to the question of equilibrium of international trade. But there always have been heterodox approaches. Underlying Keynes' theory was the idea of a direct connection between capital market integration and the loss of national monetary independence. From the 'Indian Currency' to his 'Tract on Monetary Reform' and the proposals he presented in Bretton Woods, Keynes demonstrated that he held the independence of national monetary policy to be incompatible with open capital markets, because under these conditions monetary policy is forced to recognize the primacy of external stabilization. What changed in his writings was not the emphasis placed on the significance of external stabilization but the question as to how Britain's monetary policy is - under different conditions - to respond to the problem of external stabilization. As long as the stability of the international gold-Sterling standard was taken for granted, there was no alternative to the recognition of the primacy of external stabilization. Under the altered conditions of the 1920s he spoke of the dilemma expressed in the conflict between 'stability of prices versus stability of exchange'. And finally, in his proposals for the Bretton Woods conference, he made it clear that he regarded controls of capital movements as essential in order to evade the necessity of external stabilization vis-à-vis the US dollar.

> There should be the least possible interference with internal national policies. There is no country which can, in future, safely allow the flight of funds for political reasons or to evade domestic taxation or in anticipation of the owner turning refugee. Equally, there is no country that can safely receive fugitive funds, which constitute an unwanted import of capital, yet cannot safely be used for fixed investment. (Keynes 1943: 234 and 185)

Keynes was prepared to sacrifice capital market integration to the maintenance of national monetary independence in the international context.

In the 1950s Friedman took up the liberalization of the capital markets after World War II. Even if capital markets are integrated, he stated, national monetary independence can be maintained through a system of flexible exchange rates. Flexible exchange rates were supposed to guarantee the balance-of-payments equilibrium in the long run. Speculation was assumed to have stabilizing consequences. In his classic essay of 1953, 'The Case for Flexible Exchange Rates', Friedman anticipated the logic of the monetary approach to balance of payments theory.

In effect, flexible exchange rates are a means of combining interdependence among countries through trade with a maximum of internal monetary independence; they are a means of permitting each country to seek for monetary stability according to its owns lights, without either imposing its mistakes on its neighbors or having their mistakes imposed on it. (Friedman 1953: 430)

National monetary independence was to be made compatible with capital market integration via a transition to flexible parities, i.e. the 'liberation' of monetary policy from its commitment to stabilize exchange rates.

Despite all differences Friedman remained on Keynes' track to the extent that in his reasoning national monetary independence played an essential role: it was considered a prerequisite that enables a country to shield itself from imported higher inflation rates. Flexible exchange rates were justified by the benefits that accrue to a country from the possibility of pursuing national money supply rules.

But it was precisely the assumption that flexible exchange rates would overcome the restriction imposed by the budget constraint that proved to be the Achilles heel of the early monetarist approach. Outflows of foreign exchange may be stopped only if it is assumed that devaluations do not give rise to expectations of further devaluations. This presupposes the existence of a rather specific constellation of events, for devaluation implies an increase of import prices and thus of price level, which has implications for production costs and - nominal incomes remaining unchanged - is tantamount to a reduction of real incomes. If an attempt is made to compensate for such losses by raising nominal incomes, the next devaluation round will be the consequence. Flexible exchange rates are therefore, it is argued, able to overcome the dependence of monetary policy on the budget constraint at best in the short run. In the long run, an outflow of foreign exchange cannot be stopped for the simple reason that the economic agents will anticipate the next devaluation round. Nor does the counterargument (see Friedman 1953: 432) stating that a general rise in wage and price levels presupposes that the rise will be financed by monetary policy, i.e. that it could be prevented if it were not fed by the central bank, seem particularly persuasive. If it is assumed that the responsibility

45

for price development lies solely with monetary policy, it is difficult to see why the monetary authorities do not reduce the money supply far enough to render a devaluation superfluous.

The theory of optimal currency areas restricted the advantages of the exchange rate instrument to special cases. Only if nominal wages and prices are inflexible and the mobility of labour is restricted does the possibility of exchange rate adjustment entail the advantage of being able to respond to asymmetrical shocks - whether they stem from the supply side or the demand side. This would imply that exchange rate adjustments (i.e. monetary policy directed to national goals) are superfluous in all cases in which either wages are flexible or factor mobility is high. Furthermore, the notion of a more or less stable Phillips curve was challenged. If, it was argued, the relation between unemployment and inflation is not independent of the existing rate of inflation, if the Phillips curve shifts upward when expectations of inflation rise, i.e. if in the long run it represents a vertical line, then the notion of a choice between inflation and unemployment proves illusory. Higher rates of inflation would entail no benefits in the long run, i.e. inflation rates adjusted at a low level and fixed exchange rates would entail no drawbacks.

Actual developments have also confounded Friedman's hope; after the Bretton Woods system had collapsed, monetary policy was unable to operate without safeguarding its external flank (see Emminger 1977). And the experience made within the EMS confirms the observation that it is not possible to fall back at will upon the instrument of devaluation; the conditions under which this is possible are indeed limited. De Grauwe (1992: 42-5) cites successful examples from the initial period of the EMS (Belgium in 1982, France in 1982-83, and Denmark in 1982), all of which required devaluation to be shored up by fiscal policy and income formation.

Monetarism Mach Two, assuming 'new classical-rational expectations', thrust into the open flank. National monetary independence in the global economic context - including adjustments of exchange rates - no longer appeared merely superfluous. The line of reasoning was reversed; the budget constraint and restrictions on national monetary policy could be viewed as beneficial, for they permitted the 'import' of monetary credibility. Now, in view of a position that starts from the assumption that monetary policy - if it is not neutral - implies a disturbance of equilibrium, the call for a halt to national monetary policy can be no surprise. Still, the call for fixed exchange rates buttressed by the argument of importing credibility does represent a turning point in the discussion.

If we assume that the current decisions of the economic agents depend at least in part upon their expectations of future policy actions, this implies that monetary policy can, in the short as well as in the long term, generate no real effects when the policy measures are anticipated by the private sector. It is only unanticipated changes in money supply and exchange rates that give rise to real effects: monetary policy therefore has an incentive to surprise the private sector with an expansion of the money supply, i.e. to let the inflation rate rise above the stated target, in order to achieve a combination of unemployment and inflation more optimal in its eyes. But the economic agents cannot be surprised systematically and are likely to anticipate the increased growth of the money supply and devaluation in the next period. Inflation would rise until the monetary authorities had no more incentive to 'cheat', because any further rise of the inflation rate would fail to enhance their position. The resulting equilibrium would be at the level of the 'natural' rate of unemployment, but would be suboptimal to the extent that the rate of inflation would be higher than necessary. Time inconsistency, monetary discipline, the credibility of monetary policy, and the reputation of the central bank form the focus of interest. The reduction of inflation seems possible only to the extent that a stability oriented monetary policy achieves greater credibility, i.e. to the extent that a country's monetary authorities built up their reputation by tying their policy to a rule.

If devaluations, to the extent that they are anticipated by the economic subjects, give rise merely to (negative) monetary consequences, without entailing any - even short term - real effects, countries with above average inflation might increase the credibility of a restrictive policy by fixing their exchange rate against a key currency, thus enhancing their reputation by 'importing' credibility. To be sure, fixing exchange rates need not necessarily be more credible than tying them to an internal money supply rule. But - the argument continues - if, in the face of integrated capital markets, the costs of adjusting exchange rates should prove high (one need only think of the political costs in Europe, the agricultural market, the loss of government prestige stemming from the perception of devaluations as failures of economic policy, etc.), the coercive pressures stemming from the budget constraint would in the end lead to adjustment of price level development to that of the key currency (Giavazzi and Pagano 1988).

The progress of the credibility approach consists in having demonstrated that flexible exchange rates only seemingly imply a 'liberation' of monetary policy from the primacy of external stabilization. But the question remains as to whether the budget constraint will lead to a convergence of monetary development. Within the discussion on European monetary integration this issue is addressed under the heading of 'transition to monetary union'. Let us look somewhat more closely at the problem of harmonizing monetary policy.

Key-currency system and the dilemma of monetary policy

Given unrestricted capital markets between several countries, the monetary budget constraint constitutes a particular structure of international relations, a key-currency system. The international economic system develops coherence because the loss of foreign exchange reserves functions as an sanction mechanism, forcing the monetary authorities of the individual countries to recognize the primacy of external stabilization, i.e. to defend the country's liquidity in foreign exchange. A key-currency system can be viewed as a 'spontaneous order' to the extent that it is constituted by the interplay of capital markets and central banks and not by international agreements. In fact key-currency systems such as the international gold-Sterling Standard have developed independently of special institutional regulations or - as in the cases of the Bretton Woods system and (even more clearly) the EMS - prevailed against planned structures. To remain with the latter example: contrary to the intentions of the founding fathers and contrary to international agreements, the EMS has never developed in the direction of a symmetrical system. From the very start it was the D-mark - and not the ECU - that assumed the role of the key currency. Within the EMS it was the logic of the key currency system that prevailed against the initiative aimed at coordination and monetary cooperation. It is this 'spontaneous order', the specific structure of a key-currency system, that makes it possible to speak of capital market integration.

Mundell's (1963: 487) definition of capital mobility, aiming at the alignment of interest rates, is misleading. A key-currency system is not the same thing as a single currency, and not only because, as Eichengreen (1993: 1354) puts it, '(e)xchange rates exist only to be changed'. Uniform interest rates are not a condition for capital market equilibrium, even when expectations of exchange rate adjustments tend toward zero. Even in an international regime with integrated money and capital markets (and fixed exchange rates), different currencies do not represent perfect substitutes. Asset holders can choose not only whether to hold or to relinquish money, they can likewise choose whether to relinquish their national currency and hold a foreign one (or assets denominated accordingly). On the one hand the establishment of a system of integrated capital markets implies placing internationally active asset holders, banks, etc., in a position to choose the currency in which they wish to hold their assets, without taking into consideration any specific foreign exchange budget constraint. Japanese banks may buy huge amounts of dollar assets if they have confidence in the American economy, and they may sell them when confidence is diminishing. 'Speculation' is only one aspect, the same is true for long term investment. On the other hand it presupposes the willingness and the ability of the monetary authorities of different countries to maintain their foreign exchange liquidity entirely by means of monetary policy.

What to asset holders appears as alternative, a choice between different currencies, constitutes from the perspective of the currencies - or the countries concerned and their monetary authorities - a relationship of competition. In open capital markets the different currencies compete with one another for the favor of the asset holders. When the capital markets are integrated, it is the competition in currency - and not its neutrality or independence - that forms the basis of international monetary relations, that restrains the options open to monetary policy and forces central banks to recognize the primacy of external stabilization.

Integrated capital markets imply the formation of a hierarchy of currencies. Just as in a closed economy, a hierarchy will emerge among financial assets with ascending degrees of liquidity. The competition between currencies in the international capital markets gives rise to a hierarchy of currencies reflecting the differences in the international liquidity premiums. The currency with the highest degree of liquidity assumes a pronounced position, it becomes the key currency of the system. We may express the different confidence bestowed by the capital markets on various currencies, in terms of price theory by conceiving it as a non-pecuniary liquidity premium (Thomasberger 1993: 19-62). If we designate the international liquidity premium of a currency as l, the interest rate as i, the two currencies as 1 and 2, equilibrium will be at:

$$l_1 + i_1 = l_2 + i_2$$

Open capital markets call for a monetary policy prepared to adjust interest rates in order to maintain the sum of the liquidity premium of domestic currency and the internal interest rate at the level prevailing abroad. If the individual economic agents are given the chance to choose the currency in which they wish to hold their assets or conduct their transactions, the central banks must take on the function of maintaining a country's liquidity against all other countries. Central banks must be conceived not as institutions acting above the markets but as market participants or - to take up a concept from the post-Keynesian discussion - as market makers, simply because integrated capital markets cannot be presupposed. Discount policy is necessary in order to create and sustain a stable market process.

The interpretation of a key-currency system in terms of 'spontaneous order' should not lead to the conclusion that a key-currency system must be regarded as a closed system. The reason is that the budget constraint and the market-endogenous sanction mechanism are effective only vis-à-vis the central banks of the countries with weaker currencies. The system is open in two respects. First, only a loss, not an inflow, of foreign exchange functions as a sanction mechanism; the necessity of recognizing the

49

primacy of external stabilization has no direct impact on the key-currency country. Secondly, the sanction mechanism affects only monetary policy, it ties neither the process of income formation nor fiscal policy (which may here be used as abbreviated expressions for the totality of economic processes for which the loss of foreign exchange reserves does not represent an effective budget constraint) into the system.

Conventional reasoning slips into the 'fallacy of symmetry' because it is unable to recognize the importance of the fact that it is only the threat of loss, and not of increase, of foreign exchange reserves that functions - as seen above - as a sanction mechanism. It is the central banks affected by an outflow of foreign exchange reserves that are forced to take action, not the monetary authorities of the countries receiving inflows of foreign exchange. Maintaining foreign exchange liquidity becomes a problem to be faced by the countries with weaker - or dependent - currencies. The latter are forced to counter the outflow of capital via an appropriate discount policy. The market has no sanction mechanism at its disposal to enforce a policy of external stabilization against the key currency. Relying on the logic of the key-currency system, the Bundesbank in the EMS has, as did the American Fed under the Bretton Woods system, assigned the responsibility for maintaining foreign exchange liquidity and fixing exchange rates to the dependent currencies. And the Bundesbank was de facto the only central bank in the EMS that was able to meet the criterion of internal stability. Notwithstanding, the Bundesbank has never been able to renounce external stabilization completely (see Riese 1986, Spahn 1988, Thomasberger 1993a). This is not only an explanation of why the key-currency country commands a special position, it also explains why all attempts to force German monetary policy to collaborate and cooperate have been bound to fail; the foreign exchange markets have no sanction mechanism that would take effect when the key-currency country refuses to cooperate.

The fallacy of convergence is closely related to the second aspect. If monetary policy is successful in maintaining foreign exchange liquidity via interest rate policy, other economic agents appear to be released from any direct consideration of external constraints. Capital market integration therefore does not restrict the independence of the fiscal policy of individual countries in the same way that it restricts monetary policy. Put differently: If the central bank assumes the function of maintaining foreign exchange liquidity, there is no market-endogenous sanction mechanism that might occasion fiscal policy and the private economic subjects, in conducting their normal transactions, to include external economic concerns in their calculations. International capital flows respond sensitively to interest rate differentials, but their influence on income formation is dependent on the impact of interest rates on investment activity and employment. The question of 'crowding out' is misleading. If a country's fiscal deficit is growing, the confidence in the internal economic and monetary stability may diminish, and the outflow of capital may increase. The monetary authorities will have to raise interest rates in order to stimulate the influx of capital and to defend their foreign exchange reserves. The case of Italy shows clearly that increasing interest rates constitute only a weak constraint on fiscal policy. On the contrary, the fiscal deficit may even tend to grow parallel with interest rates as a result of both increasing payments for national debt and diminishing tax revenues. In modern circumstances, the loss of foreign exchange reserves functions as an sanction mechanism against the monetary authorities, but not against the state and private economic agents. The fact that a market-endogenous sanction mechanism is effective only vis-à-vis monetary, but not fiscal policy explains why the framers of the Maastricht treaty specified 'reference values' for budget deficits and public debts to be met as political preconditions for participating in the monetary union.

If fiscal policy or the process of income formation are to be conceived as autonomous vis-à-vis monetary policy, capital market integration is not sufficient to ensure the convergence of monetary development in different countries. Because its hands are tied by the necessity of maintaining external stability, monetary policy is unable to respond to internal impulses, be they from fiscal policy or from the process of income formation. The persistence of inflation rate differentials between the Member States of the EMS in the face of largely integrated capital markets can therefore not be interpreted as the consequence of an ill-conceived monetary policy, but as the result of a fundamental conflict. If fiscal policy or the process of income formation in two countries do not converge, monetary policy may end up in a dilemma: the central bank looses the ability to guarantee not only external stability in the sense of stable exchange rates, but also - if a devaluation fails to restore confidence - the convertibility of the currency (see Thomasberger (1993: 232-45). Pointing one's finger at errors in monetary policy is not very convincing for the simple reason that the presupposition of a budget constraint ('tying the hands' of monetary policy) is inconsistent with the assumption of national monetary independence (otherwise monetary policy could not be made responsible). The inflation differentials are the expression of social and institutional differences, different rates of productivity development in various industries, specific features of the process of income formation, fiscal orientations, etc. This is the reason why systems that combine integrated capital markets with fixed exchange rates, like the 'new EMS' (Giavazzi and Spaventa 1990), appear fundamentally unstable (Eichengreen 1993: 1328), and flexible exchange rates or a single currency seem in the end the only alternatives.

Seen from a monetary perspective, it would in fact be purely accidental if the monetary policy induced by necessities of external stabilization should result in equivalent inflation rate levels in different countries. Monetary policy in the European Community in recent years has been unable to contribute in a significant way toward the goal of convergence because its 'hands have been tied' by integrated capital markets. A strategy that seeks to instrumentalize the opening of the capital markets toward the end of convergence is doomed to failure. It is precisely capital market integration that is preventing monetary policy from controlling internal monetary variables, be it in the form of a money supply target or price level stability. And this provides an explanation of the fact that the initial tendency toward convergence of inflation rates within the EMS began to falter in 1988. For all countries except Germany, capital market integration rendered impossible any consistent orientation of monetary policy in terms of internal stability.

What is crucial is not the credibility of monetary policy - the risk of being 'surprised' by decisions made by the central bank - it is the expectations of the capital markets as regards the ensemble of all factors (including income formation and fiscal policy) that are relevant to a country's monetary development. The economic agents would not be rational if they failed to take account of the budget constraint and the necessity of external stabilization. Nor would they be rational if, in forming their expectations, they failed to consider differences in the process of income formation, fiscal policy, etc. And, as far as parities are concerned, the credibility of exchange rates is not conditioned on confidence in the willingness of the monetary authorities to respect any money supply rules. It depends far more on expectations concerning the ability of monetary policy to sustain existing exchange rates.

The weakness of the recent credibility literature is not the assumption that the current decisions of economic agents depend upon expectations but the other assumption that the formation of expectations follows neoclassical lines of reasoning. The rational expectations literature has yielded to the temptation - already implied in the separation of the monetary from the real economy - of, in the end, denying monetary policy any influence on the real economy. The consequence is to conceive the monetary sphere as a 'superstructure' located above markets and controlled solely by governmental activities. If it were correct to suppose that an adjustment to the conditions of the key currency could be instantaneously effected by linking exchange rates, then bringing about a convergence of monetary development in Europe would in fact pose no problem. But if this is not the case, the recent credibility literature is unable to point out a path toward convergence. In fact, the contributions relying on the 'new classical-rational expectation' assumptions are obliged to presuppose what ought to be the result of development: the convergence of monetary performance. The criticisms of the procedure underlying the Maastricht Treaty - especially of the idea that the transition to monetary union be conditional on the convergence of monetary performance - and of the policy recommendation, the 'big leap' proposal (Eichengreen 1993: 1353-54; Giovannini 1990: 265) are, however, not only unrealistic. They express nothing other than capitulation to the divergences that, de facto, continue to exist.

Capital market integration as a gradual concept

Capital market integration at the European as well as at the global level alters the socioeconomic context in which monetary policy acts. The asymmetric and limited impact of the budget constraint makes it clear why capital market integration - and the resultant restrictions on national monetary independence - was unsuccessful in tying the hands of fiscal policy and income formation, and in committing the Bundesbank to a policy recognizing the primacy of external stability. The consequence of the former was continuing divergences. The latter permitted the monetary policy exercised by the monetary authorities of the key-currency country to treat external stabilization as the task of the 'other countries'. De facto, persistent inflation differentials entailed the emergence of new imbalances, such as growing current account disequilibria and increasing creditor-debtor dependencies.

This makes evident why the laissez faire strategy toward economic and monetary union was bound to fail. Integrated capital markets constitute a socioeconomic context unconducive to the convergence of monetary performance, precisely because they tie the hands of monetary policy. Conventional theory poses the wrong question; the crucial point is not whether national monetary dependence must be seen as beneficial or as disadvantageous. The decisive point is how much capital market integration is suitable to support the process of economic integration.

Today capital market integration has become, as paradoxical as it may sound, a threat to the transition to a European economic and monetary union. The laissez faire strategy that sees the capital markets as the starting point of integration in Europe runs the risk of coming to a deadlock, because, given its concentration on establishing market constraints, it relinquishes its instruments for responding to persisting divergences and compensating for the instabilities resulting from them. The problem is no longer that this conditions progress in integration on the functional logic of the foreign exchange markets. Worse yet, in absolutizing the integration of capital markets it is today creating the constraints to which tomorrow's monetary policy will be forced to submit. Attempts to cooperate and coordinate monetary policy at the European level are bound to fail, firstly, because the establishment of a key-currency system leaves the countries with dependent currencies no choice other than to safeguard external stability and, secondly, because the latter relinquish the instruments required to influence the monetary policy of the key-currency country. But there is no need to take capital market integration as the point of departure of integration as a whole. The proposition that capital markets engender constraints on monetary policy is not identical with the proposition that there are constraints to subordinate monetary integration to the logic of the capital markets.

A glance at the development of international economic relations in this century is sufficient to recognize that there does not exist any continuous tendency toward integration of capital markets. In retrospect, the 1970s and, even more so, the 1980s constituted a rather exceptional period. If, however, it is correct that capital market integration contributes automatically neither to a stabilization of international relations nor to a convergence of monetary performance, one essential justification for the laissez faire strategy dominant in the past decades collapses. On the one hand, we are again faced with the old question of how much convergence is desirable and/or necessary. On the other hand, it becomes evident that room for monetary manoeuvre must be kept open if monetary policy is to provide a positive contribution toward convergence. Certainly, national monetary independence is no guarantor of convergence. But the fact that an instrument can be used for purposes other than those for which it is conceived is no excuse for not using it.

References

Commission of the European Communities (ed.) (1988), 'Creation of a European financial area - liberalization of capital movements and financial integration in the Community', *European Economy 36,* Office for the Official Publications of the European Community, Brussels and Luxembourg.

Commission of the European Communities (ed.) (1990), 'One market, one money. An evaluation of the potential benefits and costs of forming an economic and monetary union', *European Economy 44*, Office for the Official Publications of the European Community, Brussels and Luxembourg.

De Grauwe, P. (1992), *The Economics of Monetary Integration,* Oxford University Press, Oxford.

Dornbusch, R. (1988), 'The European Monetary System, the dollar and the yen', in Giavazzi, F., S. Micossa, and M. Miller 1988.

Eichengreen, B. (1990), 'One money for Europe? Lessons from the US currency union', *Economic Policy*, 10, April.

Eichengreen, B. (1993), 'European monetary unification', *Journal of Economic Literature* vol. 31, September.

Eichengreen, B., and C. Wyplosz (1993), 'The Unstable EMS', *Brooking Papers on Economic Activity*, vol. 1.

Emminger, O. (1977), *The D-Mark in the Conflict between Internal and External Equilibrium 1948-1975*, Princeton University Press, Princeton.

Friedman, M. (1953), 'The case for flexible exchange rates', in Friedman, M. *Essays in Positive Economics*, University of Chicago Press, Chicago; quoted after the republication in:Caves, R.E., and H.G. Johnson (eds) (1960) *Readings in International Economics* (The Series of Republished Articles on Economics vol. 11), George Allen and Unwin, London.

Giavazzi, F., S. Micossa, and M. Miller (1988), *The European Monetary System*, Cambridge University Press, Cambridge.

Giavazzi, F. and M. Pagano (1988), 'The advantage of tying one's hands: EWS discipline and central bank credibility', *European Economic Review*, 32.

Giavazzi, F. and L. Spaventa (1990), 'The "New" EMS', in De Grauwe, P., and L. Papademos (eds) *The European Monetary System in the 1990's*, Longmans, London.

Giovannini, A. (1990), 'European monetary reform: progress and pros-- pects', *Brooking Papers on Economic Activity*, no. 2.

Giovannini, A. (1990a), *The Transition to European Monetary Union* Princeton University Press, Princeton.

Hayek, F.A. v. (1978), *Denationalisation of Money - The Argument Refined,* The Institute of Economic Affairs, London.

Keynes, J. (1943), *Proposals for an International Clearing Union*, The Collected Writings of J. M. Keynes, vol. 25, MacMillan Cambridge University Press, London.

Mundell, R.A. (1961), 'A theory of optimum currency areas', *American Economic Review*, vol. 51.

Mundell, R.A. (1963), 'Capital mobility and stabilization policy under fixed and flexible exchange rates', *Canadian Journal of Economics and Political Sciences,* vol. 29, no. 4; quoted after the republication in Caves, R.E., and H.G. Johnson (eds) (1968) *Readings in International Economics, The Series of Republished Articles on Economics vol. 11,* George Allen and Unwin, London.

Padoa-Schioppa, T. (1987), *Efficiency, Stability, and Equity: A Strategy for the Evolution of the Economic System of the European Community,* Oxford University Press, Oxford.

Polanyi, K. (1944), *The Great Transformation*, Beacon Press, Boston.

Riese, H. (1986), *Theorie der Inflation*, Mohr, Tübingen.

Röpke, W. (1959), 'Zwischenbilanz der europäischen Wirtschaftsintegration. Kritische Nachlese.', *Ordo* 11.

Spahn, H.-P. (1988), *Bundesbank und Wirtschaftskrise*, Transfer, Regensburg.

Thomasberger, C. (1993), *Europäische Währungsintegration und globale Währungskonkurrenz*, Mohr, Tübingen.

Thomasberger, C. (1993a), '"Schlingerkurs" oder externe Stabilisierung. Anmerkungen zur Politik der Deutschen Bundesbank nach den Währungsturbulenzen vom Herbst "92"', *Konjunkturpolitik,* vol. 39, no. 5.

Wyplosz, C. (1988), 'Capital flow liberalization and the EMS: A French perspective', in Commission of the European Communities (ed.) (1988).

3 European integration and fiscal policy options[1]

Brigitte Unger

EU
F36
F15
E62

Summary

The differences between an (irrevocable) fixed exchange rate system (stage IIIa of the Delors plan) and a currency union with a common currency (stage IIIb) are often undervalued. Forming a currency union would be a huge institutional shock, and would clearly alter the scenario of a future Europe. Transferring monetary and currency policy to a European Central Bank would mean a clear diminution of national sovereignty. 'Spill-over' effects could lead to decreases in national sovereignty in other policy areas, or could lead to conflicts among the Member States and the collapse of the Monetary Union. The scope for state action is in this scenario different from that in a system of fixed exchange rates. Small countries can free ride in both currency regimes. Yet the restrictions and demands on economic policy are different. In a system of fixed exchange rates, the disciplining function of the currency reserves and the vulnerability to speculation in foreign exchange markets present barriers for a small country. In a currency union, barriers are created by the disciplining function of capital markets and speculation on the price of government bonds. Monetary policy can not be pursued autonomously by a small country in either regime. Differences exist, however, in the possibility to use wage policy and fiscal policy. Institutional differences between countries become clearer in a currency union, because they must make a greater contribution to competition policy than they have in the past. A strong convergence of economic variables can not be expected in a currency union, because corrective mechanisms are absent. Given the significantly larger institutional differences in Europe in comparison to the USA, differences in the real variables, such as unemployment rates, will increase with convergence of the monetary variables.

To make a prairie it takes a clover and a bee,
One clover, and a bee,
And revery.
The revery alone will do,
If bees are few.

Emily Dickinson (1830-1886)

Introduction

After the Second World War, economic policy succeeded in making a prairie full of clover and bees in many European countries. Full employment and a prosperous economy were the outcome of Keynesian expansionary budget policy in the 1970s. In the 1980s international financial trends and financing problems reduced the options of fiscal policy, by which I understand all measures concerning the budget. Given the new premises of budget consolidation under surveillance of financial markets, it became more and more difficult for politicians to realize stabilization goals. Full employment is more difficult to realize, if budgets have to be cut. The prairie is more difficult to make, if bees are few. More imagination will be needed in the future, to create the prairie. Revery alone will, unfortunately, not do it, but will help us to maintain our visions and to explore the options left for economic policy making.

Does national economic policy still have room for manoeuvre in an 'international and integrated world', i.e. in a world with increased goods and factor mobility and professed commitments to common economic policies? The latest changes in Europe, such as the lifting of borders for labour, capital, goods, and services in parts of Western Europe, raise the question of the possibilities and limits of national economic policy. The discussion about a future currency union makes this question even more urgent.

International trends and fiscal policy

The increase in the speed, importance and volume of international financial transactions since the early 1980s is striking. The liberalization of capital markets resulted in an enormous increase of international capital flows. Mooslechner (1995: 98f) gives some empirical indicators for the growth of financial markets: In the US, the volume of border crossing transactions in bonds was about three times the US gross domestic product in 1970, nine times in 1980, but ninety-two times in 1990. Hence, in the last ten years international bond transactions of the US were ten times as large as before. If financial transactions were solely meant to buy goods, they should have approximately the size of an economy's exports and imports of goods and services. In most industrial countries financial transactions exceed by far the volume of trade. The international capital transactions in the financial center of London amount to 700 per cent of the GDP! The volume of foreign exchange transactions in the world's most important financial centers amounts to 880 billions of dollars per day, i.e. about sixty times world trade. On a single day, the volume of transactions in foreign exchange markets exceeds the foreign exchange reserves of industrial countries' national banks by fifty percent. Since the currency reserve position is the main variable to control the exchange rate and the domestic supply of money, national monetary policy could be counteracted by financial markets within less than a day.

The increase of international financial markets also puts pressure on the budget. First, the debt problem of the 1980s was partly due to the growth of international financial markets, transmitting the high interests rates of the US to European countries. In a growing economy, debts can be managed as long as the economy grows faster than the debt. The debt as long as it is not paid back, grows automatically every year with the interest rate. If real growth rates are higher than interest rates, the economy grows faster than its debts, and there is room for increasing budget deficits. With increasing interest rates, however, the debt burden became suddenly an issue. Even without adding new budget deficits, the old debt burden would grow faster than the economy if interest rates exceed growth rates. Budget consolidation became the issue of the 1980s. It would be economistic, to see the reason for budget consolidation in economic factors alone. The general trend towards more conservative politics in many Western European countries certainly contributed to budget cut backs as well. Second, budget deficits can stimulate the economy, but can also lead to inflation and to exchange rate problems, effects that can be an incentive for financial markets to withdraw their capital. Nowadays, the ministers of finance plan their budgets not only under financing constraints, but also under the constraints not to irritate the expectations of financial markets. It seems as if financial markets became more sensitive towards budget issues lately. This can have to do with the fact, that the convergence criteria of Maastricht for the first time shed light on the causal relationship between the budget and the overall economic performance of a country. A light, which is, perhaps, too bright. A country with sound fundamentals and a high budget deficit could still perform well, since budget problems are long term problems, and usually not of much concern of short term speculative financial markets. But as soon as budget criteria enter into the expectations of speculators, they become a constraint for fiscal policymaking.

Beside economic factors of internationalization, legal factors are important constraints for fiscal policy. The Maastricht Treaty set convergence criteria for inflation rates, nominal interest rates, which influence the budget size indirectly. Too expansive budget policies would drive inflation rates and interest rates up. The Treaty sets further convergence criteria, which influence the budget size directly. Countries that want to join the planned European Monetary Union must not exceed net budget deficits of three percent of GDP and gross public debts of sixty percent of GDP. Even if, in the process of negotiation, some exceptions or softer constraints are likely to appear, the general political trend of cutting budgets is reinforced by the Maastricht criteria.

Table 3.1 shows, that many countries are far from fulfilling the Maastricht budget criteria. In the forecasts for 1995, only Germany, Denmark, Ireland and Luxembourg fulfill the net borrowing constraint of three per cent of GDP. Only Germany, France, Luxembourg and the United Kingdom fulfill the constraint on public debt. Altogether, only Germany and Luxembourg fulfill both budget criteria. Furthermore, the convergence process does not seem to occur smoothly. Convergence of fiscal policies would mean, that countries would move in the direction of the Maastricht box, which lies between zero and three per cent of net borrowing and zero and sixty per cent of public debt. But, as Table 3.1 indicates, countries develop in all directions. Germany and Luxembourg are already in the box. Greece and Italy reduce their net deficits, but increase their public debt ratio. The Netherlands reduces its net deficits, but keeps its public debt ration constant. The former EFTA countries Austria, Finland and Sweden, as well as Portugal and the UK increase both their net deficits and their public debt ratio.

The crisis of the early 1990s has shown, that strict budget criteria cannot be fulfilled in a recession. The simple working of the automatic stabilizers (increased government spending for unemployment benefits and decreased tax incomes) was enough to lead to a significant deterioration of the fiscal position of the Member States (Cabral 1995: 13). There seems to be more room for manoeuvre left for fiscal policy than the tight budget criteria of Maastricht indicate. Furthermore, the criteria are 'softened'. Countries are now judged according to the reliability of their convergence programmes. Convergence is interpreted as 'going in the right direction' rather than reaching the less than three or less than sixty per cent box.

Scenarios for a currency union in the future Europe

Before discussing the national scope of action, it is appropriate to consider if the 'nation' will still exist in the integrated Europe of the future?

Economic theory has almost always assumed the nation, or rather the country, to be the largest tax collecting entity, either explicitly (as for example Adam Smith in 1776 in the 'Welfare of Nations') or implicitly. In German it is actually called the national economy (Nationaloekonomie). Stabilization policy was discussed as the objective of taxation in states (with the exception of regional aspects). The task of economic policy was to do the 'best' for one's own state, in an international environment (two-country, three-country model). Either to go on with macroeconomic theory in which the supernational entity is henceforth the object of analysis, seen as 'a big country or nation' confronted with 'the rest of the world'. The other possibility is to switch to the regional economy, analyze the former nations as regions within the supernation, and discuss center-periphery problems.

Problems emerge if the newly developing territorial and functional 'patterns' divide from one another. If, for instance, certain spheres of politics were dealt with at the European level and others at the national level. Schmitter (1993) depicts various scenarios for the future of european politics. Scenario one represents europe as a nation-state (a 'stato' in Schmitter 1993's terminology), characterized by a fixed territory (the twelve or however many EU Member States) and well defined tasks. Macroeconomic policy would then be a competence of the supranational state. The individual states would resolve, sooner or later, to transfer ever more policy areas to the supranational authority. Does the discussion about a unified financial and currency policy point in this direction for a future Europe? Even though it is always emphasized that national sovereignty should to a large degree be maintained (for instance in the area of fiscal policy), would not political and economic integration, the creation of a common currency and the central governance of monetary policy eventually have spill-over effects on other political and economic sectors, that undermine the nation-state? For economic analysis, this would mean that the traditional macroeconomic theory can be used for the external relations of the EU, while for the internal relations between the individual members, primarily the regional aspects (such as regional unemployment) of macroeconomic measures are relevant.

In Schmitter's second scenario, the 'confederatio', the nation-states maintain their sovereignty and join an alliance for specific, fixed tasks. For each task their may be more or less Member States, i.e. the territory is variable. For example there could be some states within the EU that join together around fiscal policy, while others join to a common environmental or social policy. Does the discussion of a economic and currency union point in this direction for a new Europe? One in which certain EU States join the currency union whereas others do not (as Great Britain has signalled)? In this scenario, the nation-states would retain the largest

61

degree of sovereignty and cooperation would be attempted only for certain tasks. In the area of currency policy, fixed (irreversible) exchange rates correspond most closely to this scenario.

Or do we have two (contradictory) images of a future Europe? An integrated supranational Europe in the area of monetary and exchange rate policy and a nation-state based Europe in other areas of stabilization policy, as for example in fiscal and wage policy? This raises the question of whether these two different scenarios can exist next to one another. It is much more likely, that either the supranational state assumes ever more responsibilities and thus eliminates the individual state (scenario one), or that the competition of the individual states for autonomy and sovereignty hinders the supranational state (scenario two). This could lead to the collapse of the planned currency union. The introduction of a monetary union is therefore to be viewed as an unstable solution (compare also the unstable solutions of a currency union from Casella and Feinstein 1989).

Scenario three depicts the future Europe as a 'consortio' (Schmitter 1993), as a loose association of nation-states, with fixed territory, that come together for certain, varying tasks according to necessity. For example, they might cooperate on boycotts of third parties, or on the formulation of common technical standards etc. In the area of currency policy this would correspond to a system of fixed exchange rates, in which, for example, the central banks would meet together to agree on realignments or on exchange rates parities with third countries. It remains difficult in this scenario, however, to keep the territory fixed, if other countries simply fix their currencies to the same currency basket. In this variant of a future Europe, the nation-states remain in place.

Scenario four depicts Europe as a regional network (a 'condominium' in Schmitter's terminology 1993). Functions and territory are variable in this model. This would be the case, for example, if the city of Munich set up an exhibition together with France, or if a bank reached a credit agreement with the firms of a region, or if a branch reached agreements with all countries etc. Here Europe would form an overlapping, territorial pattern. Europe would then be a melting pot of varying tasks and different sizes and hierarchically, fully indeterminate territorial units. There would be (in the condominium) neither a supranational state (stato) nor nation-states (confederatio, consortio). While this scenario is quite imaginable for the areas of trade and industry, it is not plausible for financial or currency policy, because a supranational entity or a nation-state is necessary to carry them out (except if one supports Hayek's (1978) demand for a denationalization of money).

The history of monetary unions in the Europe of the nineteenth century shows, that monetary unions, that were not also political unions, did not endure. Examples of this include the German-Austrian Münzunion 1857-

1867, or the Scandinavian Münzunion 1872-1931. As opposed to that, where currency areas were adapted to new political borders, where political unification of the members existed, they were irreversible. Examples of this are the Swiss Confederation, or the Italian Kingdom. (see Theurl 1992: 34 and 337f). If we extrapolate from these historical patterns, it would mean that a currency union can only exist in a politically unified Europe, in which the sovereignty of the nation-states is eliminated in many areas (Scenario one). If it occurs without political adjustment, i.e. if the sovereignty of the nation-states is maintained (Scenarios two and three) then it is reversible and unstable. For Scenario four, where supranational- and nation-states do not exist, it is not defined.

The only thing that seems quite sure for the time being is that the European Monetary Unions (EMU) will not be established in 1997, if it ever will. It, furthermore, seems quite sure, that not all of the countries will participate. A Europe of several speeds (Bogdandy 1993) is likely. If the Maastricht criteria have some relevance for potential access to the currency club, than countries such as Italy, Greece and Spain are far from joining it.

Differences between a fixed exchange rate regime and a currency union

Some economists see no difference between an irrevocable fixed exchange rate system and a currency union (see Delors 1989, Branson 1991). In both cases there is, from this perspective, no expectation of exchange rate changes. Therefore, the same economic conditions hold, regardless of whether currencies are fixed to one another or whether there is only one currency.

By contrast, De Grauwe (1992), Casella and Feinstein (1990), and Thomasberger (1993) all clearly differentiate between the two currency systems. The demand in the Delors report for an irrevocable fixed exchange rate and for irrevocable and unlimited convertibility of the currencies is nothing other 'than a proclamation of the irrevocability of the EMS, i.e. a political declaration of the commitment to a key currency system'. (Thomasberger 1993: 221). A belief in keeping with scenarios two or three from above.

A further demand of the Delors report, the creation of a unified currency (ECU) with autonomous, centralized monetary policy and the correspondingly necessary institutions, is by contrast something quite different. It is a demand in keeping with scenario one of above.

The hybrid form of these two exchange rate regimes, that is discussed now, is an irrevocable fixed exchange rate system under surveillance of a European Central Bank. As will be shown below, this is a very peculiar mixture between a fixed currency regime and a currency union, which might politically appropriate, but not economically. I will first show the differences between an irrevocable fixed exchange rate system and a currency union and then try to evaluate, whether the hybrid form of an irrevocable fixed exchange rate under European Central Bank surveillance belongs to the former or to the latter regime.

The following differences exist between both regimes:

A currency union has either a common currency (the ECU) or perfectly substitutable currencies. This is the case when on a given day the old currencies can be converted into new ones, such that 1 new DM = 1 new Franc = 1 new Lira = 1 new Guilder = 1 new pound = 1 new ECU. Also, the idea of printing the ECU on one side and the national currency on the other side would be acceptable, as long as 1 DM = 1 Franc etc. In this case, only one price must be displayed on a product, rather than a price list in every country for all currencies. Furthermore, one must be able to pay with any currency in every country. A common currency or perfectly substitutable currencies have advantages that can be deduced from the function of money as a unit of account, a medium of exchange, and as a store of value (see Qvigstad 1992: 3f). A common unit of account reduces accounting costs and facilitates cost comparisons. A common medium of exchange reduces transaction costs, in that it eliminates costs of converting currency. With money as a store of value the exchange rate risk drops. With the end of the currency risk premia, the interest rates of the Union members will drop.

The cost of a common currency is the diminution of the responsibilities of sovereign states (at the very least in exchange rate and monetary policy). Furthermore, the exchange rate can no longer serve as a regulating instrument to filter exogenous shocks. As long as labour and capital are not perfectly mobile, which would provide an automatic balancing mechanism (i.e. an optimal currency zone), or as long as some kind of centralized institutions (Finanzausgleich) would create an economic and financial balance, economic swings and crises could be intensified by it. Within this magic polygon, the options open to national economic policy narrow, because ever fewer goals can be achieved nationally. Is the currency union a 'price lowering union'? Could higher unemployment rates be the cost of the common price stability and currency policies? Is the trade-off between inflation and unemployment (e.g. institutionally conditioned) different in the different countries? Are the real costs of the unions likewise different from country to country? In that case, convergence of sinking inflation rates means divergence of climbing unemployment rates (Grandner and Unger 1993). The currency union would then create further costs because of increased unemployment.

By contrast, a system of irrevocable, fixed exchange rates means that the problems that having different units of account cause for price comparisons persist. Also the transaction costs of the currency exchange remain if every country retains its own currency as a medium of exchange. The foreign exchange markets for the individual currencies would remain. Also the risk premia for money as a store of value would not disappear. This is true because even with an irrevocable fixed exchange rate, the possibility still exists that rates will be changed. Thus, insecurity regarding the irrevocability of the parities remains. Therefore the assessment of the credibility of irrevocable fixed exchange rates by the money and foreign exchange markets is of significance. A debtor country in danger of a devaluation will, as before, pay higher risk premia than countries with higher credit worthiness and secured exchange rates. The insecurity over future developments in the exchange rates will also lead banks to use domestic currency for their short term interbank transfers, i.e. the substitutability of the currencies is limited (see De Grauwe 1992: 154). 'In essence this fixed exchange rate system is just a further development of the present EMS regime' (De Grauwe 1992: 155).

The planned irrevocable fixed exchange rate system under surveillance of a European Central Bank (stage IIIa of the Delors plan) is a mixture of both regimes. As long as exchange rates still exist, even if declared 'irrevocable', we still have a fixed exchange rate system and not a currency union. The fact, that a European Central Bank declares them irrevocable makes the commitment more reliable than if left to the member countries. Nevertheless, though the exchange rate risk is diminished, it is not eliminated as long as different currencies with different values exist. Economically this stage does not provide any advantage of a currency union. The accounting costs of calculation in different currencies still exist, cash registers of the Member countries would have to have many subcompartments for the different currencies, convertibility costs would still exist, foreign exchange markets would still exist and the substitutability of the currency would simply not be perfect.

Banks would continue to do their domestic affairs in domestic currencies, and for the rest, the former key currency of the German Mark would continue to be the predominant currency.

If we define a currency system not by the exchange rate risk and the predominance of a key currency, but by common monetary policy followed by the Member Countries, the hybrid form of stage IIIa looks more like a currency union. Not Germany's monetary policy will have to be followed anymore, not asymmetric shocks will prevail, but a common monetary policy with more symmetric shocks. The European Central Bank fixes the common money supply and the quota for each central bank of its Member Countries. Nevertheless, the interest rates among member countries will not be the same. Even if capital markets believed, that the exchange rate

65

will be kept fixed, the liquidity premium charged on the interest rate will differ among currency. The German Mark will still have the lowest liquidity premium. Stage IIIa in its actual design seems economically thus like a very improvised solution.

The differing scopes for action in a currency union and in a fixed exchange rate system

Austria is occasionally cited as an example of a small country that already has more than ten years of experience with a currency union, because through stable currency policy it fixed the Schilling to the German Mark. Because the nominal exchange rate was to be held at 7.04 Schillings per German Mark consistently since 1981, one can view it as an laboratory experiment for the Economic and Currency Union (see Breuss 1992, Guger and Marterbauer 1993). Viewing the Austrian hard currency policy a currency union with Germany is based on a misunderstanding of diverse currency regimes. Pegging ones currency to a key currency is not a currency union. The exchange rate pegged to the German Mark is not an irrevocably fixed exchange rate either. Although the Austrian National Bank was able to defend the currency against unfounded, rumor-based speculation against the Schilling in 1993, its limited currency reserves would leave it powerless against massive, long term speculation against the Schilling. The exchange rate is, therefore, much less 'irrevocable' than in the European Union, where at least intervention in support of the currency by the other Member States can be expected. A currency union is a completely different system, in which there are no exchange rate risks, foreign exchange markets, transaction costs for currency exchange or opportunities for currency speculation.

In this context the following questions are of interest, first, if a small country still has room for manoeuvre to conduct autonomous economic policy, and, second, if this room for manoeuvre differs in the various currency regimes.

First, can economic variables remain different with fixed exchange rates, or do they converge such that national economic policy becomes powerless? A common argument claims that internationalization leads to the impotence of national economic policies (especially those of small countries), because ever more parameters, or limitations on policy choices, are set from abroad. If financial capital crosses borders instantly without obstacles, if firms can move their operations quickly and without resistance, and if workers can easily change jobs, i.e. if the factors of production can be allocated to their best use, then interest rates, prices and wages of different countries must converge. Thus the leeway for monetary, price, wage, income and fiscal policies decreases systematically with increasing factor mobility. At the same time, (from an allocative point of view) increases in efficiency are achieved. In this 'best of all worlds' economic policy is not only powerless, it is also superfluous. It can make, at best, a few distributional corrections, if the market determined outcome is unacceptable on ethnic, moral or social grounds.

If, however, markets do not function perfectly, if factor mobility is not perfect, if there are reasons that factors of production can not cross borders quickly and without resistance, then there will be no alignment of economic variables. By contrast, with the increased insecurity and higher tempo with which adjustments and disturbances can cross borders, comes a new demand on economic policy. It must now filter out more sudden and drastic disturbances which are increased from abroad.

Factors are never perfectly mobile. In general, financial capital is more mobile than physical assets. This means that financial disturbances are transferred to other countries much faster than are physical phenomena. While there are no intrinsic barriers to the increase of mobility of financial capital (in a fully computerized world it could be infinite), there are intrinsic barriers to the mobility of physical assets. Their dependence on geographical proximity of sales markets and raw materials markets, their high fixed costs, transport costs etc. limit the speed with which physical assets can be transferred from one country to another. Labour mobility (except for very high and very low level jobs) is even more limited. In general, country specific training patterns and skills, language barriers and cultural ties limit the increase of labour mobility. This, in turn, has an effect on the mobility of physical assets which often rely on the specific skills of workers (see Unger 1990). Although factor mobility has increased and will continue to increase, there are clear limits on future increases in mobility.

Such increases in mobility limit the room for maneuver of small countries. The possible means of controlling the money supply and interest rates decrease drastically. By contrast, fiscal policy, labour market policy, wage policy and other institutional arrangements increase in their importance for reducing insecurity and filtering shocks. From the last fifteen years we know, that strongly centralized wage negotiation systems with macroeconomic oriented Unions can mitigate international shocks with more success than can wage negotiation systems at the branch level (see Grandner and Unger 1993). Countries where participants in the negotiations share stable, long term relationships based on cooperation and trust (so called 'trust societies') reduce uncertainty and mitigate shocks with more success than do countries with higher flexibility but less certainty that negotiating partners will even be around come tomorrow. Also, the elasticity of wages with respect to changes in unemployment varies institutionally (see Carlin and Soskice 1990).

The second question is, what different options do a fixed exchange rate system and a unified currency leave for a small country? Small, open economies are, on one hand, confronted with exogenous, predetermined economic variables such as foreign interest rates, price levels and incomes. They must adapt their domestic economic variables to these exogenous ones. On the other hand, the smallness of the country allows for actions which are not open, or are open only under restricted conditions, to a large country. Small countries can 'free-ride' with much less fear of facing sanctions.

Small countries can free ride in either currency regime. However, different modes of behavior are more likely in the respective regimes. In the area of monetary policy, the money supply is not more controllable with fixed exchange rates, because an integral component of the money supply, the currency reserves, must be bought and sold in order to maintain the fixed rate. This remains the control function of the currency reserves. In the case of long lasting imbalances, the loss of foreign currency reserves would endanger the fixed exchange rate.

In a currency union (without a European Central Bank) the money supply is not controllable, because it would be determined by the sum total of the participants. Every country would have an incentive to put more money in circulation, because the costs of higher inflation would be divided among all states, while the benefits of seigniorage would be exclusive to the country issuing the money. (Seigniorage amounts to approximately ten per cent of the State revenues of the Southern EU States, see Hermann, Leibfritz, Sorensen, and Wegner 1992: 41.) A small country has a particularly strong incentive, because the costs, the negative effects of higher inflation for all other states, are negligible. Small states have the advantage that they can take advantage of large states, without inflicting noticeable damages on them. The disciplining function of currency reserves ends, because there is no longer an exchange rate that needs to be maintained.

The fact that the money supply of the Union would no longer be controllable if every country issued money at its on discretion led to the demand for a European Central Bank to control the money supply. In this case, the free-rider problem associated with increasing the money supply disappears.

Therefore, in the realm of monetary policy, small countries can only expect to maintain room for maneuver in the absence of a central monetary institution. Otherwise neither currency regime allows room for maneuver in monetary policy.

In the area of wage policy, institutional arrangements of individual countries play an especially important role. In Austria, the hard currency policy (that implied a revaluation of the effective real exchange rate) was viewed as 'a whip for employers' (Handler 1982). It was viewed in this light because, given the overvaluation of the currency, increases in exports were only achievable through increases in productivity. At the same time this was also a signal to the unions to make moderate wage demands, less they endanger the competitiveness of the export sector. Hard currency policy was thus a disciplining instrument for both employers and workers. Actual wage flexibility was guaranteed through the system of 'Social Partnership', because, among other things, the dependence on foreign countries and the threat of exogenous shocks existed for both industrialists and workers. Katzenstein (1985) sees this phenomenon as typical for small, open economies.

In a currency union countries become regions. They lose the opportunity to control the real exchange rate (i.e. the relationship between the prices of tradeable and non-tradeable goods) through influencing the nominal exchange. (Eichengreen (1991) assumes prices to be given and sees fiscal policy as the only means to remedy the resulting regional problems of unemployment.) Because of that wage (and structural) policy is of significance for the regional problem. It is true that the Austrian system of using hard currency policy as a 'whip' for the interest groups becomes untenable. It is, however, replaced by a new whip effect: the pressure for productivity increases and moderate wage increases could increase in significance in a currency union where there is otherwise no opportunity for the regions to influence price levels. This, however, requires that the mobility of labour and physical assets does not greatly increase, because that would lead inevitably to a convergence of wages and productivity. In the future, the institutional arrangements of the individual countries and their more or less solidaristic wage policies will, therefore, play an important role in their competitiveness. It is also important that small countries show more room for maneuver regarding real wage flexibility and regarding influencing the terms of trade than do large countries. For large countries low wages and prices have impact on the price and wage level abroad. Their price diminishing policy results also in lower wages and prices abroad, while small countries do not have this impact.

In the area of fiscal policy opportunities for free-riding exist in a system of fixed exchange rates, as Austrian economic policy of the 1970s and early 1980s (the so-called 'Austro-keynesianism') demonstrates. Through hard currency policy, pegging to the currency of an important trading partner with stable prices, low inflation rates could be imported, while an expansive fiscal policy provided for a high level of unemployment. The balance of payments deficit induced as a result could be matched by higher interest rates and surpluses on the capital account. The moderate wage policy of labour inhibited domestically induced inflation. Limits on the opportunity for free-riding are set by the disciplining function of the overall balance of payments and again by the currency reserves. Room for maneuver for fiscal policy remains, even if differences in interest rates can no longer be used as a policy instrument in a world of high capital mobility. Bredenkamp and Deppler (1990) show that the room for using budget deficits and debts in Europe, that is still compatible with fixed exchange rates, is considerable. The distinctly lower rates of unemployment that Austria maintained, with rates of inflation nearly identical to Germany's, serve as evidence that large countries normally do not sanction the free-riding behavior of small countries.

In a currency union the impact of fiscal policy on the balance of payments looses significance, because no sanctions of currency reserves losses will occur. Regional imbalances of payment can persist without a self-correcting mechanism. Without a superstate with a central government, flexible budget policy is the means with which to filter shocks from abroad: a negative (asymmetric) shock in Country A decreases the tax revenue and increases the automatic expenditures, such as unemployment insurance. Therefore the budget deficit grows in Country A, while Country B, with a positive shock, shows a decreasing budget deficit. Fiscal policy is the sole shock absorber, because nominal and (with prices given) real exchange rates disappear as corrective mechanisms (Eichengreen 1991). (As Herr 1995: 209) points out, it is, however, not very likely, that poor regions will be able to enjoy the unpunished and almost unlimited financing of their balance of payments deficits. The more realistic scenario, according to him, is that investments in a poor regions are small but savings are still smaller. A regional balance of payment surplus instead of a deficit will then occur together with low regional growth).

With a central government the balance between the countries would automatically succeed: the tax revenue of the European government from Country A would be lower than that from Country B, while the expenditures for Country A would be greater than those for Country B. In this case, however, we would be back in Scenario 1 with a European Superstate. States without monetary, currency or fiscal policy would be divested of virtually all their sovereignty.

Which free-riding opportunities exist for countries, and if they will actually use them, is contested in the literature. Some authors (among others Delors 1989) fear that incentives for free-riding exist in a currency union, which can only be controlled with strict budget rules. A moral hazard problem would exist. Country A could go ever deeper into debt and thus create negative effects for all in that it would increase interest rates in the Union's capital market. That would, in turn, pressure the European Central Bank to follow a loose monetary policy, and would endanger the Union's price stability. This argument does not apply to a small country,

70

because its debt has no influence on the interest rate of the Union. A small country can, therefore, costlessly take a free-rider position. (If, however, many 'small' countries follow this strategy, problems could result.)

As De Grauwe (1990: 170f) demonstrates, the moral hazard problem is based on the assumption of imperfect capital markets. With efficient capital markets, the bad debtor country would pay higher interest than the good one. Thus, as before, there would be different rates of interest for different risk premia on government debts. Only the exchange rate risk would be missing. Here the question reappears of whether the Union would allow a country to go into bankruptcy. Even the most solemn declaration by the Union of a 'no bail-out clause' would only matter if it was believed by financial markets (De Grauwe 1990: 172). In fact, in so far as strict budget rules are set, questions arise regarding recoverability and its credibility. (On the controversy regarding the necessity of 'budget straight jackets' see Buiter 1992 and Buiter, Corsetti and Roubini 1992.) The disciplining function of currency reserves in a fixed exchange rate system are replaced by the disciplining function of the capital market. The individual states must finance the state debt exclusively in capital markets. Limits on debt will be set by the capital markets. By contrast the central unit has a much softer budget constraint, since it still has the option to monetarize its debt by printing money (Moesen and Van Rompuy 1990 quoted in De Grauwe 1990).

Whether the disciplining function of the currency reserves and the dependence on foreign exchange market speculation, or that of the capital markets and their speculation leaves small states more options depends on the behavior of the capital markets and the other Member States. In both exchange rate regimes, opportunities for free-riding by small states exist.

There is hardly an area of the economy in which forecasts of actor's actions differ as greatly as they due when discussing the currency union (for an excellent, brief overview see De Grauwe 1990, chapter seven and eight). Whether budget deficits will rise or fall, if interest rates will rise or fall, if external effects will appear or will be automatically internalized by the capital markets, if shocks will be filtered or intensified, etc. depends on assumptions regarding the strategic behavior of actors. That involves (implicit) speculation in the areas of psychology, sociology and political science.

Basically, it deals with problems of collective action. What Mancur Olson (1965) showed about interest groups in his 'Logic of Collective Action', can be applied in part to the Member States of a Union:

First, Olson shows that large firms have more incentive to found an interest group than do small ones, because due to their size they benefit disproportionately from lower costs and more advantageous sector regulations. If one carries this analysis to the currency union, the economic

71

incentive for large countries to build a union is greater than that for small countries, as concerns the gain in sales markets volume and the amount of lower transaction costs. Also, large countries often have relatively closed economies, such that an opening of markets can reveal wholly new perspectives. Olson's argument can not be applied if effects of scale are taken into account. Small countries can realize larger economies of scale than big countries, since - under 'normal' conditions - they are located at the beginning of the decreasing part of the cost curve.

Their dependence on export markets is also larger, which makes an expansion of the sales markets beneficial for them. Politically, large countries have a power advantage vis a vis small ones. Therefore, they offer small countries a disproportionately large say in Union affairs to partially compensate them and to convince them to participate in the Union. Large countries might, given their considerable economic and political interest in forming a Union, allow small countries to free-ride. Small countries also have less sanctions to fear, because the negative externalities their free-riding creates is negligible. On the negative side, small states face unequal power relations, the enormous financial and economic threat potential of large countries, and the potential for legal threat-potential of the European Court of Justice.

Second, Olson has argued that unions with few participants are 'privileged groups', as long as no free-rider problem emerges. The more members a Union has, the larger the free-rider problem will be. In a small group, everyone will be required to contribute to the production of the collective good. The larger the group, the more likely the good will be produced even without the contribution of a given individual. In larger groups there is less, and more distant, social control than in small ones. An increase in the number of members of a currency union heightens the free-rider problem. Eichengreen (1992: 54), who finds that the efficiency gains of a unified currency are a positive function of the number of participating countries, overlooks the fact that increasing costs associated with the free-rider problem could emerge. EU-enlargement increases the likelihood of free-riding of Member States.

Third, free-riding can become contagious. One country starts to free-ride, and the next one follows. This is consistent with the results Axelrod (1987) found in his computer-generated prisoner's dilemma tournaments. The best strategy was not to defect first, but to cooperate in the first round and to mimic the opponents previous move in subsequent rounds. ('tit-for-tat')

Fourth, Starbatty (1990) shows that in the history of European currency systems, too large defection did not become a problem for the international arrangements. Rather, it became a problem for the defectors themselves. As long as the leaders of the main participants were coordinated, the small countries would again conform (Starbatty 1990: 105). This means that free-riding is only possible to a limited degree. If the policies of the small country are too expansive or restrictive in comparison to the policies of other states, they face problems competing. In a system of fixed exchange rates, policies which are too expansionary generate pressure for devaluation (e.g. Sweden), whereas policies which are too restrictive generate pressure for revaluation (e.g. Switzerland) (see Starbatty 1990: 105). In a currency union competitiveness problems arise in one of two ways. Policies which are too expansionary create high wages and prices, whereas policies which are too restrictive lead to high unemployment rates. The example of Austria shows clearly, however, that there is considerable leeway for free-riding through expansionary policies, without generating competitiveness problems.

Fifth, empirical studies of the USA supply surprising findings regarding the scope for economic policy in a currency union. The US-Dollar area has existed for more than a hundred years and is even today far from homogenous in crucial economic policy variables. The unemployment rates in 1991 varied between 2.7 per cent in Nebraska and 10.5 per cent in West Virginia (Rauch 1994). (In Europe they vary between 2.7 per cent in Luxembourg and 23.8 per cent in Spain in 1994!) This although the USA is far more homogenous in this respect than Europe would be. Reasons for the higher American homogeneity in unemployment rates, in addition to the much stronger individualization of American society, include the absence of language barriers, which also result in a higher labour mobility (on parallels and differences between the USA and Europe see Klatzer and Unger 1992).

Fiscal policy shows considerable differences between the fifty States. Tax systems, income tax and sales tax differ between the states. The revenues of the states in 1989 differ between 7.1 per cent of the gross state product in Texas to 22.2 per cent in Alaska (see Ranch 1994). The federal government is, however, much stronger in comparison to its European counterpart. It is responsible for about sixty per cent of budget agenda. Thus it has considerably more authority than in Europe. According to Sachs and Sala-I-Martin (1991), this clearly moderates regional shocks between the US states. According to their calculations, if incomes decrease by one dollar, then tax payments by the residents decrease by 30 cents, while transfer payments from Washington increase by 10 cents. Von Hagen (1991), who analyzes short term shocks and uses a different definition of the region, comes to more moderate results. He holds the regional redistribution effects of the federal budget to be at most moderate.

One can find clear differences not only in the revenues, but also in the expenditures of the states. The states are responsible for, among other things, unemployment, pension payments and health care. Big differences can still be found in social affairs, such as the recognition and treatment of the homeless, and health care, which were among the earliest tasks of local governments. Welfare payments in rich states like Alaska and California are approximately 550 dollars per month, nearly five times as high as in Alabama. (see Dye 1991: 472)

Looking at the USA suggests that states and regions in a currency union differ not only in geographical, historical and political factors, but also in constitutional, legal and economic factors such as taxes, social welfare spending, income and income distribution.

One can also learn something about the potential free-rider problem and the trustworthiness of regulations on indebtedness from the US experience. The vast majority of American States have voluntary debt restrictions in their constitutions (see Hermann, Leibfritz, Soerensen, and Wegner 1992: 63 for a detailed overview of the regulations). Despite that, debt behavior varies greatly. As Von Hagen (1991) shows, states often circumvent these limits through 'flight from the budget' in that they leave specific expenditures out of the budget. There is no universal definition of 'debt' in American legal language. (Hermann et al. 1992: 67 take the opposite view, namely that debt restrictions are effective, and that the US debt crisis results mainly from the federal budget.) 'Flight from the budget' succeeds in calming capital markets, which would reduce the bond-rating and greatly increase interest rates if the state went deeper into debt (Eichengreen 1991). The US capital markets thus serve a disciplining function, because the municipal bond rates differ. Goldstein and Woglom (1991), who find a correlation between low budget deficits and low costs for debts on the US Municipal Bond Market, also come to this conclusion.

Nevertheless, we do not know, how financial markets will interpret debts in the European Union. In the US they obviously do believe in no bailing-out among the fifty states. Also, the fact, that for the first time a whole county (Orange County) bankrupt in California in 1994, is a clear signal to financial markets, that bailing-out does not take place. But would the same be the case in Europe? Would the European Central Bank let a debtor country go bankrupt? Would market forces bring about the budget adjustments, by sanctioning higher debtor countries by means of higher interest rates charged? If we could be sure about this, if we could rely on market forces, the Maastricht criteria would be completely obsolete! As long as frictions have to be expected and as long as the strategic action of players is not determined, there is room for manoeuver left for fiscal policies. The prairie of clover can still be made, even if the bees seem to have diminished.

Conclusion

The differences between an (irrevocable) fixed exchange rate system and a currency union with a common currency are often undervalued. Forming a currency union would be a huge institutional shock, and would clearly alter the scenario of a future Europe. Transferring monetary and currency policy to a European Central Bank would mean a clear diminution of national sovereignty. 'Spill-over' effects could lead to decreases in national sovereignty in other policy areas, or could lead to conflicts among the Member States and the collapse of the Monetary Union. The scope for state action is different in this scenario than in a system of fixed exchange rates. Small countries can free-ride in both currency regimes. Yet the restrictions and demands on economic policy are different. In a system of fixed exchange rates, the disciplining function of the currency reserves and the vulnerability to speculation in foreign exchange markets present barriers for a small country. In a currency union, barriers are created by the disciplining function of capital markets and speculation on the price of government bonds. Monetary policy can not be pursued autonomously by a small country in either regime. Differences exist, however, in the possibility to use wage policy and fiscal policy. Institutional differences between countries become clearer in a currency union, because they must make a greater contribution to competition policy than they have in the past. A strong convergence of economic variables can not be expected in a currency union, because corrective mechanisms are absent. Given the larger institutional differences in Europe compared to the USA, differences in the real variables will increase with convergence of the monetary variables.

Note

1. I thank Gerhard Munduch, Ewald Nowotny (Vienna University of Economics), Heinz Handler (Ministry of Economic Affairs, Vienna), Edith Kitzmantel (Ministry of Finance, Vienna) and Frans van Waarden (Utrecht University) for helpful comments on an earlier draft. Parts of the paper have been translated from German by Dan Kelemen. I thank my generous sponsor, the Austrian National Bank and its president Dr. Maria Schaumayer, whose fellowship allowed me to spend six months at Stanford University. By granting post doctoral fellowships to women of her Alma Mater, Dr. Maria Schaumayer contributes in her very personal way to Austria's catching up with the EU level of womens' participation in academics. With one clover and a bee a year, Emily Dickinson's prairie is not left to revery alone, anymore.

Table 3.1
General government net borrowing and gross general government debt

Country	General government net borrowing (a) in % of GDP		Gross general government debt in % of GDP	
	1990	1995	1990	1995
Belgium	5.4	4.7	130.8	138.7
Denmark	1.5	3.0	59.6	78.0
Germany	2.1	2.4	43.8	59.4
Greece	14.0	13.3	82.6	125.4
Spain	3.9	6.0	45.1	65.8
France	1.6	4.9	35.4	53.4
Ireland	2.2	2.0	96.8	83.7
Italy	10.9	8.6	97.9	126.8
Luxembourg	-5.9	-1.6	5.4	9.8
Netherlands	5.1	3.5	78.8	78.8
Portugal	5.5	5.8	67.7	71.7
United Kingdom	1.5	4.6	34.9	52.4
Austria	2.0	4.4	31.7	64.4
Finland	-1.4	5.0	55.1	70.0 (b)
Sweden	-3.9	9.6	44.7	78.9 (b)
Maastricht-criterion	---	3.0	---	60.0

Source: Cabral, 1995, Commission services, economic forecasts (Autumn 1994), OECD Economic Outlook, December 1992

Notes:
(a) A minus indicates a budget surplus. (b) Values for 1994.

References

Argy, V., and P. de Grauwe (eds) (1990), *Choosing an Exchange Rate Regime. The Challenge for Smaller Industrial Countries*, Belgium International Monetary Fund, Katholieke Universiteit Leuven, Macquarie University.

Axelrod, R. (1987), *Die Evolution der Kooperation*, Munich.

Branson, W. H. (1991), 'Exchange rate policies for the EFTA countries in the 1990s', *EFTA Occasional Paper* No. 35, European Free Trade Association, Geneva.

Bredenkamp, H., and M. Deppler (1990), 'Fiscal constraints of a fixed exchange rate regime' in Argy, V., and P. De Grauwe (eds).

Breuss, F. (1992), Was erwartet Oesterreich in der Wirtschafts- and Waehrungsunion der EG? in *Monatsberichte des Oesterreichischen Instituts fuer Wirtschaftsforschung*, vol. 65, no. 10.

Buiter, W. (1992), 'Should we worry about the fiscal numerology of Maastricht?', *CEPR Discussion Paper* no. 668, June, Center for European Policy Research, London.

Buiter, W., G. Corsetti, and N. Roubini (1992), '"Excessive deficits": sense and nonsense in the Treaty of Maastricht', *CEPR Discussion Paper* no. 750, December, Center for European Policy Research, London.

Cabral, A.J. (1995), 'Is convergence towards EMU making enough progress?', paper presented at the Austrian Conference in Stanford 'Options for the European Union: Meeting the Challenge of Enlargement', March, Stanford.

Casella, A., and J. Feinstein (1989), 'Management of a common currency'. in De Cecco, M., and A. Giovannini (eds).

De Cecco, M., and A. Giovannini (eds) (1989), *A European Central Bank? Perspectives on Monetary Unification after Ten Years of the EMS*, Cambridge University Press, Cambridge, UK.

De Grauwe, P. (1992), *The Economics of Monetary Integration*, Oxford University Press, Oxford.

Delors, J. (1989), *Bericht zur Wirtschafts- and Währungunion in der Europäischen Gemeinschaft*, s.l.

Dye, T.R. (1991), *Politics in States and Communities*, New Jersey.

Eichengreen, B. (1991), 'Is Europe an optimum currency area?', *NBER Working Paper* no. 3579, January, National Bureau of Economic Research, Cambridge.

Eichengreen, B. (1991), 'Will European currency unification exacerbate regional unemployment problems?', paper prepared for the Conference on Labor's Response to 1992, April, Berkeley.

Eichengreen, B. (1993), 'European monetary unification', *Journal of Economic Literature*, vol. 31, September.

Grandner, T., and B. Unger (1993), 'The role of governance institutions for the future of European policy', paper presented at the SASE-Conference, New School for Social Research, New York, April.

Guger, A., and M. Marterbauer (1993), 'Europäische Währungsunion und Konsequenzen für die Kollektivvertragspolitik', *Department of Economics Working Paper* no. 17, January, University of Economics and Business Administration, Vienna.

Handler, H. (1982), 'Die österreichische Hartwährungspolitik', in Abele, H., E. Nowotny, S. Schleicher, and G. Winckler (eds), *Handbuch der österreichischen Wirtschaftspolitik*, Mantz Verlag, Vienna.

Hansen, J.D., H. Heinrich, and J.U. Nielsen (1991), *An Economic Analysis of the EC*, McGraw-Hill, London.

Hayek, F. von (1978), *Denationalization of Money*, Institute of Economic Affairs, London.

Hermann, A., W. Leibfritz, P.B. Soerensen, and M. Wegner (1992), *Probleme und Chancen einer Koordinierung der Finanzpolitik in der EG*, Schriftenreihe des Ifo-Instituts für Wirtschaftsforschung nr. 130, Duncker und Humblot, Berlin and Munich.

Herr, H. (1995), 'Die europaeische Waehrungsunion als politisches Projekt', in Thomasberger, C. (ed), *Europaeische Geldpolitik zwischen Marktzwängen und neuen institutionellen Regelungen*, Metropolis, Marburg.

Klatzer E., and B. Unger (1992), 'Will internationalization lead to a convergence of national economic policies?', *Department of Economics Working Paper* no. 12, June, University of Economics and Businesss Administration, Vienna.

Moesen, W., and O. van Rompuy (1990), 'The growth of government size and fiscal decentralization', paper prepared for the IIPF Congress, Brussels.

Mooslechner, P. (1995), 'Finanzmarktliberalisierung and Wirtschaftspolitik', in Thomasberger, C. (ed), *Europäische Geldpolitik zwischen Marktzwängen and neuen institutionellen Regelungen*, Metropolis, Marburg.

Olson, M. (1965), *The Logic of Collective Action*, Harvard University Press, Cambridge.

Qvigstad, J.F. (1992), 'Economic and Monetary Union (EMU), A survey of the EMU and empirical evidence on convergence for the EC and the EFTA Countries', *EFTA Occasional Paper* no.36, European Free Trade Association, Geneva.

Sbragia, A.M. (ed.) (1992), *Euro-Politics, Institutions and Policymaking in the 'New' European Community*, The Brookings Institution, Washington, DC.

Sbragia, A.M. (1992), 'Thinking about the European future: the uses of comparison', in Sbragia, A. (ed.).

Schaumeyer, M. (1993), 'Die Notenbank hat die kurzfristige Attacke des Auslands auf den Schilling souverän abgewehrt', *Handelsblatt* 14.10.1993.

Schmitter, P.C. (1993), 'The future of the European polity', unpublished manuscript, Stanford University.

Starbatty, J. (1990), 'Sanktionsregeln bei internationaler Politikkoordination', in Kantzenbach, E. (ed.), *Probleme der internationalen Koordinierung der Wirtschaftspolitik*, Duncker und Humblot, Berlin.

Theurl, T. (1992), *Eine gemeinsame Währung für Europa, 12 Lehren aus der Geschichte*, Österreichischer Studien Verlag, Innsbrück.

Thomasberger, C. (1993), *Europäische Währungsintegration und globale Währungskonkurrenz*, J.C.B. Mohr, Tübingen.

Traxler F., and B. Unger (1994), 'Governance, economic restructuring and international competitiveness', *Journal of Economic Issues*, vol. 28, no 1, March.

Unger, B. (1990), 'Possibilities and constraints of national economic policies for small countries: the case of Austria', *West German Policy Studies*, no. 3, Harvard University, Cambridge.

Unger B., and F. van Waarden (1994), 'Interest associations and economic growth. A critique of Mancur Olson's "Rise and Decline of Nations"', *CEPR-Working Paper*, no. 894, April, Centre for Economic Policy Research, London.

Weber, M. (ed.) (1991), *Europa auf dem Weg zur Währungsunion*, Wissenschaftliche Buchgesellschaft, Darmstadt.

4 International trade, multinational enterprises, and industrial policy choice

Christian Bellak

$L52$
$F21$
$F13$
$F23$
$F10$

Summary

This chapter analyses whether the process of globalization by means of international trade and foreign direct investment will lead to convergence of national industrial policies. In particular, two questions will be discussed: First, what is the nature of international competition. And, second, what are its consequences for national industrial policy choice. It is argued, that the conduct of multinational enterprises as international hierarchies reduces the number of industrial policy strategies open to national governments, since they have to compete for foreign direct investments with other countries. This common trend of reduced policy options does not necessarily lead to convergent industrial policies. Altogether, it seems even more likely that industrial policies will diverge rather than converge, since the interrelatedness of countries by means of firms leads to an increasing specialization of industrial policy strategies.

Introduction

International competition in the form of international trade is an old phenomenon. International competition in the form of foreign direct investment (FDI) carried out by Multinational Enterprises (MNEs) is an old phenomenon as well. In fact, the degree of internationalization (i.e. international investment stock relative to domestic output) never again reached the level at which it stood around the beginning of the century (Dunning 1983, Roth 1984) in the major capitalist countries (see Table 4.2).

Yet, the interrelatedness of countries and firms is much more complex and multifaceted than it was at the beginning of this century. The nature of internationalization, or better, globalization, has changed dramatically and so have the main actors, the MNEs. The international links between countries via firms have increased due to new technologies and new institutionalized settings on the national, inter- and supra-national levels. These developments have been paralleled by considerable government interventions into industries on various levels seeking to maximize national and/or global welfare. This article concentrates on how national industrial policy and international competition are interlinked in this global environment, emphasizing FDI and MNEs. In particular, two main questions are discussed:

1   What is the nature of international competition with respect to its extent and principles of organization?

2   What consequences arise for national industrial policy choice in an increasingly internationalized (globalized) environment?

The first part of the chapter concentrates on international competition in the form of international trade, FDI and MNEs and their role in capitalist economies. The second part of the paper assesses the options open to governments in shaping their national industrial policies. A short overview on industrial policy in Europe is followed by subsections assessing the bargaining process of governments, labour and international businesses as well as their changing bargaining positions due to the increased importance of international competition and MNEs in particular. Most of what is said about industrial policy is with reference to the European context (the European Union (EU), in particular). There is a short concluding section summarizing the arguments for convergence and/or divergence of national industrial policies. The chapter concludes that although we will see some cases of convergent industrial policies, generally we will see more divergent industrial policies in the future, due to the role of MNEs and the nature of international competition. The interrelatedness of countries via firms leads to an increasing 'individualization of national industrial policy strategies' towards MNEs.

The nature of international competition

International competition was originally based on inter-firm trade and took place on markets. Independent firms competed from their (national) home base by exporting their goods to markets of other nations. (Relative)

81

comparative advantage determined what and how much was traded on foreign markets. The nature of international competition changed rapidly from the beginning of the twentieth century, when the 'new-capitalism' emerged, with firms investing abroad. *Inter alia*, firms started to internalize trade-flows by means of intra-firm trade. By using their subsidiaries for foreign production or 'exchange of threats', firms competed directly in the competitors' markets (i.e. intra-industry FDI and international trade flows took place in oligopolistic markets).

Thus, the degree of international competition increased sharply with three main consequences:

1   More countries, such as newly industrialized countries, taking part (a widening process).

2   A higher degree of integration, particularly among the advanced economies (a deepening process).

3   New forms of international investment such as contractual agreements, networks, strategic alliances, in addition to traditional FDI on a capital basis, (an intertwining process).

These developments are also termed globalization, which refers to the multiplicity of linkages and interconnections between the states and societies which make up the present world system. It describes the process by which events, decisions, and activities in one part of the world come to have significant consequences for individuals and communities in quite distant parts of the globe. Globalization has two distinct phenomena: scope (or stretching) and intensity (or deepening).

> On the one hand, it defines a set of processes which embrace most of the globe or which operate worldwide; the concept therefore has a spatial connotation. ... On the other hand, it also implies an intensification on the levels of interaction, interconnectedness or *interdependence* between the states and societies which constitute the world community (McGrew and Lewis 1992: 23, quoted from Dunning 1994b).

Globalization is thus a phenomenon that comprises all markets: goods, services, capital and labour markets. See Table 4.1 for a first quantitative assessment of the globalization phenomenon. Globalization can be summarized as follows:

> Technological progress and international competition, combined with

82

liberalization, have lowered barriers to international flows of goods, services and factors of production, increased the scope for international specialization and led to an unprecedented expansion of international economic transactions (UNCTAD-DTCI 1994: xxi).

At the forefront of globalization and internationalization are MNEs as the main players in the economic arena and national governments as well as inter- and supranational bodies in the political arena. The following subsection assesses the question of the nature of international competition and highlights some quantitative measures of globalization.

International trade

International trade is still the main subject of integration on a global (e.g. GATT, World Trade Organization) as well as on a regional scale (e.g. NAFTA). Its nature has changed dramatically, and a good deal of change was brought about by MNEs.

1   Today, about one-third of total trade is free trade, one-third is managed trade, between 30 and 40 per cent is intrafirm trade by MNEs (and in the case of intangible assets such as technology and organizational skills even 60 to 70 per cent, see UNCTAD-DTCI 1994, Dunning 1994c).

2   International trade patterns are increasingly shifting regionally as intra-industry trade replaces traditional trade based on comparative advantages in some industries.

3   Intraregional exports are increasing their share in total exports in regions with liberalization and deepening integration (Western Europe 4 percentage points, Asia 9.7 percentage points, North America minus 6.1 percentage points real growth between 1986 and 1991) and thus growing faster than interregional trade.

4   An ever increasing share of World trade is accounted for by MNEs (e.g. indigenous and foreign MNEs are responsible for 80 per cent of British exports).

It would go beyond the scope of this chapter to describe quantitative trade developments in general, hence only two characteristics relevant in relation to MNEs are highlighted:

1   World exports of goods and non-factor services amount to about 4.5

83

trillion USD or 3 trillion USD excluding estimated intrafirm trade in 1993.

2   Some 80 percent of international payments for royalties and fees (as a measure of transfer of technology via MNEs) are undertaken on an intrafirm basis.

Foreign Direct Investment (FDI)

FDI has shaped trade flows and domestic economic activities alike. The OECD benchmark definition (2nd ed., 1992) defines FDI as:

> Investment that involves a long-term relationship reflecting a lasting interest of a resident entity in one economy (direct investor) in an entity resident in an economy other than that of the investor. The direct investor's purpose is to exert a significant degree of influence on the management of the enterprise resident in the other economy. Direct investment involves both initial transaction between the two entities and all subsequent transactions between them and among affiliated enterprises, both incorporated and unincorporated (OECD 1992).

The key phrase here is 'to exert a significant degree of influence' which distinguishes FDI from portfolio investment (i.e. international investment without strategic interest in the use of the capital by the foreign enterprises). By investing in foreign countries, national firms become MNEs and their legal, economic and political environment changes and produces new opportunities and threats. The motives for FDI are numerous and can be grouped into six categories: resource seeking (natural as well as created), efficiency seeking (production cost, location etc.), strategic asset seeking (i.e. strategic alliances, mergers, acquisitions), market seeking (i.e. localization of activities, distribution), agglomeration seeking, and know how seeking. Especially in the 1980s and 1990s, international competition via FDI increased heavily. Dunning 1994c: 2a) enumerates two sets of factors that were responsible for this development.

First, from a country's perspective: the renaissance of the market system, an enhanced mobility of wealth creating assets; an increasing number of countries approaching 'take off' stage of development; convergence of economic structures among advanced countries and some industrializing countries and changing criteria by which governments evaluate FDI.

Second, from a firm's perspective: an increasing need to exploit global markets (e.g. to cover escalating research and development costs); regional integration that has prompted more efficiency seeking investment; growing ease of trans-border communications and reduced transport costs; heightened oligopolistic competition among leading firms; an opening up of new territorial opportunities for FDI; a need to 'tap into' foreign sources of technology and organizational capabilities; and to exploit economies of agglomeration.

FDI and other types of international business operations are instruments to transfer whole packages of physical, financial or human capital or technology across borders and to extend the hierarchy of firms internationally (see MNEs below). Again, a few selected numbers should provide a picture of the relative importance of FDI:

1   In the early 1990s FDI (FDI book values 2,000 billion USD, turnover of MNEs: 5,500 billion USD) has reached the importance of international trade (4,000 billion USD) and other economic activities (see Table 4.1). The outward FDI flows from the five major home countries (France, Germany, Japan, UK and US) account for two-thirds of worldwide outflows. The worldwide FDI stock - as a proxy for the productive capacity of transnational companies outside their home countries - continued to increase, reaching an estimated 2.1 trillion USD at the end of 1993. This stock is even higher when revalued at constant or current replacement values (Cantwell and Bellak 1994).

2   The outward FDI stocks of Japan, Germany, US and UK grew (real, on average, per annum) faster than their exports and GDP between 1960 and 1990, especially between 1980 and 1990 (FDI growth: 6 per cent; GDP growth: 2.9 per cent; trade growth: 2.6 per cent; Cantwell and Bellak 1994: 19). Thus, international production has gained relative importance even in periods of an overall slowdown in growth of GDP and trade.

3   Services are the largest sector in the outward FDI stock (46-66 per cent) of the five major investor countries. Table 4.2 shows the main monetary indicators of globalization and relates domestic economic activity (GDP, investment) to FDI. Given the many *caveats* related to FDI figures in particular (e.g. Bellak 1994), one should treat them as trend indicators rather than as absolute figures.

Since most of what will be said in this chapter refers to the European Union (EU) or former European Community (EC) a few numbers should be given (based on UN 1992, EUROSTAT 1991, Commission of the European Community 1994):

1   At historic values, the FDI stock of the European Community in North America (269.7 billion USD, 1989) grew by 12.4 per cent and in Japan (7 billion USD, 1989) by 15.6 per cent annually between 1980 and 1989.

2   Intra-EC FDI flows grew at a rate of 45.4 per cent between 1984 and 1988 and thus faster than extra-EC FDI flows (15.3 per cent) reflecting the liberalization of capital flows and anticipatory effects of the Single Market Project.

Multinational enterprises and transnational corporations

MNEs are the main economic players in the globalization process and are often said to be the 'secret government' of the world, which is due to their economic importance and political influence. Their global orientation and independence of nations renders meaningless traditional paradigms which assume that firms have a specific nationality: 'For internationally dispersed companies the nationality of ownership does not coincide with the nationality of output' (Thomsen and Nicolaides 1990). The question of 'corporate citizenship' (OECD 1991) becomes particularly crucial, when we turn to industrial-policy matters. Firms change their nationality and migrate. Hence, the nationality of a national government's bargaining partner (the MNE) may change. To cite the often used example, ICL, which was taken over by a Japanese firm, received subsidies from the EC.

Another recent example is the German car company BMW taking over Rover, mainly owned by British Aerospace, which was owned and subsidized by the British government before it was privatized some years ago. The BMW takeover was followed by the pullout of Honda (Japan) which previously controlled a twenty per cent stake in Rover. Originally, Honda's investment in Rover was mainly intended to secure efficient access to European markets and became obsolete and even threatened its technological competitiveness when the major competitor (BMW) acquired Rover.

These examples and numerous others show that by creating an inter-and supranational infrastructure (i.e. governance institutions and policies), national governments may have responded insufficiently to MNEs. Thus, MNEs may employ the mainly nation-based systems of industrial policy to their own advantage, because in an ever more complex environment of capital and contractual relationships between firms (sometimes termed 'virtual companies' to emphasize their dynamic nature) the options of national governments for intervening at the firm level are greatly reduced. The numbers concerning MNEs are impressive, but should again be treated with caution:

1   In the beginning of the 1990s there were about 37,000 parent firms with 200,000 foreign affiliates.

2   They accounted for 73 million employees at home and abroad (i.e. ten per cent of paid employment in non-agricultural activities worldwide) plus even more employees indirectly connected to MNEs (suppliers, distributors, etc.).

3   Their sales reached 4.8 trillion USD (more than trade in goods and non-factor services).

4   'The world's largest hundred transnational corporations (not including those in banking and finance) ranked by foreign assets, had about 3.4 trillion USD in global assets in 1992, of which about 1.3 trillion USD were held outside their respective home countries. These firms are estimated to account for about one-third of the combined outward FDI of their countries of origin' (UNCTAD-DTCI 1994: 5; Table 4.3).

5   The fifty largest firms (by turnover) worldwide had a total turnover of 1,771.8 billion ECU (average 35.4 billion ECU) and 8,858,000 (average 177,160) employees, while the fifty largest firms in Europe had a turnover of 1,157.7 billion ECU (average 23.3 billion ECU) and 7,572,104 employees (average 151,442; all figures refer to 1992). The fifty largest European companies are thus much smaller by turnover than the fifty largest worldwide, but there is less difference in terms of employees. These large firms are responsible for a very large share of FDI stocks and flows worldwide.

6   '90 per cent of parent firms are based in developing countries' (UNCTAD-DTCI 1994: 3; thus, a major part of the globe is actually excluded from 'globalization').

All figures suggest, that multinational enterprises and transnational corporations are increasingly important bargaining partners to national governments. The attitude of governments towards MNEs is thus influencing national industrial policy and supra- and international governance institutions. 'The relationship between international companies and national governments has always been an uneasy, if not a schizophrenic, one' (Dunning 1994a: 10). Since about 1900 we observe waves of 'love and hate' in the relationship of home and host governments and MNEs, yet there seems to be consensus that the influence of MNEs in politics has increased steadily. The period up to World War I was characterized by a peaceful co-existence of MNEs and governments, the latter supporting the former and *vice versa*. Before the late 1970s, several waves of nationalization occurred - among them in Russia after the 1917 revolution; in Eastern Europe after World War II; in Third World countries about 1400 cases between 1960 and 1976 in more than 70 countries (Hofer 1987).

The critical view of MNEs by host governments then changed to a more positive view in the 1980s, which was due among others to an increasingly supply-side oriented economic policy favoring deregulation and privatization; a diversification of home and host countries; a reduction of the FDI imbalance (so called 'peace by investment'); the debt-crisis reducing the critical attitude of many Third World countries; the creation of new forms of investment changing the shape and type of MNEs; and a more sophisticated bargaining process between home and host governments and MNEs. During the early 1990s, the favourable view of MNEs by home and host countries was further supported by their role in (European) integration (MNEs as 'integrating agents'); by their positive judgement of East European developments; by a further reduction of the bargaining power of third world countries due to a steadily decreasing share in total FDI; and not least because of the ongoing recession, by governments increasingly focusing on employment (MNEs as 'engines of growth'). Yet some more critical attitudes are perceivable, e.g. the environmental and atomic-energy question; radical religious movements against the 'imperialistic capital'; and the accusation by home countries that FDI 'export' competitive advantages and jobs.

As with national firms, the existence of positive transaction costs favour a hierarchical or contractual organization of resources over market transactions (eg. Hollingsworth, Streeck and Schmitter 1994). By creating their own 'sphere of discretion', MNEs are not as accessible to governments as are markets. Yet, internalization alone is not sufficient for a firm to engage in FDI and to become an MNE. Two other conditions must be satisfied (e.g. Dunning 1981). Firstly, there must be a location advantage abroad (such as resource availability and low production costs) and secondly, there must be an ownership-specific advantage (such as technology, marketing) to compensate for possible disadvantages in the foreign market (due to, for example, less information). Yet, MNEs form organizational channels across nations, which do not only channel trade and investment, but also other production factors, such as financial capital, labour, machinery, technology, know how, patents, access to raw materials, ownership rights and in particular information. They are governing centers of business, not nationally fixed, they are international 'hierarchies'.

The substantial impact of MNEs in economic as well as in a political sense suggests that MNEs have wider responsibilities than national firms. 'However, firms are not well placed to act as agents of international governance, particularly if the insertion of public policy objectives in the decision making process is thought to be desirable. International firms create the need for improved international governance, but they do not and cannot provide it' (Grant 1992: 1).

The following subsections assess the consequences of the globalization process for national industrial policy choice. It is preceded by a short overview on industrial policy in Europe and the emergence of a European industrial policy.

Consequences for national industrial policy choice

Orthodox arguments for intervention by the state into industrial markets are based on the incidence of market failure (i.e. because of monopolies, public goods, positive or negative externalities, lack of ownership rights, divergence of public and private time preference etc.). Industrial policy should help to 'correct' for market failure and maximize total welfare. At the national level, we find measures like competition policy, internalization of social cost, subsidization of infant industries which are consequently also applied at the inter- and supranational level through, for example, the removal of barriers, international competition rules, and free trade. Modern approaches to industrial policy emerge from trade theory and growth theory. Given the assumption of market imperfections or differentiated goods in modern trade theory, transaction costs are no longer zero. In such an environment, protectionism may raise welfare above a scenario with free trade, since welfare gains of free competition are not distributed equally over countries. The so-called 'strategic trade and industrial policy' may shift rents towards the home country by subsidizing large firms (with high barriers to entry for foreign firms) or by facilitating entry of domestic firms into foreign markets. Modern growth theory suggests national industrial policy measures in two scenarii.

First, externalities arising in the process of growth (from technology, human capital etc.) have to be internalized (by means of patenting, monopolies etc) in order to provide an incentive for their creation. Second, the cost of growth in the form of structural change and structural adaptation (e.g. bankruptcy of firms, obsolete human capital) requires counteracting industrial policies such as training, subsidization of new investment, seed capital, and other social schemes. The former of these measures is often termed 'accelerative' and the latter 'decelerative' but in practice both types of measures are applied to externalities and structural change.

National industrial policies in Europe during the 1980s ranged from 'laissez-faire' to 'planning' approaches. In Britain, the renaissance of the market was based on large privatization and deregulation programmes. An active industrial policy, apart from subsidization of mature industries, was rejected for ideological and other reasons. The British rejected active industrial policy even the more so at the EC level. Germany on the other hand followed a strategy of 'supportive' industrial policies in the form of a competition policy which aimed at enhancing efficiency through fostering innovation and restructuring within industries rather than relying on concentration and market power. Contrary to policy in Britain, industrial policy in Germany follows the principle of strong *Ordnungspolitik* (regulation) accompanied by *ablaufspolitische* measures (intervention). As is well known, due to the strong ownership position of the banking sector in certain industries, banks exert a unique influence on industrial policy makers in Germany. An even more active, in part 'planning' oriented, industrial policy is pursued by France (*économie concertée* or *planification*). France is, therefore, one of the counterparts of Germany in the industrial policy discussion at a European level. In France, the main thrust of industrial policy is the creation of market power for large and successful firms, as opposed to the German 'efficiency' approach. This requires a wide spectrum of interventionist measures in public industrial enterprises and their relationships to other firms (*politique des filières*) and banks. Privatization in France is consequently implemented under a careful regime to secure French strategic ownership in privatized enterprises.

The wide range of national industrial policies in Europe creates conflict at an inter- or supranational level, particularly with regard to the issue of a common European industrial policy. The origins of a European industrial policy date back to the foundations of the European Community. The Treaty of Rome, which included investment subsidies but not industrial policy as such, and the Treaty of Paris (European Coal and Steel Community) constitute early examples of European industrial policy measures. In 1972 in the communiqué of Paris, several programmes and measures were agreed upon to develop a common industrial basis and in 1973, a memorandum about a common 'Research and Technology Policy' was issued. Subsequently,

> Governments in the early 1980s felt hard pressed, or saw a golden opportunity, depending on their political complexion, to withdraw the political full employment promise of the post war period and yield control over the restoration of prosperity and employment in their

internationalized nation economies to "the market", including a deregulated labour market thereby in effect accepting the increasingly demanding conditions placed by capital holders on industrial investment (Streeck and Schmitter 1991: 146).

The 'Transnational Plan' of 1983 aimed for better coordination and organization of national policies. However, the main European industrial policy measures of the 1980s were certainly the creation of the Single Market, the 'Strategy for a European Industrial Policy in an open and competition oriented environment' of 1990 (the so called *Bangemann Plan*') and the first reform of the Structural Funds to enhance structural change under 'socially acceptable conditions'. Thus, until 1991 industrial policy on a European level was confined to the areas of primary Community law (Article 130ff; research and development, science, competition policy, structural funds etc.). An important explanation for the strengthening of European integration in the 1980s was 'the result of an alignment between two broad interests - that of large European firms struggling to overcome perceived competitive disadvantages in relation to Japanese and US capital and that of state elites seeking to restore at least part of the political sovereignty they had gradually lost at the national level as a result of growing international interdependence' (Streeck and Schmitter 1991: 148).

MNEs were certainly on the forefront of lobbies for a Single European Market, since liberalization increases their 'freedom' to internalize markets across borders. In the 'Treaty of Maastricht' (1991), after a revision of Article 3 and a new Article 130, industrial policy was declared a European matter in its own right for the first time. The main objectives of a European industrial policy were the enhancement of innovation and improvement of European competitiveness vis-à-vis Japan and the US through international coordination (e.g. Article 129b: trans-European networks in transport, telecommunications and energy infrastructure). (For the main Articles of the Treaty concerning industrial policy see Note 1).

Comparable to industrial policy on the national level, European industrial policy has to serve the main objectives of the EU. Yet, several points can be put forward to predict a limited relevance of a future European industrial policy.

Firstly, there is the unanimity requirement which will likely not be met on key issues. As should be clear from what has been said above, national identification and industrial policy strategies vary in Member States. Germany, Britain and the Netherlands support a competition oriented European industrial policy (so called horizontal, because it creates equal regulations for all industries), while France, Italy, Spain and Greece favour an interventionist, sectoral (or vertical) industrial policy. This

91

reduces the discussion to the issue of whether 'picking winners' is the strategy to survive in international competition or whether competition per se creates enterprises which compete successfully in world markets. Depending on the structure of the industry (number of suppliers, characteristic of goods or services supplied, extent of international competition, regulations etc.), MNEs may favour either strategy.

Secondly, industrial policy is still considered a national responsibility. The huge differences between Member States in industrial structures, in industrial policy traditions, in the participation of interest groups and in the share of mature industries make it neither likely nor logical to transfer too many national competencies to a supranational level. Thirdly, the discrepancy between sector specific programmes and measures which should be designed horizontally will not be easily overcome. Competition policy, domestic as well as foreign, has been a principle of EC policy since the treaty of Rome. In 'Maastricht', a compromise between both approaches mentioned above has been reached. As a consequence, the competencies stated in the Treaty are fluid and leave many options open. MNEs may, however, play a crucial role in the process of formulating an accepted European industrial policy strategy, because they show interest for both types of European industrial policy.

The following conclusion may serve as an example for the non-market approach by MNEs: 'A second exception, in the early 1980s, was constituted by multinational high-tech industrial firms. These wanted European protection for their price setting and financial support for their R&D' (van Schendelen 1993: 284).

Industrial policy at the European level is still subject to heavy debate and will not emerge on a broad scale or scope in the near future. Instead, we have systems of national industrial policies and MNEs which have learned to 'live' with these and to exert influence to get protection and support on a wider basis (i.e. vis-à-vis foreign competition in the triad, see also Prize 1991).

The effect of MNEs on national industrial policy

National industrial policy alone is no longer able to influence all firms' activities on its territory - foreign subsidiaries depend on foreign parent firms while indigenous firms are generating investment and production overseas. Thus, national welfare depends increasingly not only on national industrial policy but also on industrial policies of other nations. For example, in exporting, tariff and tax policies of other nations in part determine export revenues. In FDI, capital controls, infrastructure and political stability are only 'created national relative advantages' versus other nations. This interrelatedness of countries via firms puts the pressure

92

of international competition on national governments. 'The essence of the policy challenges in a more integrated international production system is how best to insure that the forces of international competition and cooperation work in a complementary manner to enhance global economic welfare and contribute to a more equitable distribution of the resulting benefits' (UNCTAD-DTCI 1994: xxviii). The internationalization process via international trade and FDI affects the position of governments in two major fields:

1   The loss of sovereignty due to international and supranational regulations.

2   The weakening of bargaining power of nations by the relocation and restructuring process of MNEs leading to the need for new industrial policy strategies.

In the first of these major fields, as internationalization and globalization prevail in more and more industries, national industrial policies are neither sufficient nor efficient for regulating the competition of MNEs. Therefore, international trade agreements like GATT or supranational competition policy like EC-competition rules have been introduced. Although there is some room for national policy, it has to be in conformity with the international and supranational rules. Thus, external policy (trade policy, capital control policy, etc.) is gradually shifted away from nation states. Yet, policies traditionally termed internal policies (competition policy, structural policy and industrial policy) are also increasingly determined and constrained by international rules. For example, MNEs are increasingly included in talks about international trade in the GATT under TRIMS (trade related investment measures), and in talks about subsidies and mergers and acquisitions via the EC merger control system of 1989. Or consider, for example structural policy, which (especially for small, trade dependent states) depends largely on external structural changes in global industries and on demand which is in part generated abroad (i.e. exogenously given). It should be emphasized that loss of sovereignty must not be interpreted as only disadvantageous for the nation state, since global competitiveness may only be secured by a supranational competition policy. Moreover, in practice, national policies are quite innovative in undermining the objectives of international and supranational policies in order to counteract some of the effects of these rules (e.g. protecting food industries from imports with safety regulations).

The second of the major fields mentioned above is the weakening of the bargaining power of nations due to the relocation and restructuring process of MNEs leading to the need for new industrial policy strategies. The

93

threatened bargaining position of governments vis-à-vis firms is based on the spatial mobility and flexibility of capital. The key aspects relating to MNEs are 'restructuring' and 'relocation'. As van Liemt (1992) demonstrated impressively in his study 'Industry On the Move' on the 'causes and consequences of international relocation in the manufacturing industry', it is exactly these two dynamic features of international competition between firms which influence their relative bargaining position vis-à-vis governments. The fact that neither restructuring (which depends on the global structural change) nor relocation (which depends on the global strategy of the firm) may be influenced directly and effectively by the state threatens its bargaining power. Interstate competition for FDI further weakens the power of the states. When trying to attract FDI or prevent disinvestment, states can be played off each other by the MNEs. This can force states to reduce burdens on firms (high wages, labour protection legislation, environmental regulation). Since states are now competing more for the means to create wealth within their territory than for power over more territory, 'the implication is that national choices of industrial policy and efficiency in economic management are beginning to override choices of foreign or defense policy as the primary influences on how resources are allocated' (Stopford et al. 1991: 1).

On the other hand, with reference to the argument above that governments control less and less of their firms, industrial policies toward MNEs might take a backseat to industrial policies toward national firms, because 'also, as firms become increasingly transnational in orientation, the domestic payoffs - in terms of employment and wealth generation - of state assistance to firms may decline' (Kenworthy 1990: 255). National industrial policy is thus challenged to be innovative and flexible enough to secure the welfare of the state, and to be competitive in comparison to other national policies. Again, the source of the new imperatives in national industrial policy is international competition of MNEs via trade and FDI - without MNEs states would not have to compete actively for FDI and market shares in exporting. In this respect, national industrial policy comprises location policy (*Standortpolitik*), strategic industrial and trade policy, cluster policy and integration policy measures.

Another influence of MNEs on the national governments' position stems from the fact that MNEs might influence the behavior of national firms by introducing certain standards which apply in plants or companies of the MNE in foreign countries. For example, the MNE might introduce more flexible working hour regulations - which are in place in a foreign country - in a country with rather inflexible rules. This would certainly put pressure on national firms. Through their activities in many different local environments, MNEs have large opportunities to learn which set of regulations best fit their activities and consequently try to 'skim the cream'

- a strategy which is less likely for national firms. It is more the relationship between MNEs and national firms which is crucial and not the multinationality of firms *per se*: 'Therefore, industrial relations difficulties do not arise in TNCs (transnational corporations C.B.) more frequently than in domestic firms. This is all the more important because the pattern of industrial relations adopted by TNCs may become a model for domestic firms and that part of the labour force that is not organized' (UNCTAD-DTCI 1994: 250).

However, internationalization creates not only conflicting interests of national governments and multiple policy approaches. Exporting (or trade in general), capital flows (FDI in particular) and international migration also lead to the convergence of nations' GDP growth, GDP per capita, etc. (see Narula 1993 for an overview). Consequently, the convergence of countries would bring about similar needs for industrial policy measures. This may, in fact, be true on a macrolevel, but at the meso- or microlevel where industrial policy measures normally apply, substantial differences between countries still exist. These differences are partly brought about by the location decisions of MNEs.

Industrial policy of the 1990s: location and cluster policy high on the agenda

In many advanced industrial countries we observe two basic industrial policy strategies, (i) directed toward the domestic economy and (ii) directed to the international economy. Both are directly oriented to MNEs and we present one example for each; location policy in the first case and cluster policy in the second. What is even more interesting is that both employ different sets of national measures in order to improve internal and external competitiveness.

Our example of a domestically oriented strategy, location policy, basically aims to differentiate the nation from others in order to succeed in the international competition of states for FDI. It consists of industrial policy measures to improve location related factors such as tax policy, education, infrastructure and productivity. These measures serve to attract FDI and at the same time strengthen the competitiveness of domestic firms. Some countries have already fully adopted a strategy of economic policy to compete actively for FDI (e.g. Ireland). They try to undercut production cost of and provide infrastructure superior to that of other countries in order to attract MNEs. Many West European countries have tried to improve on such location related factors as a result of their MNEs' activities in Eastern Europe, which offers a high level of education and low-cost production in some industries. Of course, productivity in Eastern

Europe is still low and hence relative-labour-unit cost high, but their improvement is a real threat to basic industries in Western Europe.

Location policy also includes measures summarized by the term strategic industrial and trade policy à la Krugman (1987). Besides the improvement and upgrading of location factors, location policy intends to differentiate countries as to their location factors, i.e. to emphasize or create some comparative advantage of the location. However, *de facto* we could see a convergence of infrastructure, if all countries concentrate on the same factors. Usually, priority is given to immaterial infrastructure such as education, telecommunication in advanced countries. In addition, location policy might differentiate between national and foreign firms, granting exceptions for the foreign firm for example in the labour market (additional shifts during the night, etc.) which may consequently have to be granted to the local firms as well. In this respect, the MNEs are initiators of industrial policy changes on a national level. There is a case for an overall convergence with respect to FDI flows but this, as explained, may call for differentiation.

Yet, this process of liberalization has been far from homogenous, and there are still considerable differences in the nature, breadth and depth of the measures taken. As the normative frameworks for FDI around the world become increasingly similar, these differences become more important for attracting foreign investors, and there is a real possibility that efforts to attract FDI can lead to increased 'policy competition' among governments. Such competition could potentially be carried into more policy areas than in the past, since the increasingly integrated nature of international production elevates more and more policies from the domestic to the regional and international domains (UNCTAD-DTCI 1994: xxviii).

The second type of policy in response to the international competition of MNEs aims at differentiation of industries at an international level. Cluster policy is an example. Even if not always termed 'cluster policy', this type of industrial policy is frequently found in more and more countries. (For the concept of clusters see Porter 1990.) It aims to directly or indirectly support certain (sub)sectors of the economy in order to create sustainable competitive advantages over industries of other nations. It is distinct from a 'picking the winner' concept in that it is broader in scope, and it is more applicable in large than in small economies. Clusters are thus a form of national specialization, determined largely by created resources and the countries' historical experiences. A cluster goes beyond the traditional industry classification in that it includes all activities of the value added chain of a certain product or service. A cluster policy is compatible with a horizontal approach to industrial policy à la the EU (see above) but also with sectoral or vertical elements of industrial policy. Yet, as with location policy, these are merely the intentions. Whether cluster policy will prove

96

more successful than other types of industrial policy remains to be seen. To date, states have generated a variety of concepts and approaches relevant to 'cluster policy', but it is too early to evaluate these measures.

Conclusions

This chapter set out to discuss the nature and extent of international competition via trade, Foreign Direct Investments and Multinational Enterprises. It then proceeded to ask how national industrial policies are affected by international competition, emphasizing the bargaining position of national governments. We can now bring together the strands of our arguments and ask whether these developments will lead to convergence or divergence of industrial policies in the future.

As a first overall conclusion we can stress that governments have less choice regarding national industrial policy strategies, because globalization creates more necessities than options for national governments. FDI, trade and MNEs give rise to a situation in which national industrial policies cover less of the activities of the nation's firms (foreign and indigenous). Hence, one country's national industrial policy is constrained by other countries' national industrial policies which also influence the behaviour of these firms. The conduct of MNEs as international hierarchies reduces further the number of national industrial policy strategies of national governments vis-à-vis other countries with which they compete for FDI. MNEs themselves reduce the freedom of national governments in industrial policy by lobbying for each government to meet the optimum conditions they experience in any of their subsidiaries (perhaps supporting this with the relocation threat).

Since there is no straightforward answer to the question of national industrial policy choice, we distinguish two scenarii of the consequences of international competition on national industrial policy: first, the case for convergence of national industrial policies, which admittedly is the less likely outcome, and second, the more likely case for divergence of national industrial policies.

The case for convergence

A first argument in favour of convergence is that the nature and logic of international competition creates pressure for more policy coordination and for substitution of supranational for national governance structures. For example, Dunning (1994b: 44ff) identifies two general instances that will lead to supranational regimes: first, negative externalities from national government actions and second, the possibility of cross-border market failure (e.g. in satellite communications, environmental issues). Supranational industrial policy is one possibility for convergence, while similar national industrial policies are the other.

Second, MNEs may lobby for equal, non-discriminatory EU policies in an *ésprit de corps* in some areas, but it is very difficult to detect homogenous interests of MNEs in general, since the nature of their goods and services as well as competition differ substantially between industries. Rather, there are strong sectoral common interests or firm-specific interests which do not require a general convergence of national industrial policies in many fields. Especially in times of recession and weak economic performance of MNEs, their solidarity will be quite low.

Third, a convergence in FDI positions would require similar industrial policies of nations of a similar welfare level. Regulation of MNEs, FDI, ownership structure, size and competition would have to be treated similarly. There is, however, no clearcut evidence so far on a significant convergence of FDI positions between countries.

Fourth, location policy may prompt a convergence of national industrial policies if countries focus their resources in the same fields. National governments may compete for FDI and MNEs in the same basic infrastructure, which would imply similar industrial policy measures. This is, however, only one location strategy. It is also possible to see more differentiation and specialization strategies which would imply divergent national policies towards different location factors of production. For governments it might yet be rational to follow other governments' strategies in order to minimize the risk of falling behind in the quality of location factors.

The case for divergence

There are also a number of arguments for divergence. First, the nature of international competition, i.e. concentration of economic activity combined with a higher mobility of assets, requires more short term and reactive industrial policy toward MNEs and single large firms. This process is likely to result in more divergent measures. Also, the size of MNEs may create dependence of national governments in some cases.

Second, governments compete for wealth creating assets of firms partly by trying to differentiate a nation's location factors from those of other nations. They apply different industrial policy measures in order to create a unique environment to attract FDI of certain industries and MNEs. This may lead to a certain specialization of countries in certain industries which require different national industrial policy measures.

Third, the renaissance of market forces with a strong competition policy and deregulated labour markets leaves less room for broad, long term agreements between governments and MNEs. For MNEs, corporatist agreements on a national level become less important, because they have the option of replacing a certain environment with another by relocating their resources. Industrial policy measures will for this reason be more 'unstable'.

Fourth, due to the regional expansion of international competition, competitive advantages of MNEs may be shifted more easily between locations and are hence less sustainable from a country's point of view. Standardized solutions like those in the past are too rigid or even, 'counterproductive, when what is demanded are policies tailored to improving the productivity and international competitiveness of specific sectors and individual enterprises' (Streeck and Schmitter 1991: 147). The specialization strategy of small and large countries which is enforced by high entry barriers in certain industries due to high research and development expenditures and tough global competition calls for more narrow industrial policy strategies and measures.

Fifth, as has been explained above, there are many obstacles in the way of implementing a European industrial policy à la Maastricht. Since the competencies in the Treaty of Maastricht as well as the *realpolitische Ausgestaltung* are weak and fluid, industrial policy will be on the national agenda for the foreseeable future. Given the many different experiences and historical paths of national industrial policies and the structural differences of the economies, despite a macroconvergence, it seems unlikely that there is chance of more convergent industrial policies. The Maastricht Treaty is the best example for open options and divergent industrial policy strategies of Member States. In addition, the globalization process has not yet brought about a level of economic convergence in the structure of industries which would require or justify more convergent industrial policies at national levels.

Sixth, we observe national industrial policies counteracting certain international or harmonized industrial policies on a supranational level. These counteractive national industrial policies will differ according to the sectors affected by the international industrial policy in each country. As long as this schizophrenic attitude of governments prevails, we will see sector-specific national industrial policies in order to support national MNEs.

But - seventh - since industrial policy is on the national agenda, the importance of MNEs will have a great deal of influence on the direction in which industrial policy will move. We have shown that MNEs tend to favour divergence of industrial policies, but favour convergence in some areas. European MNEs have learned to cope with different national industrial policy systems and are able to take advantage from this knowledge, at least versus their US and Japanese competitors. In addition, the EU is 'organized by sector' (van Schendelen 1993: 287) with different needs and problems in different sectors in each Member State.

It has become clear then that there is a strong case for divergence of industrial policies, since:

1   National governments transfer as little as possible national industrial policy competencies on MNE regulation to the supranational level.

2   National governments are unlikely to employ similar industrial policy measures at the same time. As has been shown above, this is mainly due to the required flexibility and firm / industry specificity of measures and to differentiation strategies on a local and international level.

Notes

1 Treaty of Maastricht: Articles concerning a European Industry Policy
Article 3.

For the purposes set out in Article 2, the activities of the Community shall include, as provided in this Treaty and in accordance with the timetable set out therein:

(g) a system ensuring that competition in the internal market is not distorted;

(j) the strengthening of economic and social cohesion;

(l) the strengthening of the competitiveness of Community industry;

(m) the promotion of research and technological development;

(n) encouragement for the establishment and development of trans-European networks;

Article 130.

1 The Community and the Member States shall ensure that the conditions necessary for the competitiveness of the Community's industry exist. For that purpose, in accordance with a system of open and competitive markets, their actions shall be aimed at

- speeding up the adjustment of industry to structural changes;

- encouraging an environment favourable to initiative and to the development of undertakings throughout the Community, particularly small and medium-sized undertakings;

- encouraging an environment favourable to cooperation between undertakings;

- fostering better exploitation of the industrial potential of policies of innovation, research and technological developments.

... This shall not provide a basis for the introduction by the Commu-

nity of any measure which could lead to a distortion of competition.
Article 130c.

The European Regional Development Fund is intended to help to redress the main regional imbalances in the Community through participation in the development and structural adjustment of regions whose development is lagging behind and in the conversion of declining industrial regions.

Article 130f

1 The Community shall have the objective of strengthening the scientific and technological bases of Community industry and encouraging it to become more competitive at international levels, while promoting all the research activities deemed necessary by virtue of other Chapters of this Treaty.

2 For this purpose the Community shall, throughout the Community, encourage undertakings, including small and medium sized undertakings, research centers and universities in their research and technological development activities of high quality; it shall support their efforts to cooperate with one another, aiming, notably, at enabling undertakings to exploit the internal market potential to the full, in particular through the opening up of national public contracts, the definition of common standards and the removal of legal and fiscal obstacles to that cooperation.

Table 4.1

Worldwide foreign direct investment and selected economic indicators for 1992 and growth rates for selected years

(billions of dollars and percentage)

Indicator	Value at current prices 1992	Annual growth rate (per cent) 1981-85(a)	1986-90(a)	1991	1992
FDI outflows	171	3	24	-17	-11
FDI outward stock	2,125 (b)	5	11	10	6
Sales of foreign affiliates of TNCs (c)	4,800 (d)	2 (e)	15	-13	---
Current gross domestic product at factor cost	23,300	2	9	4	5
Gross domestic investment	5,120	0.4	10	4	5
Export of goods and non-factor services	4,500 (d)	-0.2	13	3	---
Royalty and fees receipts	37	0.1	19	8	5

Source: UNCTAD-DTCI, 1994: 20

Notes:

(a) Compunded growth rate estimates, base on semi-logarithmic regression equation. (b) 1993. (c) TNCS: Transnational Companies; estimated by extrapolating the worldwide sales of foreign affiliates of TNCs from Germany, Japan and the United States on the basis of the relative importance of these countries in worldwide outward FDI stock. (d) 1991. (e) 1982-85.

Table 4.2
The role of FDI in world economic activity, 1913 to 1991

Item	1913	1960	1975	1980	1985	1991
World FDI stock as a share of world output	9.0 (a)	4.4	4.5	4.8	6.4	8.5
World FDI inflows as a share of world output	----	0.3	0.3	0.5	0.5	0.7
World FDI inflows as a share of world gorss fixed capital formation	----	1.1	1.4	2.0	1.8	3.5
World sales of foreign affiliates as a share of world exports	----	84 (b)	97 (c)	99 (d)	99 (d)	122

Source: UNCTAD-DTCI, 1994: 130

Notes:
(a) Estimate. (b) 1967 based on United States figures. (c) Based on United States and Japanese figures. (d) 1982 based on German, Japanese and United States data.

Table 4.3
World FDI stock and estimated employment in transnational
corporations, 1975 to 1992
(millions of dollars and millions of employees)

Item	1975	1985	1990	1992
Outward FDI stock	282	674	1,649	1,932
Estimated employment in TNCs	40	65	70	73 (a)
Employment in parent companies at home	----	43	44	44 (a)
Employment in foreign affiliates	----	22	26	29 (a)
Developed countries	----	15	17	17 (a)
Developing countries	----	7	9	12 (a)
China	----	----	3	6
Memorandum				
Employment in United States TNCs	26 (b)	25	25	----
Of which: employment in foreign affiliate	7	6	7	----

Source: UNCTAD-DTCI, 1994: 175

Notes:
(a) Preliminary estimate. (b) 1977.

References

Atkinson, Michael M., and William D. Coleman (1985), 'Corporatism and industrial policy', in Cawson, Alan (ed.) *Organized Interests and the State*, Sage, London.

Bellak, Christian (1994), 'FDI - fairly disappointing indicator?', *Transnational Corporations*, August.

Cantwell, John, and Christian Bellak (1994), 'Measuring the importance of international production: the re-estimation of foreign direct investment at current values', *Discussion Papers in International Investment and Business Studies*, no. 192, University of Reading.

Commission of the European Community (1994), *Panorama of EC Industry 1994*, Brussels.

Contractor, Farok J. (1990), 'Do government policies toward foreign investment matter? An empirical investigation of the link between national policies and FDI flows', *GSM Working Paper*, 90-15, Rutgers University, Newark.

Dörrenbächer, Christoph, and Michael Wortmann (1994), 'Multinational companies in the EU and European works councils', *Intereconomics*, July/August.

Dunning, John H. (1981), Explaining the international direct investment position of countries: towards a dynamic or developmental approach, *Review of World Economics*, vol. 117, no. 1.

Dunning, John H. (1983), 'Changes in the level and structure of international production: the last one hundred years', in Casson, Mark (ed.) *The Growth of International Business*, Allen and Unwin, London.

Dunning, John H. (1991), 'European integration and transatlantic foreign direct investment: The record assessed', *DSRI Working Paper* 3, Copenhagen.

Dunning, John H. (1994a), 'Globalization: The challenge for national economic regimes', *University of Reading Discussion Papers in International Investment and Business Studies*, no. 186, Reading.

Dunning, John H. (1994b), 'Globalization, economic restructuring and development', *University of Reading Discussion Papers in International Investment and Business Studies*, no. 187, Reading.

Dunning, John H. (1994c), 'Revaluating the benefits of foreign direct investment', *University of Reading Discussion Papers in International Investment and Business Studies*, no. 188, Reading.

Dunning, John H., and Peter Robson (1988), 'Multinational corporate integration and regional economic integration', in Dunning, John H., and Peter Robson (eds) *Multinationals and the European Community*, Basil Blackwell, Oxford.

EUROSTAT (1991), *European Community Direct Investment 1984-1988*, Office for Official Publications of the European Communities, Luxembourg.

Grant, Wyn (1992), 'Economic globalisation, stateless firms and international governance', University of Warwick, Department of Politics and International Studies, *Working Paper*, no. 105, April.

Grant, Wyn, and William Paterson (1987), 'Large firms as political actors: the case of the chemical industries in Britain and West Germany', paper presented to the *Annual Conference of the Political Studies Association*, University of Aberdeen, April.

Grant, Wyn, and Wolfgang Streeck (1985), 'Large firms and the representation of business interests in the UK and West German construction industry', in Cawson, Alan (ed.) *Organized Interests and the State*, Sage, London.

Henley, Andrew, and Euclid Tsakalotos (1993), *Corporatism and Economic Performance*, Edward Elgar, Aldershot.

Hofer, Erwin H. (1987), 'Der Wandel des Verhältnisses zwischen Staat und multinationaler Gesellschaft', *Aussenwirtschaft*, vol. 42, no. 4.

Hollingsworth, J. Rogers, Philippe C. Schmitter, and Wolfgang Streeck (1994), *Governing Capitalist Economies: Performance and Control of Sectors*, Oxford University Press, Oxford and New York.

International Monetary Fund (1993), *International Financial Statistics Yearbook*, Washington.

Katzenstein, Peter J. (1985), *Small States in World Markets, Industrial Policy in Europe*, Cornell University Press, Ithaca and London.

Kenworthy, Lane (1990), 'Are industrial policy and corporatism compatible?', *Journal of Public Policy*, vol. 10, no. 3.

Krugman, Paul (1987), 'Is free trade passé?', *Journal of Economic Perspectives*, vol. 1, no. 2, Autumn.

Landesmann, Michael (1992), 'Industrial policies and social corporatism', in Pekkarinen, J., M. Pohjula, and R.E. Rowthorn (eds) *Social Corporatism: A Superior Economic System?*, Clarendon Press, Oxford.

Liemt, Gijsbert van (ed.) (1992), *Industry On the Move: Causes and Consequences of International Relocation in the Manufacturing Industry*, ILO, Geneva.

Narula, Rajneesh (1993), *An Examination of the Evolution and Interdependence of Foreign Direct Investment and Economic Structure: The Case of the Industrialized Countries*, Ph.D. Thesis, Rutgers University, Newark.

OECD (1991), *Globalization, Corporate Citizenship and Industrial Policy*, DSTI. IIND, vol. 38, OECD, Paris.

OECD (1992), *Detailed Benchmark Definition of Foreign Direct Invest-*

106

ment, 2nd Ed., Report prepared by the Group of Financial Statisticians at the request of the Committee on International Investment and Multinational Enterprises, OECD, Paris.

Porter, Michael (1990), *The Competitiveness of Nations*, Harvard University Press, Cambridge.

Price, Curzon V. (1991), 'The threat of "Fortress Europe" from the development of social and industrial policies at a European level', *Aussenwirtschaft*, vol. 46, no. 2.

Roth, Bernhard (1984), *Weltökonomie oder Nationalökonomie? Tendenzen des Internationalisierungsprozesses seit Mitte des 19. Jahrhunderts*, Schriftenreihe der Studiengesellschaft für Sozialgeschichte und Arbeiterbewegung, vol. 46, Verlag Arbeiterbewegung und Gesellschaftswissenschaften, Marburg.

Schendelen, M.P.C.M. van (ed.) (1993), *National Public and Private EC Lobbying*, Dartmouth, Aldershot.

Stopford, J.M., and Susan Strange (with J.S. Henley) (1991), *Rival States, Rival Firms: Competition for World Market Shares*, Cambridge University Press, Cambridge.

Streeck, Wolfgang, and Philippe C. Schmitter (1991), 'From national corporatism to transnational pluralism: Organized interests in the Single European Market', *Politics & Society*, vol. 19, no. 2, June.

Streeck, Wolfgang, and Sigurt Vitols (1993), 'European works councils: Between statutory enactment and voluntary adoption', *Social Science Research Centre Discussion Paper*, 312, Wissenschaftszentrum Berlin.

Thomsen, S., and P. Nicolaides (1990), 'Foreign Direct Investment: 1992 and global markets', *RIIA Discussion Papers* 28, London.

Tolentino, Paz E. (1993), *Technological Innovation and Third World Multinationals*, Routledge and Kagan Paul, London.

UNCTAD-DTCI (1993), *From the Common Market to EC92: Regional Economic Integration in the European Community and Transnational Corporations*, United Nations Publications, Sales no. E.93.II.A.2, New York.

UNCTAD-DTCI (1994), *World Investment Report 1994: Transnational Corporations, Employment and the Workplace*, United Nations, New York.

Williamson, Peter J. (1989), *Corporatism in Perspective*, London (Sage).

5 Labour mobility and migration policy: Lessons from Japan and the US[1]

Saskia Sassen

Japan
USA
F22
J61

Summary

The general proposition organizing the analysis is that international migrations are embedded in larger social, economic and political processes, and that economic internationalization is one form of this embeddedness. This then raises a question about the viability of the immigration framework in developed countries which rests on older notions of the importance of borders and assumes that immigration begins at the borders. The growing convergence in immigration policies in developed countries is happening in a context of on the one hand, inefficacy in regulating international migration and, on the other hand, rapid deregulation of international trade and investment. The case of Japan allows us to capture the intersection of economic transnationalization and immigration at its inception, something no longer possible in Europe or the US. The particular processes through which economic internationalization binds major immigration receiving countries to their emigration sending countries will vary for different periods and different countries or regions. Yet one fact in all of these situations is the existence of a multiplicity of economic, geopolitical and ethnic linkages.

Introduction

Current immigration policy in developed countries is increasingly at odds with other major policy frameworks in the international system and with the growth of global economic integration. All highly developed countries have received rapidly growing numbers of legal and undocumented immigrants over the last decade; none has found its immigration policy effective. These countries are opening up their economies to foreign investment and trade, and deregulating their financial markets. The emergence of a new economic regime in developed countries sharply reduces the role of national governments and national borders in the control of international transactions.

Yet the framework of immigration policy in these countries remains centered on older conceptions of the nation-state and of national borders. Notwithstanding differences in the details of their immigration policies and the attendant operational apparatus, all these countries reveal a fundamental convergence regarding immigration. Further, immigration policy in these countries is shaped by an understanding of immigration as the consequence of the individual actions of emigrants. The receiving country is taken as a passive agent, one not implicated in the process of migration. Immigration is then conceived of as a process that begins at the borders. This in turn provides an additional rationale for the emphasis on border control, whether land borders or airports, as the heart of the regulatory effort.

We are seeing the agglutination of diverse elements of immigration policy and legislation into convergent immigration frameworks across the developed world. Clearly, how we define convergence or divergence is subject to debate. What matters for this paper is first, the contrast between the ongoing emphasis on borders as sites for enforcement of immigration policy and the neutralization of borders when it comes to other types of flows, and, second, the view of immigration as the result of the actions of individuals. I will elaborate on these distinctions later.

The question of convergence takes on an ironic twist in this matter. There is a trend towards convergence in neutralizing borders when it comes to flows of capital, information and goods, and a convergence in maintaining borders when it comes to the flow of immigrants (and refugees). It points to the existence of distinct epistemic communities in each case, and the fact that these communities are transnational. At the same time there is a fundamental divergence in the emergent regime for the flow of capital, goods, information and services on the one hand, and the regime for immigration flows on the other. (For a full discussion of these issues see Sassen, 1995 and in progress a, b.)

The general proposition organizing the analysis in this paper is that international migrations are embedded in larger social, economic and political processes, and that economic internationalization is one form of this embeddedness. This then raises a question about the viability of an immigration framework that rests on older notions of the importance of borders in today's context of growing transnationalization. The particular processes through which economic internationalization binds major immigration receiving countries to their emigration sending countries will vary for different periods and different countries or regions. The transatlantic economy of the 1800s was bound through process that are different from the ones binding the US to the Caribbean today, and these in turn diverge from those binding major European receiving countries to their labour sending countries. Yet one fact in all of these situations is the existence of a multiplicity of economic, geopolitical and ethnic linkages. What is distinct about today's period is a) the growing formation of economic linkages where states play a sharply reduced role, a condition now increasingly referred to as transnationalization or globalization, and b) the fact that the state has developed the technical and bureaucratic capacity to control its borders which it lacked in the 1800s during the period of massive transatlantic migration. Elsewhere I have developed such an analysis for the cases of the US and Europe (Sassen 1988 and 1995).

The recent illegal immigration into Japan is a first in its long history. It raises a question as to the impact of Japan's emergence as a global economic power, particularly its impact on the economies of the emigration sending regions, on the formation of this new immigration. Japan is a country that has never had immigration, although it has a history, even if at times brief, of forced labour recruitment, colonization, and emigration. It lacks the belief in the positive contributions of immigration that is still a trait in the US. The concept immigration did not exist in Japan's law on the entry and exit of aliens. Yet, over the last decade Japan has seen a rapidly growing illegal immigration from, among others, Bangladesh, Thailand, Philippines, Pakistan, and most recently Malaysia and Iran. Japan is now a major foreign aid donor, investor, and exporter of a wide range of consumer goods in the countries where most of its new immigrants originate. This may have created objective and subjective bridges between these countries and Japan, reducing the sociological distance by familiarizing people with Japan. The US has played a similar role in the regions and countries where most of its immigrants originate.

These developments in Japan capture the intersection of economic internationalization and immigration. They also allow us to explore the intersection of immigration policy and immigration reality. Japan's closed door policy has not prevented a growing influx of immigrants. Nor has its 1990 immigration law - which opens up the country to high skill foreign workers but closes it to all low wage workers - actually kept out the latter. Furthermore, despite a strong anti-immigration culture, immigrants have become incorporated into several kinds of labour markets and have begun to form immigrant communities in several major cities in Japan. A detailed exploration of the dynamic at work in the Japanese case should thus provide useful insights into immigration processes in the context of economic internationalization.

The first section of the paper discusses the impact of economic internationalization and geopolitical factors on the formation of immigration flows both in Europe and the US over the last twenty-five years. The second section examines the magnitude and forms of Japan's recent economic presence in the South and Southeast Asian region from where its new immigrants originate. The third section describes the evidence on the new illegal immigration in Japan. The fourth section of the paper briefly reviews the intense debate regarding immigration policy in Japan over the last few years. The final section of the paper is an attempt to understand what conditions in receiving countries make possible the incorporation of immigrants. The underlying concern here is to understand how recent illegal immigrants became part of the Japanese economy, since they had to be accepted by Japanese employers deeply steeped in an anti-immigration culture.

Economic internationalization and geopolitical linkages

Each country is unique and each migration flow is produced by specific conditions. Yet, the dynamic I have identified for the case of the US (Sassen 1988) is at a sufficiently high level of generalization that one could posit its occurrence also in other countries characterized by economic dominance and the formation of transnational spaces for economic activity. This type of analysis seeks to capture the impact of the internationalization of the economy on the formation and direction of migration flows.

The mechanisms binding immigration countries to emigration countries can, in principle, assume many forms. But two appear to be dominant and account for most of the flows. One mechanism is past colonial and current neo- or quasi-colonial bonds, including the types of military presence the US has taken in such diverse situations as El Salvador and the Philippines. The other is the economic linkages brought about by economic internationalization, ranging from the offshoring of production, to the implantation of export oriented agriculture through foreign investment, to the weight of multinationals in the consumer markets of sending countries. There is a third type of linkage, characterized by far higher degrees of specificity and including a variety of mechanisms; among the most important ones are organized recruitment of workers, either directly by the government or in the framework of a government supported initiative by employers, and ethnic linkages established between communities of origin and destination typically via the formation of transnational households or broader kinship structures. These recruitment and ethnic linkages tend to operate within the broader transnational spaces constituted via neo-colonial processes and/or economic internationalization.

Some form of organized recruitment by employers or governments on behalf of employers often lies at the origin of immigration flows, both in

111

the 1800s and today. But eventually most migration flows gain a certain autonomy from the organized recruitment mechanisms. While organized recruitment, and therewith the constitution of certain countries as labour exporting countries, is in many ways radically different from the migrations engendered by erstwhile colonial bonds, there are also similarities. In many ways the labour exporting country is put in a subordinate position, and keeps being represented in the media and in political discourse as a labour exporting country. This was also the case last century when some labour sending areas existed in conditions of economic subordination and often also quasipolitical subordination. The former Polish territories partioned off to Germany were such a region, a region which generated significant migration of 'ethnic' Poles to Western Germany and beyond. It is the case of the Irish in England; and of Italy, which repeatedly served as a labour supplier for the rest of Europe.

The large mass migrations of the 1800s emerged as part of the formation of a trans-Atlantic economic system binding several nation-states through economic transactions and wars. The trans-Atlantic economy was at the core of US development. There were massive flows of capital, goods and workers and specific structures that produced this trans-Atlantic system. Before this period, labour movements across the Atlantic had been largely forced, notably slavery, and mostly from colonized African and Asian territories. Similarly, the migrations to England in the 1950s originated in what had once been British territories. Finally, the migrations into Western Europe of the 1960s and 1970s occurred in a context of direct recruitment and of European regional dominance over the Mediterranean and over some of the Eastern European countries. There are, I would say, few if any innocent bystanders among countries receiving large labour migrations. Receiving countries have typically been participants in the processes leading to the formation of international migration.

The renewal of mass immigration into the US in the 1960s, after five decades of little or no immigration, took place in a context of expanded US economic and military activity in Asia and the Caribbean Basin. The United States is at the heart of an international system of investment and production that binds these various regions. In the 1960s and 1970s, the United States played a crucial role in the development of a world economic system. It passed legislation aimed at opening its own and other countries' economies to the flow of capital, goods, services and information. This central military, political and economic role contributed, I argue, both to the creation of conditions that mobilized people into migrations, whether local or international, and to the formation of links with the United States that subsequently were to serve as often unintended bridges for international migration. Measures commonly thought to deter emigration - foreign investment and the promotion of export oriented growth in developing countries - seem to have had precisely the opposite effect. Among the leading senders of immigrants to the United States in the 1970s and 1980s have been several of the newly industrialized countries of South and Southeast Asia whose extremely high growth rates are generally recognized to be a result, initially, of foreign direct investment in export manufacturing.

That migrations are patterned is further reflected in the figures on the US share of global immigration. Though inadequate, the available evidence compiled by the United Nations *Demographic Yearbook* and *World Population Prospects* shows that in the mid-1980s the United States received about 19 per cent of global emigration. This figure is derived from data on permanent settlement, which excludes illegal immigration and unofficial refugee flows between countries, a growing category. A breakdown by region and country of origin points to a distinct patterning. The US received 27 per cent of total Asian emigration, but 81.5 per cent of all Korean emigration and almost 100 per cent of emigration from the Philippines. It received 70 per cent of Caribbean emigration, but almost 100 per cent of emigration from the Dominican Republic and Jamaica. And it received 19.5 per cent of all emigration from Central America, but 52 per cent of emigration from El Salvador, the country with the greatest US involvement in the region.

Elsewhere (1988) I identify three processes as constituting the larger framework within which to place the new US immigration phase that began after 1965: the offshoring of production; the internationalization of major cities in the US, which emerge as centers for international business and for the coordination and management of a global economic system; and, thirdly, the development of conditions in the US that make it an attractive location for foreign manufacturers and other types of firms and, at the limit, make certain areas of the US competitive with Third World countries as production sites. At least two of these conditions have emerged in Japan as well: the rapid growth in offshore manufacturing and the rapid growth of Tokyo and other major Japanese cities as international business centers. The third development clearly is not found in Japan, nor is it likely to happen. Even though direct foreign investment in Japan is gradually increasing it is at such low levels that it lacks systemic weight at this point (see Sassen 1991).

The implications of these developments for migration are briefly as follows. The internationalization of production established linkages between the US and several Third World countries and, furthermore, uprooted and mobilized people into migrations. Developments in major cities not only have brought about growth in high-income jobs but also a mass of low-income jobs and casualization of the labour market. This has created conditions for the absorption of a large supply of immigrant workers.

113

Finally, the growing presence of foreign manufacturing and other firms in the territory of the US has contributed to create transnational spaces for economic activity. Immigrant workers are emerging as a key labour supply for manufacturing and tend to lower the cost of producing in the US.

On a more conceptual level one could generalize these tendencies and posit that immigration flows take place within systems and that these systems can be specified in a variety of ways. The type of economic specification contained in this particular paper represents but one of several possibilities. However, in other cases, the system within which immigration takes place is to be specified in political or ethnic terms. One could ask, for example, if there are systemic linkages underlying the current Central European migrations to Germany and Austria. Rather than simply posit the push factor of poverty, unemployment and the general failure of socialism, we might inquire as to the existence of linkages which operate as bridges. Thus, before the Second World War both Berlin and Vienna were major receivers of large migrations from a vast Eastern region. Furthermore, these practices produced and reproduced migration systems as such. Finally, the aggressive campaign during the cold war years showing the West as a place where economic well being is the norm and well-paying jobs are easy to get, must also have had some effect in inducing people to migrate westward; a more accurate portrayal of conditions in the West might have deterred potential migrants beyond the absolutely convinced ones who can be seen as constituting a pent-up demand - in other words, beyond those that would have come at all costs. These historical and current conditions contain elements for specifying the systems within which the current Eastern migration to Germany and Austria take place.

The backgrounds of immigrants in Europe suggest that there is a geopolitics of migration. In the case of the United Kingdom, sixty per cent of the foreign residents in the United Kingdom are from Asian or African countries which were former dominions or colonies. Immigration from European countries is rather low, and almost three-fourths of European immigrants come from Ireland - also once a colony. There are almost no immigrants from such countries as Turkey or Yugoslavia which provide the largest share to Germany. On the other side of the coin, almost all immigrants from the Indian subcontinent and from the English Caribbean residing in Europe are in the United Kingdom.

Continuing along these lines, in the first ten years after WWII, the vast majority of 'immigrants' to Germany were the eight million displaced ethnic Germans that resettled there. Another major group were the three million who came from the GDR before the Berlin Wall was erected in 1961. Almost all ethnic Germans went to Germany; and those that did not go to Germany went overseas. But also 86 per cent of Greek immigrants,

80 per cent of Turks and 76 per cent of Yugoslavs in Europe reside in Germany. More recently Germany expanded its labour recruitment or sourcing area to include Portugal, Algeria, Morocco and Tunisia, even though the vast majority of immigrants from these countries reside in France. In brief, what we see in the case of Germany is first, a large migration rooted in a long history of domination over the eastern region. Then an immigration originating in less developed countries following a by now classical dynamic between labour import/labour export countries.

France, for long Europe's main immigration country, is since the late 1960s its second largest, after Germany. Decolonization brought about the return of two million Frenchmen from overseas. During the period of sharp post-war growth a whole new migration developed originating in France's former zone of influence in North Africa. Almost all Algerians residing in Europe are in France; and so are 86 per cent of Tunisians and 61 per cent of Moroccans. Almost all immigrants in Europe from overseas territories still under French control - such as the French Antilles, Tahiti, French Guyana - reside in France. But so do 84 per cent of Portuguese and of Spaniards residing in Europe outside their country. France has a long history of recruiting/receiving migrant workers from these countries for its vineyards going back to the 1800s.

The Netherlands and Belgium both received significant numbers of people from their former colonial empires. They also received foreign workers from labour exporting countries, such as Italy, Morocco and Turkey. Switzerland similarly receives workers from traditional labour exporting countries: Italy, Spain, Portugal, Yugoslavia and Turkey. All three countries originally organized the recruitment of these workers, until eventually a somewhat autonomous set of flows was in place. Sweden receives 93 per cent of Finnish immigrants. Also in Sweden as in the other countries, there is a large expansion of the recruitment area to include workers from the traditional labour exporting countries on the Mediterranean.

As a given labour migration flow ages, it tends to become more diversified in terms of destination. It suggests that a certain autonomy from older colonial and neo-colonial bonds sets in. Immigrants from Italy and Spain are now distributed among several countries. Among Italian immigrants in Europe, one-third reside in Germany, 27 per cent in France, 24 per cent in Switzerland, and 15 per cent in Belgium. The fact that it is still a limited diversity of destinations could be seen as signaling the presence of migration systems. On the other hand, more recent labour migrations reveal very high levels of geographic concentration. The largest single immigrant group in any of Europe's labour receiving countries today are the Turks, with 1.5 million in Germany.

It does seem, and the history of economic development supports this,

115

that once an area becomes a significant emigration region it does not easily catch up in terms of development with those areas that emerge as labour importing areas. Precisely because these have high growth, or at least relatively high growth, it seems that there is an accumulation of advantage. History suggests that this is an advantage which labour sending areas either a) cannot catch up with, and/or b) are structurally not going to be part of because growth is precisely characterized by this type of spatial concentration. One cannot be too rigid and mechanical about these generalizations. But it is clear that Italy and Ireland, even if they now receive immigrants, have for two centuries been labour exporters and this has not necessarily been a macroeconomic advantage, even though individuals and localities may have benefitted.

In short, we could argue that as today's labour receiving countries grew richer and more developed, they kept expanding their zone of recruitment or influence. They covered a larger and larger set of countries and included a variety of emigration-immigration dynamics, some rooted in past imperial conditions, others in the newer development asymmetries that underlie much migration today. There is a dynamic of inequality that keeps on marking regions as labour sending and labour receiving, notwithstanding a blurring of the definitions as is evident with Central Europe and Italy, both of which are now also receiving immigrants.

Some migration characteristics in the Japanese case

Japan, a country long proud of its homogeneity, has traditionally kept its doors closed to immigration - though not to emigration and forced labour recruitment. (The notion that Japan is a racially homogenous country is contested by the resident Korean population many of whom insist on their right to maintain their Korean ethnicity and by the indigenous Ainu people, who consider themselves the oldest ethnic people in Japan). Japan is now facing an influx of illegal immigrants from several Asian countries with whom it has strong economic ties. These flows have taken place despite a closed doors policy. Has the internationalization of the Japanese economy created conditions that contribute to building 'bridges' with those countries which may eventually facilitate the migration of people? There is also a growing number of legal immigrant workers both for low-wage jobs and for high-level positions, especially in the financial sector. All these workers fall under categories of entry that were either introduced or expanded in the new 1990 immigration law discussed below. High-level manpower flows are clearly related to the internationalization of the Japanese economy. But this is far less evident in the case of the new illegal immigration from Asia.

After being centered on trade, Japan's role in the post-World War II global economy has now expanded onto a number of other arenas: foreign direct investment, foreign aid, the export of culture in various forms including fashion, architectural styles, and - especially to Asia - new models of success. Along with the export of consumer goods, these various flows have contributed to a strong Japanese presence in many Asian countries.

Japan's role in global foreign direct investment (FDI) has grown rapidly. By 1982, Japan had become the leading net exporter of FDI, with a gross outflow of $4.5 billion. That particular year Japan surpassed the United Kingdom's $4.4 billion. Although this level was still far below the $7 billion and the $10 billion gross outflows registered for the UK in 1980 and 1981, it signalled Japan's major position among capital exporting countries. In 1983, when a general contraction in direct foreign investment occurred, Japan's decline was relatively smaller than that of other leading countries. This is particularly evident for the period beginning in the late 1970s, when the realignment of investment patterns began to consolidate. By 1986, Japan's direct foreign investment flows had risen to $14.3 billion and by 1987 to $19.4 billion, for a cumulated stock of almost $80 billion. In 1990 they reached $36.3 billion compared to $40 billion for the US and $24 billion for the UK. Japan has surpassed most of the leading Western European capital exporters, including West Germany, the Netherlands, and France.

Although much of Japan's investment has gone to the United States, its impact is much greater in South and Southeast Asia where Japan has a strong, complex, and multifaceted past and current presence. Over the last few years, a rapidly rising share of Japan's foreign direct investment has been going to Asia. By 1986 Japan's FDI stock in South, Southeast and East Asia stood at $22.1 billion compared to $16 billion for the US.

Since 1986 Japanese direct investment in Thailand, Malaysia, Singapore, Philippines and Indonesia has grown rapidly. Most of this investment is in export oriented businesses centering on the auto and electronics industries. Some Japanese companies have also shifted their plants from NIEs to ASEAN countries.

Another important aspect of Japan's internationalization is the rapid growth in overseas development assistance in the 1980s. While Japan's overseas development assistance is a small share of its GNP, in absolute terms it has made Japan the leading donor in the world (given US retrenchment). Though less so today than in the past, much of this aid consists of loans that are tied to specific purposes and have been viewed as serving the interests of Japanese firms to expand their markets and operations overseas. The 1980s saw a major change in Japan's understanding of the role of foreign aid, with a greater emphasis on broader political aims linked to Japan's becoming a global power. This is evident in the much larger share of grants rather than loans in overall Japanese aid Japan's aid began with the Colombo Plan and the signing of the Reparations Treaty with Burma in 1954. Many institutions were founded in the 1950s aimed at overseas economic and technical cooperation and assistance. But it was not until the late 1970s that Japan emerged as an important foreign aid donor. In the 1960s loans began to replace reparations. By the 1980s aid was more diversified with at least half of all money going for grants and technical cooperation loans.

Japan surpassed West Germany in 1983 and France in 1984 becoming the second largest donor country behind the US. In 1988 it surpassed the US, becoming the largest donor. Japan has played a particularly prominent role in aid to Asia. In the 1980s Japan became the largest single donor of overseas development assistance in Asia. By the mid-1980s, Japan's foreign aid to Asia reached $15 billion, or 70 per cent of all Japanese aid. Meanwhile, the US provided aid of only $1.11 billion for Asia and only $500 million for Southeast Asia. In 1989-90 Japan's foreign aid in Asia was $4.8 billion compared to 1.4 billion by the US. Japan accounts for about one fourth of all foreign aid in Asia, but it is now the single largest donor in China, Thailand, Philippines, Indonesia, Malaysia. Japan provides for almost 70 per cent of foreign aid to Thailand, and about half of all aid to Malaysia and Philippines. While it accounts only for about a fifth of all aid to Pakistan and Bangladesh it is the largest single donor.

The new illegal immigration in Japan

The legal foreign workforce in Japan consists of a broad spectrum of categories from professional workers to unskilled company trainees. It is largely of Asian origin; China, Philippines, Thailand and Malaysia are major sending countries. A majority are women who come in as 'entertainers', still largely from the Philippines. The direct recruitment of women for the 'entertainment industry', initially mostly confined to the Philippines, has increased sharply, spread to several other countries, and gone beyond the stipulations of the law (see Asian Women's Association, 1988; and AMPO, 1987). Most recently there have been growing numbers of entrants classified as company trainees, and students in post-secondary non-university institutions, mostly language and vocational schools. The descendants of Japanese born abroad up to the third generation can come and work legally in Japan. Their numbers have been growing rapidly since 1987. This group, along with 'company trainees' and non-university students are seen as providing a legal supply of foreign workers for low-wage, typically unskilled, undesirable jobs. Since the new 1990 law was

118

passed, it is estimated that about 150,000 have entered each year under these provisions (Morita 1992).

There is a population of Koreans and Chinese whose origins go back to the period of Japanese colonization at the turn of the century. In 1985, before the rapid growth in unauthorized immigration began, the total number of permanent resident aliens in Japan stood at 850,000, of whom 683,000 were of Korean origin, many third generation. By 1990 there were about 700,000 Koreans and 140,000 Chinese, accounting for 85 per cent of all registered alien residents and 0.5 per cent of Japan's population. Many are third generation and slowly growing numbers are becoming naturalized, mostly through having a Japanese parent. The vast majority of the legal foreign population reside in the large metropolitan areas, particularly Tokyo, Osaka and Nagoya.

Though fragmentary, the evidence indicates a rapid increase over the last five years in the numbers of foreigners working illegally in Japan - mostly in the Tokyo metropolitan area, Nagoya and Osaka, though they are also employed in agriculture. Typically they have entered the country on tourist visas and have overstayed their officially permitted time. (The new Hispanic immigration to New York City began in much the same manner.) Labour contractors, mostly members of organized crime groups, often use illegal documents to bring foreign workers in.

Juxtaposing entries with departures shows that, compared to much earlier years, there were significantly more entries than departures. This may be explained by a number of reasons, from a legal multiple year stay to an administrative miscount. But together with other evidence, these data suggest that among certain nationality groups an increasing number of entrants with short term visas are coming to work illegally. Figures after 1988 show a distinct increase in entries. Entries from the Philippines have more than doubled, from about 48,000 in 1983 to 108,300 in 1990. If what we have seen in the United States should take place in Japan, a growing number of 'tourists' and 'visitors' are coming into the country not to visit but to find gainful employment. I spent many hours interviewing illegal immigrants in Tokyo in an attempt to learn how they decided to migrate to Japan, given Japan's reputation as a closed society (see Sassen 1991). It is impossible to do justice to their answers here, but the main points were as follows: first, they were individuals who, in one way or another, had been mobilized into becoming migrant labour; second, Japan's growing presence in their home countries, together with the consequent availability of information about Japan, had indeed created linkages and made Japan seem a good option for migration.

It is important not to read too much into the above figures on entries from the Philippines - entries may have been registered in one year, departures in another; but the figures do support other information indicating growing illegal immigration through the overstaying of tourist visas.

Estimates based on apprehensions and on entry and exit figures suggest that by 1994 there were up to 500,000 illegal immigrants working in Japan, mostly in construction, manufacturing, and bar and restaurant work. Almost all were from Asia, the largest groups from South Korea, Bangladesh, the Philippines, Pakistan, Thailand. About 100,000 of these are estimated to be from South Korea. Since 1988 when the government fully recognized the existence of this new immigration, it is estimated that the numbers have kept increasing. In early 1990 there may have been a temporary halt in new entries - though not in apprehensions.

Data on apprehensions from the Immigration Office of the Ministry of Justice analyzed by Morita (1990, 1992) point to a pre- and post-1990 pattern. In mid- and late 1980s the data for apprehended immigrants show that the largest single country of origin was the Philippines followed by Pakistan, Bangladesh, Thailand and Korea. Two-thirds of Filipinos were women; this was also the case with Thai apprehensions. But women were small minorities in the other major groups. In 1989, only two each in Pakistani and Bangladashi groups were women. Up to the mid-1980s the majority of apprehensions had been of women, because almost all illegal immigrants were 'entertainers' recruited for the sex industry. However, they accounted for only twenty-five per cent of apprehensions in 1989 and in 1990. Alongside this shift toward increased male apprehensions, there was also a shift in nationalities due to the passing of the new 1990 immigration law and the greater difficulty of obtaining visas. After the new law (in 1991), there was a sharp decline in apprehensions of Bangladeshi and Pakistani. This coincided with a) a sharp fall in tourist entries from these two countries due to Japan's cancellation of its visa exemption agreement; b) a sharp increase in apprehensions of Iranians, who could enter without visas due to an agreement signed between Iran and Japan during the oil crisis of the 1970s. Iranians replaced the Bangladeshi and Pakistani as the most visible unauthorized population in the early 1990s. Japan has now canceled its visa exemption agreement with Iran; tourist entries and, by inference, illegal overstays, have dropped sharply.

Figures on apprehensions from 1980 to 1991 show clearly that visa overstaying is the single largest category. Overall apprehensions rose from 2,536 in 1980 to 10,573 in 1986 and 35,903 in 1991. In 1991 overstayers were 32,820 out of 35,903 apprehensions. Only about 2,000 of those apprehended had *entered* the country illegally in each of these two years. This pattern held throughout the 1980s. A new category of illegal entry that is growing fast is illegal boat landing. There is no record of such apprehensions up to 1982, but they had risen to 2,751 in 1986 and 27,100 by 1991. Other changes are the rapid increases in apprehensions of South Koreans, Thais, and Malaysians (the latter a migration that only began

120

around 1987). Except for the Philippines, Taiwan and Thailand - still the main countries for the recruitment of women for the entertainment industry - a majority of apprehensions are of men.

Why immigration now?

If immigration were simply a matter of the push of poverty in sending countries and the pull of plentiful jobs in Japan, then one would have expected a large immigration during Japan's period of rapid industrialization when there was a huge demand for labour and many of Japan's poor neighbors still had not become industrialized. During this period there was large scale construction of public and private infrastructure to accommodate the industrialization of the economy and the urbanization of the people. The demand for labour was immense. It was filled, however, by rural migrations to major urban areas. Although Japan had large rural labour reserves, they were outstripped by job growth, a fact that made headlines worldwide and conceivably could have 'pulled' immigrants from Asian countries with high levels of poverty and unemployment. But becoming a labour migrant to Japan in the 1950s and 1960s was simply inconceivable for reasons that probably go far beyond legal restrictions to entry. That legal restrictions are not the central factor is suggested by the fact that today labourers try to come to Japan despite the ongoing legal restrictions against their entry.

While individuals may experience their migration as the outcome of their personal decisions, the option to migrate is itself socially produced. Because immigration flows tend to share many characteristics, this embeddedness is easily lost in much immigration analysis or made so general as to lose explanatory power. An example of this is the notion that poverty as such is a migration push factor; yet many countries with great poverty lack any significant emigration history. It takes a number of other conditions to activate poverty into a push factor.

If immigration were simply a matter of policy, then the current unauthorized immigration in Japan should not have happened. The law forbids the entry of workers for unskilled jobs, which is precisely where most of the unauthorized immigrants are employed. In the case of the US, the law passed in 1965 which opened the country to immigration had an immense impact, because it happened at a time when the US had a far flung network of production sites and military operations in several Third World countries. There was not only a pent-up demand for emigration but also a broad network of linkages between those countries and the US. These linkages then activated poverty into a migration 'push' factor. Immigration policy by itself cannot engender migrations.

In its period of high growth, Japan lacked the types of networks and

121

linkages with potential immigrant sending countries that could have facilitated the formation of international migration flows given considerable poverty and unemployment in many Asian countries. Could it be that as Japan internationalizes its economy and becomes a key investor in South and Southeast Asia, it creates - wittingly or not - a transnational space for the circulation of its goods, capital, and culture which in turn may create conditions for the circulation of people? We may be seeing the early stages in the formation of an international labour market, a market to which both labour contractors and illegal immigrants have access.

The new 1990 immigration law in Japan

The Immigration Control and Refugee Recognition Law passed by the Diet in Dec. 8, 1989, which became effective June 1, 1990, is a revision of a 1981 revision of an earlier law. On the one hand the amendments expand the number of job categories for which the country will accept foreign workers, typically on three-year stays. These are mostly in professional occupations such as lawyers, investment bankers, accountants with international expertise and medical personnel. On the other hand, it seeks to restrict and control the inflow of unskilled and semiskilled workers. For the first time the law imposes sanctions on those employing and contracting illegal workers. Japan is, then, in many ways replicating the efforts of the United States to control who is coming into the country.

Morita (1990) points out that there had been a set of regulations and practices covering the granting of residence and work permits to foreigners. But the numbers involved were smaller and the overall situation was one of stability in all types of entries. In 1980 work permits were granted to 30,000 foreigners, mostly business managers, professors, artists, entertainers, foreign instructors and skilled workers. By 1989 such permits had grown to 72,000, and by 1991 to over 200,000; though this is a very small number in a workforce of 65 million, it represents a sharp increase since 1980.

The 1990 law establishes a total of twenty-eight categories for legal residence and work. It basically allows a variety of professional workers as well as the descendants of Japanese immigrants abroad (up to the third generation) to work and reside legally in Japan, with specific lengths in the allowable stay. There are three classifications which allow foreigners to work in Japan. A first classification covers diplomats, artists, religious personnel and journalists. These are clearly all categories of workers that will tend to operate internationally and do not represent the typical migrant worker. The second classification describes rather precise categories of professional and technical occupations ranging from financial and accounting experts to engineers and highly skilled craft workers. A third classification describes very specific forms of expertise. Temporary visitors, students, family visitors, are all prohibited from work. The law also includes a stipulation whereby a foreigner already residing in Japan may apply to the Immigration Office for a work permit. This is clearly more likely to cover the children of foreigners legally residing in Japan when they reach work-age than illegal workers in unskilled jobs.

In terms of the control of unauthorized immigration, one of the central aims of the new law, two effects are becoming evident in the short run. The new law has had at least a temporary deterrent effect, as had the 1986 IRCA in US. Before the law took effect, about 30,000 Bangladeshi and Pakistanis illegally in the country left, presumably to avoid arrest. It should be noted that in order to avoid the pattern familiar in other countries, Japan canceled its visa exemption for visitors with Bangladesh and Pakistan in 1989 (prior to the passage of the new law) to prevent a great rush of visitors intending to become illegal workers before the new law was to be implemented. The new visa agreement made it very difficult to obtain a visa and contributed to reducing the number of visitors drastically, both genuine visitors and those intending to overstay and become illegal workers. This policy is not unlike that which evolved in the US in the late 1980s with known emigration countries. The US law requires visa applicants from these countries (e.g. Colombia, the Dominican Republic, Peru, Ecuador) to demonstrate means and ties that suggest they are definitely on a tourist, short term business trip or some such kind of visit, and plan to return to their countries of origin. In 1991 Japan also revoked the visa exemption agreement it had signed with Iran in 1975. As with Bangladeshi and Pakistani tourists, the effect was a sharp drop in Iranian tourist entries.

Secondly, the new law allows some unskilled labour in through other categories: 'company trainees', students, Japanese descendants up to the third generation. It has, in many cases, become a vehicle to bring in low-wage foreign workers for unskilled routine jobs where little if any training is involved. Furthermore, the new law also allows students of post-secondary (but not university) institutions, including language and vocational schools, to work for a limited number of hours per week; universities are excluded from this provision. This provision has also become largely a device to obtain workers for unskilled, lowly-paid jobs.

Employers can be fined up to 2 million yen (about $16,000) if they knowingly hire an illegal immigrant and imprisoned for up to three years if they continue to employ illegal workers. This is a fairly heavy punishment for employers in view of the acute labour shortage especially in manufacturing. As for the contractors and criminal gangs that have gotten involved in procuring illegal workers, Morita (1990) considers that the law as it stands now is weak in provisions concerning their punishment. The new law also completely leaves out any discussion of the human rights of immigrant workers (Miyajima, 1989). (For detailed accounts of abuses against illegal immigrants, especially by contractors who are typically part of or working for 'yakuza' (organized crime) organizations, see *AMPO*, 1992).

Enforcement of the new law appears to be checkered. Apprehensions have risen, but so have the numbers of estimated illegal workers. Apprehensions rose from 22,629 in 1989 to 36,264 in 1990 and 35,903 in 1991. In addition, 27,137 mostly Chinese in boats, were denied landing in 1991, up from 13,934 in 1990 and 10,404 in 1989. There have been no large scale deportation efforts, even though immigrants tend to live in known residential concentrations (See Sassen 1991: Chapter 9). Just a few hundred employers have received sanctions for knowingly hiring illegals. In a country with millions of enterprises and a large number of labour contractors, there are fewer than 2,000 immigration inspectors authorized to check on employers. Alongside weak enforcement of the new law, there appears to be a pattern of growing abuse of illegal immigrants by labour brokers *and* by immigration officers and police (AMPO 1992; Miyajima 1988).

The new law is already being criticized because it does not address the labour shortage in unskilled, low-paying or undesirable jobs and pushes at least some employers either to risk sanctions for hiring illegal immigrants or to close their factories. These employers include not only small, technologically backward factories, but also highly mechanized, technologically advanced factories (Morita 1990). One strategy being used particularly by large firms is replacing illegal workers with the descendants of Japanese in South America (Komai 1992); large firms are better positioned for access to these labour supplies because they can make use of existing international channels. While in Brazil recently I spoke with some of those who had returned. The stories they tell are quite dismal; the jobs were hard and dirty, they received no respect, they were not seen as Japanese. Many have returned defeated and humiliated. The press in Brazil has written considerably about this and it is seen as a scandal. Japanese recruiting agents in Brazil are allowed only to hire Japanese descendants; this has in turn caused a furor in Brazil since it is seen as discriminatory hiring.

Another problem with the new law is that insofar as control relies on restricting visitors' visas, it has to travel a fine line between remaining open to vast numbers of genuine tourists and business people *and* closing up to potentially unauthorized immigrants. Two-thirds of tourists and business people come from Asia, as do almost all unauthorized immigrants. In fact the main nationalities identified by the government in the detected unauthorized population and in the inferred overstayers population are mostly also those with a large share of Asian tourists and business people. Furthermore, with Japan becoming a strong presence in more and more countries, there is likely to be a growing number of countries that will be coded as potential emigration countries. Thus, for example, it was only in the late 1980s that Japan set up offshore factories and other types of investment in Malaysia. It appears from apprehensions data that there now is an unauthorized migration of Malaysians, one of the newest flows. Many of these countries are likely to be also large senders of tourists and business people.

In the late 1980s before the new law was passed, there was a long debate about the nature of immigration in Japan (see Sassen 1991: 311-4). The centrality this issue assumed for the Japanese government is evident from the fact that all the major ministries set up working parties to study and consult on the issue and to develop position papers. A review of the main positions of the ministries points to the complexity of the issue and to the fact that the employment of illegal foreign workers is generally recognized as a given and growing development. At the heart of the immigration debate were the Ministry of Justice, mainly concerned with the maintenance of public order, and the Ministry of Labour, centrally concerned with employment conditions of domestic workers and the nature of labour shortages in Japan. Morita (1990) notes that the debate on immigration, originally conceived purely as a labour market issue, eventually became a broader debate about the incorporation of foreigners in a homogeneous society such as the Japanese, a development akin to that in the West. The possibility of ethnic conflict and of racism can no longer be overlooked. In the view of Morita (1990), one of the leading analysts of immigration in Japan, the demand for immigrant workers is structural not cyclical, and the inflow of foreign workers will further rigidify the segmentation in the labour market, therewith contributing to a rise in demand for foreign workers. In addition, some Japanese analysts have argued that Japan should take a broader view and see immigration from Asia and Latin America as part of the larger issue of international inequality in social and economic development, and that it should make immigration policy part of development policy (Nanami and Kuwabara, 1989).

Labour demand in receiving countries: post-industrial growth and increased casual employment

In the case of advanced economies, no analysis of immigration is complete without an explanation of the changes in labour demand. In the case of the US, which I analyze elsewhere (1988: Chapter 2; 1991: Chapter 8), beginning in the late 1970s there was a rapid expansion in the supply of low-wage jobs and a casualization of the labour market, both associated with the new growth industries, but also with the decline and reorganization of manufacturing.

Such tendencies toward casualization are an important process facilitating the incorporation of illegal immigration into the labour market. Casualization opens up the hiring process, lifts restrictions on employers and typically lowers the direct and indirect costs of labour. The increase in low-wage jobs in the United States is in part a result of the same international economic processes that have channeled investment and manufacturing jobs to low-wage countries. As industrial production has moved overseas or to low-wage areas in the South, traditional US manufacturing organization based on high wages has eroded and partly been replaced in many industries by a downgraded manufacturing sector characterized by a supply of poorly paid, semi-skilled or unskilled production jobs and extensive subcontracting. At the same time, the rapid growth of the service sector has created vast numbers of low-wage jobs in addition to the more publicized increase in highly paid investment banking, management and professional jobs. Income inequality increased. In the decade from 1963 to 1973, nine out of 10 new jobs were in the middle earnings group whereas after 1973 only one in two new jobs was in the middle earnings category. If one were to add the increase in the number of workers who are not employed full-time and year-round, then the inequality becomes even more pronounced. Part-time workers (including all types of non-full-time workers) increased from 15 per cent in 1955 to 22 per cent in 1977; by 1990 they were a third of the labour force. Approximately 80 per cent of these 50 million workers earn less than $11,000 a year.

Can we detect growing casualization of labour markets also in Japan during the late 1980s, the period of rapid immigration growth? There are indications of structural change in Japan in the 1980s. Elsewhere (Sassen 1991: chapters 8 and 9) I have described in detail the growth of service jobs in Japan, the replacement of many full-time male workers with part-time women, the growth of forms of subcontracting that weaken the claims of workers on their firms, the fact that most new jobs created in Tokyo in the 1980s were part-time or temporary jobs. Since the mid-1980s, average real earnings in Japan have been decreasing and the manufacturing sector has been losing its wage-setting influence (Japan Economic Planning Agency, various years). Data from the labour Force Survey in Japan (Japan Ministry of Labour, various years) show that the share of part-time workers increased from under 7 per cent of all workers in 1970 to 12 per cent in 1987, or 5 million workers. Among women workers, this share almost doubled, from about 12 per cent in 1970 to 22 per cent in 1985 and over 23 per cent in 1987, or a total of about 3.65 million women. Almost 24 per cent of part-time women workers were in manufacturing, an indication of the growth of a casualized employment relation in that sector.

126

Unemployment, though minor by Western standards, is growing; it used to be largely frictional, but now distinct patterns are emerging. In 1986 unemployment reached almost three per cent, one of its highest levels since the mid-1950s. Furthermore, with few exceptions, most of the service industries which are growing have significantly lower average earnings than do manufacturing and transport and communications. Hotel and catering had among the lowest average earnings, along with health services and retail. Many of the industries that are growing either pay above-average wages, as is the case with finance, insurance and real estate, or pay below-average wages as is the case with many of the other services. There is a growing split between high and low wage jobs. The same trends found in many western cities are beginning to be evident in Tokyo. (For a full discussion, see Sassen 1991, Chapters 8 and 9.)

We need to ask whether these conditions facilitate the employment of unauthorized immigrants in a society where this is not part of the cultural heritage. We cannot take for granted that the labour shortage ipso facto explains the incorporation of unauthorized immigrants. My research suggests other mediating conditions must be present in order to facilitate their incorporation. During my fieldwork in one of the large day labourer markets, it became clear to me that these markets are a key mechanism for the incorporation of illegal immigrants into the Japanese labour market; they also make it possible for immigrants to get a job without a labour contractor. Several of the return illegal immigrants I spoke with had come by themselves and gotten jobs without contractors.

The evidence on detected unauthorized immigrants from the Ministry of Justice analyzed by Morita (1990) shows that over 80 per cent of men apprehended from 1987 to 1990 held construction and factory jobs. Clearly, factories and construction sites lend themselves to apprehension activity unlike small service operations in the center of Tokyo or Osaka. Thus we cannot assume that this level is an adequate representation of the occupational distribution of unauthorized immigrants. But it does indicate that factories are employing unauthorized immigrants. According to a study of unauthorized immigrant employment in the major urban areas in Japan carried out by the Immigration Office of the Ministry of Justice, factories employing unauthorized immigrants are in a broad range of industries: metal processing, plastic processing, printing and binding, plating, press operating and materials coating. Most recently a growing number of women have been apprehended in factories in metals and plastic processing and in autoparts manufacturing (Morita 1990). Most unauthorized immigrants were found in medium sized and small factories. The figures for 1991 point to a continuation of these patterns. Almost half of illegals detected by the government were in construction, followed by 14 per cent in manufacturing and certain jobs in the retail industry, in particular backroom jobs in restaurants.

Estimates about the evolution of unauthorized immigration for unskilled jobs vary considerably, but all point to growing demand. The Ministry of Labour estimates the labour shortage will reach half a million by the end of the decade. Japan's most powerful business organization, Keidaren, puts the shortage at five million. Specialists estimate the shortage will range between one and two million by the end of the decade. Currently the largest shortages are in manufacturing, particularly small and medium-sized firms. But there is considerable agreement that the service sector will be a major source of new shortages. As the current generation of Japanese employees in low-skill service jobs retires and young highly educated Japanese reject these jobs, there may well be a gradual acceptance of immigrant workers.

All highly industrialized countries have resorted to immigrant workers for many of the low-wage jobs in manufacturing and in services. But not all have experienced the combination of conditions evident in Japan today. Japan has the lowest fertility rate among developed countries and one of the fastest growing old-age populations. It also experienced one of the fastest urbanization rates and has exhausted its rural labour reserves to the point that agriculture now has severe labour shortages and farmers have resorted to immigrant workers (and importing brides, given the shortage of young Japanese women willing to be farmers' wives). The high educational level of young Japanese and the ongoing demand in high-paying jobs further reduces the effective supply of labour for low-wage, unskilled jobs. Even if the current trends continue beyond the recession and more Japanese are laid off, it is unlikely they would take the low-wage jobs where most of the shortages are expected. As in all advanced economies, the labour market is segmented and shortages can coexist with unemployment.

The case of Japan shows in great starkness patterns that are vague and ill-shaped in other advanced economies with long immigration histories. Advanced economies tend to have high average levels of education and a growth in high-income jobs; but, we are discovering, they also engender a large supply of low-wage, unskilled jobs *and* a devaluing of most production jobs in manufacturing. Japan shows us that even in a society that is fairly homogeneous and thinks of itself as one-nation, one-people, these processes of differentiation will produce relative labour shortages.

Conclusion

The worldwide evidence shows rather clearly that there is considerable patterning in the geography of migrations, and that the major receiving countries tend to get immigrants from their zones of influence. This holds for countries as diverse as the US, France and Japan. Immigration is at least partly an outcome of the actions of the governments and major private economic actors in receiving countries. Economic internationalization and the geopolitics resulting from older colonial patterns suggest that the responsibility for immigration may not be exclusively the immigrant's.

Yet the policy framework for immigration treats the flow of labour as the result of individual actions, particularly the individual's decision to migrate in search of better opportunities. Such a policy puts responsibility for immigration on the shoulders of immigrants. Policy commentary which speaks of an immigrant 'influx' or 'invasion' treats the receiving country as a passive agent. The causes for immigration appear to be fundamentally unconnected to past or current actions of receiving countries. Immigration policy becomes a decision to be more or less benevolent in admitting immigrants. Absent from this understanding is the notion that the international activities of the governments or firms of receiving countries may have contributed to the formation of economic linkages with emigration countries, linkages that may function as bridges not only for capital but also for migration flows.

Refugee policy in some countries does lift the burden of immigration from the immigrant's shoulders. US refugee policy, particularly for the case of Indochinese refugees, does acknowledge partial responsibility on the part of the government. Clearly, in the case of economic migrations, such responsibility is far more difficult to establish, and by its nature far more indirect.

The case of Japan is of interest here because it allows us to capture the intersection of economic internationalization and immigration in its inception and to do so in a country with a radically different history, culture and, to a lesser extent, a different economic organization from those of other advanced economies. One of the areas where this difference is evident is in Japan's lack of an immigration history. Yet, though much later than most advanced economies, Japan now has a growing unauthorized immigrant workforce in low wage, unskilled jobs in a context where Japanese youth are rejecting such jobs.

Why has this happened now rather than during the period of extremely rapid economic growth in the 1950s and 1960s when Japan experienced very sharp labour shortages? Japan is a major presence in a regional Asian economic system where it is the leading investor, foreign aid donor, and exporter of consumer goods (including cultural products). And while Japan is not quite as open to foreign firms as the US, there is a growing presence of such firms. Is the new immigration to Japan unrelated to these processes of internationalization? This paper argues that the new immigration is part of the globalization of Japan's economy. This is easy to recognize in the case of foreign high level manpower for the financial industry in Tokyo. It is less clearly so in the case of the new, mostly unauthorized immigration of manual workers employed in construction, manufacturing and low-wage jobs in services. In this latter case internationalization a) provides a context within which bridges are built with the countries of origin of potential emigrants and b) makes the Japanese economy more porous, particularly so in the case of large cities.

We are seeing the formation of similar migration processes in all major advanced economies. These are forming at a very specific juncture: what we identified analytically as the intersection of processes of economic internationalization and labour market developments. Placing the formation of immigration flows and their continuation at this juncture allows us to see important parallels in advanced economies with significant differences in terms of history and culture. The parallels result from the condition of being global powers with strong economic presences in transnational zones of influence and from major processes of economic restructuring evident in all advanced economies in the 1980s. The differences stem in part from the specifics of each country's culture and history. In Japan we see the beginnings of processes which are longer-standing in the US and in Western Europe.

This type of analysis opens up the immigration policy question beyond the familiar range of border control. It signals that international migrations are partly embedded in conditions produced by economic internationalization both in sending and in receiving areas. This would suggest that the basic framework for immigration policy shared by these advanced economies should be reworked towards the incorporation of the facts of economic internationalization. It would thereby achieve greater convergence with other major policy frameworks aimed at further facilitating economic internationalization. Indeed, the global integration of economies on the one hand, and, on the other, the growth of a broad network of rights and court decisions supporting the social and civic rights of immigrants are already reducing the autonomy of the state in immigration policy making. This should not be surprising given the trends towards transnationalization in economies, in culture, and in the battle around human rights.

Note

1. The author wishes to acknowledge the two larger projects on which this paper is based: *Immigrants and Refugees: A European Dilemma?* (Frankfurt: Fischer Verlag, 1995) and *On Governing the Global Economy* (in print with Columbia University Press). They contain full bibliographic information about the many subjects covered in the paper.

References

AMPO (1988), *Japan's Human Imports: As Capital Flows Out, Foreign Labour Flows In*, vol. 19, no. 4.

AMPO (1992). vol. 23, no. 4.

Asian Women's Association (1988), *Women from Across the Seas: Migrant Workers in Japan*, Asian Women's Association, Tokyo.

Cornelius, Wayne et al. (1992), 'Controlling illegal immigration: A global perspective', Work in progress, Center for United States-Mexican Studies, University of California, San Diego.

Iyotani, Toshio, and Toshio Naito (1989), 'Tokyo no Kokusaika de Tenkan Semarareru Chusho Kigyo' (Medium- and small-sized corporations under pressure of change by Tokyo's internationalization), *Ekonomisuto*, September 5.

Komai, Hiroshi (1992), 'Are foreign trainees in Japan disguised cheap labourers?', *Migration World*, vol. 20, no. 13-17.

Miyajima, Takashi (1989), *The Logic of Receiving Foreign Workers: Amongst Dilemmas of Advanced Societies* (Gaikokujin Rodosha Mukaeire no Ronri: Senshin shakai no Jirenma no naka de), Akashi Shoten, Tokyo.

Morita, Kiriro (1992), 'Japan and the problem of foreign workers', Research Institute for the Japanese Economy, Faculty of Economics, University of Tokyo-Hongo.

Morita, Kiriro (1990), 'Foreign workers in Japan', Research Institute for the Japanese Economy, Faculty of Economics, University of Tokyo-Hongo.

Nanami, Tadashi, and Yasuo Kuwabara (eds) (1989), *Tomorrow's Neighbors: Foreign Workers* (Asu no Rinjin: Gaikokujin Rodosha), Toyo Keizai Shimposha, Tokyo.

Sassen, Saskia (1988), *The Mobility of Labour and Capital: A Study in International Investment and Labour Flow*, Cambridge University Press, Cambridge and New York.

Sassen, Saskia (1991), *The Global City: New York London Tokyo*, Princeton University Press, Princeton.

Sassen, Saskia (1995), *Immigrants and Refugees: A European Dilemma?*, Fischer Verlag, Frankfurt/M.

Sassen, Saskia (in progress a) *On Governing the Global Economy*, The 1995 Leonard Hastings Memorial Schoff Lectures delivered ar Columbia University, to be published by Columbia University Press.

Sassen, Saskia (in progress b) *Immigration Policy in a World Economy*, book in progress for the Twentieth Century Fund.

Part 2
DISTRIBUTIVE POLICIES

6 State competition with tax policy

OECD
EU
H73
H87
E62

Edith Kitzmantel and Erhard Moser

Summary

The most significant recent development in tax policies, as with economic policies in general, has been that international considerations have gained unprecedented importance. One characteristic element of the tax reforms of the 1980s has thus been the effort to create an 'internationally attractive' tax system. This is most obvious in the case of the most mobile and price sensitive resource, financial capital, where foreign operators are typically exempted from income taxation whilst domestic operators are not.

By competing for mobile resources, tax systems have increasingly distorted allocation decisions, thus raising questions of efficiency. Perhaps even more importantly, as tax reforms in the 1980s were typically financed out of the 'cyclical dividend', they have eroded public finances. This feature explains partly why, after 'the longest recovery in postwar history' and somewhat sizable spending cuts, deficits in industrial countries are as high as they were before whilst the debt burden has grown 1.5 times as fast as overall production. Finally, the tax burden has been shifted from upper to lower income groups, accentuating the combined effects of labour market deregulation, globalization of markets and technological change. These developments are still in full process, and no early international agreements are in sight that would bring about more cooperative strategies.

Apart from efficiency losses through distortion of allocation decisions, tax competition will intensify two worrisome developments. Firstly, public budgets - already burdened by historically high debt ratios, high unemployment rates and an aging population - will be restrained further. Secondly, the shifting of the tax burden from the better-off to the less well-off, and likely further cuts in welfare spending, will accentuate the polarization in income and wealth brought about by global market forces.

135

Changes in the external environment of tax policies

The environment in which national economic policies operate has changed enormously during the past decade or so. This is mostly due to three interrelated factors; a focus on the 'supply side' of the economy, an unprecedented wave of liberalization and deregulation, and rapid progression of regional and global integration.

The initial motivation of 'supply side policies' was to inject new dynamism into a stagflation plagued economy, by removing or lowering barriers on business operations. From the mid-1980s on however liberalization and deregulation gained an important international dimension. The first important step was the launching of the 'Single Market Project' by the European Community. The project's main objective was to strengthen the competitiveness of the region vis-à-vis the United States and Japan, by allowing economic agents, in particular enterprises, to operate across a vast economic area with uniform rules as freely as their overseas competitors did. Similarly, all the important international agreements that were subsequently concluded (e.g., NAFTA, EU- and EFTA-agreements with some Eastern European Reform Countries) aimed at strengthening regional competitiveness.

As a consequence, the economic regulatory framework changed dramatically in less than a decade. Remaining legal obstacles to cross-border trade of goods were also largely dismantled, with the notable exceptions of agriculture and some sensitive industrial products. But even in those areas, tariff and non-tariff barriers were lowered. New areas, like services and intellectual property rights, were taken up at world wide level ('GATT Uruguay Round'). To varying extents, regional integration agreements also included the politically most sensitive area of liberalization: freedom of movement of labour. The area where liberalization and deregulation has gone the furthest has clearly been capital flows.

'Tax competition' and mobility of the tax object

The most obvious economic result of these changes has been a rapid move towards globalization of markets, and with it, an increased competition. Capital flows have grown fastest, reflecting both the liberal policy regime and high physical mobility. As a matter of fact, gross capital flows seem to be about 8.5 times as high today as they were a decade ago, and have also by far outpaced current account transactions.

The globalization of markets in a liberal regulatory environment has had two important effects on tax policies: firstly, demand for goods, services, capital and labour has become more price-elastic, accentuating the role of taxes as a price determinant; and secondly, the potential of and the incenti-

136

ve for tax avoidance and tax evasion have become higher. This in turn has meant that migration of resources and transactions has partly become tax-induced, and that, at given tax rates, global tax receipts will have fallen.

To understand the nature and consequences of these changes, it is important to note that whilst these programmes were negotiated and implemented by governments, the initial driving forces behind them were internationally mobile economic operators, in particular industrial and financial interests to whom previous restrictions had been most limiting.

In the industrial countries taxes are relatively high, ranging from less than 30 per cent of GDP in the United States, Japan and Australia, to more than 45 per cent in Benelux and Scandinavian countries (1992). The regional pattern is such that European countries typically record higher tax ratios than overseas countries do, reflecting mostly differences in social welfare arrangements. As welfare spending is largely financed through earmarked payroll taxes, such differences will largely be mirrored in differences in non-wage labour costs. However, national tax legislation in industrial countries also varies widely for all other types of transactions - consumer spending, business profits and, last but not least, capital income.

National tax policies have thus increasingly been subject to the following dilemma: Tax revenues may fall if rates are not brought down because economic operators may move abroad, thus compressing the tax base. However, unless internationally mobile operations are very price-elastic, lowering rates may result in even higher tax losses. Some countries however will be able to build up free rider positions, the extent of which will depend on the price sensitivity of demand, of the relative size of the economy (e.g., how large the tax base diverted from abroad is compared to the domestic component), on the regulatory homogeneity (jurisdiction, etc.) as well as on geographic proximity.

Given this dilemma, one may wonder why global international tax agreements have so far been limited to a very small segment, namely international double taxation, and why so far efforts to harmonize taxes in increasingly integrated markets has mostly as a history of major failures and small successes (see 2.1.).

Tax reforms in OECD countries

Increasing economic integration, along with the general tendency to reduce the size of the public sector and to shift tax policy towards more 'economic neutrality', has led to some convergence of tax regimes over the past decades. Examples are the introduction of the Value Added Tax (VAT) in many countries during the 1970s, the implementation of VAT - minimum rates in EU - countries at the beginning of the 1990s, and the unprecedentedly widespread reforms in the field of personal and company income taxation during the second half of the 1980s.

However, it would be wrong to think that tax systems are now largely aligned and that this is the result of cooperative effort: Considerable discrepancies between national tax systems still exist with respect to both tax rates and tax exemptions. Convergence has to a large extent come about via tax competition rather than via joint action. Concerted measures have been mainly limited to harmonizing indirect taxes (VAT, excise duties), whereas direct taxation (company taxes, personal income taxes) has remained largely subject of national initiatives.

As far as indirect taxes are concerned, harmonization has been a salient issue in Western Europe since the establishing of the EEC. It was already recognized in the Treaty of Rome that differences in the taxation of goods may distort international trade and that a certain degree of harmonization may be needed. Consequently, all Member States had to introduce the VAT-system of and to adjust the tax base according to some common rules. With regard to tax rates, however, this could only be achieved in connection with the completion of the internal market and the removal of fiscal frontiers in 1993.

At present, VAT-standard rates in EU-member states vary from 15 per cent, the harmonized minimum rate (Germany, Spain, Luxembourg), to 25 per cent (Denmark). Reduced rates cover a range from 3 per cent to more than 10 per cent. All Member States have meanwhile abolished additional rates above the standard rate (Table 6.1).

Direct taxation on the other hand has up to now remained the domain of individual countries. This phenomenon might be explained by the fact that taxes on income particularly reflect national economic and social policies. The application of specific investment allowances, or incentive schemes for savings, which are provided for in almost all OECD-countries, may be seen in this context. However, de facto national systems have converged somewhat in the past years. A typical feature of the tax reforms in most OECD countries was to broaden the tax base by abolishing or curtailing tax exemptions, and, at the same time, to cut nominal marginal rates.

Despite some de jure and de facto convergence over the past decade, comparisons still indicate considerable differences: At present, top rates of corporate tax at central government level vary from 33 per cent (UK) to 50 per cent (Germany), those of personal income tax from 40 per cent (UK, Denmark, Portugal) to 60 per cent (Netherlands). In addition, investment incentives, depreciation rules, and provisions concerning the offset of losses still differ between EU-members as well as their main trading partners.

As a result of controversial positions between Member States towards harmonization in this field, the European Commission has meanwhile reduced previous ambitions. A draft directive on corporate taxation, submitted already in 1975 and proposing statutory rates within a band of 45 to 55 per cent, has been withdrawn.

Now a more pragmatic approach is envisaged, emphasizing the principles of subsidiarity and tax coordination. Priority is given to measures which are designed to eliminate or reduce obstacles to cross- border activities. Major steps in this direction are the adoption of two directives (Parent/Subsidiary Directive, Merger Directive) and the ratification of a convention on transfer-pricing disputes (Arbitrage Convention).

Finally, no progress has been made so far with regard to the taxation of interest income, in spite of considerable risks of relocation of investments due to tax disparities and tendencies of tax competition. Presently, almost half of the OECD-countries apply a flat rate withholding tax on interest income of their residents, which is designed as a final tax in some countries (e.g. Austria, Belgium). Others (e.g. USA, UK, Denmark, the Netherlands) operate reporting systems, where financial institutions are obliged to inform tax authorities about interest payments to residents (Table 6.1).

A proposal by the European Commission released in 1989 called for a unified withholding tax of 15 per cent on bonds and deposits. It failed because of the conflicting positions taken by Member States. However, the Commission's White Book (1992) has provided fresh impetus to take up the discussion again. There it is argued that a reduction of payroll taxes, which might be one precondition for curtailing labour costs and improving economic competitiveness, could be compensated for with a more efficient taxation of interest income.

At present a system is under consideration which would allow for a final withholding tax of 10 per cent on interest income of residents as well as non-residents. Countries with reporting systems should be entitled to apply such systems also in future.

Recent developments in tax burden and tax structure

Changes in tax policy over the past decade have also been reflected in developments of tax revenues and tax structures. In almost all countries covered by this comparison, the overall tax rate (taxes and social contributions as percentage of GDP) has only slightly increased since the mid-1980s. In some countries the tax burden as measured by the tax to GDP ratio has even been reduced. At the same time, differences between individual overall tax rates have declined.

From 1980 to 1992 the average overall tax rate (taxes and social contribution as a percentage of GDP) in the EU rose by over 4.5 percentage points, from 36.8 per cent to 41.4 per cent (Table 6.2). Roughly two-thirds of this increase relates to the years before 1985, whereas in the years after 1985 the further rise in social security contributions was largely compensated for with lower direct taxes as the tax reforms described above took effect. Over the same period, the range of average overall tax rates has fallen from more than 22 to 16 percentage points.

Apart from four countries (Italy, Spain, the Netherlands and Greece) which recorded increases significantly above one-third, all other EU Member States and their main trading partners experienced only modest changes in the overall tax burden. In many countries, such as the United Kingdom, Belgium and Luxembourg, the average overall tax rate in 1992 was even lower than it had been in 1985.

As far as the tax structure is concerned, a slight shift from income-related taxes to consumption taxes can be identified, mainly for the period after 1985. In addition, in many EU countries the relative share of payroll taxes used to finance social security benefits has increased significantly. Finally, there is also some evidence that over the last couple of years, the collected corporate tax lost some importance. Whereas this tax in EU countries amounted to 2,5 per cent of GDP in 1980 and 3 per cent in 1985 on average, the share decreased again to approximately 2,8 per cent in 1992.

Economic and distributive effects of tax policy

The changes in tax structure described above follow the expected pattern of shifting the tax burden from the relatively mobile resources and transactions to the less mobile ones: Taxes on income, the most mobile tax base, have grown least, by 0.6 points or about 4 per cent between 1980 and 1993, whereas taxes on labour inputs, the least mobile resource, have grown most, by 1.5 points or about 18 per cent. Taxes on consumption lie in between, as expected, with an increase of 1.2 points or about 11 per cent over the same period.

One of the conclusions might be that tax policy in OECD-countries has taken an undesirable course over the past years. National systems are now much more constrained in enacting an efficient and fair tax system. In addition, international cooperation between tax authorities may not be sufficiently organized to avoid allowing a sizable share of international transactions to escape taxation.

Both points can be illustrated best by the example of taxation of interest income: At present almost all EU Member States are reluctant to impose withholding taxes on foreign investors, due to the desire to attract or to maintain financial services. At the same time, countries of residence frequently cannot monitor interest income from foreign sources because of the insufficient exchange of information. Consequently, taxation in this area has increasingly become a beggar-thy-neighbour policy. As the internationally mobile operators are typically found in the upper range of income and wealth distribution, it also affects the principle of vertical equity. As far as taxation of domestic income is concerned, a number of countries at present apply withholding taxes, and some others operate reporting systems. Since withholding taxes are usually significantly lower than the marginal personal income rate, it is likely that significant amounts of domestic interest income escape taxation. This development also counters the principle of horizontal equity which was a major concern of the tax reforms of the 1980s. This shift in the tax burden comes on top of the income-polarizing effects of labour market deregulation, globalization of markets and technological change.

The preferential tax treatment which is de jure or de facto granted to capital income also discriminates against investment in 'productive' capital, i.e. against business investment in plants and equipment. This applies even though in many countries, effective tax rates were lowered to improve the return on equity-financed investment.

Finally, the under-taxation of interest income has also contributed to increasing deficits in public households, in a period when progress in budget consolidation was seen as important both in itself and as a means to reduce pressures on real interest rates. As in almost all OECD countries, the brunt of spending cuts has fallen on investment and social benefits. This should have exacerbated the allocative and distributive problems mentioned above.

Outlook

At present, the developments described above are still in progress: Globalization can be expected to proceed further, as recent integration and liberalization agreements will gradually come to full effect. However, present negotiations within the EC - where unanimity is required in tax matters - as well as discussions at OECD level do not point to a rapid transition to more cooperative strategies. Arrangements to contain tax evasion are being discussed, but are in too early a phase to allow an evaluation of their effectiveness.

As a consequence, the most likely scenario is that the erosion of the tax base, and the efficiency and equity problems associated with it, will progress further.

Table 6.1
Tax rates and tax provisions in OECD countries (as of January 1, 1994)

	Top Marginal Tax Rates (a)		Withholding tax on interest (b)	Depreciation Rates (c)		Other Tax Reliefs (d)	Offset of Losses (e)		Value Added Tax		Overall Tax Burden (f)
	Corporate Tax	Personal Income Tax		Buildings	Machinery		Back	Forward	Reduced Rate(s)	Standard Rate(s)	
EU Member States											
Denmark	34	40	(g)	SL	DB	no	--	5	--	25	50.0
Luxembourg	39	56	--	SL	DB; SL	yes	--	no limit	3; 6	12; 15	48.4
Netherlands	40	60	(g)	DB	DB; SL	yes	3	8	6	6	48.2
Belgium	40	55	10	DB; SL	DB; SL	yes	--	no limit	1; 6; 12	20.5	45.7
France	33	57	15; 38	SL	DB; SL	no	3	5	2.1; 5.5	18.6	44.0
Italy	52	50	12.5; 15.3	SL	SL	no	--	5	4; 9; 13	19	43.2
Greece	40/35	40	15	SL	SL	yes	--	5	4; 8	18	40.5
Germany	45/30	53	30	SL	DB; SL	no	2	no limit	7	15	39.7
Ireland	40	48	10	DB; SL	DB	no	1	no limit	2.5; 12.5	21	37.1
Spain	35	56	25	SL	DB	yes	--	5	3; 6	15	34.7
United Kingdom	33	40	25	SL	DB	no	3	no limit	--	8; 17.5	34.4
Portugal	39	40	20; 25	SL	DB	no	--	5	5	16	31.1
Main Trading Partners											
USA	38	44	(g)	SL	DB; SL	no	3	15	--	--	29.4
Japan	50	50	20	DB	DB	no	1	5	--	--	29.4
Switzerland	39	38	35	DB	DB	no	--	6	--	--	32.5

Source: OECD, European Commission

Notes:

(a) Including immediate and local governments. (b) Figures refer to the taxation of residents. Interest income earned by non-residents is in general not subject to withholding taxes. (c) SL: straight line; DB: declining balance. (d) General investment allowance or credit. (e) Maximum of years authorized. (f) Taxes and social contributions of GDP. (g) Countries with reporting systems.

Table 6.2
Tax burden and tax structure in OECD countries, 1980 to 1993

	Overall Tax Burden (a)			Changes in the Tax Structure (1993/80) (b)						
				Total		Income &	Social	Goods &		
	1993	1985	1980	1993/80	1993/85	Profits	Security	Services	Property	Others
EU Member States										
Italy	43.2	34.5	30.2	13.0	8.7	7.8	2.0	3.3	-0.1	0.0
Greece	40.5	35.1	29.4	11.1	5.4	1.7	2.7	6.6	0.5	-0.4
Spain	34.7	28.8	24.1	10.6	5.9	4.2	1.5	4.3	0.6	0.0
Denmark	50.0	49.0	45.5	4.5	1.0	4.9	0.8	-1.2	-0.6	0.6
Netherlands	48.2	44.1	44.7	3.5	4.1	0.9	1.5	0.8	0.2	0.1
Ireland	37.1	36.4	33.8	3.3	0.7	2.7	0.9	-0.5	-0.2	0.4
Portugal	31.1	31.5	28.7	2.4	-0.4	2.9	-0.1	0.3	0.4	-1.1
Luxembourg	48.4	50.1	46.0	2.4	-1.7	-2.8	0.2	4.0	1.2	-0.2
France	44.0	44.5	41.7	2.3	-0.5	0.1	1.8	-1.0	0.8	0.6
Germany	39.7	38.1	38.2	1.5	1.6	-1.2	2.3	0.7	-0.2	-0.1
Belgium	45.7	47.9	44.4	1.3	-2.2	-1.7	2.8	1.3	0.1	-1.2
United Kingdom	34.4	37.9	35.3	-0.9	-3.5	-1.4	0.4	1.8	-1.6	-0.1
Main Trading Partners										
USA	29.4	28.7	29.3	0.7	0.7	-1.6	1.1	0.1	0.4	0.1
Japan	29.4	27.6	25.4	1.8	1.8	0.8	2.3	-0.1	1.0	0.0
Switzerland	32.5	32.0	30.8	0.5	0.5	0.0	2.5	-0.8	0.2	-0.2
OECD Total	**38.8**	**37.0**	**35.1 (c)**	**—**	**1.8**	**0.6**	**1.5**	**1.2**	**0.3**	**0.1**
OECD Europe	**40.6**	**38.7**	**36.6**	**4.0**	**1.9**	**0.9**	**1.6**	**1.4**	**0.2**	**-0.1**
EU countries	**41.4**	**39.8**	**36.8**	**4.6**	**1.6**	**1.5**	**1.4**	**1.8**	**0.1**	**-0.2**

Source: OECD, Revenue Statistics 1965-1993, Paris 1993

Notes: (a) Taxes and social security contributions as a percentage of GDP. (b) In percentage points. (c) Of which: Taxes on Incomes & Profits 13.7%; Social security contributions 8.4%, Taxes on Goods & Services 10.6%.

7 A pendulum swing in conceptions of the welfare state[1]

Anton Hemerijck and Wieger Bakker

Summary

In this chapter the evolution of perspectives in the study of comparative social policy will be described in terms of a pendulum swing. Three representative authors play leading parts in a heuristic 'tour d'horizon'. The explication of the convergence perspective, which prevailed in the 1950s and 1960s, will be based on the work of the sociologist Harold Wilensky, a pioneer in the study of comparative social policy, The divergence perspective, which came to fruition during the late 1970s and early 1980s, will be discussed in terms of the studies of the political economist Gøsta Esping-Andersen. Finally, the recent work of the sociologist Abram de Swaan, represents a good illustration of the renewed interest in the dynamic of convergence in the 1980s and 1990s. The three representative perspectives will be placed against the background of a number of important political, social and economic developments of the episodes in the postwar era under which the authors gained prominence in the contemporary welfare state debate. The overview concludes with a 'thought experiment' whereby the convergence/divergence controversy will be confronted with the process of European integration. By so doing we hope, albeit tentatively, both theoretically and empirically, to explore the changing boundaries of domestic patterns of social care and the problems and prospects for transnational European social policy harmonization.

The internationalization of the welfare state debate

For more than two decades the academic and public debate on the future of the welfare state in Western Europe and North America has been predominantly cast in terms of financial distress, ungovernability, inefficiency and inefficacy, perverse effects, and the perceived lack of normative foundations of the welfare state. Since the mid-1970s the general tenor has been that the modern welfare state will be irrevocably undermined by domestic and international social, political and economic inevitabilities in the near future. Notwithstanding the rather bleak constant in the welfare state debate, an important shift in emphasis has taken place over the past twenty years. Gradually, the academic interest has shifted from a rather narrow focus on internal steering problems of national systems of social care, confronted with an overload of new societal and political demands, to a wider concern with external developments in the international political and economic environment of the welfare state. Especially in Europe, in light of the ongoing process of economic integration, the codification of the free movement of capital, labour and commodities by the Single European Act (1986), discussions about the future of the welfare state have come to be placed against the background of the efforts harmonize social policy.

The internationalization of the welfare state debate is best described in terms of a stylized confrontation between two dominant models of thought in the literature. Since the establishment of the welfare state during the first decade after World War II, its evolution has come to be analyzed in terms of convergence and divergence. The concept of convergence here relates to the long term process of growing institutional and policy uniformity of advanced industrial societies. The notion of convergence concerns an elusive concept with numerous analytical problems with respect to time, policy goals, content, instruments, outcomes and means. Yet, its proponents in comparative social policy have argued that domestic systems of social care are in the process of becoming increasingly alike, under the influence of common demographic, economic and technological developments, and similar social, political, and financial problems. With time, variation in country-specific institutional characteristics and national policy styles will narrow and may eventually disappear altogether. The suggestion is that current highly variegated systems will converge towards a singular homogenous domestic welfare state regime in the future. By contrast, the advocates of the divergence perspective emphasize the extent to which various advanced industrial societies are able to maintain the extraordinary diversity of policies and institutions when confronted with common international pressures and similar domestic problems. Divergence authors maintain that perceived homogenizing pressures continue to be mediated through highly country-specific institutional structures, national policy styles and cultural traditions, the outcome of which more likely accentuates country-specific features and persistent exceptionalism. Put strongly, domestic welfare state regimes are more likely to grow apart than towards one another in the future.

145

In this chapter the evolution of perspectives in the study of comparative social policy will be described in terms of a pendulum swing. Three representative authors of three rather dissimilar approaches to the study of the welfare stare play leading parts in our heuristic 'tour d'horizon'. The explication of the convergence perspective, which prevailed in the 1950s and 1960s, will be based on the work of the American sociologist Harold Wilensky, a pioneer in the study of comparative social policy, The divergence perspective, which came to fruition during the late 1970s and early 1980s, will be discussed in terms of the studies of the Danish political economist Gøsta Esping-Andersen. Finally, the recent work of the Dutch sociologist Abram de Swaan, while not solidly ingrained in the comparative welfare state debate, represents a good illustration of the renewed interest in the dynamic of convergence in the 1980s and 1990s. The three representative perspectives will be placed against the background of a number of important political, social and economic developments during episodes in which the authors gained prominence in the contemporary welfare state debate. The overview concludes with a 'thought experiment' whereby the convergence/divergence controversy will be confronted with the process of European integration. By so doing we hope, albeit tentatively, both theoretically and empirically, to explore the changing boundaries of domestic patterns of social care and the problems and prospects for transnational European social policy harmonization.

The welfare state as a social compromise

During World War II, the foundations of the contemporary welfare state were laid. William Beveridge's report to the British wartime government, *Social Insurance and Allied Services* (1942), has often been cited as the formative manifesto of the contemporary welfare state. In his subsequent, and probably even more influential publication, *Full Employment in a Free Society* (1944), Beveridge proposed wholesale social policy innovation to counter, what he called, the 'Five Great Evils of Want, Disease, Idleness, Ignorance and Squalor'. The welfare state's founding launched a novel vocabulary of national unity, collective action and social citizenship after a decade of economic depression, social friction, political chaos, and war. Beveridge's conception of the postwar welfare state was based on the normative principle that all citizens should share equal life chances. It also embraced the assumption of political responsibility for social and economic distress, especially employment. Placing full employment as the major goal of social and economic policymaking required the state to take a prominent and active role in social and economic policy. The innovations that Beveridge proposed in economic policy and social security, in terms of a

146

committed effort to institutionalize universal social rights for all citizens on the basis of redistributive principles, clearly required strong state intervention.

Political intervention in governing the economy was theoretically justified by the Keynesian revolution in economic theory. The novel economic ideas of Lord Keynes had a profound political impact on the development of the welfare state after 1945. A fair number of his conclusions on the Great Depression were directly translated into economic policymaking in many western countries. While the prominent role of state intervention in the postwar welfare state should not be viewed as the direct corollary of the insights of Lord Keynes, Peter Hall argues that:

> Keynesian ideas were a potent weapon in the hands of those who sought to justify a new role for the state against the arguments of the old laissez faire. (Hall 1989: 365-6)

Keynes justified intervention to stabilize the economy and legitimized a reorientation of monetary and fiscal policy to support high levels of employment and sustained economic growth. His seminal *General Theory of Employment, Interest and Money* (1936) offered the first theoretically convincing rationalization for a policy of running public deficits in order to stimulate effective demand through the mechanism of the 'multiplier effect' by which fiscal and monetary policy could enhance demand, growth, and, consequently, employment. To be sure, smoothing out business cycles required a high degree of coordination between monetary and fiscal policy. Because monetary policy stood at the heart of Keynesian economics, many central banks were brought more closely under political control in the immediate postwar years. Keynesian economics allowed democratic governments to endorse political responsibility for full employment and expansion of public works without affecting the primacy of the free market. Many economic policy elites in the advanced industrial world remained skeptical about the practice of deliberately running deficits as a key instrument of macroeconomic policy. Such skepticism notwithstanding, the shift to the Keynesian economic policy paradigm created a supportive cognitive environment for the expansion of the welfare state in the postwar era.

The strategic economic and social policy collaboration between the interwar antagonists, organized labour and capital, constitutes another prominent political-institutional characteristic of the emerging postwar welfare state. It has been argued that the concerted effort of the social partners and the democratic state to administer responsible incomes policies stood at the basis of the so-called 'golden age' of capitalism; the longest period (1945-1973) of economic growth, market expansion and increasing welfare in Western Europe and North America (Marglin and Schor 1990). The so-called 'postwar settlement' between workers and employers can be viewed as the pragmatic and concerted postwar response to the disruptive economic, political and social crises of the interwar period (Crouch 1979). Moderate representatives of organized labour and capital were eager to endorse Keynesian economics, as it held out the promise of a favourable circle of full employment, high wages, growing aggregate demand, investment incentives, increased productivity, and high standards of living for everyone (Scharpf 1991). Employers came to appreciate trade unions as the legitimate representatives in collective bargaining, supported social policy innovation and pledged to create high levels of employment. Meanwhile, organized labour came to recognize the prerogative of private ownership and the legitimate authority of management over crucial economic decisions, especially investment. The social-democratic labour movement abandoned its traditional demand for the socialization of production. In exchange, labour was rewarded with minimum wage legislation, the extension of social policy, and the attribution of public status within the decisionmaking format of social and economic policy.

The democratic state was granted an active role in orchestrating consensual industrial relations and collective bargaining agreements. Especially, tripartite incomes policies were considered highly effective in promoting growth and employment. The prevalent postwar emphasis on output and growth triggered what Charles Maier has called the 'politics of productivity' (Maier 1987: 121-52). Moderate governments and pragmatic organized interests assumed responsibility for growth and productivity by endorsing incomes policies based on wage restraint, keeping pay increases below productivity growth. To be sure, the labour movement did emerge as a strong political force from the depression and the second world war. Changes in labour legislation, in part already adopted in the 1930s, promoted postwar trade union strength, organization and centralization. The presence of a powerful and moderate labour movement, both in party politics and in the industrial arena, inspired social-democratic and christian democratic governments to invite trade union representatives in the participation, formulation, administration and implementation of social and economic policy.

At the international level of geopolitics, welfare state development was backed by the success of what John Gerard Ruggie has aptly coined the regime of 'embedded liberalism' (Ruggie 1982). A multilateral commitment to open international trade was 'embedded' in a recognition of an extensive role for the state, both in governing the economy and administrating the expanding welfare state. The international regime of embedded liberalism allowed for the domestic extension of social rights and the 'politics of productivity'. Embedded liberalism centered around the compatibility of international monetary policy with domestic social and economic stability. The relatively flexible monetary regime created at the Bretton Woods conference in 1944 was based on a compromise over multilateral trade, predicated upon domestic interventionism. Again the ideas of Keynes were highly influential in drafting the Bretton Woods agreement that stood at the heart of the postwar order of embedded liberalism. The constraints imposed upon national economic policy during the 1920s and 1930s by the Gold Standard were relaxed, while the doctrine of price stability was somehow eased in order to sustain multilateralism and peaceful prosperity (Hirsch 1978).

It should be emphasized that the regime of embedded liberalism was highly dependent on the leadership of the United States in the international political economy. Keohane goes as far as to argue that the European welfare state was in fact built on the foundations of American hegemony (Keohane 1984: 22). The United States supported the system of Bretton Woods by pegging the dollar to gold at a fixed price, while allowing free convertibility of currencies and stable exchange rates at levels that enabled their exports to be competitive on world markets. During the 1950s and 1960s the United States continued to pursue policies which reinforced the regime of embedded liberalism. Partly to buy off the communist threat, the United States provided massive funding to the economic reconstruction of Western European nations through the Marshall Plan after 1947. Marshall Plan aid strongly divided the European labour movement between the pragmatic and constructive growth oriented moderate Christian and Social-Democratic unions and the highly politicized, conflict-prone, and anti-American Communist trade union movement.

A largely hidden and often ignored feature of the 'historical compromise' pertains to the welfare state's role in consolidating the traditional nuclear family. The central policy objective of full employment was defined in terms of full-time jobs for only male workers, for 48 hours a week, with fourty-eight working-weeks in a year, for a period of 48 years. The male provider was supposed to financially cover the unpaid full-time dedication of his spouse to the family. Keynes, Beveridge, postwar governments, and the representatives of capital and labour, all implicitly relied on a traditional family structure model. It has been argued that the postwar establishment of the welfare state had in effect come to undermine the nuclear family as social care was institutionalized as a right of citizenship. While indeed social services no longer are the exclusive domain of the church, the neighbourhood, or the extended family, it should be emphasized that the welfare state has consolidated the traditional family structure, rather than caused it to subside in the face of professional social services. Because of the consolidation of the traditional family, the financial burden of the postwar welfare state remained rather limited (Esping-Andersen 1993). General job security for men, with dedicated housewives at home, allowed the welfare state responsibilities to be kept at bay for the period of unprecedented growth between 1945 and 1973. Public provisions only came into play at the beginning (education) and at the near the end (old-age pensions), with only brief intermittent periods of social dependence on social security and state-sponsored assistance.

The emergence of the fully-fledged welfare state after 1945 can be viewed as the result of a Weberian mutually reinforcing 'elective affinity' between and among Lord Beveridge's social-liberal social consciousness, the more technocratically oriented novel economic ideas of Lord Keynes, a strengthened state apparatus run by astute and self-assured political elites and a truly historical class-compromise marked by a strong labour voice which was supported internationally by a regime of embedded liberalism and undergirded by the consolidation of the nuclear family at the level of the household.

The welfare state as an industrial product

Under the aegis of postwar social harmony, expanding world markets, economic growth and full employment, the convergence perspective in the study of social, economic and political development gained prominence in academic circles of advanced industrial societies in the 1950s and 1960s. To be sure, a host of convergence theses flourished during the 'Golden Age' of postwar prosperity; from Galbraith's coming of the 'affluent society'(1958), to Bell's 'end of ideology' (1960), Lipset's decline of class warfare (1969), Kerr's 'industrial man' (1960), and Kirchheimer's emergence of 'catch-all' parties (1957). These authors observed a general reduction in the diversity of the policies and institutions of advanced industrial countries. They all believed that most nations were converging towards homogeneous polities dominated by large corporate firms, with increasingly fluid social structures, declining inequalities, pluralist industrial relations, technocratic macroeconomic management, and a declining importance of ideological strife in politics.

Harold Wilensky was the first to advance a convergence argument in the field of social policy. In his classical study *The Welfare State and Equality* (1975), Wilensky established a direct correlation between economic development and the advancement of social policy by employing multivariate statistical techniques in an extensive cross-national quantitative comparative analysis. By comparing social policy expenditure as a proportion of GNP of no less than sixty-four countries, including both liberal and communist polities, using data from 1966, he came to the conclusion that per capita GNP 'overwhelms regime type as a predictor of social security effort' in the long run. In short: the proliferation of the welfare state is positively correlated with affluence. Following structural functionalist reasoning, Wilensky derived from his empirical material the hypothesis that different national systems of social care were converging towards similar goals and institutions of social policy as a result of economic development. Welfare state growth seem to follow the so-called 'logic of industrialism', a convergence thesis of the labour sociologist Clark Kerr (Kerr, Dunlop, Harbison and Myers 1960).

Wilensky and Kerr, both supporters of Talcott Parsons' modernization theory, viewed the proliferation of standard methods of mass production, based on Taylorist and Fordist principles, as the driving force behind a worldwide convergence of modern societies. The emergence of the welfare state is no more than the imperative corrolary of the dynamic of economic progress, which fosters a society-wide movement toward the policies and institutions of the contemporary welfare state. Clark Kerr goes as far as to suggest that eventually the Cold War cleavage between capitalist and socialist societies will become irrelevant. Western polities will slowly but surely allow more state intervention in their market economies, while communist regimes are likely to create room for market arrangements within their planned economies. Heavy industry requires healthy, literate and reliable workers in all advanced industrial societies, whether in East or West. Industrialization and economic growth stand at the basis of the expected move towards a dominant 'best practice' national welfare state model across the globe. The organization of mass production, which lies at the heart of Wilensky's functionalist argument, corresponded neatly with the paternalistic, top-down, technocratic decisionmaking procedures of the expanding welfare systems of the 1950s and 1960s in the advanced capitalist and communist economies. Perhaps, planned industrialization in the former Soviet Union and its satellites was even more inspired by Fordist production and Taylorist organizational principles than was the reconstruction of the West European economies (Maier 1987: 43-4).

Wilensky's functionalist convergence argument characteristically leaves little room for institutional variation and political choice in the process of welfare state convergence. In agreement with Bell, Wilensky claims that political variables are of little significance for social policy development:

> Economic growth and its demographic and bureaucratic outcomes are the root cause of the general emergence of the welfare state ... such heavy brittle categories as 'socialist' versus 'capitalist' economies, 'collectivist' versus 'individualist' ideologies, 'democratic' versus 'totalitarian' political systems ... are almost useless in explaining the origins and general development of the welfare state. (1975: xiii)

Economic growth makes countries with contrasting political traditions more and more alike in their welfare state policies (1975: 27). In the long run, the effect of industrial development clearly prevails over the institutional effect of country-specific collective arrangements of social care. In agreement with both liberal Parsonian and leftist Marxian developmental perspectives, Wilensky's suggests that institutional leftovers from the past are of little consequence to welfare state proliferation. Existing institutional diversity between different national welfare states is likely to disappear in the process of industrialization. Variation in ideology and political institutions is far less significant than levels of economic development and related differences in demographic structures in explaining differences in social security spending across nation-states. Ideology as a source of social, political, and economic organization and mobilization is of decreasing importance in the inevitable process of welfare state modernization. He believes that in all advanced industrial societies collectivist values and individualist sentiments are equally prevalent. It could be argued that the end of the cold war in 1989 in fact belatedly corroborates Wilensky and Kerr's functionalist reasoning. However convergence did not lead toward the expected mix of planification and laissez faire liberalism, but instead toward the Western institutions of the market economy and liberal democracy (Fukuyama 1989).

From Wilensky's analysis it follows that national and international political elites only have a limited scope for choice between alternative goals, content and instruments of economic and social policy. Domestically, the democratic state, the key political actor in the administration of the welfare state apparatus, is apparently no more than the bureaucratic-technocratic clearinghouse of modern industrial development. Also, the social partners are expected to more or less follow the technological requirements of standard mass production. Pathbreaking insights may perhaps accelerate social policy innovation, which could lead to time lags between countries in the proliferation of the welfare state. However, faced with increasingly similar social, economic, technological and demographic problems, developed industrial societies are more likely to administer rather homogeneous national systems of social care (Wilensky 1975: 27,47; Wilensky 1976: 21-3). In the long run the homogeneous size, scope, form and content of the welfare state will be determined unilaterally by the functional imperatives of economic development.

By assuming a deterministic relationship between economic development and social policy progress, Wilensky's functionalism completely overlooks the unique historical, domestic and international political setting of postwar prosperity. Not only is Wilensky ignorant of the harsh experiences of the depression and the war, which critically shaped postwar social policy innovation, he is also largely oblivious to the reorganization of the interna-

152

tional economic order in the 1940s and 1950s, which established the framework of 'embedded liberalism' under American hegemony. By deliberately breaking with the deflationary episode of the Great Depression, postwar domestic and international political elites, promoted a rapid convergence in the policies and institutions of the postwar welfare state. Postwar convergence, however, contained an explicit political enterprise prompted by the memory of war and depression. The European economies benefited enormously from trade liberalization and the cheap oil supplies of embedded liberalism. Unparalleled prosperity, in turn, contributed effortlessly to the financing of the expanding welfare states under protracted full employment. On a superficial level, Wilensky offers a persuasive argument in explaining social policy leads and lags in rich and poor polities. However, his analysis is of little help in explaining variation between the welfare programmes of the OECD democracies. Moreover, similar expenditures do not tell us much about how money is spent on various programmes.

The welfare state as a political choice

Until the mid-1970s the advanced welfare states of Western Europe and North America experienced similar trajectories of welfare state growth, roughly in agreement with Wilensky's convergence claims. With relatively little cross-national variation, the bulk of public resources was spent on social programmes in the policy areas of education, health and old age care. The 'productivist' postwar era of unprecedented economic growth, full employment, unparalleled capital formation and social peace only saw a moderate growth of social security provisions to limit the social risks of the market economy. The growth of social security entitlements largely took place during the 1960s. The crisis-prone 1970s and 1980s experienced a dramatic increase in expenditures on social security. The breakdown of the Bretton Woods monetary system in 1971, the steep rise in oil prices between 1973 and 1979, accelerating inflation and rising unemployment brought an end to the 'golden age' of postwar prosperity. The crisis of the 1970s brought domestic diversity in the policies and institutions of national welfare states to the surface as the recession gave rise to distinct national patterns of economic adjustment and industrial restructuring. The plethora of national responses discredited Wilensky's convergence claim (Goldthorpe 1984: 315-43). With hindsight, it seems that the postwar boom masked divergent trajectories of welfare state development. To be sure, the 1970s recession created rather similar economic problems of public sector management across advanced countries. That notwithstanding, the experience of the 1970s and 1980s revealed that advanced market economies reacted surprisingly differently to similar societal and political demands and common pressures in the world economy, as a result of past history, prevailing institutional arrangements, and strategic choices.

Country-specific divergences constituted a productive ground for the emergence of a form of comparative analysis with a distinct focus on domestic institutional structures as critical intervening variables in the explanation of diverse trajectories of industrial restructuring. The 1970s crisis prompted a paradigm shift in comparative welfare state analysis, away from cross-national generalizing toward 'middle range' matched comparison argumentation. A new generation of welfare state scholarship explicitly centered their analyses around the political structure of the sovereign state with its characteristic institutional arrangements for combatting unemployment, poverty, and deprivation. Academically, this revival of the Weberian comparative political economy in the 1970s and 1980s was in part inspired by increased frustration with the type of structural-functionalist reasoning that Wilensky and others practiced. The Weberian political economy perspective centered around the comparative analysis of political actors, both individual and collective, who were engaged in a struggle over the control of political and economic resources in pursuit of largely conflicting goals. Evans and Stephens highlight that particularly the 'historical-materialist' side of the intellectual heritage of Max Weber, with its preoccupation with social class, state structure, and the historical evolution of the institutions of capitalism, was recovered during the period of economic crisis and industrial restructuring (Evans and Stephens 1988).

With the advent of stagflation in the OECD-economies, the institution of the labour market in advanced industrial societies acquired a prominent place in the renaissance of comparative political economy. Perhaps the most successful attempt to bring domestic institutions back into comparative analysis as relatively independent variables has been developed by the students of modern corporatism (Berger 1981; Goldthorpe 1984; Lehmbruch and Schmitter 1982; Schmitter and Lehmbruch 1979). In the midst of the alleged ungovernable 1970s, corporatist scholars found that advanced industrial societies, employing institutional devices for integrating business and labour interests in public policy platforms, were best able to alleviate the destructive impact of the social, political, and economic shocks from the late 1960s through to the early 1980s. The central argument that corporatist authors put forward was that the ability of advanced countries to manage social conflict and enhance economic performance was highly contingent on the presence of an institutional infrastructure which incorporated the societal interests of organized capital and labour into nation-wide economic policy formation. Corporatist researchers centered their institutional arguments around the administrative structures of the state and the organizational attributes of functional organized interests. Corporatist scholars conclusively argued that institutional variation in

154

business-government relations is directly linked to public policy outcomes. The economic crisis and restructuring has also been critically influential in transforming the welfare state debate. Different trends of what has been termed 'welfare state retrenchment' gave rise to gave rise to a growth industry of divergence arguments about the welfare state (Castles 1987; Korpi 1978; Leibfried 1979; Schmidt 1983; Therborn 1984; Esping-Andersen 1990). In contrast to Wilensky's structural functionalism, a number of academics found a superior explanation for institutional diversity among welfare states in the social and political distribution of power among the electorate, political parties, government and interests groups in various decisionmaking arenas. Politics seemed to account for divergent cross-national trends of welfare state development and social security expenditure (Alber 1982; Castles 1982). The idea that domestic politics and institutions make a difference led researchers to study the extent to which domestic welfare state arrangements and traditions were consequential in shaping divergent outcomes and away from studies of the general development of social care in terms of expenditure growth. Wilensky's convergence claim, with the economy as the prime mover, clearly lacked an adequate answer to the divergent experience of welfare state retrenchment among highly developed welfare states. A variety of so-called welfare state typologies were developed; ranging from strong to weak welfare states, institutional and residual welfare systems, social-democratic, conservative-corporatist and liberal regimes of welfare capitalism.

The most encompassing divergence perspective has been advanced by the Danish political economist Gøsta Esping-Andersen. His recent study *The Three Worlds of Welfare Capitalism*, published in 1990, can already be labelled a social science classic. Esping-Andersen's landmark study of contemporary welfare state diversity is critically sensitive to the idea that social rights as outcomes of political struggle, once institutionalized, evolve rather independently, or with considerable time lags, from changes in the world economy. Although clearly a product of the 1980s period of welfare state retrenchment, Esping-Andersen's divergence perspective, like Wilensky's convergence theory, is primarily concerned with welfare state growth and development. In agreement with Max Weber's essentially political understanding of society, Esping-Andersen claims that the welfare state redraws the boundaries of politics and economics in a manner that strengthens the domain of politics. He views the welfare state as a political institution that enables citizens to make ends meet without relying on the labour market. Social rights, in Esping-Anderson's usage, 'permit people to make their living standards independent of pure market forces' (Esping-Andersen 1990: 3). Esping-Andersen coins this measure of public protection against labour market forces as *decommodification*. Decommodification refers to 'the degree to which individuals, or families, can uphold a socially acceptable standard of living independently of market participation' (1990: 37). High degrees of decommodification render citizens of the welfare state less vulnerable to loss of income from jobs, in the sense that the welfare state makes their living conditions essentially less dependent on the labour market within which people have to trade their capacity to work as a commodity. The level of decommodification determines the extent to which social security benefits exempt citizens from labour force participation. For Esping-Andersen, the scope, strength, content and degree to which decommodification takes place render the key to a better understanding of cross-national welfare state diversity.

Esping-Andersen is critically interested in the manner and the extent to which domestic welfare state arrangements structure the labour market and the status of the family in advanced societies. By explicitly including family structure in his analysis, he introduces a gender element into the comparative welfare state debate. Esping-Andersen maintains that family status is structured by social policy. Consequently, social policy directly translates into a gender-specific social division of labour. For instance, increased female participation in the labour market generates a higher demand for reproductive services, such as day care and catering, which in turn creates an additional labour market segment for working women. By contrast, the predominance of traditional family patterns in more conservative polities is likely to consolidate social reproduction by full-time housewives. In comparative terms, Esping-Anderson shows that especially the political status of the family in the welfare state almost directly translates into a gender-specific formal and informal division of labour between men and women in the modern welfare state (Esping-Andersen 1990: 108-214).

Esping-Andersen's argument is both voluntarist and historicist. On the one hand, he emphasizes strategic political choice and coalition building behind social policy innovation. On the other hand, he highlights the constraints of institutional legacies for political agency. Esping-Andersen's overall claim is that 'politics is decisive' in the historical evolution of welfare state diversity (1990: 5). The voluntarist side of Esping-Andersen adheres to a so-called power resources argument, associated with the work of Walter Korpi (Esping-Andersen and Korpi 1984; Korpi 1978). Social policy development requires a mobilization of sufficient power resources to overcome opposition to social reform. Following a power resources argument, the nature and scope of the contemporary welfare state is closely related to the social and political mobilization of the working class. It is not the labour power per se that explains divergent paths of welfare state development in Europe and North America, but the historical forging of coalitions of organized workers with opponents within parliamentary arenas and the sphere of industrial relations. The critical variables that are considered to contribute to welfare state growth are the strength of leftist political parties, the number of years leftist parties participate in government, the size, unity and concentration of the trade union movement, and the weakness and division of the right.

The institutionalist side of Esping-Andersen deviates from a narrow class mobilization perspective by suggesting that political legacies have long term consequences for subsequent political struggles. Esping Andersen highlights the historical legacies of Catholicism and absolutism, or lack thereof, as consequential structures in the evolution of national welfare states. He maintains that no contemporary welfare state can be understood without looking at the historical development of each nation-state. The history of nation-state building goes back further than the days of the inaugural watershed of the establishment of the welfare state in 1945. The institutional effect of previous choices over for instance electoral systems set certain limits to the freedom of action of social actors in the field of social policy innovation. In other words, in Esping-Andersen's analysis, the existing diversity of welfare state regimes and their divergent trajectories are determined, on the one hand, by the persistence or 'path dependence' of leftover institutional arrangements, and, on the other, by strategic policy choices of contemporary social actors. A combination of 'path dependent' historical legacies and pre-existing institutions channel and constrain contemporary political agency in a 'path dependent' fashion, which in turn structures divergent trajectories for welfare states.

Following Esping-Andersen the explanation of the divergent trajectories of the national welfare states in Western Europe and North America should be answered in terms of the historical legacies. The mobilization of social classes in the nineteenth century and the forging of a political coalition between Left and Right in the twentieth century occurred against the background of the political legacies of Catholicism and absolutism in Western Europe, while these legacies were absent in North America. Esping-Andersen distinguishes three welfare state regimes: the liberal, the conservative-corporatist, and the social-democratic welfare regime. With respect to decommodification of labour, the social-democratic welfare state regime clearly is a welfare front runner, while the liberal regime is a welfare laggard, with the conservative-corporatist regime taking the middle position.

The liberal regime is characterized by the primacy of the market. A low tax burden, a limited degree of redistribution of incomes, together with a rather modest means-tested individualized system of social benefits are its key features. The market-led liberal regime, moreover, stimulates labour force participation of women in the labour market, especially, in commercial personal services. The liberal welfare state of the Anglosaxon polities lack the legacies of both absolutism and Catholicism.

The conservative-corporatist welfare state of continental Europe, inspired by Bismarck, administers a 'quasi-private' system of rather generous means-tested social security provisions, which is intimately related to previously earned income and family status. A rather heavy tax burden is compensated for by a high level of income redistribution towards 'non-active' segments of the population. With respect to the position of the family, the conservative-corporatists are very much geared towards consolidation of the traditional family structures. As such, it very much discourages the participation of (married) women in the labour market. The social partners play important roles in the administration and implementation of social security in a bipartite fashion. Both absolutism and Catholicism left strong historical markings in the conservative-corporatist welfare state. It should be emphasized that Esping-Andersen's usage of the term 'corporatist' here is quite different from that employed in neocorporatist literature on labour market institutions.

The social-democratic welfare state of the Scandinavian countries, in which united labour movements have come to occupy hegemonic political positions, executes a universal system of generous universal and highly redistributive benefits, which do not depend on any individual contribution. The social-democratic regime type, which is most familiar to the Dane Esping-Andersen, enables citizens to make ends meet independent of labour market participation for relatively long periods of time, when unemployed, ill or incapacitated, for educational purposes and/or for raising children. Although this regime offers rather few market incentives to do paid work, the Swedish model is notorious for its strong political emphasis on maximum labour participation, as Esping-Andersen concisely argues (1990: 28):

> Perhaps the most salient characteristic of the social-democratic regime is its fusion of welfare and work. It is at once genuinely committed to a full-employment guarantee, and entirely dependent on its attainment. On the one side, the right to work has equal status to the right of income protection. On the other side, the enormous costs of maintaining a solidaristic, and de-commodifying welfare system means that it must minimize social problems and maximize revenue income. This is obviously best done with most people working, and the fewest possible living off of social transfers.

Like the liberal regime type, the state-led social-democratic regime type favours female participation in the formal labour market, particularly in the public care sector. As a result of the heavy tax burden to finance a massive public sector and far-reaching levelling of income, two incomes per household are almost a prerequisite for a decent standard of living. Analogous to the conservative-corporatist welfare state, the social partners play important roles in social policy administration and implementation. While conservative-corporatist 'quasi-private' welfare programmes are generally administered in a bipartite fashion, the social partners play a subsidiary role in the social-democratic regime type (Esping-Andersen 1990: 26-8). The social-democratic regime type lacks the historical imprint of Catholicism and absolutism, again in agreement with the liberal welfare state.

Esping-Andersen divergence perspective in effect turns Wilensky's convergence argument theoretically on its head in two respects. First of all, Esping-Andersen argues that the political effect is stronger than the effect of economic development, as he finds no significant correlation between a country's gross national product and its type of welfare state regime, in a quantitative comparison of eighteen OECD countries based on the basis of a 1980 survey (1990: 52). In contrast to Wilensky's structural functionalism, Esping-Andersen successfully introduces a voluntaristic element of political choice into the comparative study of social policy. Secondly, Esping-Andersen attaches much greater value to the institutional effect of historical legacies of Catholicism in explaining social policy innovation and, consequently, the degree of gender-specific labour market protection under various welfare state regimes. It should, however, be emphasized that in the 1980s Harold Wilensky has partly come to endorse a divergence perspective, as he found that Catholic party incumbency represents a strong indicator for social security expenditure growth (1981: 356-70). In addition, Wilensky also contributed to the corporatist debate by increasingly emphasizing political and institutional factors in his analysis (Wilensky 1976; Wilensky 1981; Wilensky and Turner 1987). Finally, also Clark Kerr reformulated his logic of industrialism argument to allow institutional diversity (Kerr 1983).

With the development of a divergence perspective in the comparative study of welfare state development, Esping-Andersen and other authors have made an important contribution to the welfare state debate. Certainly their political voluntarism and historical institutionalism were welcome and necessary counter arguments to structural functionalism. Yet there is also place for criticism. The narrow focus on national institutional configurations and domestic political action and collective action represents both the strength and the weakness of the divergence perspective. Esping-Andersen for example passes over important aspects of the economic preconditions of the contemporary welfare state under welfare capitalism. By taking the extent of decommodification as the indicator of the level of 'social citizenship', he really obscures the primacy of capital accumulation as 'raison d'etre' of the prevailing welfare state regime types. Under capitalist conditions the relation between commodity growth and political decommodification remain asymmetrical. Decommodification is dependent on economics to create employment, wealth and a tax base for social policy

159

development. There are distinct boundaries to disengaging politics from economics in the modern welfare state.

The more striking shortcoming, however, as is the case with the convergence perspective, concerns the absence of an international geopolitical dimension in the divergence literature. Recent changes within the international political economy have obviously undermined the sovereignty and effectiveness of national institutions for social policy. This especially with respect to monetary, fiscal and incomes policy. The growing vulnerability of national economies has partly been caused by the increasing international mobility of capital, resultant from the discrete liberalization of capital transactions. Consequently, a growing capital market instability together with an ongoing process of deindustrialization in Western Europe and North America and the emergence of industrial competition from the newly industrializing low-wage economies of Eastern Europe, Mexico and South-East Asia, impose serious restraints on domestic social and industrial policy. Furthermore, West European were not at all prepared for the collapse of communism in 1989, German unification in 1991, and the resultant massive migration from Eastern Europe.

The divergence perspective, with its distinct emphasis on the institutions of the nation-state, runs the risk of overrating national sovereignty and the scope for independent action and underestimating the consequences of international interdependence in the world political economy. Similarly, by placing the primacy of social policy too close to domestic institutions and political choice, the possibilities of international coordination and integration are likely to be overlooked and underestimated. Notwithstanding, continuous efforts of the European Union towards supranational economic and political integration, and agreements within the GATT and the IMF, have decisively contributed to the creation of regulatory institutions above and beyond the traditional nation-state. And any transfer of regulatory powers, however limited and small, will consequently curtail the importance of domestic institutions for social and economic policy. In countering this critique, the proponents of the divergence perspective counter that developments in the international political economy still have to be mediated through national institutions. They maintain that the nation-state is far from losing its salience in the face of globalization. According to Alexander Gourevitch, domestic arrangements remain of crucial importance. He argues that it is not so much a question of whether the international political economy determines national policy, but rather of in what way, through which institutions and with what forms of legitimacy the international economy influences national policy:

> The international economy presses on individual countries, and it does so through working on domestic actors. It is these domestic

160

actors who are affected by changes in the international market conditions and who, as a result, seek changes in national policy. (Gourevitch 1986: 235)

The welfare state as a strategy of elite control

The parallel rise and decline of the divergence and convergence perspectives over the 1970s and 1980s is intrinsically related to demise of the postwar settlement. The 1970s showed how vulnerable the social compromise under the regime of embedded liberalism really was. The cross-national breakdown of the postwar settlement over the 1970s and 1980s was characterized by a protracted weakening of the labour movement, state withdrawal from the politics of productivity, and increasing globalization of capital.

In the latter half of the 1960s, the labour movement was the first to abandon the postwar settlement. Pressed by tight labour markets, radical trade unionists regenerated a resurgent confidence in class conflict (Crouch and Pizzorno 1978). The subsequent decentralization of collective bargaining towards sectoral and company agreements seriously undermined the public status of trade union representatives in the economic policy decisionmaking arenas. In addition, internal strife came to fragment the trade union movement from within due to conflicts between the export-oriented and internationally exposed industrial unions and the more domestically oriented unions of the protected public sector, which had become the largest under the 1960s and 1970s expansion of the welfare state. The process of deindustrialization resulted in a tremendous loss of employment in the heartland of the labour movement and set in a persistent decline in union membership. The industrial job loss was only partly compensated for by the creation of new jobs in an expanding service sector. However, service sector union mobilization lagged significantly behind employment growth. Post-industrial job growth offered new opportunities for female labour force participation, mostly under part-time contracts in small and medium-sized firms and organizations. To be sure, the expanding post-industrial labour force of women and youngsters working under atypical labour relations is not easily mobilized after the traditional industrial ideology of class solidarity (Baglioni and Crouch 1990).

When tripartite incomes policies lost efficacy in the wake of the 1970s recession, the political center, inspired by a revival of neoliberalism, subsequently also withdrew its support of the postwar practice of class reconciliation. In the ideological environment of the crisis, the ideas of state-led governability precipitously lost sway in the face of the emergent philosophy of 'state failure'. The consequent electoral gains of conserva-

161

tive governments at the turn of the decade in Western Europe and North America set in a distinct economic policy reversal. In the 1980s, public governance of the economy has been marked by deregulation, privatization, a move away from Keynesian to monetarist macroeconomic policy, cutbacks in public expenditure, and a distinct shift from progressive taxation toward flatter tax rates. Especially, the neoliberal fight against inflation and budget deficits seriously undermined the postwar politics of productivity. The paradigm shift in economic policy goals from growth and employment to more restrictive policy priorities caused grave unemployment problems. As Forsyth and Notermans observe, under the episode of embedded liberalism exchange control was strategically designed to allow individual economies to pursue divergent policies oriented towards growth and employment. Once the containment of inflation became the main economic policy imperative exchange control lost its rationale (Forsyth and Notermans 1994).

The sea-change in domestic economic policy priorities was provoked by the breakdown of the regime of embedded liberalism. Since the fall of the international monetary system of Bretton Woods in 1971, major adjustments have taken place in the international political economy. Especially, initiatives at financial deregulation had the effect of abolishing exchange control, which facilitated the free flow of capital around the globe. The liberalization of world financial markets has in turn imposed a deflationary bias on the world economy.

The postwar proliferation of the welfare state was built on the politics of productivity oriented towards growth and employment. The reversal of economic policy in 1970s and 1980s put the welfare state on the defensive throughout the OECD world of rich nations. While significant cross-national differences persist, major cutbacks in social security provisions have been introduced with more or less enthusiasm everywhere. To be sure, while cross-national diversity in generosity, policies and institutions remained, comparative political economy analysis with its rather narrow interests in domestic factors, has clearly not been able to shed much light on the basic 1980s trend of 'welfare state retrenchment' in North America and Western Europe in the context of the globalization of the world economy.

Globalization in the 1980s has been accompanied by novel efforts at supranational cooperation, especially in Europe, where the signing of Single European Act in 1986 laid the foundation for further European monetary and political integration. The cross-national trend of welfare state retrenchment in the context of economic globalization and transnational political integration has markedly rekindled the convergence perspective in the study of comparative social policy in the 1980s and 1990s.

162

The convergence perspective has recently been brought back to life by the Dutch sociologist Abram de Swaan. His *In Care of the State* (1988), theoretically resembles Wilensky's concern with the general logic behind welfare state development. De Swaan does not emphasize national institutional diversity. Rather, drawing on secondary source empirical material from Britain, the Netherlands, Germany, France, and the United States, he highlights the common cross-national process behind the evolution of national systems of social care. In contrast to Wilensky's functionalism, and in agreement with Esping-Andersen's emphasis on political choice, De Swaan is principally interested in the role of political factors in the historical evolution of the welfare state, which he names as the 'collectivization process'. The collectivization process pertains to the increasingly dominant regulatory role of the state in the formulation, implementation and administration of social policy.

De Swaan's analysis draws on two rather dissimilar strands of thought in social theory. The study tries to synthesize, on the one hand, the historical sociology of Norbert Elias, and on the other, Mancur Olson's theory of collective action (Elias 1982; Olson 1965). De Swaan celebrates his combination of historical sociology and microeconomics as a true 'paradigm shift' through which the neoclassical reduction from dynamics to statics is overcome (1988: 4). As an ardent disciple of Norbert Elias' developmental civilization, De Swaan claims that human beings are fundamentally interdependent, and that in the course of history their mutual interdependencies grow more and more complex and intense. The civilization process thus entails the unremittant lengthening and intensification of human interdependence chains. Urbanization, the creation of states, and industrialization are part and parcel of an increasingly complex and extended civilization process. Consequently, also the welfare state is a product of the converging logic of increased social interdependence.

For his explication of important political innovations in the evolution of social policy, De Swaan reverts to welfare economics and collective action theory (Baumol 1952; Olson 1965). From welfare economics, De Swaan eclectically imputes the problem of 'market failures' as the 'external effects' with socially harmful consequences. The predicament of external effects provoke a distinct dilemma of collective action over the provision of public goods to overcome external effects. Olson has concisely argued that the production and allocation of public goods is inherently problematic. As they cannot be sustained on a voluntaristic basis, they should be brought under coercive regulation.

De Swaan employs welfare economics and collective action theory to analyze the complex constellations of interdependence, while relying on Elias' civilization theory to identify accumulative handling of external effects in the historical process. Following De Swaan, episodic social

163

policy innovations are the outcome of past conflicts between different established elites over the provision of the public good of social care. The central tenet of his argument runs as follows: poverty constitutes a problem for established elites in terms of the external effects of social upheaval. The predicament of social upheaval provokes a typical collective action dilemma for these elites. They have a common interest to pacify the poor with relief. However, voluntary arrangements, especially on a large scale, are intrinsically threatened by Olsonian 'free rider' problems over the distribution of costs in the provision of the public good of poor relief. Coercive 'third party' arrangements are therefore required to solve this dilemma of collective action. Consequently, national welfare states emerge in the collectivizing process as the focal solution to the external effects of poverty for established elites. The evolution of social care thus tends to episodically develop from small scale to large scale regulation and from voluntary to mandatory social policy. In the words of De Swaan:

> In the course of the collectivizing process, collective action produces both a collectivity capable of coordinating the actions of its members effectively and a collective good which corresponds to this level of integration, but cannot exist apart from it. (De Swaan 1988: 4)

Increased social interdependence generates intensification of both the scope and potential of negative external effects in social life. So far, this has enticed the nation-state to embark on social policy, as it constitutes the most solid institutional structure for regulating, administrating and implementing binding arrangements of social care.

With respect to the institutional origins of social care, De Swaan's genealogy of the welfare state begins with the institutions of medieval poor relief (De Swaan 1988: 21). In response to the threat of roaming vagabonds, the parish church took over the responsibility for social care, given the lack of central authority under feudalism. In the course of the seventeenth century, Poor Laws instituted the first public provision of social care, administered by separate regions and financed through local taxes. Subsequently, the eighteenth century workhouse enabled cities to control the inflow of the vagrant poor by forcing them to work. Nineteenth century industrialization unleashed the serious social risk of contagious disease. Persistent dangers of contamination prompted the rich to cater for infrastructural city hygiene. Sanitation provisions were initiated for rich neighbourhoods and were later extended to poorer neighbourhoods.

The historical development of the twentieth century national welfare state has to be understood against the background of two important social changes. First, the growth of organized capitalism around the turn of the century, brought the labour movement to institutionalize social benefit funds to counter the social risks for industrial workers. As these so-called 'friendly societies' were unable to manage cyclical industrial unemployment, the current system of mandatory national social insurance was gradually introduced in the interwar period. After World War II, the extension and consolidation of the national welfare states was further encouraged by important value changes. Poverty and unemployment were no longer understood as individual moral shortcomings. Modern interdependent citizens came to realize that everybody can be struck by the externalities of the dynamic capitalist economy. This form of society-wide social consciousness since 1945, subsequently reinforced the increased willingness among citizens to contribute to state-led social policy through redistributive taxes. A kind of societal learning seems to have taken place in the face increased human interdependence of the twentieth century which underscores the legitimacy of the national welfare state (De Swaan 1988: 252-7).

De Swaan's provocative study constitutes a bold contribution to the international welfare state debate. His analysis of the collectivization of social care can be understood as an attempt to integrate historical and political factors, neglected by Wilensky, into an encompassing developmental perspective. De Swaan's political explanation of the collectivization of social care arrangements in history, nevertheless, remains conspicuously onesided. Its most striking shortcoming concerns the neo-Hobbesian predicament which in fact lies at the heart of both the intellectual traditions upon which he builds his argument. Elias and Olson, both adhere to a conception of social order imposed upon by central authorities (Hemerijck 1990). The historical motive of elites to institutionalize poor relief, health care, education and social security is aroused through time by fear of social upheaval of the poor against the rich. As new social problems promise to provoke social unrest on an increasingly large scale, a Hobbesian 'state of war' can only be pacified by an even stronger Leviathan. Social upheaval must be managed externally and centrally at ever higher and more coercive levels of social integration. The major social policy innovations in the evolution of the welfare state are the result of the historical conflict between the established elites about the coordination and provision of public social care, under the continuous threat of social unrest. Faced with the danger of social disruption, the contemporary welfare state has 'become a vast conglomerate of nationwide, compulsory and collective arrangements to remedy and control the external effects of adversity and deficiency' (De Swaan 1988: 218). The role attributed to central government in the process is that of an enlightened interventionist despot, pacifying the poor in the name of established elites with an efficient public apparatus of national social care.

165

According to De Swaan, the welfare state can be understood as the historical institutional effect of well-understood self-interest of established elites. The support of the middle class has clearly been crucial to the development of the welfare state. Disadvantaged groups in his analysis are merely understood as potentially disruptive forces, that pose a threat to social order, and should consequently be pacified by the enlightened elites. To be sure, interdependence is never symmetrical. Dependency relationships are sources of power, that give rise to structural social inequalities and political struggles with contingent outcomes. The manner in which political power is employed by elites under dilemmas of collective action is in any case not necessarily informed by the benign aspects of increased interdependence. Increased interdependence certainly does not as a matter of course lead to a predestined state administered system of universalistic social policy.

De Swaan's convergence perspective departs considerably from Esping-Andersen's historical-institutionalist divergence perspective, in which the mobilization of the labour movement is seen as a crucial collective force behind the development of the contemporary welfare state. De Swaan's neo-Hobbesian top-down conception of social order prevents him from seriously recognizing the formative influence of the mobilization of subordinate classes in the evolution of social policy. Contrary to De Swaan, Esping-Andersen assigns great importance to innovative capacities of class mobilization in channelling scope and content of social policy development. Especially, the introduction of universal suffrage has enabled the labour movement to establish strong political parties. Supported by closely allied trade unions, the parties have become coalition partners in democratic governments, which have enacted major social reforms in the initial postwar era. Historically, the middle class was merely interested in the proper functioning of markets, i.e. the political protection of property rights by a non-interventionist minimalist state. The mobilization of the labour movement in support of universal suffrage was partly inspired by the contrary demand for political protection of wage earners against injuries of the market. Esping-Andersen is not at all blind to the interests of the middle class. Provisions for the middle classes in education and health care constitute important preconditions for welfare state development. By merely analyzing the evolution of the welfare state in terms of an elite control strategy, De Swaan's convergence thesis fails to do justice to the divergent mobilization of social classes in support of different trajectories of social policy development across North America and Western Europe.

Convergence, divergence and European integration

Since January 1, 1993, the European Single Market guarantees the free movement of goods, services, capital, and labour among the twelve Member States of the European Union. The completion of the internal market and the ongoing attempt at monetary and political integration inescapably raise the fundamental question whether the Maastricht treaty and its associated Social Protocol signed by the Member States, except Britain, has set the stage for more European social policy coordination and harmonization in the 1990s. To what extent is social policy harmonization likely to invite a truly transnational European welfare state? Is institutional diversity finally on the way out, or, to the contrary, are domestic differences in social policy goals and institutions between Members States further accentuated by the realization of the single market? And what about the dissimilar impact of European integration on the institutions and policies of the more advanced welfare states of the rich North and the poor residual welfare systems of South? What kind of novel institutional linkages between market dependency and social protection - commodification and decommodification - will emerge in the European Union?

For the last part of this essay we wish to explore questions by way of a 'thought experiment', based on the different perspectives of welfare state advanced by Wilensky, Esping-Andersen and De Swaan. Consequently, three heuristic scenarios will be contemplated with respect to future of the European welfare state. To be sure, these scenarios have to be treated with extreme caution. The extraordinary character of European integration, whereby independent Member States voluntarily transfer sovereignty to a semi-sovereign transnational entity, very much complicates our endeavour. Moreover, the different perspectives from which we borrow our 'thought experiment' have all primarily dealt with processes social policy expansion up until 1980. They are not made to explain the process of welfare state contraction or retrenchment since, under which the drive for European unity regained momentum. Paul Pierson rightly underlines that, 'retrenchment does not mirror expansion' (Pierson 1994). Notwithstanding these daunting reservations, we believe that the above arguments about the importance of economic factors, power resources and institutional legacies, and neo-Hobbesian collective action predicaments, as developed respectively by Wilensky, Esping-Andersen, and De Swaan, allow us to offer tentative insights in the form of three possible scenarios.

First of all, inspired by Harold Wilensky's 'logic of industrialism' argument, the domestic European welfare state can be expected to evolve toward a convergence of national systems of social care. Under the functionalist, exogenously triggered, economic pressure of further European integration, the policies and institutional characteristics of national welfare states are brought closer together. Secondly, in agreement with Esping-Andersen's emphasis on domestic power resources and institutional leftovers, it could be argued that further European integration is not likely to undermine current domestic diversity. Strongly put, further integration is most likely to endogenously accentuate the already existing national patterns and trajectories of social care within the internal market. Finally, under the aegis of increased global international interdependence, De Swaan's developmental neo-Hobbesian logic of collective action implies an international, endogenously driven trend toward an ever more encompassing transnational system of social care. This implies a distinct transfer of social policy responsibilities from the nation-state to the European Union.

Up until the mid-1980s, the process of European integration can been portrayed as one of 'two steps forward, one step back'. In their stimulating contribution on interest group politics in the European Community, Streeck and Schmitter (1991) distinguish three periods of rise and decline in the process of European integration. From 1948 until the mid 1960s, Jean Monnet and Robert Schumann, the founding fathers of European unity, have with great zeal laid the institutional foundation of the European community. In 1952 the European Coal and Steel Community was established. In 1956 the Benelux countries, Germany, France, and Italy signed the Treaty of Rome. The European Economic Community was subsequently founded in 1958. The 1970s multifold recessions and the failure of the monetary policy experiment of the so-called 'snake' provoked a period of 'Eurosclerosis' after the United Kingdom, Ireland, and Denmark joined the Community in 1973. In the wake of the entry of Greece in 1981, and Spain and Portugal in 1986, the integration effort regained momentum under the chairmanship of Jacques Delors. Stiff economic competition with Japanese and American industries brought enlightened European political elites to rekindle the European ideals of Monnet and Schumann. The Single European Act of 1986, which launched plans of monetary and political union, consequently ushered a brief episode of 'Euroforia'.

In the field of social policy, the integration process, so far, has been, as Peter Lange aptly puts it, a period of 'good intentions, high principles, and little action' (Lange 1993: 7). Initiatives for a 'social Europe' have clearly lagged behind progress towards the economic integration process. Social policy has clearly been the 'stepchild' of European integration. Nonetheless, the completion of the internal market is likely to make it increasingly difficult to exclude social issues from entering the agenda of the Commission.

A scenario of social dumping

Ironically, the Treaty of Rome was very much inspired by the type of functionalistic reasoning that Harold Wilensky adheres to. After two disastrous nationalist wars, European elites believed that transnational integration could help transcend the prewar nationalist aspirations of the continental nation-state. Monnet and Schumann held that economic integration would encourage political unification in Western Europe. Moderate and pragmatic functional organized interests were deemed of critical importance in the construction of a European-wide policy of class reconciliation. Policy success in the sectors of coal, steel and agriculture could generate favourable spillovers to other policy fields, including social policy. Following this kind of structural functionalist reasoning, it could be argued that a uniform European welfare state was in the making. By giving primacy to economic development, once internal borders disappeared, competition between Member States would intensify. This logic applies as much to the productivist, employment and growth oriented postwar era as to the restrictive and deflationary decades of 1980s and 1990s.

If the welfare state is a product of economic development, as Wilensky believes, increased competition among the Member States within the single market under recessionary conditions can encourage downward adjustment in levels of social protection. Such an argument deviates strongly from Wilensky's original convergence thesis which focussed on economic progress promoting ever higher levels of social protection among advanced industrial societies. However, such an argument is still consistent with Wilensky's functionalist economic reasoning.

It has to be emphasized that the Single European Act was part and parcel of the deregulatory and restrictive economic policy reversal that swept the OECD world after the second oil crisis in 1979. The project of Europe 1992, with the internal market as its primary objective, turned into a project of 'external economic assertiveness' through policies of deregulation, liberalization, and decentralization. The Single European Act was explicitly not about 'internal social intervention' and the establishment of European standards for social protection. For European business leaders the main attractions of the Single Market were the liberalization of capital markets, deregulation of the labour market, and welfare state retrenchment. Today, global economic integration takes place through the volatile financial markets of a 'disembedded' liberal international regime. The restrictive requirements for the European Monetary Union in the Maastricht treaty, which in fact embody a clearcut prohibition on European Keynesianism, are likely to result in a downward pressure on social protection. The rather tough convergence criteria under which Member States are allowed to join the EMU, with extremely restrictive requirements for budgetary discipline and inflation, will put severe restrictions of monetary and fiscal policy (Holtman 1993; Scharpf 1991: 257-75). Once containment of domestic inflation, becomes the main macroeconomic priority, this may very well encourage downward adjustment of the standard of social protection under stringent budgetary requirements. This has been termed 'social dumping'. When standards of social protection and employment condition vary significantly across Europe, social rights are likely come to play a part in policy competition. Countries with a high level of social protection could price themselves out of the market in favour of economies with lower levels of social protection. The fear that freeing up competition will lead to 'social dumping' is widespread among the rich welfare states of North-Western Europe. They fear that the relative low wage advantage of the Southern European economies will tempt entrepreneurs to relocate production to the low wage regions of Europe, which, in turn, forces the more advanced welfare state with their high level of social protection to lower social standards by tax cuts and labour market deregulation so as to lower labour costs in order to persuade capital from migrating to the South. While the rich North fear social dumping and capital migration, the poor South fear the migration of their skilled workers to the North. In addition, the South also dread European minimum wage legislation which is likely to undermine its primary source of competitive advantage.

It should, however, be emphasized, that the social wage is only one factor in investment decisions. Not so much labour costs, but productivity differences decisively influence investment decisions. Moreover, investments are also influenced by other factors such as interests rates, skill levels, infrastructure and the stability of industrial relations. High levels of productivity and encompassing standards of social protection seem to go together and vice versa. So far, the evidence of social dumping and its opposite has remained patchy.

A scenario of domestic and supranational institutional obstacles

Assuming that the welfare state is the product of domestic political choice, determined by national power resources and pre-existing institutional factors, it seems that the welfare systems of the Member States will not become identical overnight. Increased policy competition will not overcome the immense institutional diversity among the Members State. For the same reason, it is highly unlikely that national systems of social care can be easily absorbed into the more encompassing transnational collectivity of the European Union with significant measures of autonomy in social policy legislation, administration, and implementation.

To be sure, a rather narrowing of power resources indeed suggests a serious social dumping scenario for the European welfare state. The shift to disinflationary macroeconomic policy since the mid-1970s, which invited a massive surge of unemployment, has seriously weakened the

170

political influence of the labour movement in domestic politics and industrial relations. At the transnational level, the European trade union movement is notoriously weak. The European Trade Union Confederation has great difficulty organizing on a transnational scale, due to lack of resources and cultural and ideological heterogeneity, language and economic barriers. Moreover, the wide disparity in economic development between the North and the South has generated important differences in social interests which further undermine a unified labour voice at the level of the Union. Under the deregulatory agenda of the Maastricht treaty, employers have been more successful in having their voice heard in Brussels (Streeck and Schmitter 1991).

The factor of labour weakness in Europe should however not be taken at face value. Relative European labour weakness should be placed against the background of pre-existing institutional arrangements, both at the national level and at the level of the European Union. Stephan Leibfried and Paul Pierson offer some intelligent insights into the preemptive role of existing institutions against European social policy convergence. First, they underscore that the institutions of the European Union inhibit pathbreaking initiatives in the sphere of social policy. While the Maastricht Treaty extended qualified majority voting on issues of the internal market, social policy initiatives remain subject to unanimous consent. Second, they emphasize that European integration occurs in the context of an extensive and diverse array of national policies and institutions. While the integration process challenges these national provisions, domestic social programmes will decisively remain an enduring part of the European political landscape. Moreover, national social programmes not only pre-empt an European social policy space, they also leave the European Union with weak administrative capacities and fiscal room to fund and implement social policy initiatives (Leibfried and Pierson 1994: 30-37).

Perhaps the most important institutional obstacle to European social policy harmonization concerns the strong popular attachments to particular social programmes. Leibfried and Pierson conclude that the national welfare state, despite mounting external economic pressures, probably still is the most popular component of the postwar settlement, as the efforts to scale back social provisions have met with stiff resistance in the 1970s and 1980s.

While the European economies have clearly become more interdependent, the immense diversity in culture, policy goals and networks, institutions, national traditions of administration and implementation, and economic development, make any simple process of national or transnational convergence unthinkable for the near future. In short, domestic political choices continue to play a crucial role in transforming the national welfare state.

171

A scenario for the united welfare state of Europe

Recently Abram De Swaan has surveyed the prospects for transnational social policy, in which he again takes as a point of departure the dilemma of action that rich nations must overcome if they are to jointly fund social provisions for the poor. He observes a further intensification of the interdependence between rich and poor on a global scale, which he sees reflected in the growth in the flows of migration from the poor to rich regions of the world. Poverty in poor regions constitutes a problem for the rich parts of Europe as the external effects of poverty present themselves in violent social conflict and labour migration to the rich welfare states of Western Europe. When the integration process intensifies, there will be mounting pressure in the form of external of intra-union migration, which will encourage European political elites to develop social policies to buy off migration. De Swaan clearly finds the perspective of a transnational European welfare a realistic scenario. He boldly states, with little knowledge of international economics and decisionmaking structures and procedures of the European Union, that the free movement of capital, commodities, and labour, will inevitably level off differences in wages, interests, and profits. Moreover, he simply claims that 'once general elections are held for a united Europe, the less wealthy groups of voters in their own interest will attempt to tax the wealthier ones'. He concludes, therefore, that a supranational welfare state within the 'United States of Europe' is quite conceivable.

Subsequently, he goes on to address the predicaments of the former communist economies in Eastern Europe. Deprivation in the East will lead to mass migration to the West. Once this threat materializes the European nations have a common interest to stop the flow of people crossing the former Iron Curtain. This, De Swaan believes, activates a classical mechanism of collective action: 'time and again the fear for vagrant poor has persuaded the rich to pacify the poor with relief'. He subsequently portrays the European Union as a reasonably effective central coordinating agency, which during this transitional stage might be capable of organizing and funding some minimal system of social benefits so that the poor Eastern European citizens can remain where they are (De Swaan 1994: 106-110). While De Swaan's argument is challenging, it is not at all clear that the European Union represents a solid collective actor with the kind of extensive transnational bureaucratic and administrative competencies, judicial control, democratic governance, and, most importantly, significant autonomy, to engage in welfare state building in the West, let alone the East.

Delors' original proposal to include a 'social chapter' to strengthen the social dimension in the Maastricht Treaty, next to the plans for monetary and political union, corresponds with De Swaan convergence perspective.

However, what in fact followed at Maastricht did not agree with De Swaan's benign conception of enlightened elite collective action solutions, as the Social Paragraph was not included in the Treaty. The alternative Article 117 of the Treaty, referred to as 'the agreement of the Eleven', excluding the United Kingdom, concerns, in the best tradition of European Unity, again a celebration of good intentions (job growth, social dialogue), high principles (improving living standards, working conditions, and adequate social protection), but little action. It definitely does amount to European social policy harmonization, binding rules directed at the uniformation of national programmes at the European level, which De Swaan assumes already exists. The only area where the European Union has effectively forced social policy harmonization concerns the equal treatment of men and women at the work place and in social security together with minimal health and safety requirements.

It appears highly unlikely that the European Union will overshadow domestic politics as the center of social policy in the medium to long run. The intergovernmental institutional structure of the European Community is far too fragmented to undertake a massive expansion of transnational social policy. The principal institutional obstacles for an effective European social policy is undoubtedly the requirement of unanimous consent over harmonization. This requirement has caused the watering down of many Commission plans, as Member States exert direct control over policy proposals through the Council of Ministers. The individual ministers are guided by national preferences and personal views rather than by the collective interest of the community. The proposal for accepting decisions by qualified majorities, has definitely facilitated decisionmaking within the European Union. The Single European Act has definitely strengthened the legal basis for action by the Commission. With respect to social policy, the Treaty stipulates that the qualified majority does not apply to 'provisions concerning the rights and interests of employees', for which the unanimous consent is required. The subsidiarity principle determines that the Union can only intervene when policy objectives are better achieved at the level of the political union than by Member States. Centralization is only considered when there are obvious advantages over national policymaking. To be sure, the implementation of directives through legal means is left to the Member States. The fact that national styles and practices of implementation differ widely across Europe, and the European Union cannot adequately guide and govern compliance with regulatory decisions, encourages divergent policy outcomes practices, which frustrates social policy coordination. So much for De Swaan's conjecture of the European Union as an autonomous regulatory actor.

The current delay in the unification process is not so much due to the fact that national states cannot jump their own shadows, but has its roots in the original functionalist logic upon which the European ideal was based. Progress in European social policy development presupposes a political union which precedes economic integration. The heroic choice of Monnet and Schumann, however, was to bet on the horse of economic progress, that would as a matter of course pull the cart of social policy and political integration. The vicissitudes around the Social Protocol in Maastricht in 1991, the EMS crisis of 1993, and the election of Santer to succeed Delors in 1994, once again demonstrate the fundamental functionalist fallacy upon which European integration was erected. The mounting problems confronting the European Monetary Union reveal that the European Union remains a utopia as long as there is no real political authority in Brussels. Put strongly, the irony is that the success of the European integration effort from Monnet to Delors in terms of economic prosperity has strengthened the nation-state more than it has promoted actual unification (Milward 1984). The current crisis, like the episode of Eurosclerosis of the 1970s, really shows that the European Union is a 'fair weather' product. As long as the Member States prosper, integration is stimulated and projects towards the deepening and widening of the Union rank high on the European agenda. When the economic tide turns, however, the European Union lacks political clout for a truly concerted effort, because it lacks political capacity since it was built on the functionalist fallacy of economic development. The Commission does not lack good intentions, but in times of economic distress no coordinated collective action is to be expected from Europe.

Conclusion

The most important conclusion that can be drawn from our tentative 'thought experiment' is that currently convergent tendencies go together with divergent developments. With respect to policy convergence, we observe everywhere in Europe labour weakness, the strength of business, restrictive macroeconomic policy, and the globalization of the finance market with a deflationary bias on a 'disembedded' world economy. These trends definitely put the national welfare state on the defensive. However, convergent pressures do not point in the direction of system uniformity at the national or supranational level. Despite increased global economic interdependence, we believe that social policy reform for a more restricted national welfare state will for the near future continue to be characterized by a high degree of institutional diversity. European integration under a deregulatory agenda might stimulate a gradual and rather indirect process of domestic social policy erosion. Such a common trend, however, under widely heterogeneous national welfare state regimes makes any simple

174

process of harmonization practically inconceivable. Similar tendencies will necessarily be coloured and mediated by the existing country-specific institutional arrangements. To be sure, the increased pressure on the national welfare state cannot simply be read off from economic trends and predicaments.

Nostalgia for the stable postwar social compromise of the national welfare state is both misplaced and unrealistic. The domestic ingredients upon which the welfare state of Lord Keynes and Lord Beveridge was built included a homogeneous national society, expansionary growth and full employment oriented macroeconomic policies, a traditional industrial production structure, a strong labour movement engaged in centralized and highly institutionalized industrial relations, an astute and selfconscious interventionist state, and a traditional family structure. The historical postwar settlement was based on the international regime of 'embedded liberalism' which allowed national polities to institutionalize generous social policies. Today, none of these conditions can be fulfilled. While the post-Cold War international order remains an obscure and fragile entity, apart from the enormous technological developments in the production structure, the Keynesian recipe of demand stimulation can no longer be effectively pursued on a domestic scale in a world of global competition and free movement of capital. Along with its economic borders, the nation-state has lost its sovereignty over monetary and fiscal policy. Under the deflationary criteria of the EMU, even within a truly integrated European political economy, Keynesian policy initiatives would be foiled. Within the rapidly globalizing international economy, wherein national regimes compete under only a thin layer of European legislation, the nation-state, unable to guarantee full employment, has become too small an entitity for encompassing economic regulation. Likewise the nation-state is really too big to respond flexibly to disperse regional and local social problems. Also with respect to employment patterns a return to the postwar compromise is improbable. Persistent high unemployment, the decline of heavy manufacturing, rapid technological innovation, expanding service industries, the advent of white collar unionism, the growth of atypical post-industrial employment patterns, increased female labour force participation, the internal strife between 'exposed' industrial unions and 'protected' public sector unions, together with strains between the trade union movement and social-democratic parties, has further politically weakened the labour movement, the traditional supporter of the postwar welfare state. In terms of family relations a return the traditional family is undesirable. The traditional family clearly is no longer the universal household type. Whereas the family structure of the postwar order remained uniform, homogeneous, and highly predictable in terms of mobility, current post-industrial life style patterns are far more heterogeneous,

175

multicultural, diverse, atypical, and unpredictable (Esping-Andersen 1993). Today women constitute about half of the labour force in the advanced welfare state. A majority of women and a minority of men are working part-time for at least part of their working life. A double income is almost the new standard.

We would still like to emphasize that while the adaptive capacity of domestic social policy is restricted, it should not be underestimated. Even under unfavourable national and international economic conditions, a novel sustainable compromise can be drafted, that allows for further decentralization and a deconcentration of the welfare state between the small margins of national social policy and supranational regulation. Administrative capacities are being transferred partly to lower levels of local and regional authorities and private care institutions (Sabel 1989; Simonis and Kreukels 1991). Social policy is best linked to local needs. This process of subnational devolution of the national welfare state would, secondly, correspond to the ongoing trend of the (re)regionalization of post-Fordist production processes in industry and in the services, and agrees with a renewed interest in the importance of a rich social infrastructure on the supply side of the economy (Streeck 1992).

In order to maintain high standards of social protection, the advanced welfare states of the North will have to secure a position on the international markets for products with high added values. On this market of diversified quality production, competition is not based on price competition and the economies of scale of standardized mass production, but on advanced manufacturing technologies and organization structures with strong innovative capacities, stable industrial relations, good training and education provisions and high levels of practical training (Boyer 1988; Kern and Schumann 1984; Piore and Sabel 1984; Sorge and Streeck 1988). According to Wolfgang Streeck, such a flexible and specialized production concept can thrive only within a rich and comprehensive social infrastructure at all levels between state and society (Streeck 1992). The challenge of the highly developed national welfare state in this respect is to transform its passive system of domestic compensation on the demand side of the economy towards activating a flexible social infrastructure on the supply side, explicitly aimed at the development of human resources (Reich 1991).

Gøsta Esping-Andersen has recently argued that the advanced welfare state is faced with a tragic. The postwar welfare state has been able to realize two treasured goals of the labour movement: full employment and income equality. Under today's economic predicaments the achievement of this twin objective is no longer realistic. A choice has to be made between employment and equality. Following Esping-Andersen, we prioritize employment and thus allow for more inequality. The price that has to be

176

paid for this tragic choice does not necessarily increase poverty, as long as active social policies guarantee sufficient training and education and generate sufficient turnover on the labour market to counter underclass ghettoization (Esping-Andersen 1993). The current conjunction of convergent trends and divergent tendencies also has consequences for theory development and empirical research. Any substantive debate on the future of the welfare state will remain fruitless as long as various perspectives discussed in this chapter are conceived of as mutually exclusive models of thought. The analysis of the problems and prospects of social policy will have to concentrate on the relationship between international interdependence and institutional diversity within national polities, both with their respective strengths and weaknesses. The focus of comparative research should be on the interaction between general processes of social change under specific national, regional, local and sectoral institutional configurations of a newly emerging sustainable post-industrial compromise.

Notes

1 This chapter is a much revised English translation of the Dutch article published as 'De pendule van perspectief' in Engbersen, G., A.C. Hemerijck, and W.E. Bakker (eds) (1994), *Zorgen in het Europese huis*, Boom, Amsterdam).

References

Alber, J. (1982), *Vom Armenhaus zum Wohlfahrtsstaat*, Campus, Frankfurt am Main.

Baglioni, G., and C.J. Crouch (eds) (1990), *European Industrial Relations: the Challenge of Flexibility*, Sage, London.

Baumol, W. (1952), *Welfare Economics and the Theory of the State*, Princeton University Press, Cambridge, Mass.

Bell, D. (1960, 1988), *The End of Ideology*, Harvard University Press, Cambridge, Mass.)

Berger, S. (1981), *Organizing Interests in Western Europe, Pluralism, Corporatism, and the Transformation of Politics*, Cambridge University Press, Cambridge.

Beveridge, W.H. (1942), *Social Insurance and Allied Services*, HMSO, London.

Beveridge, W.H. (1944), *Full Employment in a Free Society*, George Allen & Unwin, London.

Boyer, R. (1988), *The Search for Labour Market Flexibility: the European Economies in Transition*, Oxford University Press, Oxford.

Castles, F.G. (ed.) (1982), *The Impact of Parties: Politics and Policies in Democratic Capitalist States*, Sage, London.

Castles, F.G. (1987), 'Neo-corporatism and the happiness index', *European Journal of Political Research*, vol. 15.

Crouch, C. (1979), 'The state, capital and liberal democracy', in ders. (ed.) *State and Economy in Contemporary Capitalism*, Croom Helm, London.

Crouch, C. (1993), *European Industrial Relations and State Traditions*, Oxford University Press, Oxford.

Crouch, C., and A. Pizzorno (eds) (1978), *The Resurgence of Class Conflict in Western Europe since 1968*, Macmillan, London.

Elias, N. (1939, 1982), *The Civilizing Process*, Basil Blackwell, Oxford.

Esping-Andersen, G. (1990), *The Three Worlds of Welfare Capitalism*, Princeton University Press, Princeton.

Esping-Andersen, G. (1993), *Changing Classes: Stratification and Mobility in Post-industrial Societies*, Sage, London.

Esping-Andersen, G., and W. Korpi (1984), 'Social policy as class politics in post-war capitalism: Scandinavia, Austria and Germany', in Goldthorpe, J.H. *Order and Conflict in Contemporary Capitalism*, Oxford University Press, Oxford.

Evans, P., and J.D. Stephens (1988), 'Studying development since the 1960s: The emergence of a new comparative political economy', *Theory and Society*, vol. 17.

Forsyth, D., and T. Notermans (1994), 'Macroeconomic policy regimes and financial regulation in Europe, 1931-1994', mimeo, Massachusetts Institute of Technology.

Fukuyama, F. (1989), 'The end of history?', *The national Interest*, no. 16.

Galbraith, J.K. (1985, 1962), *The Affluent Society*, Penguin Books, Harmondsworth.

Goldthorpe, J.H. (1984), 'The end of convergence: Corporatist and dualist tendencies in modern western societies', in Goldthorpe, J.H. *Order and Conflict in Contemporary Capitalism*, Oxford University Press, Oxford.

Gourevitch, P. (1986), *Politics in Hard Times*, Comparative Responses to International Economic Crisis, Cornell University Press, Ithaca.

Hall, Peter A. (1990), *The Political Power of Economic Ideas: Keynesianism across Nations*, Princeton University Press, Princeton.

Hemerijck, A.C. (1990), 'De verzorgingsimperatief', *Beleid en Maatschappij*, no. 5.

Hemerijck, A.C. (1993), *The Historical Contingencies of Dutch Corporatism*, D.Phil. Balliol College, Oxford.

Hirsch, F. (1978), 'The ideological underlay of inflation' in Hirsch, F., and J.H. Goldthorpe, *The Political Economy of Inflation*, Martin Robertson, London.

Holtman, G. (1993), 'Economic integration after Maastricht', *Occasional paper Institute of Public Policy Research*, London.

Keohane, R.O. (1984), *After Hegemony. Cooperation and Discord in the World Political Economy*, Princeton University Press, Princeton.

Kern, H., and M. Schumann (1984), *Das Ende der Arbeitsteilung? Rationalisierung in der industriellen Produktion*, C.H. Beck, Munich.

Kerr, C. (1983), *The Future of Industrial Societies*, Harvard University Press, Cambridge, Mass.

Kerr, C., J.T. Dunlop, H. Harbison, C. Myers (1960), *Industrialism and Industrial Man*, Harvard University Press, Cambridge, Mass.

Keynes, J.M. (1936), *The General Theory of Employment, Interest and Money*, Macmillan, London.

Kirchheimer, O. (1957), 'The waning of opposition in parliamentary regimes', *Social Research*, vol. 24, no. 2.

Korpi, W. (1978), *The Working Class in Welfare Capitalism*, Routledge, Kegan Paul, London.

Lange, P. (1993), 'Maastricht and the Social Protocol: Why did they do it?', *Politics and Society*, vol. 21, no. 1 (March).

Lehmbruch, G., and P.C. Schmitter (1982), *Patterns of Corporatist Policy-Making*, Sage, London and Beverly Hills.

Leibfried, S. (1979), 'The United States and West-German welfare systems', *Cornell International Law Journal*, vol.12.

Leibfried, S., and P. Pierson (1994), 'The prospects for social Europe', in Swaan, A. de (ed.) *Social Policy Beyond Borders*, Amsterdam University Press, Amsterdam.

Lipset, S.M. (1969), *Political Man*, Heinemann, London.

Maier, C.S. (1987), 'The politics of productivity: Foundations of American international economic policy after World War II', in Maier, C.S. (ed.), *In Search of Stability: Explorations in Historical Political Economy*, Cambridge University Press, Cambridge.

Marglin, S.A., and J. Schor (eds) (1990), *The Golden Age of Capitalism. Reinterpreting the Postwar Experience*, Oxford University Press, Oxford.

Milward, A.S. (1984), *The Reconstruction of Western Europe*, Methuen & Co., London.

Olson, M. (1965), *The Logic of Collective Action; Public Goods and the Theory of Groups*, Harvard University Press, Cambridge, Mass.

Pierson, C. (1994), 'The new politics of the welfare state', paper prepared for the Conference of Europeanists (preliminary draft), April 1994

Piore, M.J., and C.S. Sabel (1984), *The Second Industrial Divide, Possibilities for Prosperity*, Basic Books, New York.

Reich, R.B (1991), *The Work of Nations, Preparing Ourselves for the 21st Century*, Vintage, New York.

Ruggie (1982), 'International regimes, transactions and change: Embedded liberalism in the postwar economic order', in Krasner, S. (ed.) *International Regimes*, Cornell University Press, Ithaca.

Sabel, C.S. (1989), 'Equity and efficiency in the federal welfare state', paper presented to the Nordic Working Group on the New Welfare State, Copenhagen.

Scharpf, F.W. (1991), *Crisis and Choice in European Social Democracy*, Cornell University Press, Ithaca.

Schmidt, M.G. (1983), 'The welfare state and the economy in periods of economic crisis: A comparative study of 23 OECD nations', *European Journal of Political Research*, vol. 11.

Schmitter, P.C., and G. Lehmbruch (eds) (1979), *Trends Toward Corporatist Intermediation*, Sage, London.

Simonis, J.B.D., and A.M.J. Kreukels (1991), 'De erosie van de nationale staat; de hernieuwde scheiding tussen imperium en dominium', *Beleid & Maatschappij*, no. 6.

Sorge, A., and W. Streeck (1988), 'Industrial relations and technical change: The case for an extended perspective', in Hyman, R., and W. Streeck (eds), *New Technology and Industrial Relations*, Basil Blackwell, Oxford.

Streeck, W. (1992), *Social Institutions and Economic Performance*, Sage, London.

Streeck, W., and P.C. Schmitter (1991), 'From national corporatism to transnational pluralism: Organized interests in the Single European Market, *Politics and Society*, vol. 19, no. 2.

Swaan, A. de (1988), *In Care of the State. Health care, Education and Welfare in Europe and the USA in the Modern Era*, Polity Press, London.

Swaan, A. de (1994), 'Perspectives for transnational social policy in Europe: social transfers from West to East', in Swaan, A. de (ed.), *Social Policy Beyond Borders: The Social Question in Transnational Perspective*, Amsterdam University Press, Amsterdam.

Therborn, G. (1984), 'Does corporatism really matter? The economic crisis and issues of political theory', *Journal of Public Policy*, vol. 7.

Wilensky, H.L. (1975), *The Welfare State and Equality*, University of California Press, Berkeley.

Wilensky, H.L. (1976), *The New Corporatism, Centralization and the Welfare State*, Sage, London and Beverly Hills.

Wilensky, H.L. (1981), 'Democratic corporatism, consensus and social policy: Reflections on changing values and the crisis of the welfare state', in OECD, *The Welfare State in Crisis: An Account of the Conference on the Social Policies in the 1980s*, OECD, Paris.

Wilensky, H.L., and Turner, L. (1987), *Democratic Corporatism and Policy Linkages*, University of California Press, Berkeley.

8 The 'social dumping' threat of European integration: A critique

Hugh Mosley

EU
FO2
P16
P17

Summary

This paper examines the implications of European economic integration for the welfare state. One possible scenario ('Euro-welfare') is the establishment of supranational EU-standards of social protection. Another more pessimistic scenario ('social dumping') sees economic liberalization as resulting in de facto deregulation, leading to an erosion of national standards of social protection. After reviewing efforts to institutionalize a European social dimension commensurate with the European Union's economic programme, the paper focuses on the question of whether 'social dumping' is a threat to the welfare state. It concludes that this scenario is based on questionable assumptions and is not supported by historical evidence.

Introduction

There has been considerable concern, especially in high labour cost countries like Germany, that increased competition as a consequence of European economic integration may lead to an erosion of national standards of social protection, or at least inhibit further progress. Although similar concerns have been raised in the US and elsewhere, there appear to be important differences that distinguish the European case: first, the completion of the European internal market and, in the long run, monetary union entail a degree of integration of product, capital and labour markets that far exceeds that on world markets. Second, there is the parallel process of European political integration, which brings at least a partial transfer of sovereignty. This means that, in contrast to the situation on the world market, the European Union (EU) has central political institutions capable, in principle, of regulating internal competition by imposing EU-wide supranational standards. Third, as a customs union with central political institutions the EU not only promotes internal competition but regulates external competition and can buffer its impact.

What are the implications of European integration for national regimes of social policy? The actual outcome depends, of course, on developments that cannot be foreseen: Whether the EU internal market and monetary union is fully realized as envisioned, the extent to which there is an offsetting market closure vis-à-vis third countries, whether the European Commission, trade unions and other actors are able to develop adequate policy responses on the European level.

This paper examines two aspects of the impact of European integration on the welfare state: First (more briefly) the prospects for meaningful EU-wide social regulation and second (at somewhat greater length) the potential for destructive 'social competition' in the absence of such regulation.

European social policy

The development of EU-level social policies can be conveniently divided into three distinct periods (Mosley 1990). The first period of benign neglect (1958-73) lasted from its establishment in 1958 down to the end of the postwar period of sustained economic growth and very low rates of unemployment in the early 1970s. In this period the EU was preoccupied with the establishment of the common market and limited its involvement in social policy largely to the problems of the coordination of social security for EU-migrant workers. The second period of increased social activism (1974-75) coincides with the end of the postwar economic boom and the onset of mass unemployment. In response the EU adopted several important directives in the field of labour law in the latter part of the 1970s:

1   Requiring advance notice of mass layoffs to labour market authorities and to the affected employees;

2   Protecting employees' rights in the event of transfers of businesses or parts of businesses by making collective agreements applicable to new employers and requiring that representatives of employees be informed and consulted;

3   Requiring the establishment of a fund to guarantee employee wage claims in bankrupt firms;

4   Numerous directives on specific aspects of work health and safety.

Moreover, a number of important directives were adopted in the area of sex discrimination in employment, prohibiting discrimination in pay, recruitment, promotion, vocational training, and working conditions. The third period from the adoption of the Single European Act in 1986 to the ratification of the Maastricht Treaty in 1994 has been dominated by new initiatives for a 'social dimension' to the internal market programme, of which the 'Social Charter' has been the centerpiece.

The Social Charter

The 'Social Charter', which was adopted in December 1989, is an extensive catalog of employee rights. Whereas most countries supported it, at least in principle, the Charter and subsequent directives to implement it have been resolutely opposed by the British government. Although the Charter itself has only the status of a non-binding declaration, the Commission, under strong political pressure, subsequently proposed an action programme to implement it. In many cases the Commission chose - probably wisely in view of the diversity even within the European Community - to limit EU involvement to the issuance of recommendations (e.g. minimum wages, convergence of social security systems, collective bargaining rights). Nevertheless, the Commission did propose new directives, i.e. binding Community law, in a number of potentially controversial areas. The most important subjects affected are part-time and other non-standard forms of employment, consultation and participation rights of workers in so-called 'Euro-companies', working time, protection of pregnant women at work, and a revision of the earlier directive on procedures to be followed in collective redundancies to take into account situations in which decisions are taken by a controlling transnational undertaking. Several other proposed directives in the field of occupational health and safety were not controversial.

Many of these 'new' proposals are in fact reincarnations of earlier initiatives that were rejected by the Council of Ministers, the principal lawmaking organ of the EU, due to the earlier requirement of unanimity. For example, a proposed directive requiring that part-time workers receive equal treatment, except where the difference in hours worked objectively justifies different treatment, which was first proposed by the Commission in 1981; a directive on temporary workers first proposed in 1982, which would have given them the same rights a permanent employees and limited their use; a directive on parental leave for family reasons first proposed in 1983; a draft directive on working time considered by the Council in 1984. This logjam in European social policy regulation could only be broken through an extension of qualified majority voting on social policy issues in the Council of Ministers.

Under the 1986 Single European Act community law related to the completion of the internal market programme now requires, with some exceptions, merely a 'qualified majority' instead of unanimity - overcoming a major obstacle to the development of European-level policies. Moreover, Article 118 provides for decision by qualified majority where the health and safety of workers and the improvement of the work environment is concerned and Article 49 provides for qualified majority voting in the implementation of the right of freedom of movement for workers from EU-Member States. A 'qualified majority' is roughly the equivalent of a two-thirds majority based on weighted national voting in the Council, the EU's main decisionmaking body.

Other treaty provisions limit the scope of qualified majority voting, especially in the area of social policy: Article 100a.2 of the EU-Treaty explicitly exempts fiscal provisions, those relating to freedom of movement of persons, and 'the rights and interests of employed persons' from majority voting. The fact that measures of economic integration related to the completion of the internal market are unambiguously subject to qualified majority voting, while accompanying social measures are not, constitutes a fundamental asymmetry in the development of European integration.

It is the European Commission that determines the legal basis of the proposed action and thus whether majority voting or unanimity is appropriate. Whereas the socialist majority in the European Parliament called for an expansive interpretation of the scope of majority voting in the area of social policy others (most vociferously the UK government) insist on a narrow interpretation.

The Commission did in fact adopt such an approach. In more controversial draft directives on employee participation in Euro-companies, limiting working hours, and on equal treatment of part-time and temporary workers in social security legislation, the Commission has asserted that qualified majority voting is applicable. In the first case because it is deemed part of the internal market programme, in the second because it is deemed to be a work health and safety issue, and in the latter case because such discriminatory treatment is said to constitute unfair competition within the internal market. This important 'constitutional' issue will ultimately be decided by the European Court of Justice, which is the ultimate interpreter of European law.

By 1994 a significant part of the Commission's 'action plan' has been implemented including numerous Council Directives, which national governments are required to implement through legislation. These include seven health and safety directives setting minimum standards in various work situations; four major directives on employment rights, including the amendment to the directive on collective redundancies referred to above; an important directive on the rights of pregnant workers, a directive on working time, and on the protection of young people at work.

The Maastricht Treaty on European Union established a two-tier system of social policy in the EU. The scope of qualified majority voting in social policy is significantly extended in a new procedure. The UK, which has been the most vocal opponent of European social policy, would not participate and not be bound by the resulting directives. One controversial directive on European works councils has now been adopted under the new procedure. Two controversial proposed directives on non-standard forms of employment (part-time and temporary workers), which failed to be adopted under the pre-Maastricht rules, may also win approval under the new procedure.

Although significant, these ad hoc regulatory interventions are reminiscent of the early development of national welfare states. At best they serve to establish basic standards in employment protection aimed at preventing more extreme forms of 'social dumping'. Mainline social security programmes are not affected at all, except for the requirement of non-discrimination in the case of EU-migrant workers and women.

Indeed, harmonization appears neither desirable nor feasible. 'Downward' harmonization would be unacceptable to countries with generally higher standards of social security and 'upward' harmonization is beyond the financial means of the poorer countries and consequently rejected by their governments (e.g. Spain). There will thus, in any case, continue to be a broad diversity of welfare state regimes within the EU, both in terms of levels and styles of social protection, and not a common European welfare state regime.

The welfare state and competitiveness

The European Union's project of economic liberalization may entail a de facto form of social deregulation. While existing national regimes of social protection remain in place, they must compete with one another as the economic space in which goods, capital and persons move freely is extended. Are marked differences in the quality of social regulation economically sustainable or are national policy options increasingly constrained by the impact of the competitive pressures resulting from the increasing economic interdependence? For theoretical reasons it seems plausible (in a neoclassical framework) to expect that market forces will lead to such a result (convergence of factor costs) in the absence of supranational regulation. These concerns are in practice exacerbated by the

186

fact that the original European Community, which consisted of six relatively homogeneous continental welfare states, now includes states with markedly lower wage levels and less developed social welfare systems (e.g. Greece, Portugal and Spain).

Social competition?

In European policy discussions one can identify a recurrent paradigm of the linkage between the welfare state and international competitiveness, which is a more or less explicit common assumption of both trade unions and employers' organizations (and their respective political representatives). 'Social dumping' as a type social competition seems to be conceived of as taking place in at least three (interrelated) ways (Mosley 1990:

1   Through the displacement of high cost producers by low cost producers from countries in which not only wages but also social benefits and the direct and indirect costs entailed by protective labour legislation are markedly lower;

2   Firms in high labour cost countries would be increasingly free to relocate their operations and/or be in a strong bargaining position vis-à-vis their current workforce (or national authorities), exerting downward pressure on wages and working conditions;

3   It is sometimes assumed that individual states will be tempted to pursue a low-wage and perhaps even anti-union policies as part of a catch-up economic strategy.

While these concerns are widely shared, spokesmen for capital and labour differ in their policy conclusions. Whereas trade union representatives advocate compensating regulating at the European or international levels (e.g. through a 'social clause' in the GATT) in order to exclude certain basic standards from being factors in competition, employers' representatives generally emphasize the necessity of controlling labour costs in the light of competitive conditions not only by moderating wage demands but also by welfare state retrenchments and labour market deregulation.

This pessimistic scenario in which social competition puts welfare states at risk is open to criticism on a number of points. Although any effort to assess the threat to the welfare state that European economic integration entails is inevitably speculative, it does seem possible to provide some approximation of the order of magnitude of the problem by examining some of the scenario's assumptions: How much do EU welfare states differ

187

in their level of provision? Is there a clear hierarchy in social protection or are there different social policy dimensions with different rank orders, for example, among levels of social security provision and protective labour legislation regulating employment contracts or working time? How are social programmes financed and in particular what share of overall financing is borne by employers? How important are such 'social costs' for international competitiveness in relationship to other factors? To what extent is a higher cost 'social constitution' of employment associated with offsetting competitive advantages? What historical trends are observable in the EU's first 35 years and has there been an EU effect?

Regime diversity: multiple dimensions

Welfare state spending There is considerable diversity in social security expenditures as a percentage of GDP (see Table 8.1). It is especially the new Member States (Spain, Portugal, Greece) that show markedly lower levels of expenditure, whereas The Netherlands, Belgium, France, Denmark and the Federal Republic of Germany are high expenditure countries. These national differences are even more dramatic (at the extreme almost four to one) when expressed in terms of per capita expenditures at purchase price parities. Generally the data reflect not a North/South but rather a center-periphery (Greece, Ireland, Portugal and Spain) pattern. Welfare state effort is greatest in the wealthier core countries of the European Community, as measured by per capita GDP.

Welfare state financing The potential welfare state 'burden' on competitiveness via labour costs is a function not only of the level of welfare state spending but also of differences in the mode of financing. While some countries such as Spain, Italy and France rely heavily on employers' contributions to finance social security, others - most notably Ireland and especially Denmark - have primarily state-financed systems (see Table 8.1). The relative burden directly placed on employers is frequently highest in Mediterranean countries with otherwise lower levels of welfare state effort. The potential impact of this institutional factor can be illustrated by calculating the employers' GDP share of social protection expenditures (total expenditures multiplied by the employers' share in financing), which yields a rank order quite different from that based on welfare state spending as a percentage of GDP. France and Italy place the highest (relative) welfare burden on employers as a percentage of GDP and Denmark by far the lowest. Some welfare state laggards, most notably Spain and Portugal, move up on this index, with Spain actually approaching Germany and the Netherlands because of the high percentage share of costs borne directly by employers.

188

These observations cast doubt on any simple notions of 'unfair' competition within the EU between welfare state 'leaders' and 'laggards' since the mode of financing also has important implications for costs and competitiveness. Indeed governments may be tempted to shift the burden of social security financing, which in many countries accounts for one third or more of total labour costs, toward the state and general revenues in order to improve their competitive position. State financing clearly shifts the incidence of taxation away from employers and the factor labour and, in some forms (e.g. value added taxes), away from export goods (Commission 1993).

The actual incidence of security costs, which may be shifted forward to consumers or backward to employees, is in fact difficult to assess. Moreover, it may be argued on theoretical grounds that, in the long run, the division of social security financing shares between employers and employees does not affect the total wage bill. Even on this view, increases in these charges, which have been frequent, probably will. Furthermore, this argument has an interesting implication that is discussed below, namely, that welfare state provision may in the first instance affect only the form (public versus private) and not the level of costs and compensation.

Protective labour legislation   Quite a different picture emerges if we compare European welfare states in terms of the relatively neglected dimension of protective labour legislation (e.g. employment protection regulations, restrictions on fixed-term or temporary employment, notice and severance pay requirements.) Although regulatory measures in the labour market were the initial form of welfare state intervention, it has become identified with transfer programmes in the post World War II era. Since regulatory interventions do not entail public expenditures, their impact is underestimated by expenditure data (Mosley 1994b).

Regulatory interventions are still relatively more important in some European countries, particularly in some of the institutionally less developed states of the 'Latin rim' (Leibfried 1990). It is Mediterranean countries such as Italy, Greece, Spain and Portugal with below average levels of welfare state expenditure that frequently impose the heaviest regulatory burdens in the labour market, whereas Denmark and the UK are the states with the lowest level of regulatory restraint (Table 8.3, see Emerson 1988, Mosley 1993b, Mosley 1994a, OECD 1994). For example, Greece, Italy, Portugal and Spain (along with the Netherlands) are among the states with the most severe restraints on dismissals with three of them (Greece, Portugal, and Spain) requiring prior authorization of collective redundancies by public labour market authorities. Although all EU States have some type of notice and severance pay requirements, there is considerable variation in the level of protection provided (and the costs imposed on employers). The average entitlement to statutory compensation ranged from a high of 45 weeks' pay in Italy, 43 weeks in Spain, and 29 in Greece to a low 8 weeks of pay in Ireland.

Other areas of labour market regulation important for international competitiveness show a similarly complex pattern. For example, regulation of working time, including both individual work schedules and the operating hours of plant and equipment, vary greatly, and flexibility in working time is often greater in the core high-wage high-benefit countries of the European Union (Bosch, Dawkins, Michon 1994, Carolath 1988).

In summary, the multiple dimensions of the welfare state examined indicate that - contrary to a principal assumption of the 'social dumping' thesis - there is in fact no simple hierarchy in Europe with regard to the costs and restraints imposed by welfare states on enterprises.

Private versus public provision

Differences in welfare state expenditures are not necessarily reflected in employers' labour costs. A higher public 'social wage' may reflect merely the allocation of a larger share of total labour costs to indirect compensation in the form of social security or other social services. Moreover, there is clearly a trade off between public and private social programmes in which the former represent an alternative form of institutionalization of social provision (Mosley 1983, Rein and Rainwater 1986). For example, the relative underdevelopment of the welfare state in the US and UK is offset, in part, by a greater development of employer-financed schemes.

Other factors in competitiveness

Competitiveness depends not merely on (indirect and direct) wages but on productivity-adjusted compensation. A key question is the extent to which the prevailing levels of labour productivity are able to sustain higher levels of wages and welfare in the most advanced economies of the European Community (Pfaller, Gough, and Therborn 1989). Productivity is of course a complicated result of numerous factors that affect competitiveness in product markets and in the locational decisions of firms: infrastructure, qualifications of the labour force, industrial relations climate, proximity to customers and suppliers, research and education centers, political stability, etc. The social competition paradigm, like much public debate, places an undue emphasis on labour costs as a factor in competitiveness (Mosley and Schmid 1993).

Is the welfare state only a competitive burden?

Discussions of the relationship between the welfare state and competitiveness focuses too often on the supposed 'welfare burden'. Although the direct beneficiaries or 'users' of public social services and social security programmes are, in most instances, not firms but individuals, it would be erroneous to regard such programmes as representing merely public consumption or redistribution. The greater part of such expenditures, i.e. for education, health, labour market services (training, placement, information services, etc.) and social security programmes, are closely related functionally to the labour market and production. It is generally recognized that this is the case for education and training systems. Other types of social programmes also supply (or finance) services which, in the absence of public programmes, would in many cases have to be directly purchased by firms in the form of employee benefits (Mosley and Schmid 1993).

Public provision of welfare state services is relevant not only to equity considerations but also to efficiency and competitiveness. This point can be illustrated by the example of public health insurance, or the lack of it, in the United States. Although the lack of a public health insurance system in the US means that public (welfare state) health expenditures are relatively low (4.6 per cent of GDP in 1987, OECD 1990), the health costs of American workers are in fact largely borne by employer-financed company health care programmes, which currently insure an estimated 136 million workers and their family members. By most accounts this health care system has the distinction of being not only inequitable (i.e. ca. 30 million uninsured persons) but also patently inefficient. The fact that cost of health care services - one of the industry's largest cost components - are significantly higher in the USA than in Canada has led the US auto industry to become an important advocate of public health insurance. According to Chrysler's former chairman, Lee Iacocca, the company's health care costs averaged 700 dollars per vehicle in the US but only 233 dollars in Canada (Financial Times, September 1, 1989).

How can this difference in costs be explained? The following factors illustrate the potential for rationalization of service provision, cost containment and conflict avoidance in publicly organized social services (Kosterlitz 1989a and 1989b, Mosley and Schmid 1993).

1   A unified national health insurance programme exhibits important economies of scale in contrast to the fragmented and competitive public (Medicare, Medicaid), private, and employer-based US system. For example, an estimated fifteen to twenty per cent of US health care expenditures are for administrative costs compared to two to three per cent in Canada. Moreover, in contrast to competitive

191

private carriers, there are no sales costs or profit mark-ups.

2   As the sole purchaser of health care services the government is better able to constrain costs than in the fragmented and competitive US system by negotiating doctor's and hospital fees, limiting the availability of certain kinds of health care providers, services, and high technology medical equipment. Doctors and dentists not only earn less than in the entrepreneurial US system, but their numbers are also limited (on the theory that medical services are supply driven). Hospital occupancy rates and the utilization of specialized high-tech equipment are higher.

3   Since corporate health plans usually commit the company to supply certain services, their actual costs are in part unpredictable, depending on the rise in costs for such services. The reliance on employer-based health programmes means that the firms become the locus of conflicts over health care costs: efforts of US companies to cut back health care costs have been important factors in many industrial conflicts in recent years. Health insurance was a major issue in work stoppages affecting 78 per cent of all striking workers in 1989.

Trends in European welfare state expenditure

Past trends in the development of the welfare states of the European Community show a distinctive regional pattern, particularly in the case of the six original Member States. Table 8.3 summarizes data on social security expenditures as a percentage of gross domestic product (GDP) over the period 1950-86. This measure of welfare state effort provides comparable data based on ILO definitions but of course fails to include developments in the social regulation of employment (e.g. working time regimes, employment protection, employee representation, etc.), on which information is less readily available. Overall the data show a strong and general upward trend in welfare state effort in both EU and OECD states as a whole (measured in terms of expenditures on GDP) during the postwar up until 1975, slower growth between 1975 and 1980, and thereafter stagnation and decline. Within the European Community there was an initial trend toward convergence in the rates of social spending in the 1950s and 1960s for the six original EU states (as measured by the coefficient of variation). This trend, which is already broken in 1970, is reversed after 1975 under the impact of the economic crisis and above all the expansion of the original six-nation EU to include states with markedly lower rates of social spending (the UK and Ireland after 1973 and especially Greece, Portugal and Spain in the 1980s). For the EU as a whole, the impact of its expansion from six to twelve states clearly outweighs any internal dynamic.

Separate examination of the development of expenditures in the original six EU-states shows them to be a decidedly homogeneous group with a markedly higher average rate (mean) of social spending on GDP over the entire period in contrast to the OECD as a whole (or even the expanded EU-12). The earlier pattern of convergence from 1950 to 1965 comes to an end in the 1970s and appears to have stabilized at a low level (as indicated by the coefficient of variation) in contrast to the OECD, or the expanded EU-12. The relative homogeneity of the levels of social expenditure for the original EU-6 group and earlier pattern of convergence appear to largely predate the impact of the Common Market itself (established in 1958). In both the EU and the OECD as a whole economic growth appear to be the principal determinant of the rising level of welfare state expenditures and there is no apparent evidence for a retarding effect of European economic integration on welfare state effort. Among the EU-6, the earlier phase of convergence and later divergence also coincides with the period of relatively higher economic growth in the 1950s and 1960s and the generally slower growth particularly after 1973, suggesting again that broader economic parameters have been of overriding importance. The EU, and especially the old EU-6, are distinctive groups of states with a lower level of dispersion of welfare state effort than in the OECD as a whole. Until the membership of Spain and Portugal, mean welfare state expenditures were also higher in the EU, and remain so for the core six. On the basis of these past trends, we find no evidence that the Common Market itself has been a significant causal factor in the development of European welfare states. However, the past expansion of the EU to include twelve quite diverse Member States (and future plans to include not only EFTA but East European states) as well as the surge in economic integration now taking place may make past experience an unreliable guide.

Conclusions

Our survey suggests that concerns about 'social dumping' as a form of welfare state regime competition within the EU are exaggerated. While direct welfare state costs now constitute a large proportion of GDP (non-wage labour costs now average almost 40 per cent of total labour costs in the EU), their prospective impact on international competitiveness depends first of all on national differentials in levels of social expenditure. These differentials are in fact not great for the six original core states of the European Community, which display a high degree of regional homogeneity in this and other respects (in comparison with the OECD as a whole or

193

the expanded EU). The differentials are relatively large only for the three least developed Mediterranean states (Greece, Portugal and Spain), as are wage cost differentials. The potential impact of these new differentials within the European Union is offset by the small size of these economies, relative to the EU as a whole, and by these states' overwhelming disadvantages in other factors important to productivity and competitiveness.

The impact of the protective labour legislation component of welfare states further complicates the picture. Again some Mediterranean countries that score lower on overall welfare (spending) effort score higher on this measure of welfare state standards and some big spenders both within and outside of the EU score low. Thus Italy has by far the most stringent regulatory constraints, while France and Spain are at least as strict as Germany, and the UK and Denmark appear to have the least regulated labour markets. Other labour market regulations (e.g. working time) further complicate the picture in the area of regulatory intervention.

If all dimensions of the welfare state are taken into account, any hierarchy that exists in the overall 'burden' on enterprises is difficult to discern since these different dimensions are cross-cutting rather than congruent.

Last but not least, the simplistic notion of welfare state as merely a competitive burden is clearly mistaken. To a large extent welfare state social services and income maintenance programmes represent not additional social protection (and costs) but an alternative to private provision. Moreover, as the example of health care illustrates, public provision may, in many cases, be superior on efficiency as well as on equity grounds.

Lest my message be misunderstood as being too sanguine, it should be emphasized that this essay addresses only the limited issue of 'social dumping', i.e. the thesis that European economic integration poses a significant threat to national standards of social protection. We found that this argument rests on questionable assumptions and that past trends provide no plausible evidence for a retarding effect of European economic integration on social protection.

While social benefits and protective labour legislation are on the ideological defensive even in Germany and in other older EU welfare states (particularly Belgium, the Netherlands and Great Britain), we do not think European economic integration has been a significant cause. These trends appear to be rooted in broader economic changes (especially slower growth and resulting fiscal constraints), in the social structure (especially the shift toward a post-industrial service and information society), and in the rightward shift in the ideological and political center of gravity in the 1980s (Cusack 1994). Traditional regulatory and transfer programmes of the welfare state were already being reassessed even prior to the recent surge in European economic integration and this has been occurring outside (e.g. in the US or Sweden) as well as within the European Union.

194

Table 8.1

Social protection expenditures in the European Union, 1991

Country	GDP (per cent)	Per capita (ECU)	Financing shares (per cent)			
			Employers	Employees	Government	Other (a)
Belgium	27.60	4374.10	40.52	24.45	22.83	12.20
France (b)	28.50	4826.00	52.17	22.73	16.69	8.41
Germany	27.00	5446.30	40.24	21.93	26.24	11.59
Italy	24.60	4035.20	51.39	10.44	30.06	8.11
Luxembourg	27.60	5385.10	31.11	18.72	39.41	10.76
Netherlands	32.50	5049.40	19.98	31.19	24.01	24.82
Denmark (b)	30.70	6284.40	8.73	4.78	79.78	6.71
Ireland	20.90	2141.40	23.93	13.79	60.09	2.19
United Kingdom	24.70	3491.50	27.14	15.06	41.82	15.98
Greece	20.20	1124.90	47.79	26.99	16.42	8.80
Portugal	19.90	1085.70	45.33	19.90	27.69	7.08
Spain	21.70	2374.10	53.09	8.76	26.95	11.20
EU unweighted average	25.49	3801.51	36.79	18.23	34.33	10.65

Source: Eurostat, Social Protection Expenditure and Receipts, Tables 1, 6.2, and 4.3B (Denmark)

Notes:

(a) "Other" includes contributions by other protected persons (e.g. pensioners and self-employed) as well as miscellaneous and otherwise unallocated receipts.

(b) Financing data for France = 1990, Denmark = 1989.

Table 8.2
Regulatory labour market constraints in EU States

Country	Working time	Fixed-term contracts	Employment protection	Minimum wages	Employee representation rights	Synthetic index
Greece	2	1	2	2	1	8
Italy	1	2	2	2	0	7
Spain	2	1	2	2	0	7
France	1	1	1	2	1	6
Germany	1	1	1	1	2	6
Netherlands	1	0	1	1	2	5
Belgium	0	1	1	1	1	4
Ireland	2	0	2	0	0	4
Portugal	1	1	1	1	0	4
Denmark	0	0	0	0	2	2
United Kingdom	0	0	0	0	0	0

Source: OECD, 1994

Notes:

2 = strong; 1 = intermediate; 0 = weak. Synthetic index is sum of individual ratings.

Table 8.3

Social security expenditures as a percentage of GDP in EU and OECD States, 1950 to 1986

Country	1950	1955	1960	1965	1970	1975	1980	1981	1982	1983	1984	1985	1986
Belgium	11.6	13.0	15.3	16.1	18.1	24.0	26.2	27.5	27.5	28.5	27.2	26.4	26.4
France	11.5	10.7	13.2	15.8	15.1	23.9	26.3	27.9	28.8	28.9	29.0	28.7	28.6
Germany	14.8	14.3	15.4	16.6	17.1	23.7	24.0	24.7	24.9	24.3	24.1	23.8	23.4
Italy	8.4	10.8	11.7	13.8	14.1	19.2	21.5	23.9	24.4	25.7	25.3	25.2	25.2
Luxembourg	10.8	13.4	13.4	14.9	14.9	21.1	24.5	26.5	26.5	25.4	24.2	23.4	23.4
Netherlands	8.0	8.3	11.1	15.5	18.9	25.5	28.3	29.7	31.3	31.4	30.6	29.1	28.6
Denmark	--	--	--	--	--	20.2	26.9	28.4	28.6	28.1	26.2	25.9	26.3
Ireland	--	--	--	--	--	19.0	20.1	20.7	22.4	23.1	22.3	22.8	23.2
United Kingdom	--	--	--	--	--	16.0	17.1	18.2	19.7	20.3	20.6	20.3	20.4
Greece	--	--	--	--	--	--	12.2	14.4	16.7	17.5	18.5	19.5	20.0
Portugal	--	--	--	--	--	--	--	--	--	--	--	10.1	10.4
Spain	--	--	--	--	--	--	--	--	--	--	--	18.4	18.1
Expanding EU: EU-6, EU-9, EU-12 States													
Standard deviation	2.26	2.03	1.62	0.90	1.77	2.91	4.78	4.72	4.24	4.00	3.52	5.02	4.90
Mean	10.85	11.75	13.35	15.45	16.37	21.40	22.71	24.19	25.08	25.32	24.80	22.80	22.83
Coefficient of variation	0.21	0.17	0.12	0.06	0.11	0.14	0.21	0.19	0.17	0.16	0.14	0.22	0.21
Original six EU States only													
Standard deviation	2.26	2.03	1.62	0.90	1.77	2.10	2.14	1.96	2.35	2.45	2.44	2.21	2.15
Mean	10.85	11.75	13.35	15.45	16.37	22.90	25.13	26.70	27.23	27.37	26.73	26.10	25.93
Coefficient of variation	0.21	0.17	0.12	0.06	0.11	0.09	0.09	0.07	0.09	0.09	0.09	0.08	0.08
22 OECD States													
Standard deviation	--	--	3.26	3.91	--	5.23	6.29	6.70	6.60	6.48	6.47	6.24	--
Mean	--	--	10.16	11.26	--	17.25	19.31	20.24	20.90	21.26	21.05	21.05	--
Coefficient of variation	--	--	0.32	0.35	--	0.30	0.33	0.33	0.32	0.30	0.31	0.30	--

Sources: The Cost of Social Security, 13th International Inquiry, 1984-1986
(Geneva: ILO, 1992) and earlier editions. Greek data for 1986 and Italian data for 1980s extrapolated from Eurostat data on social expenditures.

References

Bosch, Gerhard, Peter Dawkins, and Francois Michon (1994), *Times Are Changing. Working Time in Fourteen Industrialised Countries*. ILO Publications, Geneva.

Carolath, Alexandra (1988), 'Arbeitszeitverkuerzung, Arbeitszeitflexibilisierung, Sonntagsarbeit im 19-Ländervergleich', *Recht der Arbeit* vol. 41.

Commission of the European Communities. (1993), *Growth Competitiveness, Employment: White Paper*, Office of Official Publications, Luxembourg.

Cusack, Thomas (1994), 'Economic problems in the OECD countries during the period 1950 through 1990', paper prepared for the WZB Workshop on 'Societal Problems, Political Structures, and Political Performance', March, Berlin.

Emerson, Michael (1988), 'Regulation or deregulation of the labor market', *European Economic Review*, vol. 32.

Kosterlitz. Julie (1989a), 'Taking care of Canada', *National Journal*.

Kosterlitz, Julie (1989b), 'But not for us?' *National Journal*.

Leibfried, Stephan (1990), 'Income transfers and poverty policy in EC perspective: On Europe's slipping into Anglo-American welfare models', paper presented to the EC-Seminar on 'Poverty Marginalisation and Social Exclusion in the Europe of the 1990s', Alghero, April.

McPherson, Kim (1990), 'International differences in medical care practices', in OECD 1990.

Mosley, Hugh (1983), 'Social security in the United States and in the Federal Republic of Germany', *Policy Studies Journal,* vol. 11.

Mosley, Hugh (1990), 'The social dimension of European integration', *International Labour Review*, vol. 129, no. 2.

Mosley, Hugh (1993), 'Employment protection in Europe',*InforMISEP Policies*, no. 44.

Mosley, Hugh (1994a), 'Employment protection and labor force adjustment in EC Countries', in Schmid, Günther (ed.) *Labor Market Institutions in Europe: A Socio-Economic Evaluation of Performance*, M.E. Sharpe, New York.

Mosley, Hugh (1994b), 'Employment protection in Europe: Regulatory trends, labor market impacts, regime competition', paper presented to the Ninth International Conference of Europeanists, March-April, Chicago.

Mosley, Hugh, and Günther Schmid (1993), 'Public services and competitiveness', in Hughes, Kirsty (ed.), *European Competitiveness*, Cambridge University Press, Cambridge.

OECD (1990), *Health Care Systems in Transition*, OECD, Paris.
OECD (1994), 'Labour Standards and Economic Integration', *Economic Outlook 1994*, OECD, Paris.
Pfaller, A., I. Gough, and G. Therborn (eds) (1989), *Can the Welfare State Compete?* Friedrich Ebert Stiftung, Bonn.
Rein, Martin, and Lee Rainwater (1986), *Public/Private Interplay in Social Protection: A Comparative Study*, M.E. Sharpe, Armonk, New York.

9 Poverty regimes and life chances: The road to anomia?

Godfried Engbersen

E U

I 32

I 38

P 16

Summary

H 53

In the 1980s the number of households living in poverty mushroomed in Europe. This rise had to do with the process of economic restructuring and the deterioration of welfare state arrangements. In this article three contemporary faces of modern European poverty are sketched. These sketches show the dynamics of social seclusion (the Netherlands), the creation of second class citizens (Great Britain) and growing racial tensions in multicultural neighbourhoods (France). Besides, attention is paid to the issue of illegal aliens. The author argues that the various faces of poverty are certain to merge in the near future, partly as a result of changes that take place within different European 'poverty regimes'. These changes reflect a convergent trend towards more minimal selective and provisional poverty regimes. As a consequence the life chances of many poor European citizens and newcomers will further deteriorate.

Poverty in Europe

There has recently been ample evidence of growing inequality in the Western welfare states (Wilterdink 1993). In the past decade, the differences between the rich and the poor have become greater. The income equalization brought about in the 1980s has come to a halt, and the reverse process would seem to have set in. The gap between the rich and the poor is only getting larger. This tendency toward greater social inequality in the West is reflected in the growing numbers of poor people. In the 1973-85 period, the percentage of poor people in the EC countries rose from 12.8 per cent to almost 14 per cent in 1985. This meant a rise in the number of poor people from almost 39,000,000 to 44,000,000 (Van der Ploeg 1990, O'Higgins and Jenkins 1989). More recent calculations indicated a total of 50,000,000 poor people in 1989. Transnational economic and demographic transformations and political policy shifts have influenced these income changes and the basic way national welfare states are set up and run. The quality of life of people in a vulnerable position in society has clearly deteriorated. This mainly pertains to 'flexible' workers who are unskilled or poorly educated, the unemployed, single-parent families, the disabled and other groups dependent on social benefits. Three developments should be cited here.

Firstly, Western economies have undergone a process of economic restructuring, manifesting itself in the negligible significance of industrial labour. De-industrialization has had severe ramifications for the regions, cities and inner cities unable to compensate for the loss of industrial jobs by an increase in other jobs. The economic restructuring has given rise to growing labour insecurity in Europe's welfare states, as is expressed in high rates of long term unemployment and growing numbers of part-time, temporary and flexible jobs. A new generation of workers no longer has the prospect of a steady job, but of a career of ups and downs at temporary and often poorly paid jobs. This segmentation of the labour market leads to insecurity in other aspects of life as well, as is evident from the return of poverty to Great Britain (Townsend 1979, 1993), France (Paugam 1991), Germany (Leibfried and Tennstedt 1985) and the Netherlands (Engbersen and Van der Veen 1987).

Secondly, newcomers have changed the face of large metropolises, with multicultural cities evolving in relatively homogeneous European countries. At the end of 1990, there were 800,000 refugees in the European Community, and in the 1980s, the total number of official requests for asylum rose from 160,000 in 1980 to more than 400,000 in 1990 (Refugee Work 1991). The arrival of refugees and people requesting asylum led the countries of Western Europe to tighten their admission policies, although in many cases this has not enabled them to gain adequate control over the migration patterns. In some countries, such as Italy, there has been large scale illegal immigration. In addition, the integration of migrants who have already settled and of new refugees entails various problems. Many of them are now unemployed or disabled, and their children tend to have a hard time finding a place for themselves on the labour market. In the Netherlands, eight per cent of the unemployed were of non-Dutch descent in 1980, but by 1992 the figure had risen to almost twenty-five per cent. There are now inner city districts more than half populated by people of foreign descent, many of whom are unemployed. These districts have increasingly been the target of xenophobia and racism, though their severity and frequency varies widely from country to country.

201

Thirdly, budget cuts affected the implementation of social policies in the 1980s, which came to be known as the decade of the welfare state crisis. In various countries, the level of the various welfare arrangements was reduced, be it to a limited extent. Albert (1988) and Pierson (1991) put the notion of the welfare state being dismantled into the proper perspective. They noted that although the growth of social expenditures stagnated in the 1980s, only four of the OECD countries reduced their social expenditures (the United States, Canada, Germany and the Netherlands). Albert referred to the 1980s as a period of consolidation instead of crisis, and Pierson felt the crisis of the welfare state was mainly an 'intellectual crisis' (Pierson 1991: 177). This intellectual crisis was reflected in altered ideas on social policies. In the 1990s, the debate on the welfare state crisis entered a new stage. The rhetoric of retrenchment became reality. Labour market, social security, and migration policy became tougher and more restrictive. The term 'crisis' was no longer as prominent, and was replaced by references to 'limitations' or 'borders' (see De Swaan 1994). While the discussions of the 1960s and 1970s mainly focused on the 'internal' margins of national states (Hirsch 1977), at the moment the claim is increasingly made that national states are confronted with 'external' limitations. Alongside transnational processes (migration, economic restructuring), there are the developments within the European Community (the emergence of a common market). National social protection would seem to be a costly liability in the competition on the internal European market. In efforts to improve or maintain their competitive position, Member States are cutting down on the services provided by their national social protection systems.

It has mainly been these three developments that led to Europe's debates on 'new poverty' and 'social exclusion', or on the emergence of 'ghettos', and the coming into existence of a European 'underclass'. Despite the similarity in the choice of topics, the emphasis is different in each country. In the Netherlands, the subject of labour participation in relation to social security fraud occupies a central position. In Great Britain, various authors have made references to growing class differences and the phenomenon of second class citizens, and in France there is growing concern about resentment toward people of foreign descent and the growth of ghettos. As we shall see, these national debates are informed in part by the structural features of the national 'poverty regimes'.

In addition to this selective attention focused on specific themes, one topic that keeps coming up in the debates is 'poverty'. Even the most superficial examination does, however, reveal certain dissimilarities in how poverty manifests itself in various parts of Europe. In order to comprehend the meaning of poverty, insight into the social context is required. I shall try to make it clear what poverty means in three different welfare states. By focusing on developments in the social assistance schemes ('welfare'), the issue of convergence and divergence will be addressed. One recurrent theme is the relation between the poverty regimes and the life chances of vulnerable Europeans. In this connection, I make use of Dahrendorf's concept 'life chances' (see section 3).

Social protection in Europe

According to figures compiled by Eurostat in Luxembourg, in 1990 there were 50,000,000 poor people in the twelve EC Member States. This includes everyone with an income fifty per cent below average in any specific country. Of course there are vast national differences, and a woman on social assistance in even the poorest section of Amsterdam is relatively better off than one in Brixton in London or on the outskirts of Napels. These differences among the poor of Europe are based in part upon the extent of social protection which the nations provide their citizens with. (Social protection pertains to illness, disability, old age, widows and orphans, families and unemployment. The Eurostat definition also includes supplementary pensions and rent subsidies.) Table 9.1 gives a general impression, and shows that the Netherlands spends 32.1 per cent of its gross national product on social protection as compared with 22.8 per cent in Great Britain and 28.4 per cent in France. This means the Netherlands spends the highest percentage in the EC. It is striking that with the exception of Spain and Greece, the various countries reduced their expenditures for social protection as percentage of the gross national product in the 1984-90 period.

These aggregated figures are only a slight indication of the capacity of the welfare state's *safety net*, mostly referred to as social assistance, public assistance or welfare. Due to (long term) unemployment, people often have to turn to the Welfare Department for protection, and here too there are clear differences in the systems. I mention only seven of them (Schutte 1991). These differences are based upon the situation in 1991.

1   In Belgium, Denmark, Germany, France, Ireland, Luxembourg and the Netherlands, everyone has an individual right to a guaranteed minimum income, but in Greece, Italy, Portugal and Spain, this only holds true for specific categories of the population.

2   In the group of countries where everyone has a right to a guaranteed minimum income, there is a difference between countries with a universal social assistance scheme such as Germany and the Netherlands and countries where the right to social assistance is guaranteed under specific conditions such as France.

3   There is a distinction between countries that mainly provide income such as Belgium, the Netherlands and Great Britain, and countries where social security benefits are accompanied by 'activating' or 'integrating' measures (training, work experience, counseling) to help make recipients of social assistance benefits more independent, such as Denmark, France and Germany.

4   There are differences in the degree of legislation, particularly the extent to which instructions are stipulated in detail, the discretionary competence of officials enforcing the legislation, and the existence of an appeal structure. Germany is uncompromising and strict in this respect, whereas Denmark and the Netherlands are more lenient.

5   There are differences in how centralized social assistance systems are. Great Britain, the Netherlands and Belgium have centralized systems, and the central governments exert a great deal of influence on the legislation, financing and administration of social assistance benefits. In Germany, this is much less the case. There the municipalities bear more of the responsibility for funding and managing the social assistance system.

6   There are differences in how high benefits are. Table 9.2 shows that in absolute amounts, the minimum benefits are relatively high in Denmark and the Netherlands. In the Netherlands, as compared with Germany or France, there is less of a disparity between the minimum and the average income. Thus it is not surprising that the Netherlands should score favourably in the European study on poverty. The countries that scored lowest include Spain, Greece and Portugal.

7   One last difference pertains to the duration of social security benefits. No adequate comparative figures are available, though there are figures on long term unemployment in OECD countries. After all, depending on the duration of their employment in the past, the long term unemployed run the risk of becoming dependent on social assistance benefits. Table 9.4 demonstrates that, compared with other countries, long term unemployment is relatively high in the Netherlands.

Poverty regimes as institutionalized life chances

The figures shown above inspired Leibfried (1991) to describe various *poverty regimes*. The term refers to the interrelation between social security and labour market policies and pertains to much more than merely the protection of the poor. In view of the focus of this chapter, however, I will continue to use the term poverty regime. Leibfried described four poverty regimes: (1) modern welfare states, (2) institutional welfare states, (3) residual welfare states, and (4) rudimentary welfare states. Thus he too contributed to the present-day proliferation of typologies to describe the wide range of national welfare states. The first three regimes coincide with the social democratic, corporatist and liberal welfare states described by Esping-Andersen (1990).

The rudimentary welfare state differs from the residual or liberal welfare state in that it does not recognize the right to social security. Leibfried referred to the situation in countries like Greece, Spain, Italy and Portugal. There are however similarities between the rudimentary poverty regime in the Latin rim countries and the other poverty regimes. There is for example the residual nature of some local services and the link with the care provided by the church in liberal welfare states. The Latin rim countries differ from the residual welfare states in that the family and church play a far more salient role in the provision of care, and there is a much larger (mainly rural) subsistence economy, an informal economy in which people can work to help make ends meet. One fundamental problem in the rudimentary welfare states is the absence of an administrative implementation system to keep the promises formulated in their constitutions. As Leibfried wrote, '(...) many of these countries have made strong promises pointing towards a "modern welfare state" in their constitutions; it is the legal, institutional and social implementation which seems to be lacking in the "Latin rim"' (Leibfried 1991: 19).

These poverty regimes can be viewed as institutionalized life chances. They make provisions for the protection of the poor and the alleviation of their problems. The term life chances goes back to the work of Max Weber. I use the term as Dahrendorf defined it in *Life Chances*, i.e. as 'opportunities for individual development provided by social structure' (1979: 28). Life chances are a function of two interrelated dimensions: options and ligatures. The first dimension, options, pertains to structural possibilities for making choices. In *The Modern Social Conflict* (1988), Dahrendorf mainly elaborated upon this dimension in terms of entitlements. In welfare states where social rights are unconditionally guaranteed, vulnerable groups have the most possibilities for social integration.

However, Dahrendorf felt that the options of citizens only acquire significance if they are embedded in patterns of social bonds. To refer to this second dimension of life chances, he used the term ligatures:

> Ligatures are allegiances; one might call them bonds or linkages as well. By virtue of his social position and roles, the individual is

placed into bonds or ligatures (...) the element of ligatures signifies meaning, the anchoring of persons and their actions, whereas options emphasize the objective and horizon of action" (Dahrendorf 1979: 30-1).

The dimension of ligatures not only represents the social basis, it refers to the moral dimension of human conduct. In his later work, Dahrendorf drew a link between the dimension of ligatures and the notion of a new social contract. In *Life Chances*, the terms options and ligatures were both mainly used for a cultural critique of the development of modern society. Traditional family, town and country ties have been severed, abandoned in part and altered in part by the postwar welfare state. The altered social bonds have contributed to the expansion of the citizens' options. But there is also another side to it. The multiple choice society runs the risks of turning into a meaningless society, because the acts of its citizens are no longer embedded in patterns of meaningful ties.

In this chapter, I use Dahrendorf's conceptualization of life chances in an analysis of the various poverty regimes. In Dahrendorf's footsteps, I operationalize the options dimension in terms of entitlements or social rights and the ligatures dimension in terms of the span and inclusiveness of the social contract between social classes and interest groups (Dahrendorf 1988: 17 and 1985: 161). The reasoning is obvious. The more firmly social rights are anchored and the wider the span of the social contract and the range of people who bear it, the greater the life chances of the citizens.

If we apply this model to the four poverty regimes, we get the following picture. The modern or social democratic poverty regime scores highest on both dimensions. It is founded upon (enforced) solidarity among various social classes and economic sectors, and is thus characterized by the most comprehensive social contract between the various parties (the ligatures dimension). The modern poverty regime also scores high on the options dimension. Citizens are protected by a wide range of universal provisions. In addition, it is important that a right to work is guaranteed.

The institutional or corporatist poverty regime also has a relatively high score on both dimensions. A social contract has been worked out between various parties, which nonetheless leaves the existing social stratification unaffected. Thus the social contract is less inclusive; it can be disadvantageous for women, for example, as is illustrated by their low level of labour participation. The options dimension is mainly characterized by a right to income compensation for unemployment or disability. Corporatist poverty regimes can be generous when it comes to the level of income compensation, and here the Netherlands is an excellent example. Since in the end, benefits can not provide as much security as an income based upon labour, the institutional poverty regime scores lower than the social democratic one on the options dimension.

The residual or liberal poverty regime scores low on the ligatures dimension: in this regime, social solidarity and social compassion are restricted. Individual responsibility occupies a central position. The options dimension also has a low score. Social rights are only developed to a limited extent. The regime is selective, and benefits are only given to specific categories (the deserving poor).

The rudimentary poverty regime exhibits a similarly low score; the social contract is mainly with relatives and local care institutions. The family provides the major support and protection. The options dimension is also poorly developed; social rights have been developed to an even more limited extent than in the liberal welfare states.

The Dahrendorf model makes it clear that the life chances of the European poor are not equally distributed. This does not mean that in the modern or institutional poverty regimes, the poor have no problems, although comparative studies do show that the poor in the Netherlands or Sweden are better off than in Italy or Greece. The 'rich' countries nonetheless have specific poverty problems that have to be taken seriously.

In the following section, three different poverty debates and faces of European poverty are described. I confine myself to the situation in three European countries representing different types of regimes: the Netherlands (mixture of modern and institutional), Great Britain (residual) and France (institutional). I also focus on recent developments pertaining to the social assistance schemes. The three portraits are not based upon a systematic comparison. They are impressionist sketches of certain elements of the national poverty debates and of crucial changes within the national poverty regimes. The reason I chose these countries is that they reflect three dominant trends within different poverty regimes: a more selective access, lower benefits, and the provisional nature of the distribution of benefits. Taken together, these three 'welfare policy strategies' reflect a convergent trend toward a liberalization of European poverty regimes.

Three European faces of contemporary poverty

The Netherlands: modern poverty and social seclusion

In the mid-1980s, a debate commenced in the Netherlands about the return of poverty in the welfare state. Studies by the Rotterdam Municipal Welfare Department (Oude Engberink 1984) and activities on the part of a social movement called the 'Poor Side of the Netherlands' played central roles. The Dutch poverty discussion nonetheless remained a mini debate and was soon overshadowed by the discussion on labour participation.

Reports by the Netherlands Scientific Council for Government Policy (see WRR 1990) cleared the way for this discussion. In view of the magnitude of long term unemployment and the relatively low Dutch labour participation compared with other European countries, this was not surprising. In the early 1990s, the discussion on labour participation also addressed the misuse of the social security system. This stemmed from specific features of the Dutch poverty regime, i.e. the relatively easy access to benefits, the lenient administration and the lack of an active labour market policy (Engbersen et al. 1993). For example, the present-day composition of the population receiving social assistance benefits gives rise to a number of questions. More than 30 per cent of the people on social assistance benefits have been receiving them for five years or more. Almost 25 per cent of them are younger than 35, and almost 40 per cent are younger than 40 (Committee on the Administration of the National Assistance Act 1993). Many of these relatively young unemployed people have given up any hope of ever finding a job. The distance that has grown between many of them and the labour market was evident from recent efforts to alleviate the situation. Large efforts are required to lead young, healthy people on social assistance back to the labour market (Dercksen and Engbersen 1992).

Despite the fact that the social position of people with minimum benefits, who have no chance on the labour market and are unable to earn extra money by working informally, has worsened in recent years, the debates on labour participation and the misuse of social security benefits have thrust the problem of poverty into the background.

Modern poverty in the Netherlands can be described as the structural social exclusion from dominant institutions accompanied by permanent or long term dependence on the care of the state (Engbersen 1991). Although financial problems do play a role in the lives of poor people, financial deprivation is not the most decisive feature of poverty in the Netherlands. A closer examination of the features of modern poverty shows that the emphasis has shifted from the material dimensions to the social ones, in particular to non-participation in labour, leisure activities and schooling combined with long term dependence on the state in many aspects of life (income, housing, health care, legal aid). It would seem as if the structure and implementation of the social security system have contributed toward the emergence of modern poverty. The majority of the modern poor are not familiar with the peace of mind the welfare state was designed to provide. Numerous studies have demonstrated that in the long run, dependence on the state only leads to social isolation and alienation.

Modern poverty can be geographically localized. The inner cities house a concentration of people on social security benefits, many of whom are of foreign descent. Poverty has increasingly become intertwined with the issue of people of foreign descent. At the moment, a quarter of the unemployed are of non-Dutch descent. This is almost four times as many as might be expected on the grounds of the composition of the population of the Netherlands.

Despite the rising unemployment rates and continual waves of newcomers, this has not led to public outbursts of Dutch versus non-Dutch groups on a scale comparable to what has been happening in Germany, Great Britain or France. Instead there has been a gradual social seclusion of certain poor groups from the mainstream of Dutch society (Engbersen et al. 1993).

The most important steps to combat poverty and inner city decline were initially taken at the local level. National efforts were made toward a policy of 'social innovation', but the results have been disappointing. At the moment, Dutch welfare policies are in a state of transition. Access to social assistance benefits is being made more selective, in particular for young people, and the level of the benefits is being reduced, especially for single people. At the same time, more funding is being made available for 'activating labour market policy'. Up to now, in comparison with other countries in Europe, the Dutch expenditures for these purposes have been low (De Neuborg 1992: 326).

Great Britain: class differences and second class citizens

The British poverty debate of the 1980s commenced with the study by Townsend, *Poverty in the United Kingdom* (1979). Initially an academic debate, in the mid-1980s it grew into a public debate. The Archbishop of Canterbury's report on urban poverty and the 1981 and 1985 riots played a definite role in this respect. Key words in the British debate have been 'citizenship' and 'deprivation', and to a lesser extent 'underclass'. In Great Britain, 'citizenship' is frequently used in reference to Marshall and his work. British society is said to have become an 'exclusive society' (Lister 1990) where specific categories of citizens have insufficient social rights. The British case differs from the Dutch in that not only is long term dependence on benefits a central problem there, the *exclusion* from them is even more of a problem. The level of the benefits was reduced in the 1980s, and access to other welfare state arrangements, particularly state-subsidized housing, has become more selective. As Logan et al. wrote, 'the welfare safety net has been withdrawn from some social groups' (Logan, Taylor-Gooby and Reuter 1992: 141). Indeed, according to official standards, almost 30 per cent of the 6,000,000 residents of Greater London live in poverty, and on one particular night in July 1989, approximately 75,000 people had to sleep on the streets (Logan et al. 1992: 136-138).

In the 1980s, the level and duration of unemployment insurance were reduced and there was a shift from unemployment insurance to means-tested social assistance benefits. Criteria for appropriate employment were expanded and criteria for granting social assistance benefits became stricter. The recent Dutch measures making unemployed schoolleavers no longer eligible for social assistance benefits were introduced in Great Britain as early as 1988. As Jacobs wrote,

Unemployment has increasingly come to mean poverty, stigmatization, reliance not only on means-tested benefits such as income support but through that also on the iniquitous social fund, where there are virtually no entitlements, only discretion, and no independent appeal' (Jacobs 1993: 71).

The barbed tone in analyses by poverty specialists can be accounted for by the rise in social inequality. Table 9.5 shows that in Great Britain, the distance between rich and poor increased in the 1980s on a scale comparable to that in the United States.

A focus on the material deprivation of the poor is characteristic of many of the British poverty analyses. The results of various poverty studies that work with deprivation indices are striking in this respect. Many British households do without basics like food and clothing that are taken for granted by the Dutch modern poor (see Mack & Lansley 1984, Townsend 1993).

British sociologists mainly analyze problems of poverty and inequality in terms of class. Thus a concept like underclass has been incorporated into the general class typologies. The British differ in this way from many of their American colleagues, who tend to assume poverty and inequality are based upon individual shortcomings or cultural and ethnic factors (Mead 1992, Jencks 1991). We also see that race and ethnicity still play a modest role in the analyses on poverty and inequality, though it is more of a role than in the Netherlands. The relatively homogeneous nature of British society is the underlying reason for this. However, the ethnic factor is more frequently addressed in studies on the social and economic dynamics of the London metropolis (see Cross & Waldinger 1992). In her evaluation of the British poverty debate, Silver nonetheless concluded that '(...) the social construction of the British new poor emphasizes not race, but employment, working class fragmentation, and a Marshallian conception of citizenship' (1993: 18).

France: ghetto formation and racial tension in the cités

In the 1960s and 1970s, several important poverty studies were published in France (see Klanfer 1965, Lenoir 1974). In the 1980s, despite growing concern about the unemployment rates, the debate on poverty and social exclusion subsided. At the end of the 1980s and in the early 1990s, urban riots and racial tension in Lyon and Paris served to revive the poverty debate. Problems of racism and nationalism - bearing in mind the political position of the *Front National* - were more emphatically linked to questions of immigration, unemployment and segregation. There was the fear that social problems would come to be viewed as ethnic ones, and that tension between the French and the non-French would polarize. The French press devoted ample attention to these problems, and even imported such American concepts as ghettos and the underclass. There were far more people of foreign descent residing in France than in the Netherlands. Second only to Germany, France had the second largest immigrant population in any of the European Community member countries: 3,752,200 in 1988 (Hollifield 1992: 38).

Questioning the wisdom of simply adopting an American frame of reference, the French sociologist Wacquant drew a comparison between the problems in the multicultural *cité* of La Courneuve, on the outskirts of Paris, and Woodlawn, a ghetto in Chicago. I would like to give a brief account of his analysis, because it so clearly illustrates the perimeters of poverty in France. The first relevant conclusion was that there were similarities in how the residents of the two areas perceived the problems, especially regarding feelings of insecurity, social inferiority, and a painful awareness of the stigma their neighbourhood entailed. There were also certain differences. The central problem in the French area, as in many Dutch ones, was the fragmentation of the traditional working class due to the disappearance of industrial jobs and the arrival of people of foreign descent. This led to racial tension. In America, hyper-ghettoization was the central theme: the radical exclusion of categories of Americans on the basis of race and class by the market and the state. Wacquant made it clear that the problems in La Courneuve were of a totally different nature than in Chicago. Woodlawn was much larger than the French neighbourhood, and was physically and socially much more closed off from the better neighbourhoods than La Courneuve. The same held true for the social problems in the two areas. Woodlawn had far more unemployed and homeless people than La Courneuve and its crime rate was substantially higher. There were more than twenty nationalities living in La Courneuve, but together they were still outnumbered by the French residents; the population of Woodlawn was completely racially segmented. One last difference pertained to the extent of state intervention. In Woodlawn, such public facilities as schools, health care centers, and public transport were barely in evidence or had dramatically deteriorated in quality. This was not the case in La Courneuve. Wacquant even referred to an 'over-penetration' of public agencies focused on the problems of the residents.

In part, the phenomenon of French poverty coincides with the Dutch one, particularly as regards unemployment and social security dependence, and the resulting problems of financial deprivation and social isolation. As in the Netherlands, not everyone in France who is dependent on social security lives in poverty. French studies have also noted calculating behaviour on the part of specific categories of people, and implementation practices that promote the perpetuation of social security dependence (Paugam 1991). Up to now, one important difference with the Netherlands has been that in France ethnicity plays a more prominent role in the analyses of poverty and racial tension.

A striking aspect of the French situation, unlike the British one, is that at the end of the 1980s the social problems in the *cités* led to large scale government efforts to alleviate them. A Ministry of Urban Affairs was founded, and via a broad approach it addressed the problems in 400 selected areas. In 1989 a guaranteed national minimum income (*revenu minimum d'insertion*) was introduced, and extra funding was reserved to launch an active labour market policy focused on the long term unemployed and on young people. For years, France has effectuated a more active labour market policy than the Netherlands. The percentage of the French labour market policy expenditures that are spent on active measures is above the European average, whereas the Dutch percentage is below the average (Swinnen 1993: 287). In France, categories of unemployed who submit a request for social assistance benefits sign a 'reintegration contract' stipulating their rights and obligations. Recipients have to do certain things in return, such as doing work, attending a work experience programme, or receiving special vocational training (see the American concept of *workfare*).

In addition, 'social solidarity' programmes have been developed on the local level for people at risk of falling through the welfare state's safety net. In part, the French approach resembles the Dutch social innovation policy. At the moment, it is hard to assess to what extent - like in the Netherlands - it is more rhetoric than actual policy. We do see that in France, the effectiveness of the 'reintegration' policy is questioned (Castel 1994). Many social assistance recipients would not have a chance on the formal labour market and are at risk of being permanently caught in all kinds of circuits peopled by the jobless (see Swinnen 1993).

Beyond the poverty regimes: the issue of illegal aliens

In addition to the three faces of poverty presented above, there is a fourth one, the issue of illegal aliens. The characteristic feature of this category is that most illegal aliens live their lives *beyond* the national poverty regimes. In this sense, there is a definite convergence. There would seem to be an over-representation of illegal aliens in the Latin rim countries, particularly the south of Italy. Illegal aliens are often barely able, if at all, to rely on any form of social protection. With the presence of illegal aliens, various of the old manifestations of poverty have reappeared: exploitation, dependence, and extreme material and physical deprivation (Engbersen and Burgers 1994).

There are no reliable figures on illegal aliens in Europe today. Estimates for the Netherlands vary from 30,000 to 150,000 (Under-Secretary of Justice Kosto). Ever since 1989, the Amsterdam authorities have been working on the assumption that there were anywhere from 20,000 to 40,000 illegal aliens in Amsterdam. There have also been estimates of the numbers of illegal aliens employed in the various branches of industry. For example, the number of illegal aliens employed in the garment industry at illegal sweatshops throughout the Netherlands is estimated at 8,000. Even less information is available on the qualitative conditions illegal aliens live under in the Netherlands. For the time being, the only work at hand on the lifeworld of illegal aliens in the Netherlands is the study by Vos et al. (1991). It demonstrated that they are mainly young men who have done a variety of jobs in the past and have a poor command of the Dutch language. Financial reasons were their main motivation for coming to the Netherlands. Most of the jobs they can get are off the books, and are largely in the market gardening industry, the garment industry (especially the sweatshops), cleaning business or at restaurants, nightclubs and brothels. Vos et al discussed how they were exploited by the people who employed and housed them, and referred in particular to the working, housing and living conditions of illegal aliens from Turkey and Morocco. Illegal aliens often do hard physical labour, work very long hours and are poorly paid. Many of them are abominably housed but nonetheless pay relatively high rents, are unable to make use of health care facilities and, if they are out of a job, are completely dependent on the informal help of acquaintances, relatives, or private organizations.

The study on illegal aliens also demonstrated what the role was of networks of relatives and acquaintances as 'bridgeheads' or 'quartermasters' in finding jobs and housing. The social network approach in the study on migration illustrated how difficult it is to influence migration process by way of state regulation. The same conclusion was also drawn in political economy studies on transformations of economies and the effect they have on the job situation and working population of large cities. Sassen (1991) and Castells (1989) noted that a growing informal sector was inextricably connected to changes in the employment structure. In this approach, illegal aliens constitute a link in the 'logic of economic restructuring', with a sharp rise in the number of poorly paid jobs in large cities. In other words, in all probability illegal aliens will continue to be part of Western societies.

It is thus logical to assume that the harder it is to get jobs and social security benefits, the fiercer the competition between legal and illegal workers and between legal and illegal immigrants. The lower the benefits, the more of an incitement for this competition. It should be noted here that the assumption that illegal aliens keep wages down and endanger the jobs of legal local workers is questioned in various American studies. Some studies make it clear that illegal aliens need not have any negative effects on the wages of the local population. They also demonstrate that the presence of illegal aliens on the work force can contribute toward accelerated economic growth and the upsurge of some industrial sectors. In addition, illegal aliens can prod local workers into better paid jobs. This can pertain to jobs in sectors that have expanded in part as a result of the hard work of illegal aliens (see Portes and Rumbaut 1990: 236-8).

Convergent trends: The way to an anomic Europe?

If we examine the three poverty debates, we see that they are related to the specific poverty regimes and the particular and shared problems various countries are confronted with. The Dutch debate can be related to the relatively lenient benefit distribution regime, which combines easy access with a poorly developed activating labour market policy. As in the Netherlands, in Great Britain the specific poverty discourse and the phenomenon of poverty itself can be traced in part to features of the particular poverty regime, which is selective, restrictive and strict. A striking aspect of the French case is that up until 1989, there was no National Assistance Law. In France, the introduction of this law at the time of a crisis in employment led to a political debate about social and economic exclusion. The French debate was primarily inspired by concern about the social effects of immigration in combination with unemployment.

Besides, there is (especially) in France and the Netherlands a growing concern with regard to the shared problem of illegal migration. Until recently the policy concerning illegal immigrants was based on an (implicit) double objective. First, to combat the adverse effects of illegality, especially criminality. Second, to tolerate those illegal aliens who contribute to the economy and do no harm to society. Priority was given to the first objective. As a result of the growing concern about flows of illegal aliens coming to Europe the immigrant policy have become more restrictive. This recent 'hardening' of immigrant policy towards illegals makes it more difficult for illegals to integrate in Western societies. A more restrictive policy could have unintended consequences, such as the marginalization and criminalization of categories of illegals (see also Portes and Rumbaut 1990).

It is my opinion that the various faces of poverty are certain to merge in the future. There is already evidence of this: racial tension does not solely occur in the French *cités* and the same holds true for the growing class differences. This 'merging' is promoted by changes taking place within the poverty regimes. I use both of Dahrendorf's dimensions of life chances to try and make this clear.

Firstly, in many countries, the options dimension (social rights) is being restricted. If we confine ourselves to social assistance benefits, three trends can be discerned. Firstly, access to social assistance benefits is being made more *selective*, as in Great Britain. Secondly, the *level* is being reduced, for example of benefits for young and single people, as in the Netherlands. France is an interesting exception, for in 1989, rather than being reduced, social rights were expanded via the introduction of a guaranteed minimum income. This minimum income, which is means-tested, is however of a provisional nature. This then is the third trend, i.e. to make the right to benefits *provisional*. It is clear that this trend need not necessarily imply an income reduction. Experience has shown however that there are always unemployed people who refuse to meet the requirements, are thus not eligible for benefits, and choose other ways (begging, stealing) to support themselves (see Logan et al. 1992: 141).

These changes are taking place at a time of growing labour insecurity. In the Netherlands, the number of people receiving unemployment benefits throughout 1994 has been estimated at 700,000, a postwar record. Many people who either have or would like to have a job are having a hard time finding permanent employment. In particular, the institutional poverty regimes (Germany, France, the Netherlands) based upon the social insurance model have been weakened in the process. People whose position on the labour market is unstable or virtually non-existent are not able to adequately insure themselves against unemployment and illness, so that for their social protection, they are mainly dependent upon social assistance benefits. In many countries, however, the level of these benefits is being reduced. The three 'welfare policy strategies' (more selective access, lower benefits, of a more provisional nature) reflect the trend toward liberalization, especially if they occur simultaneously. This liberalization is not only taking place within the residual poverty regime, as is the case in Great Britain, but also within the more advanced institutional poverty regimes such as the Dutch one. France would seem to be an exception, although it does subject recipients to strict work or training requirements. This French reintegration policy comes close to the American workfare idea. Pierson spoke of:

An internal transformation from a solidary, universalistic, citizenship-based welfare state towards a system based on the more generous provision of insurance-style entitlement and a further deterioration in the position of the poor and the stigmatized. (1991: 177)

Thus the danger arises of a dual welfare state, one for the properly insured and one for the poorly insured.

Secondly, we see that in many European countries the ligatures dimension (social contract) is also being affected. The social democratic and the corporatist social contract are the targets of perpetual assaults. No new historical compromises between capital and labour are to be expected. Instead there has been the gradual dismantlement of the existing social contract in the direction of a more 'minimal' social contract reducing the role of the welfare state and giving individual citizens, companies, and social agencies more responsibilities. There would not seem to be a broad support in society for the renovation of the existing welfare state arrangements. The more minimal the social contract becomes due to cutbacks in collective forms of social insurance (a point of discussion in the Netherlands) or due to the abandonment of solidary wage policies (a point of discussion in Sweden), the more of a reduction there will be in the social solidarity between various categories of citizens (poor versus rich, young versus old, ill versus healthy) and branches of trade and industry (loss-making versus profit-making, dangerous versus safe). Social bonds between categories will become looser, and as a result so will the moral obligations people feel to each other. In other words, reduced social and moral ties can lead to a reduction in solidarity and ultimately to a worsening of the life chances of the most vulnerable groups. Because the strong no longer have to support the weak.

The French policy reaction at the end of the 1980s was a different one. Wacquant noted that the growing social problems and inequality in the French *cités* gave rise to right-wing as well as left-wing concern, and led to a broadly supported campaign against poverty and pauperization formulated in a 'language of national solidarity' (1991: 19). In essence, this illustrates the two alternatives: the reformulation of the social contract and recalibration of social rights, for example by attaching certain conditions to the benefits, or the weakening of the social contract and dismantlement of social rights. It seems as if many countries opt for the second alternative.

The first alternative is the path toward social citizenship, the second one amounts to 'the road to Anomia'. Dahrendorf used this term in a Durkheimian meaning: 'Anomy then is not a state of mind, but a state of society' (1985: 23). Dahrendorf viewed the growing exclusion of citizens from the labour market (underclass formation) and the increased problems of xenophobia, racism and crime as signs of the disintegration of the moral

216

community. An 'anomic' community in which the economically established simply and effortlessly close themselves off from the outsiders (the unemployed, illegal aliens) and in which the most vulnerable groups try to make ends meet by way of bare survival strategies. The fighting in the summer of 1993 between illegal North Africans and Italians in Genoa or the problems in the German town of Solingen might well be omens of a pugnacious society in Europe. In *Law and Order*, Dahrendorf noted that:

> It is clear that a world with severely weakened ligatures is a disorienting and disconcerting world. Solidarity, faith, and a sense of history are not easily replaced. If the contraction of the normative structure of society goes hand in hand with the destruction of cultural bonds, we get dangerously close not only to Anomia, but to the most brutal imagery of a state of nature (1985: 46).

This is why he propagated the growth of new ligatures. Dahrendorf wrote:

> For a long time, the development of life chances in modern societies meant above all the development of options, for example, of civil rights (...) But it might well be (...) that today the development of life chances in some areas of advanced societies means above all the growth of new ligatures, so that the greater danger to liberty arises not from the lack of options, but from that of linkages and bonds (1979: 94).

In *The Modern Social Conflict* (1988), he shifted the emphasis and propagated the reinforcement of citizens' social rights in order to prevent an anomic OECD world from developing.

Dahrendorf's ideas on the growth of new social ligatures and the guarantee of fundamental social rights for all citizens have not been confirmed by recent policy developments, although there have been exceptions, such as France. On the EC level, social policy has never received the attention it deserves (Alcock 1993: 46). Very few people share the optimistic notion that economic integration would automatically lead to complementary social integration. In the separate European Member States, a tendency has been observed toward a lower level of social protection for the groups that would seem to need it the most. This does not directly imply that an anomic Europe is in the making, since some of the measures affecting social security can be viewed as useful corrections to social security systems that generate passivity. If this is taken too far and too many people are excluded, then the contours of a European Anomia do begin to loom on the horizon. A Europe where the life chances of many of the poor deteriorate rather than improve.

Table 9.1
Social protection expenditures in 1980, 1984 and 1990 as a percentage of GNP

Country	1980	1984	1990
Belgium	28.1	29.6	---
Denmark	29.7	28.9	27.0
Germany	28.6	28.5	26.4
Greece	13.3	20.0	20.2
Spain	15.6	17.4	18.0
France	25.9	29.4	28.4
Ireland	20.6	23.9	22.3
Italy	22.8	27.3	26.4
Luxembourg	26.4	25.2	24.4
Netherlands	30.4	32.8	32.1
Portugal	14.6	15.2	13.4
United Kingdom	21.7	24.6	22.8
EC	24.9	27.1	25.6

Source: Schutte, 1991 (Source: Eurostat)

Table 9.2

Minimum social benefits in the EC by household type, 1988

Country	Single		Single parent with 2 children (ages 6-11)		Couple without children		Couple with 2 children (ages 6-11)	
	Guilders (a)	Per cent of average income	Guilders	Per cent of average income	Guilders	Per cent of average income	Guilders	Per cent of average income
Netherlands (b)	1108	66	1689	64	1581	53	1846	50
Belgium (c)	926	57	1421	52	1295	48	1790	46
Denmark (d)								
Minimum	582	39	1560	68	1164	42	1927	50
Maximum	1417	95	1848	81	2843	102	3050	78
France (e)	674	27	1214	49	1012	25	1416	34
Spain (f)	0	0	916	51	853	42	916	31
United Kingdom (g)	633	40	1227	69	974	30	1497	40
Germany (h)	774	41	1595	54	1204	33	1860	40

Source: SCP, 1990: 105

(a) Net monthly pay based on purchasing power parity
(b) ABW/RWW including child allowance, excluding rent subsidy
(c) Guaranteed family benefit for unemployed, including child allowance
(d) Bystandsloven, including child allowance
(e) Revenue Minimum d'Insertion, including child allowance, excluding rent subsidy
(f) Subsideo Desempleo, including (extra) child allowance gross amounts
(g) Income support, including child allowance, excluding rent subsidy
(h) Sozialhilfe, including extra child allowance and average housing allowance

Table 9.3
Poverty rates for individuals and households in per cent

Country	Eurostat, 1985 (a) Individuals	Households	O'Higgins, 1985 (b) Individuals	Households
Netherlands	9.6	6.9	5.3	7.4
Belgium	7.1	6.3	7.2	6.3
Denmark	7.9	8.0	14.7	14.7
Germany	10.5	10.3	8.5	7.4
United Kindgom	14.6	14.1	11.7	11.7
France	19.1	18.0	17.5	14.5
Ireland	18.4	18.5	17.5	14.5
Spain	20.9	20.3	20.0	20.0
Greece	21.5	20.5	24.0	24.0
Portugal	32.4	31.4	28.0	28.0
EC average	14.7	14.0	13.9	12.1

Source: Deleeck and van den Bosch, 1992: 112

(a) Eurostat (1990) defines the poverty line as 50 per cent of the average equivalent household expenditure of single adults. Equivalence scale: first adult 1.00, second adult 0.7, child 0.5 (<14 years old). (b) O'Higgins and Jenkins (1990) define the poverty line as 50% of the average equivalent household income. Equivalence scale: 1.00, 0.7, 0.5.

Table 9.4
Long term unemployment in various OECD countries
(12 months and longer, percentage of total unemployment)

Country	1980	1984	1985	1986	1987	1988	1989
Netherlands	35.9	54.5	58.7	59.5	53.2	51.7	49.9
Belgium	61.5	68.4	69.2	70.3	74.5	---	76.3
France	32.6	42.3	46.8	47.8	45.5	44.8	43.9
Japan	16.4	15.1	13.1	17.2	20.2	20.2	18.7
United Kingdom	29.5	48.1	48.1	45.0	45.2	---	40.8
United States	4.2	12.3	9.5	8.7	8.1	7.4	5.7
Germany	28.7	45.1	47.9	48.9	48.1	---	49.0
Sweden	5.5	12.4	11.4	8.1	8.2	8.2	6.5

Source: SCP, 1990 and OECD, 1991

Table 9.5

Trends in income in real terms of richest and poorest 20 per cent in the US and UK

Country	Share of total disposable income				Average disposable income per person (in 1989 $ and £)			
	1979	1989	Change in percentage share	Ratio richest/ poorest	1979	1989	Increase or decrease	Per cent
United States								
richest 20%	39.0	42.1	+3.1	7.5	$33,883	$40,811	$6,928	+20.4
poorest 20%	6.4	5.6	-0.8	---	$5,536	$5,420	-$116	-2.1
United Kingdom								
richest 20%	36.0	42.0	+8.0	5.2	£13,156	£18,460	£5,304	+40.3
poorest 20%	9.0	8.0	-1.0	---	£4,212	£4,212	0	0

Source: Townsend, 1993: 15

References

Albert, J. (1988), 'Is there a crisis of the welfare state? Cross-national evidence from Europe, North America, and Japan', in *European Sociological Review*, vol. 4, no. 3.

Alcock, P. (1993), *Understanding Poverty*, Macmillan, London.

Castel, R. (1994), 'Integration politics', in Guidicini, P., and G. Pieretti (eds) *Urban poverty and Human Dignity*, Franco Angeli, Milan.

Castels, M. (1989), *The Informational City: Information Technology, Economic Restructuring and the Urban Regional Process*, Blackwell, Oxford.

Commissie Toepassing Algemene Bijstandswet (Committee on the Administration of the National Assistance Act) (1994), *Het recht op bijstand*, (The Right to Welfare), VUGA, The Hague.

Cross, M., and R. Waldinger (1992), 'Migrants, minorities, and the ethic divison of labor', in Fainstein, S.S., I. Gordon, and M. Harloe, *Divided Cities: New York & London in the Contemporary World*, Blackwell, Oxford.

Dahrendorf, R. (1979), *Life Chances*, Weidenfeld and Nicolson, London.

Dahrendorf, R. (1985), *Law and Order*, Stevens & Sons, London.

Dahrendorf, R. (1988), *The Modern Social Conflict*, Weidenfeld and Nicolson, London.

De Neubourg, C. (1992), 'The choice was ours', in Verhaar, C.H.A., and L.G. Jansma, *On the Mysteries of Unemployment: Causes, Consequences and Policies*, Kluwer Academic Publishers, Dordrecht, Boston, and London.

De Swaan, A. (ed.) (1994), *Social Policy beyond Borders*, Amsterdam University Press, Amsterdam.

Dercksen, W.J., and G. Engbersen (1992), 'Arbeid en sociaal burgerschap' (Work and citizenship), in H.R. van Gunsteren and P. den Hoed (eds) *Burgerschap in praktijk* (Part I), SDU, The Hague.

Engbersen, G. (1991), 'Moderne armoede: feit en fictie' (Modern poverty: fact and fiction), *De Sociologische Gids*.

Engbersen, G., and R. van der Veen (1987), *Moderne armoede: overleven op het sociaal minimum* (Modern Poverty; Surviving on Society's Minimum), Stenfert Kroese, Leyden and Antwerp.

Engbersen G., K. Schuyt, J. Timmer, and F. van Waarden (1993), *Cultures of Unemployment: a Comparative Look at Long-term Unemployment and Urban Poverty*, Westview Press, Boulder and Oxford.

Esping-Andersen, G. (1990), *The Three Worlds of Welfare Capitalism*, Polity Press, Cambridge.

Hirsch, F. (1977), *Social Limits to Growth*, Routledge & Kegan Paul,

223

London.

Hollifield, J.F. (1992), *Immigrants, Markets and States*, Harvard University Press, Cambridge.

Jacobs, J. (1993), 'Welfare, work and training for the unemployed in Britain: a historical review', in Coenen, H., and P. Leisink *Work and Citizenship in the New Europe*, Edward Elgar, Aldershot.

Jencks, C. (1991), *Rethinking Social Policy: Race, Poverty and the Underclass*, Harvard University Press, Cambridge.

Klanfer, J. (1965), *L'Exclusion Sociale*, Paris.

Leibfried, S. (1991), 'Towards a European welfare state: On integrating poverty regimes in the European Community', *Working Paper no. 2*, Centre for Social Policy Research, Bremen.

Leibfried, S., and F. Tennstedt (1985), *Politik der Armut und die Spaltung des Socialstaats*, Suhrkamp, Frankfurt/M.

Lenoir, R. (1974), *Les Exclus: Un Francais sur Dix*, Paris.

Lister, R. (1990), *The Exclusive Society: Citizenship and the Poor*, Calvert's Press, London.

Logan J., P. Taylor-Gooby, and M. Reuter (1992), 'Poverty and income inequality' in Fainstein, S.S., I. Gordon, and M. Harloe, *Divided Cities: New York & London in the Contemporary World*, Blackwell, Oxford.

Mack, J., and S. Lansley (1984), *Poor Britain*, Allen & Unwin, London.

Mead, L.M. (1992), *The New Politics of Poverty: the Non-working Poor in America*, Basic Books, New York.

O'Higgins, M., and S. Jenkins (1989), *Poverty in Europe: Estimates for 1975, 1980 and 1985*, Price Waterhouse Consultants and University of Bath, Bath.

Oude Engberink, G. (1984), *Minima zonder marge* (Poor without margins), Rotterdam.

Paugam, S. (1991), *La disqualification sociale: essai sur la nouvelle pauvrete*, Presses Universitaires de France, Paris.

Pierson, C. (1991), *Beyond the Welfare State?*, Polity Press, Oxford.

Ploeg, R. van der (1990), 'Armoede en ongelijkheid' (Poverty and inequality), in Noordegraaf, H., and Ph. van Engelsdorp Gastelaars (eds) *Sociaal economisch beleid en de arme kant van Nederland*, Eburon), Delft.

Portes, A., and R.G. Rumbaut (1990), *Immigrant America: A Portrait*, University of California Press, Berkeley.

Refugee Work (1991), *Refugees in Numbers: Edition 1991*, Amsterdam.

Sassen, S. (1991), *The Global City: New York, London, Tokyo*, Princeton University Press, Princeton.

Schutte, B. (1991), 'Building the welfare state: the development of poverty regimes in the USA and the "USE"', paper presented at the CES Workshop on 'Emergent supranational policy: The EC's social dimension in a comparative perspective', Cambridge.

Silver, H. (1993), 'National conceptions of the new urban poverty: social structural change in Britain, France, and the United States' *International Journal of Urban and Regional Research*, vol. 17, no. 3.

Swinnen, H. (1993), 'Revenue minimum d'insertion in Frankrijk: fair of workfare?', *Tijdschrift voor Arbeid en Bewustzijn*, no. 4.

Townsend, P. (1979), *Poverty in the United Kingdom*, Penguin, Harmondsworth.

Townsend, P. (1993), *The International Analysis of Poverty*, Harvester Wheatsheaf, Hemel Hempstead.

Vos, J., J. den Heeten, and S. Santokhi (1992), *'Eens komt de dag....'* *Een onderzoek naar het leven, wonen en werken van Haagse illegalen* ('Once Comes the Day' ... Live and Work of Illegal Aliens in The Hague), The Hague.

Wacquant, L.J.D. (1992), 'The comparative social structure and experience of urban exclusion: Race, class, and space in Chicago and Paris', in Lawson, R., C. McFate, and W.J. Wilson (eds) *Urban Marginality and Social Policy in America and Western Europe*.

Wetenschappelijke Raad voor het Regeringsbeleid (Dutch Scientific Counsel for Government Policy) (1990), *Werkend Perspectief* (Work in Perspective: Labour Participation in Holland), SDU, The Hague.

Wilterdink, N. (1993), *Ongelijkheid en interdependentie* (Inequality and Interdependence), Wolters Noordhoff, Groningen.

Part 3
ALLOCATIVE POLICIES AND POLICY STYLES

10 European health and safety regulation: No 'race to the bottom'

Volker Eichener

EU
I 18
L51
D18
F02

Summary

When the completion of the Single European Internal Market was announced in 1985, many observers from the technologically advanced countries feared a lowering of existing national levels of protection by social and ecological dumping. These expectations were based on political integration theories, which analyzed European policymaking primarily as intergovernmental bargaining that could only lead to agreements on the level of the least common denominator. European health and safety at work regulation, however, turned out to provide a surprisingly high level of safety and health and, furthermore, even to develop innovative approaches to occupational health and safety regulation. When the complete European regulation process is analyzed in detail, it turns out that European health and safety at work regulation has to be viewed as the outcome of the interactions within complex configurations of actors. These configurations include more actors than just national governments (as analyzed by intergovernmental bargaining theories), namely national partisans and European actors, particularly the EC Commission as a key actor. The institutional self-interest of the latter is an important factor in the explanation of the observed tendency of innovative social regulation.

Expectations of social dumping

In many Member States, the completion of the European internal market is regarded with mixed emotions. Although the economic benefits - though numerically moderate, as estimated by the Cecchini Report - are widely accepted, the neglect of Europe's social dimension is frequently criticized.

When the European Union started on its way to the completion of the internal market in 1985, the fear arose in the most economically and technologically advanced Member States that their social and ecological standards would be jeopardized. It was widely expected that national protective regulations, which functioned as trade barriers, would be removed by the White Paper deregulatory measures. This deregulation would leave a regulatory vacuum which would lead to a 'race to the bottom', a Community-wide competition to reduce costly health and safety standards.

This social dumping was considered a consequence of Europe's inability to achieve effective political integration. According to the currently dominant (neo-)realist integration theory, integration is mainly considered the outcome of intergovernmental bargaining. The theory assumes that each national government has an institutional self-interest in minimizing changes required by European integration and in defending national structures and regulations.

In a generalized analysis, Scharpf (1985) even characterized the EU as 'incapable of action', because its decisionmaking system suffers from a 'self-blockade'. The self-blockade arises because decisions on the (higher) European level depend on the consent of the governments on the (lower) national level and this consent must be unanimous or, since the Single European Act of 1986, almost unanimous. National governments and their bureaucracies have an institutional self-interest in keeping and enlarging their resources and authority rather than renouncing sovereignty rights. Therefore, they use their veto power to block any decision with negative consequences for them (*Politikverflechtungsfalle* or 'joint decision trap'; see also Scharpf 1985a). Hoffmann (1982: 30) sees a 'power of inertia' coming from the national bureaucracies' institutional self-interests in avoiding change. With 'package deals', 'log-rolling' or 'compensatory payments' only ad-hoc solutions with limited ranges can be achieved, because there are situations in which adequate compensation for each state cannot be achieved, especially if decisions must be made under negative-sum game conditions. Hence, the European Union is caught in an 'institutional trap' between national sovereignty and integration, with no way out, neither forwards (because of the national governments' interests in keeping their sovereignty) nor backwards (because of the economic interests in keeping the status quo of integration). Since the Member States have institutional self-interests in preserving their veto power, the institutional system of the European Community is unable to overcome the mutual blockade. In the view of realist integration theory, the Community's (partial) repeal of the principle of unanimity (introduced in 1966) by the Single Act in 1986 did not help much.

Under the qualified majority rule, Brussels' harmonization decisions are still blocked by serious interest conflicts (e.g. between the advanced and the underdeveloped industrial countries) and by at least equally serious direction conflicts (e.g. between the British and the German environmental policies). Hence, the high level of health protection, of safety at work, of environment protection and of consumer protection, which is required by the Single Act (Art. 100a (3)), can not be enforced jointly, but it comes either to harmonization decisions on the lowest common level or to a mutual recognition of the respective national regulations. (Scharpf 1990: 36, my translation)

Advancing economic integration combined with a 'blocked political integration' leads to an internal market with free access where national regulatory systems compete with one another. Market competition, according to Scharpf (1990: 37), 'can only lead to a systematic suppression of the more expensive standard by the less costly standard'. Deregulation would 'degenerate to a competition of mutual dumping' (Scharpf 1990: 38). In this competition between regulatory strategies, national regulatory 'packages' will be untied so that each single regulation will be compared with the least expensive regulation in any other Member State.

The self-interest of national governments in avoiding any changes which may be connected with costs of adjustment or a loss of powers or resources is reinforced by pressure from non-governmental actors (Streeck and Schmitter 1991: 142). The requirement of unanimity (or qualified majority voting) in decisionmaking puts pressure groups which are interested in preventing a harmonized European social policy - mainly the employers' associations - in a strong position, because they need just one (or three) national government(s) for a veto (or blocking minority) in the Council. Thus, 'the consequence of integration and deregulation become one and the same' (Streeck and Schmitter 1991: 142). Furthermore, 'a class like business, whose interest was and is essentially not in shaping but rather in preventing a centralized European social policy, could always hope to find allies in national governments concerned about their sovereignty'. Streeck and Schmitter indeed write that 'in the 1992 compromise, the project of European integration became finally and formally bound up with a deregulation project' as a concession that the governments had to make in return for business giving up previous claims for protection of the domestic markets (Streeck and Schmitter 1991: 149).

Many scholars agree that even if the high level countries succeed in preserving their levels of protection, there is no chance for improving these levels. Thus scholars expected, if not a roll-back, at least a long term standstill of innovation and improvement in the area of social regulation.

The real developments in European health and safety at work regulation

The danger of social and ecological dumping was seen clearly when the Treaty was amended by the Single Act (Lindl 1991: 46). Therefore, in the interests of the Member States with high safety standards, the proviso of subsection 3 was added to Art. 100a. The proviso that the Commission proposals 'will take as a base a *high* level of protection' (italics mine), however, is weak and not legally binding. First, the word 'high' is vague. 'High' may mean higher than the minimum common denominator but definitely does not mean 'the highest' (otherwise subsection four would be senseless). Thus, the proviso does not exclude social and ecological dumping. Secondly, the proviso is not binding, because it relates only to the Commission proposals and not to the final Council decisions.

Against this background, what really happened in European occupational safety and health regulation after 1985 was surprising. The European Community recognized the danger of competition between the Member States which could lead to a weakening of safety and health protection (see Directive 89-391-EEC, preamble), and therefore started a comprehensive regulatory programme with the 'essential aim' of preserving or improving the level of safety attained by the Member States (directive 89-392-EEC, preamble).

By passing the framework directive and two dozen more specific directives, the Council has decided to introduce a very broad and innovative conception of occupational safety and health. A conception which not only clearly goes beyond the least common denominator among the Member States, but which introduces an innovative approach first developed in Sweden and transferred via Denmark and the Netherlands to the EU.

The European regulation not only goes beyond the traditional mechanistic approaches by adopting the innovative Scandinavian conception, it is also based on at least six innovative principles: a broad scope, including virtually all employees, the employer's obligation to care for occupational safety and health, a broad concept of health including the humanization of work, the concept of the working environment including organizational aspects, the risk assessment approach, and the concept of absolute safety requirements regardless of technological restrictions.

Protection of all employees in all sectors

With the transposition of the European directives into national law, for the first time in the history of most Member States virtually all employees are provided with government protection at their workplaces. The enlarged scope of protection alone thus means a most significant improvement of protection standards.

A caring obligation for occupational health and safety

The most basic obligation of European occupational safety and health legislation is the employer's obligation to provide for and to improve the workers' health and safety with regard to all aspects of the working environment. The employer is no longer only obliged to satisfy all regulations and to react to official inspection, but must pro-actively care for the safety of the employees.

A comprehensive conception of health including psychological aspects

Traditionally, in most European countries occupational safety and health regulation was restricted to avoiding hazards to physical health like mechanical injury, poisoning or radiation. By contrast, European directives adopted the innovative conceptions of health employed by the World Health Organization and the International Labour Office which include psychological - or 'soft' - aspects of health like psychological stress, fatigue and even discomfort.

Practical consequences of this comprehensive conception of health are that occupational safety and health includes ergonomics and the humanization of work. Even monotonous work cycles have to be avoided. The revolutionary quality of this legislation can be estimated if compared with occupational safety and health regulation in Germany. In Germany the humanization of work has been a political goal since the early 1970s, yet has never been considered as an item for government regulation (only for government support).

A broad scope of regulation using the working environment concept

The European regulatory concept goes beyond the mechanistic approach in another respect. Traditionally, occupational safety and health regulation was restricted to technical components, to tools, machinery, equipment and workplaces. The European directives include the regulation of work organization and working time, the employers' obligations for risk analyses, information and training, considerable information and participation rights for workers and their representatives, medical examinations, training of workers and other aspects of social relations. All items which have traditionally not been subject to legislative regulation but to autonomous arrangements between the social partners on the firm or sectoral level.

The risk assessment approach

The risk assessment approach is the core of the Machinery Directive (89-392-EEC). The risk assessment approach is innovative, because it makes the effective prevention of hazards obligatory. Both manufacturers of machinery and employers have to anticipate risks, including those resulting from combination effects. They have to take measures to avoid them following a multi-step programme. Together with the obligation to take state of the art technologies and practices into account, the preventive character of the risk assessment approach may contribute to a new orientation toward higher levels of safety in most Member States (Pickert 1992: 88).

Defining absolute safety requirements irrespective of the state of technology

Traditional occupational safety and health regulation relates to the state of the art in technology. The safety level which is usually provided by regulation is relative, because it depends on what technology allows (e.g. automatic stopping of moving tools and parts may require a highly developed sensor technology). Whereas technology is dynamic, regulation is basically static and lags behind the technological development. Thus regulation frequently remains below the technologically achievable level of safety (Ossenbühl 1982: 156). According to progressive lawyers, the settlement of this problem requires a 'dynamization of law' (Wolf 1987: 387).

The most progressive approach to the dynamization of law is to provide absolute requirements regardless of the technological possibilities. Requirements may go beyond the current state of the art and anticipate future technological progress, meaning that the standards cannot be achieved at the time when the law is passed. This approach is taken in the Community's Machinery Directive.

Obviously, at least in the field of European occupational safety and health legislation, no social dumping has taken place. Quite to the contrary, a comprehensive, consistent and innovative regulation process has occurred. This phenomena has yet to be explained.

Negative expectations from Brussels are not restricted to the sector of occupational health. The highly industrialized countries expected ecological dumping (in environmental protection legislation), similar to the social dumping. However, Rehbinder and Stewart observed European regulation at a considerable level of protection, despite dissenting public and theoretical expectations; a phenomena similar to that in workplace health and safety regulation. They observed this phenomena as early as 1985, before the Single Act, although prior to the Single European Act the original Treaty did not specify any Community authority for environmental legislation (see also

Majone 1989: 165, who sees a 'continuous growth of Community regulation, even in the absence of explicit legal mandates' in environmental protection). Héritier et al. (1994) have even observed that Member States produce innovative regulation in environmental protection hoping to establish their regulatory approaches on the European level. Both in environmental protection policy and in occupational health protection, a high-level of protection - often higher than the level of the most advanced Member State - is achieved. The European regulations combine the different regulatory approaches, instruments and philosophies, e.g. high substantial requirements in traditional fields from Germany, innovative regulation in new fields from Denmark and the Netherlands, and procedural innovations (like risk assessment, environmental impact assessment, quality assurance, auditing and public access) from United Kingdom. Thus the best from each country is taken. What occurred is just the opposite of what was predicted: a 'race to the top' instead of a 'race to the bottom'. How is this to be explained?

Explanations: decision making in regulatory policy

During the 1970s, the integration process advanced very slowly and the technical harmonization schedule broke down because of endless bargaining and veto powered national blockades in the Council.

Prefaced by the Commission's White Paper on the Completion of the Internal Market, the breakthrough in European integration policy came in February 1986 with the Single European Act, which dispensed with the principle of unanimity and made the Community capable of efficient regulatory action. The mere shift to majority voting, however, could not alone be responsible for the Community's innovative regulatory drive since 1985 (see Scharpf 1990, 1992). The shift to qualified majority voting could only give rise to the expectation that the level of protection would have been slightly lifted, from the very lowest national level to the least common denominator of the nine or ten States needed to form a qualified majority. The fact that the Community adopted the highest level of protection to be found in the Member States has yet to be explained.

Since 1985, three significant changes have taken place in Community politics, which had not been predicted by the pessimistic intergovernmental bargaining approaches:

1   The replacement of unanimous consent by qualified majority voting. Given each nation-state's vital interest in sovereignty, why has each Member State given up its veto power?

2   The extension of European harmonization into many regulatory areas
     beyond the economic sphere in its strict sense, including European
     product and process regulation of occupational safety and health. Why
     have the Member States increasingly transferred regulatory authority to
     the European Community?

3   The high protective level of European health and safety at work
     legislation. Why have the Member States accepted the economic, social
     and political costs of standard upgrading, why have the low-level States
     given up their advantage in the Europe-wide competition for industrial
     locations?

For both realist and neofunctionalist integration theories, the 'sudden and
unexpected success' of the Single Act was, according to Keohane and
Hoffmann (1990: 283), a 'puzzle'.

> Since none of us anticipated such a dramatic and coherent revival of
> Community policymaking, any attempts to explain it should be viewed
> with skepticism. What was unpredicted by analysts working with
> established theories cannot, in general, be adequately explained, post
> hoc, through the use of such theories. (Keohane and Hoffmann 1990:
> 284; see also Wessels 1992: 36-7).

The main reason that the European Union regained its capacity for action
is that the power of the Council with its inherent blockade logic was broken
by substantial differentiation of decision making procedures. The Council
appears to be the main decision making body only at a superficial glance at
the EC Treaty. In fact, more actors participate in the legislative process: the
European Parliament (according to the procedures of Art. 189b and c of the
Treaty), the Economic and Social Committee, numerous advisory committees
to the Commission, and - most important - the Commission itself. The
Commission turns out to be a key player in European decision making,
because it is empowered by its prerogative of directive proposal and by its
leadership during the whole legislative process.
    The European Commission is the 'forgotten actor' in the process of
European integration. While the European Court of Justice has received much
attention as a promotor of integration (especially by Weiler 1982 and the
following discussions), the intergovernmental bargaining theories have
neglected the Commission's role (Schneider and Werle 1989: 418-20). It is
not untypical that, in an article analyzing the integration process, not more
than a few sentences are dedicated to the Commission's role. Hoffmann
(1982: 32), for example, states that 'the EEC's institutions are weak, because
they lack autonomy (from the Member States) and because their capacity to

act is small'. Scharpf (1985: 323) also sees the Commission in 'absolute dependency upon the national governments' in the Council. This is astonishing, since the Commission was established as the Community's 'driving force' (Hallstein) and has the prerogative of proposing directives, which is certainly more than a *quantité négligible*.

Although it was rational for each government to use its veto power to avoid economic, social and political costs of harmonization, the results of this mutual blockade were suboptimal for each State, since they could not realize the economic benefits of a single internal market. Before the Single Act, the intergovernmental situation was characterized by a fundamental discrepancy between the individual interests of the Member States in avoiding any adaptation to harmonization and the common interest in the economic effects of European integration. Assuming that every State government tried to optimize its action, it is safe to assume that each Member State wanted to profit as much as possible from the Community and, at the same time, to minimize the economic, social and political costs of adapting to the Community. There was a collective interest in a single internal market and in the degree of harmonization required to achieve this objective, but there were individual interests in keeping national regulation and in imposing each State's own national interest on the Community.

Within the logics of intergovernmental bargaining, there was no escape from this strategic dilemma. Log-rolling turned out to be a difficult business, which only allowed a slow advance towards integration. Obviously, the European Community was unable to control its own course towards integration.

The only solution to this dilemma was for all Member States to give up some of their decision making powers without transferring them to any other State, so that the balance of power between the Member States remained unchanged. This could be achieved by (partially) submitting to the regime of a set of supranational institutions which could serve as moderators of the integration process.

A second, more effective step towards overcoming the mutual blockade strategies is to create a corporate actor to which the (legal) authority and the (financial) resources to act in the Member States' common interest are transferred. The opportunities both for individual action and for exit must be restricted in order to stabilize the ability of the corporate actor to act in the common interest (Commons 1961, Coleman 1974, see also Haas 1964: 111).

Among the European institutions serving as 'corporate actors' and pushing the integration process forward are:

1   the Court of Justice, which served as such an integrative institution to a certain extent already before 1985. 'For many years, the European

Court of Justice has been the most active and creative Community organ' Dehousse and Weiler 1990: 247, and earlier Weiler 1982)

2   to a limited but growing extent the European Parliament

3   in a limited way, the 'second chamber', the Social and Economic Committee (with only advisory functions),

and, primarily

4   the Commission, whose role was clearly enhanced by the Single European Act (Bieber et al. 1988: 24 and 30, Pelkmans 1988: 373, H. Wallace 1990: 217-21. 'The Commission clearly won "the battle of the Single Act"', Dehousse et al. 1992: 8).

The submission of the Member States to the political leadership of supranational institutions, mainly the Commission, was bound to important conditions:

1   Each Member State had to feel sure that its net share of the total positive effect of the European integration would exceed the costs of adjustment. Since this conviction was a crucial prerequisite for giving up the veto power, it is understandable that the Cecchini Report (which, soberly analyzed, predicts that the internal market will have only quantitatively moderate economic effects) was (and is) quoted almost ritually. The Cecchini Report has a motivating function, presenting 'political data' (van Suntum 1992: 18), which are regarded as rather optimistic by several economists. The image of the 'global triad' and the conclusion that only a united Europe can withstand the economic challenges from East Asia and North America has the same function. Both the 'global triad picture' and the Cecchini Report formed Delors' 'clever marketing strategy' to convince the Member States to support the Commission's main goal: a revitalization of political integration in the backpack of market integration (Schneider 1992: 19-20).

2   The supranational process moderators, primarily the Commission, have to be strictly neutral. As soon as some Member States started to suspect that the Commission's policy systematically favoured another State or a group of other States, they would return to securing their interests by intergovernmental bargaining and forming permanent coalitions for blocking minorities. The logics of intergovernmental bargaining must not be transferred to the supranational institutions, otherwise the mutual blockade dilemma would just move to another level. Within the

238

Commission, there exists indeed a long tradition (since the Hallstein era) of 'European thinking' and of the *acquis communautaire*. Thinking in categories of national interests is taboo among Commission officials (von Senger and Etterlin 1992: 21).

3   The supranational process moderators must have a vital self-interest in the integration process in order to be pushy enough. This is the reason why institution-building can be very useful in overcoming mutual blockade configurations, because institutions have an institutional self-interest (and their officials a personal self-interest) in growing and maximizing their resources, authority and powers. 'The Commission officials appear to follow just one working principle: How can I secure more authority for myself and hence for the Commission?' (von Senger and Etterlin 1992: 19, my translation) The self-interest in institutional growth and the fact that the Commission officials personally profit from further integration (each step to further integration offers new career chances) appear to be the main reasons for the observed expansion of the tasks of the European institution and, hence, of the range of the Community's regulatory activities.

4   The partial surrender of power by the Member States in signing the Single European Act is not irrational in another respect. Success, not power, is the primary objective of politicians. Power is very often a means to achieve success. But power - here the veto power - is of no use if it is blocked by counter-powers. Power is always relative. Especially in situations in which power does not lead to success, relinquishing power can even be useful for politicians, because they are discharged from responsibility.
The more de facto authority is transferred to the Commission, the better the Commission can serve as a scapegoat for national politicians. The ugly word 'Eurocrats' is a good example for the notorious habit of blaming the Commission for every kind of political failure which might occur in any Member State.

5   The integration process conducted under the leadership of the Commission could be accelerated by creating time pressure. The tight schedule for integration, which was set up with the White Paper and justified with the Cecchini Report, had the function of speeding up the decision making process. Facing the huge and profitable task of creating the single internal market, all the objections of the Member States to single provisions of regulatory acts became neglectable and no longer justified blocking the decision making process. The Council set itself under time pressure and empowered the Commission to set it under an

even tighter time schedule by giving it the right of proposal and by affirming the legislative programmes of the Commission. Also, because the industries have begun to prepare for the internal market and hence have created irrevocable facts, the governments have no choice but to achieve the self-set goal of integration (Scharpf 1992: 24).

Given these conditions, dispensing with the principle of unanimity does not seem as irrational for the national governments as it once did. The strategy is justified by its success: 'Although the quantity and quality of outputs have been uneven, the substantive rewards, in terms of the interests of the participants, have been sufficient for them to be willing periodically to reinforce the process.' (H. Wallace 1990: 218) With the Single European Act (and related means), the governments of the Member States transformed their configuration of inevitable mutual blockade into a configuration which promotes further integration. Within this configuration, the supranational institutions (particularly the Commission) with their self-interest in integration, play crucial roles as driving forces of the integration process.

Once established by the Council as the driving force of the EC, the Commission turns out to be quite an independent actor. This is not atypical for corporate actors which are created to overcome the dilemma of an incongruence of individual and collective interests. Besides the common interest of the Members, corporate actors tend to develop an institutional interest of their own in securing their existence and in maximizing resources and powers. The institutional self-interest of supranational corporate actors countervails the institutional self-interests of the national bureaucracies, which have been emphasized so heavily by intergovernmentalism. There is a tendency for corporate actors to become independent vis-à-vis their members and founders (see Schneider and Werle 1989: 415).

The main power that was transferred from the Member States to the Commission is the prerogative of directive proposal. Although the final decision still lies in the hands of the Council, the Council cannot make any policies without or against the will of the Commission (Engel 1991a, b). And the Commission is rather free to develop its own ideas of regulation and to draw up proposals for directives properly.

This right of proposal is also crucial because it changes the logics of decision making within the Council fundamentally. The logic would be far different if, instead of the Commission, single States had the right of proposal. In that case, if a State presented a proposal for a directive to the Council there would be no initial support for this proposal and the State would have to do a great deal of negotiating to achieve a seventy-seven per cent majority, particularly if other States presented proposals on the same topic at the same time. The Commission, however, was given the prerogative of proposal. If the Commission presents a proposal for a directive, the logics

of decision making are reversed. The proposals of the Commission are supposed to be accepted by all States, because this is the only way to come to
decisions. A single State which disagrees has to find other States to form a
blocking minority. Integration theorists argue that the dissension of the States
is the barrier against integration. Once the Commission's right of initiative
has been introduced, it is this very dissension that prevents the States from
stopping the Commission's path to integration.

Intergovernmental bargaining theorists have acknowledged that 'members
of the Commission are independent figures rather than instructed agents'
(Keohane and Hoffmann 1990: 281). However, they argue that 'national
governments continue to play a dominant role in the decisionmaking process',
because 'there are innumerable committees of national experts and
bureaucrats, preparing the Commission's proposals and the Council's
decisions' (ibid.). Furthermore, 'the execution of the Council's directives by
the Commission is closely supervised by committees of national bureaucrats,
some of which can overrule the Commission's moves' (ibid.). According to
this argument, the Commission seems to be just an intermediary institution.
Is it true that, through the committees, a perfect cycle of control by the
Member States from directive drafting to application is completed?

After a closer analysis of the role of the committees, however, the
Council's decision on the comitology appears to be a minor victory in a
running fight. Particularly within DG III, many of the most powerful
regulatory committees (as 'little Councils of Ministers') are installed to adapt
the Council directives to the technological and scientific development, because
the Council is not able to do this highly technical work. Also, the adaptation
of the occupational safety and health directives is within the responsibility of
a committee, which is set up by Art. 17 of the Health and Safety at Work
Directive. If the Council delegates legislative tasks to committees, which are
chaired by a Commission representative, the Commission does not lose, but
rather gains influence. And the committees which deal with the genuine tasks
of the Commission, i.e. the problems of the implementation and application
of directives, are often just advisory committees, e.g., the committee set up
by the Machinery Directive, Art. 6 (2). Even the important task of checking
the directive conformity of standards is up to the discretion of the
Commission, which just takes notice of the opinion submitted by the Standing
Committee set up by the Information Directive.

Furthermore, the comitology decision of the Council seems to be a Pyrrhic
victory over the Commission. The empirical study by the *Institut für
Europäische Politik* (IEP) on the comitology found that 'the responding
Commission officials generally do not think that their committee considerably
reduced the Commission's freedom and even less so that it has been set up
to assure the Member States' control' (IEP 1989: 9). This subjective
assessment of the Commission's officials is verified by hard facts. The

Commission reported that it had received a positive opinion from regulatory committees for ninety-eight per cent of all proposals submitted since July 1987. Moreover, the Commission reported that the *contre filet* variant, which was the main point in dispute and which was finally introduced by the Council against the Commission's vote (Meng 1988: 218-9), was never used (SEC(89) 1591 final). (The *contre filet* variant, procedure III.b, was that the Council could decide with a simple majority that the Commission could not act, if the Council rejected the Commission's proposal but did not make a positive decision of its own.)

The IEP study reveals that the influence of the Commission within all three types of committees is still strong. In only 3 per cent of the cases did the Commission react to committee reservations by withdrawing its original proposal, while it insisted in spite of the committee's negative vote in 18 per cent of the cases (IEP 1989: 113). The dominant picture is that the proposals of the Commission are extended and modified by the proposals of the delegates, but usually without substantial changes to their original intentions.

However, hard bargaining is rare within the committees. Since they are groups of technical experts, the committees, like the Commission, favor technologically advanced regulations. From our own interviews with committee members and observations, a general rule for effective work in committees dealing with technical matters can be stated: the higher the interest and the higher the technological level of a Member State, the greater its influence in technical discussions. The debates tend to move quickly to a level of technical details (about what is technologically possible and at what cost) so that technical expertise is a crucial condition for effective participation. Thus, the delegations from the technologically advanced countries have an advantage, because they usually have a greater potential for expertise than the low-level countries, whose occupational health ministries chronically suffer from a lack of expert staff (see Vogel 1991). The interest in the matter is an important corresponding variable, because the higher the interest is, the more resources will be invested in the committee work. Members report that delegates from low-level countries frequently prefer to listen to discussions to get early information on regulatory acts than to actively contribute. These impressions are confirmed by the IEP study results. The study revealed a ranking of Member States according to the number of decisions where their delegation had particularly strong influence (IEP 1989: 103), as presented in Table 10.1.

The same general pattern - dominance of the technologically advanced Member States versus little if any influence of the so-called peripheral countries - appears even sharper in the distribution of key functions in the technical standardization bodies related to occupational safety and health. Table 10.2 shows the allotment of the key committee functions, the chair and the secretariat, over the various Member States. This is not unimportant, as the chairman (it is usually a man) and the manager can largely control the discussions within the committees. As a standardization manager explained: 'The sessions must be well-prepared. Everything must be pre-arranged so that chairman and manager can play into each other's hands. Nothing must be left to chance.' (interview)

Table 10.1
Rank-order of countries by the number of EU-committee decisions on which they had strong influence

France	33
United Kingdom	31
Germany	25
Italy and Netherlands	15
Denmark	13
Belgium	9
Ireland	7
Luxembourg	6
Greece, Portugal and Spain	5

Table 10.2
Distribution of key committee functions over Member States

Country	Chair		Secretariat	
	number	per cent	number	per cent
Germany	19	42	19	39
United Kingdom	10	22	10	20
France	5	11	7	14
Italy	3	7	4	8
Denmark	2	4	3	6
Switzerland	2	4	3	6
Sweden	2	4	2	4
Belgium	2	4	1	2

The differences in the abilities of the delegations of the Member States to participate effectively in the work of the committees appear to be one factor

243

contributing to the surprisingly high level of occupational safety and health legislation. Another, even more important factor is the behaviour of the Commission.

Obviously, the Commission is interested in regulation on a high level as well. Of course, Art. 100a(3) of the Treaty obliges the Commission to draft proposals on a high level of protection. Since this obligation is, as already mentioned, vague and leaves room for the discretion of the Commission, the latter must also have an intrinsic interest in regulation on quite a high level.

One reason is the self-interest of the Commission, the Commission Members, and the Commission Officials in achieving a profile as a political actor. The Commission, however, lacks the disposable financial resources for 'large scale initiatives' in distributive policy (since most of the budget is bound by agriculture and some existing distributive programmes) and therefore tends to regulatory policy. Given this constraint, the only way for the Commission to increase its role is to expand the scope of its regulatory activities. This is precisely what happened, and what will probably continue to happen in the future.

> Thus any satisfactory explanation of the remarkable growth of Community regulation must take into account both the desire of the Commission to increase its influence - a fairly uncontroversial behavioral assumption - and the possibility of escaping budgetary constraints by resorting to regulatory policy making. (Majone 1989: 167, see also Majone 1992: 137-8).

With a conservative, traditional regulatory policy, the Commission as an institution and the concerned Commission officials can hardly achieve a political image. Thus, the pursuit of a more active political role results in the attempts for innovative regulation which go beyond the traditional approaches of the Member States, extending into new regulatory areas like consumer protection, environmental protection and occupational health.

A second reason for the support of the Commission for a high level of protection is its institutional self-interest in maximizing its authority and resources. The higher the level of European regulation, the more authority and provisos of action the Commission will get.

A third reason may lie in the assumption of Rehbinder and Stewart that the interests of the more powerful (highly industrialized) States are favoured by the Commission. They argue that the Commission is attentive to interests of advanced Member States because acceptance of the EC by the populations of such states, who fear that their historical achievements are jeopardized by social and ecological dumping, is diminishing. The support of these populations can be very critical for the EC, as was seen when a majority of Denmark's population rejected the Maastricht Accord.

The actual behaviour of the Commission officials in the committees involved in directive preparation, is described by the interviewed committee members as follows:

The Commission officials listen (in the committees as in informal preconsultations) to everybody, but are free to choose whose ideas and proposals they adopt. This behaviour opens up great chances for influence by experts who, because they present ideas which are in line with the interests of the Commission, may act as 'partisans'. Usually, the technical annexes of the occupational safety and health directives are drafted by such (identifiable) partisans, who may come from the British labour inspection service, the German Federal Agency for Occupational Safety or a similar institution of another high-level country.

Committees are not 'little Councils', because their participants are in a different situation. The committee members are usually technical experts from the intermediate and even the lower hierarchical ranks within the national governments. Their careers do not depend on their success in intergovernmental bargaining (which is the task of the ministers), but rather on doing good and noiseless committee work, good drafting work (e.g. avoiding legal mistakes, not forgetting important aspects) and on coming to positive results on schedule while not neglecting their primary tasks at home.

It is not the task of the representatives of the national governments to bargain on directive proposals in the committees. Rather, it is their task 'to highlight and then iron out those elements in a proposal which will render its implementation or application in the Member States difficult' (Weiler 1988: 353). Their committee work is focused on legal and technical, not political problems (ibid.). Furthermore, the phenomenon that the actors on the technical level share more common interests than the political actors (ministers and heads of the governments) - particularly the common interest in improving the level of occupational safety and health regulation (and thus getting more authority and resources) - can be observed in practical committee work (*copinage technocratique*).

Given this configuration of interests, committees usually welcome initiatives from partisans who offer to do a great deal of the practical work. Furthermore, committees take the character of working groups, and social groups tend to follow leaders. The level of protection may be raised, since these partisans tend to be people with innovative ideas rather than conservative delegation members. Moreover, innovators sometimes try their ideas on the European level when they fail in their home countries (as in the case of the Machinery Directive), whereas conservatives do not engage themselves on the European level from which they expect no threats. In this respect, the expectation of social dumping may turn out to be a 'suicidal prophecy'. Schmitter's interpretation is that the 'rather extraordinary success of the Eurocrats in sustaining a consistently low political profile can be evidenced by the low scores for popular resistance against integration' (1992: 25). These dynamics of committees strengthen the position of the Commission, whose representatives are the chairpersons and thus control the committee work.

According to the results of the IEP study (1989: 83-5), the Commission prepares the committee work carefully. Particularly when the subject is considered important, the Commission defines its course very precisely, usually on the level of Heads of Division (30 per cent) and Directors (41 per cent), but sometimes also on the level of the Director General (11 per cent), the Commissioner (3 per cent) or the College of Commissioners (7 per cent). As already mentioned, the original ideas and, if presented, proposals of the Commission are often modified during the committee work, but very rarely rejected. The modifications reduce the level of conflict, but usually leave the essentials untouched. Proposals, however, are not binding. What happens to Commission proposals during the further steps of the legislative process?

Reviewing the history of occupational safety and health directives, a general pattern reveals itself. The level of protection is raised during the legislative process from the first Commission proposal to the final Council directive. This was especially the case when the European Parliament and the Economic and Social Committee were involved.

For example, the genesis of the Display Screen Equipment Directive is the history of an (almost) continuous tightening up. Both the Economic and Social Committee, and particularly the European Parliament, demanded stricter regulations, many of which were adopted by the Commission, and even the Council seemed to tighten up some provisions.

The behaviour of the Parliament and the Economic and Social Committee is not surprising. The EP and the ESC are European institutions which have a similar interest in overcoming intergovernmental bargaining (and blockades) and in attaining a distinct and innovative image. Furthermore, within the Economic and Social Committee and within the EP Committee - where the socialist faction plays a dominant role - phenomena similar to those in the advisory committees to the Commission occur.

The Commission itself quite often amends its proposals during the process. The measures are generally tightened up, especially when the basic intentions of the Commission and the delivered comments go in the same direction. Then, the Commission adopts and even strengthens the proposals for amendment. Similar processes occurred in environmental regulation, e.g. when the Commission adopted and even reinforced the tightening up by the Parliament of the Small Car Directive (see Strübel 1992: 286). Many of the EP proposals, which are politically controversial, however, have no chance of further consideration. The possibility of enforcing unanimous consent within the Council to outvote an EP decision is not of much use, because the EP is trapped in the logical dilemma that unanimity would reduce the chance

246

for high-level legislation. An example was the EP's proposal for more stringent limits in the Benzole Directive. The proposal for amendment failed, because it was not adopted by the Commission and because the Council (as was to be expected) did not come to a unanimous consent on sharper limits (TGB 1991: 44). Hence, the EP will be most influential, if it forms coalitions together with the Commission (Winter 1991: 163).

Finally, if the Commission proposal is above the level of protection of all Member States, relative deprivation is a lighter burden than absolute deprivation. As one representative of a German labour ministry, who belongs to an advisory committee stated:

> Naturally we are not satisfied with every aspect of the Commission proposals. But facing the high political costs within package deals, the barrier against voting negatively is high. We would not recommend voting against the proposal in the Council of Ministers, when we can tell our minister that we can live with the Directive and that all others have to adapt too. (Interview)

Reluctance of low-level countries to accept high-level legislation is also reduced by their ability to compensate for high requirements somewhat by weak implementation. The *de jure* transposition of the directives into national law already takes many years, since the directives provide generous time limits for transposition and many States still delay transposition until, on the Commission's request, the European Court of Justice compels the States to transpose appropriately. (For statistical data on the increasing number of violations of the Treaty see Joerges et al. 1988: 276-80).

Weiler made an interesting observation (1988: 355-6): Member States which appear to be 'tough and detail-minded negotiators' in the Council (like Denmark, 'verging almost on the obstructionist'), tend to implement the decisions rather correctly, while countries which are ready to compromise (like Italy, with a 'reputation as one of the most *communautaire* Member States') tend to have very poor records of compliance. (See also the Commission communication on implementation of the legal acts required to build the single market COM(89) 422 final of 7.12.1989).

But this situation might change. If the Commission has fulfilled most of its legislative duties to create the internal market, the institutional self-interest in maximizing resources and powers will make it seek additional tasks, which might be in the field of *de facto* implementation of European law. There are first indications that the Commission is tending toward implementation. Besides its increasing involvement in standardization, the Commission has already proposed the establishment of a European agency for occupational safety and health (OJ 1991 C 271-3), which has already been demanded by the unions (Konstanty and Zwingmann 1991: 268, TGB 1991: 91). Such an agency, 'would potentially enhance the Commission's health and safety capabilities significantly' (Baldwin 1992: 247). If the Commission becomes more active in implementation, the level of protection will become truly high in the Member States.

References

Note: Some of the documents and publications which appear here in the German version are also available in English.

Baldwin, Robert (1992), 'The limits of legislative harmonization', in Baldwin, Robert, and Thomas Daintith (eds), *Harmonization and Hazard: Regulating Workplace Health and Safety in the EC*, Graham and Trotman, London.

Bieber, Roland, Renaud Dehousse, John Pinder, and Joseph H.H. Weiler (eds) (1988), *One European Market?*, Nomos, Baden-Baden.

Coleman, James S. (1974), *Power and the Structure of Society*, New York, Norton, London.

Commons, John R. (1961), *Institutional Economics: Its Place in Political Economy*, University of Wisconsin Press, Madison.

Dehousse, Renaud, Christian Joerges, Giandomenico Majone, and Francis Snyder (1992), *Europe After 1992. New Regulatory Strategies*, draft version July, Florence.

Dehousse, Renaud, and Joseph H.H. Weiler (1990), 'The legal dimension', in Wallace, William (ed.), *The Dynamics of European Integration*, Pinter, London and New York.

Engel, Christian (1991a), 'Kommission der EG', in Weidenfeld, Werner, and Wolfgang Wessels (eds) (1991), *Europa von A - Z*, Europa Union Verlag, Bonn.

Engel, Christian (1991b), 'Ministerrat der EG', in Weidenfeld, Werner, and Wolfgang Wessels (eds) (1991), *Europa von A - Z*, Europa Union Verlag, Bonn.

Haas, Ernst B. (1964), *Beyond the Nation-State. Functionalism and International Organization*, Stanford University Press, Stanford.

Hoffmann, Stanley (1982), 'Reflections on the nation-state in Western Europe Today', *Journal of Common Market Studies*, vol. 21.

IEP (Institut für Europäische Politik) (1989), *'Comitology' - Characteristics, Performance and Options*, Research Project under contract by the EC Commission, Preliminary Final Report, Bonn.

Joerges, Christian, Jozef Falke, Hans-W. Micklitz, and Gert Brüggemeier (1988), *Die Sicherheit von Konsumgütern und die Entwicklung der Europäischen Gemeinschaft*, Nomos, Baden-Baden.

Keohane, Robert O., and Stanley Hoffmann (1990), 'Conclusions: community politics and institutional change', in William Wallace (ed.), *The Dynamics of European Integration*, Pinter, London and New York.

Konstanty, Reinhold, and Bruno Zwingmann (1991), 'Aussicht auf höhere Sicherheitsstandards in der Arbeitsumwelt?' *Die Mitbestimmung*, no. 4.

Kreile, Michael (ed.) (1992), *Die Integration Europas*, Politische Vierteljahresschrift Sonderheft 23.

Lindl, Ernst (1991), *Die EG-Richtlinie zur Angleichung der Rechtsvorschriften der Mitgliedstaaten für Maschinen. Grundlagen, Inhalt, Auswirkungen*, Ph.D. thesis, Free University, Berlin.

Majone, Giandomenico (1989), 'Regulating Europe: Problems and prospects', in Ellwein, Thomas, Joachim Jens Hesse, Renate Mayntz, and Fritz W. Scharpf (eds) *Jahrbuch zur Staats- und Verwaltungswissenschaft*, vol. 3, Nomos, Baden-Baden.

Majone, Giandomenico (1992), 'Market integration and regulation: Europe After 1992', *Metroeconomica*, vol. 43.

Meng, Werner (1988), 'Die Neuregelung der EG-Verwaltungsausschüsse. Streit um die "Comitologie"', *ZaöRV*, vol. 48, no. 2.

Ossenbühl, Fritz (1982), 'Die Bewertung technischer Risiken bei der Rechtsetzung', in *Risiko - Schnittstelle zwischen Recht und Technik*, VDE-Verlag, Berlin and Offenbach.

Pelkmans, Jacques (1988), 'A Grand Design by the Piece? An Appraisal of the Internal Market Strategy', in Bieber, Roland, Renaud Dehousse, John Pinder, and Joseph H.H. Weiler (eds), *One European Market?*, Nomos, Baden-Baden.

Pickert, Klaus (1992), 'Die europäischen Normungsarbeiten zur Maschinensicherheit und zur Gefahreneinschätzung', in *TGB*.

Rehbinder, Eckard, and Richard Stewart (1985), 'Environmental protection policy', *Integration Through Law*, vol. 2, De Gruyter, Berlin and New York.

Scharpf, Fritz W. (1985), 'Die Politikverflechtungs-Falle: Europäische Integration und deutscher Föderalismus', *Politische Vierteljahresschrift*, vol. 26.

Scharpf, Fritz W. (1985a), *The Joint-Decision Trap: Lessons from German Federalism and European Integration.*, Discussion Paper, Wissenschaftszentrum, Berlin.

Scharpf, Fritz W. (1990), 'Regionalisierung des europäischen Raums. Die Zukunft der Bundesländer im Spannungsfeld zwischen EG, Bund und Kommunen', in Alemann, Ulrich von, Rolf G. Heinze, and Bodo Hombach, (eds), *Die Kraft der Region: Nordrhein-Westfalen in Europa*, Dietz Verlag, Bonn.

Scharpf, Fritz W. (1992), 'Wege aus der Sackgasse. Europa: Zentralisierung und Dezentralisierung', *WZB-Mitteilungen* 56, Wissenschaftszentrum Berlin für Sozialforschung.

Schmitter, Philippe C. (1992), *Interests, Powers and Functions: Emergent Properties and Unintended Consequences in the European Polity*, Unpublished paper, Second version, Stanford University, Stanford.

Schneider, Heinrich (1992), 'Europäische Integration: die Leitbilder und die Politik', in Kreile, Michael (ed.) (1992), *Die Integration Europas*, Politische Vierteljahresschrift Sonderheft 23.

Schneider, Volker, and Raymund Werle (1989), 'Vom Regime zum korporativen Akteur. Zur institutionellen Dynamik der Europäischen Gemeinschaft', in Beate Kohler-Koch (ed.), *Regime in den internationalen Beziehungen*, Nomos, Baden-Baden.

Senger und Etterlin, Stefan von (1992), 'Das Europa der Eurokraten. Zentralismus, Partikularismus und die Rolle des Nationalstaates', *Aus Politik und Zeitgeschichte* no. B42/92, 9.10.1992.

Streeck, Wolfgang, and Philippe C. Schmitter (1991), 'From National Corporatism to Transnational Pluralism: Organized Interests in the Single European Market', *Politics and Society*, vol. 19, no. 2.

Strübel, Michael (1992), 'Nationale Interessen und europäische Politikformulierung in der Umweltpolitik', in Kreile, Michael (ed.) (1992), *Die Integration Europas*, Politische Vierteljahresschrift Sonderheft 23.

Suntum, Ulrich von (1992), 'Wettbewerb und Wachstum im europäischen Binnenmarkt', *Aus Politik und Zeitgeschichte*, 8.2.1992.

TGB (Europäisches Technikbüro der Gewerkschaften für Gesundheit und Sicherheit) (1991), *Verbesserung von Gesundheitsschutz und Sicherheit in der Europäischen Gemeinschaft*, Brussels. (English version: TUTB: Promoting Health and Safety in the European Community.)

TGB (Europäisches Technikbüro der Gewerkschaften für Gesundheit und Sicherheit) (ed.) (1992), *Die Mitwirkung der Gewerkschaften an den Europäischen Normungsarbeiten*, Brussels.

Vogel, Laurent (1991), *A Survey of Occupational Health and Safety Services in the Member States of the European Community and the European Free Trade Association. First Interim Report: The Existing Legal Frameworks in the Different States*. European Trade Union Technical Bureau for Health and Safety, Brussels

Wallace, Helen (1990), 'Making multilateral negotiations work', in William Wallace (ed.), *The Dynamics of European Integration*, Pinter, London and New York.

Wallace, William (1990), *The Dynamics of European Integration*, Pinter, London and New York.

Weidenfeld, Werner, and Wolfgang Wessels (eds) (1991), *Europa von A - Z*, Europa Union Verlag, Bonn.

Weiler, Joseph H.H. (1982), *Supranational Law and the Supranational System: Legal Structure and Political Process in the European Community.* Ph.D. thesis, European University Institute, Florence.

Weiler, Joseph H.H. (1988), 'The White Paper and the application of Community law', in Bieber, Roland, Renaud Dehousse, John Pinder, and Joseph H.H. Weiler (eds), *One European Market?*, Nomos, Baden-Baden.

Wessels, Wolfgang (1992), 'Staat und (westeuropäische) Integration. Die Fusionsthese', in Kreile, Michael (ed.) (1992), *Die Integration Europas*, Politische Vierteljahresschrift, Sonderheft 23.

Winter, Gerd (ed.) (1991), *Die Europäischen Gemeinschaften und das Öffentliche,* ZERP-Diskussionspapier 7-91, Zentrum für europäische Rechtspolitik an der Universität Bremen.

Wolf, Rainer (1987), 'Zur Antiquiertheit des Rechts in der Risikogesellschaft', *Leviathan*, vol. 15, no. 3.

11 European integration, workers' participation, and collective bargaining: A Euro-pessimistic view[1]

Berndt Keller

EU
FO2   JS2
J58   JS3

Summary

The prospects of the social dimension of the single market are limited - before and after the Maastricht Treaty. One group of reasons has to do with the corporate actors: differences of interest, of organizational structures, and of interest intermediation continue to exist. Furthermore problems of various forms of interest representation at different levels have hardly been solved. Even after the introduction of European Works Councils on a statutory-binding base problems of implementation are difficult to solve. Employee representation at the company level is far from being accomplished. Collective bargaining at the sectoral and/or European level seems to be impossible in the foreseeable future. Thus poor results of the Social Dialogue come as no surprise.

Introduction

The process of European unification which began with the signing of the Treaty of Rome in 1957 has been gaining momentum since the mid-1980s (from 'Euro-pessimism' and 'Euro-sclerosis' to 'Euro-optimism' and 'Euro-phoria'). After initial successes and then a long phase of stagnation (for a description of the various phases see Ullmann et al. 1990: 22, Däubler 1991: 307) structural changes in different product and labour markets and increasing competition from both Japan and the USA have acted as driving forces behind unification.

Two political signals, namely the Commission's 1985 White Paper on the completion of the Single Market and the 1987 Single European Act (SEA) encouraged this move towards integration. Until the SEA's signing, the EEC

Treaty required unanimity in the Council of Ministers, which to a great extent paralyzed the process of political decision making. In the 1980s, especially the British Government under Margaret Thatcher continually blocked decisions with its veto or with the threat of its use. Others could hide behind this minimalist position on European integration, without having to state publicly their own opposition.

This strategy will be more difficult to follow in the 1990s because of changed voting rules. Decisions can be reached with a qualified majority in certain, specific areas (Art. 100a and 118a EEC Treaty), which should ease and quicken decision making, as veto rights were abolished. As part of the Heads of State and Government's settlement at Maastricht at the end of 1991, the principle of qualified majority decisions was extended to other partial areas of labour and social policy. However, unlike the other eleven Member States, Great Britain refused to sign the protocol, and retained opt-out clauses (EIRR 1992a: 2, Blank and Köppen 1991: 653).

Parallel to the realization of the Economic and Monetary Union (EMU) are further steps towards a Political Union which aim at common foreign, security, social and immigration policies. Because of fundamental differences of opinion between the Member States (integrationists vs. supporters of cooperation between sovereign states), plans for the development of a European Political Union including a federal state are far less advanced than those for the EMU, although a simultaneous development would be in the interest of integration.

The Single Market was originally a project of pure economic integration without a political dimension. Labour and social policy, which were to remain entirely national responsibilities, were necessary only in as far as they created the basic conditions for economic integration (Teague 1989: 312, Mosley 1990). 'Harmonization' of differing national social standards was an intended result, but not a necessary prerequisite, of the unification process, in accordance with neoliberal legal policy ideas. Therefore, the development of the social dimension lags far behind that of economic integration (Kreile 1991: 17). The internationalization of national economies (market integration) has progressed much further than the Single Market's social dimension (political integration).

The signing of the 'Community Charter on the Fundamental Social Rights of Employees' in 1989, as a declaration of political intent (Silvia 1991, Addison and Siebert 1991), was frequently considered to be an important stage on the road to a social Europe. Following the signing, the Commission presented a programme to implement the contents of the 'Social Charter' with the help of proposed directives in a number of areas such as safety and health at the workplace, part-time work, limited-term contracts and irregular work, maternity protection, child labour and mass redundancies (Lodge 1990: 146, Lange 1992).

Opinions about the social charter are ambivalent (on the controversy between 'Euro-optimists' and 'Euro-pessimists' see Jacobi 1991, Hyman 1991; on the pessimistic view also Streeck 1991: 340). On the one hand, the Single Market's long ignored social dimension has gained in importance through effective publicity. This is the case even though the Social Charter is, because of Great Britain's disapproval, only a voluntary, legally non-binding recommendation to Member States to maintain certain European minimal standards. On the other hand, it is true that:

A range of constraints, including disagreement between Member States about Community labour market policy objectives, the strong emphasis the charter placed on 'subsidiarity', and difficulties associated with the current Treaty basis for industrial relations measures, point to a pessimistic assessment of the prospects of success for the social charter initiative, at least in the short term. (Hall 1991: 15, similarly Silvia 1991: 638).

In this paper we will discuss:

1   the internal problems of the social partners, i.e. trade unions and employers' associations (section 2),

2   the plant or establishment level, where the setting up and implementation of employee representation on a statutory basis is the decisive problem (section 3 and 4),

3   the company or firm level where different forms of employee representation on the board is of importance (section 5),

4   the sectoral level where the problem of creating a European system of collective bargaining constitutes the major issue (section 6).

These three interrelated levels in particular and the system of labour relations in general are considered the crucial areas for assessing the perspectives on the general development of the social dimension. We will present different pieces of evidence for the hypothesis that the prospects for the social dimension are less promising than frequently assumed in the current 'Euro-optimistic' literature. The probability of more economic integration but less social cohesion is greatly underestimated by a majority of scholars. The gap between economic and social integration, already quite obvious, could well become greater as a consequence of the EMU. The reason is that the EMU will deteriorate the prospects of union wage policies.

Corporate actors at the European level

Isolated national economic, social or labour policies will loose importance in the 1990s. Instead, new, European policy institutions will become more important. These will only supplement purely national ones, without, however, replacing them (horizontal vs. vertical dimension of decision making). The already complex internal and external agreement processes as well as strategic and organizational planning of all corporate actors, i.e. trade unions, employers' organizations, nation-states and 'Euro-actors', will thereby become more difficult.

For various reasons, a 'Europeanization' of labour relations will produce enormous problems for trade unions:

1   At the transnational level considerable differences of interest continue to exist among unions. These result from the necessary orientation towards nationally defined and economically limited interests. 'While for unions from advanced economies a joint European strategy is unlikely to offer improvements over what they have already gained on their own, to unions from weaker countries common demands tend to appear unrealistically ambitious and remote from their everyday practical concerns.' (Streeck and Schmitter 1991: 140). This overall orientation will change only slowly if at all and add further problems to those already existing at the national and sectoral level.

2   Considerable differences in organizational structure continue to exist, not only within, but especially between the countries, among others in:
- types of organization, with enterprise, professional, industrial and unitary trade unions;
- the strength of membership and density ratios, which vary between sseventy-five and eighty per cent in Denmark and Belgium and about ten per cent in France;
- the relation between interest representation at the plant and company level;
- the level of centralization of collective bargaining (plant, company, sector, nation) and conflict behaviour;
- and the level of centralization of decisionmaking (Däubler and Lecher 1991, Deppe and Weiner 1991).

Since World War Two, there has only been 'minimal convergence of the organizational structure of Western European trade unions' (Armingeon 1991: 379; another position is taken by Platzer 1991: 696). International comparisons show that changes in national trade unions have done little to reduce these differences (Jacobi 1992a: 20). As will be pointed out later, the necessary conditions for European-wide, institutionalized cooperation are rather underdeveloped. Thus, to cite a prominent example, there is no organization in the United Kingdom comparable to IG Metall. Also, the necessary attachment of individual national unions to European sectoral organizations (see below) creates difficulties because of different principles of organization.

These problems are difficult to overcome. Cooperation is made difficult by this 'Balkanization'. Long term international solidarity and opposition is difficult to organize and to maintain in view of rational, self-interested action of each national union. These tensions would be eased by a certain convergence of nationally specific laws and regulations to a minimal level. On the one hand, internationalization would bring some centralization of power and authority in the long run. On the other hand, framework regulations, i.e. basic standards and procedures, must be implemented not only at the national level, but also at the sectoral, company and even plant level (see chapter 6 for details). For this reason, the processes of alignment and differentiation have to take place simultaneously.

The currently existing 16 European Industrial Committees (EIC) (EIRR 1991a) are associations and/or bridgeheads of autonomous, more or less 'sectoral' trade unions with cross-border responsibilities. Since the substantial reorganization in the spring of 1991, they have, like the national peak organizations, representation on the decisionmaking bodies of the European Trade Union Congress (ETUC). They now have voting rights and formal influence on decisions regarding all matters except for finance. These European extensions of national trade unions form the basis of the ETUC's coordination authority, dovetailing national peak and 'sectoral' organizations. These EICs are expected to,

> inform their national members and coordinate their Europe-related activities; represent employee-related sectoral interests at EC-institutions; balance employers' organizations in the EC and coordinate contact to multinational companies in the EC. (Lecher 1991a: 200)

Not only will some supranational coordination of national peak organizations' policies be necessary, but also and especially a tight supranational coordination of trade union strategies at the sectoral level (horizontal-general versus vertical sector-specific organization). But the EICs are at different levels of development.

> A serious weakness is above all the lack of competent, materially and personnel well-equipped Euro-sectoral organizations. Even the IG Metall, up to now almost provocatively euro-abstinent, has seen that the

unions ... are still a long way from community wide collective bargaining. (Jacobi 1992b: 776)

At least for the time being, the majority of EICs are not well prepared for engaging in collective bargaining with employers' associations. Nor are they well prepared for general political representation of sectoral interests, especially by lobbying EC-institutions as an integrated part of the sectoral Social Dialogue.

The required 'internationalization' of interest representation implies of course a certain de-nationalization, i.e. the surrendering of national authority and power, above all bargaining autonomy, to either sector-specific institutions or to sector-unspecific peak organizations at the supranational level. Up to now, however, the supranational actors have been mostly concerned with the interests of their national members. They are primarily coalitions of national interests, not independent organizations.

This is true not only for trade unions, but also for employers' associations, though it holds less for trade associations. The EC-wide Federations of national, sector-unspecific peak organizations, the ETUC (Rath 1991: 245-52, Platzer 1991: 690-99) and Union des Industries de la Communauté Européenne (UNICE) (Tyszkiewicz 1991: 85-101) should already have become supranational actors and privileged discussion partners for EC-institutions. In reality, the UNICE and especially the ETUC are hardly policy-competent as independent 'Euro-actors'. There are various reasons for this (EIRR 1991b, Platzer 1992):

1   Structures required for collective bargaining are poorly developed.

2   The authority to take significant decisions - including the competence to enforce their implementation - remains with national organizations.

3   Divergent interests on both sides which cannot be mediated within the framework of peak associations could lead to the formation of internal factions and hinder external policy competence.

4   Consistent concepts of aims and strategies are rare.

5   Qualified personnel is lacking.

Not much has been accomplished by the Social Dialogue between the Federations of national peak organizations: binding agreements are totally absent. There are only a few non-binding common position papers on some topics proposed by the Commission, such as the introduction of new technologies, flexibility of the labour market and access to vocational training.

EC-wide employers' associations have been, for a long time, merely negative coalitions aimed at preventing European-level policy measures. The Portuguese, Greek and British associations were frequent opponents of the majority in the complex process of opinion formation. UNICE saw itself for many years only as a lobby of European institutions, especially the Commission, and as spokesman against regulatory measures. Only recently has it started to abandon its principle opposition to European-wide collective agreements and thus to the beginnings of European labour relations. It has cautiously signaled its willingness to negotiate general agreements.

But this change of opinion was purely strategic and instrumentally based. It was meant to prevent binding EC directives and decrees and to preempt such regulation with voluntary agreements more open to influence by the associations (see EIRR 1992b: 29). Only at the end of 1991 did UNICE, the European Center of Public Enterprises (CEEP), and the ETUC agree on the possibility of multinational collective framework agreements between unions and employers. This option was then included in the Maastricht Treaty on Political Unification.

Coalitions between leading national organizations are probable for certain, shared interests, such as the Mutual Declaration on the Social Dimension of the Single Market of 1989. Still realistic is the scenario where unions and employers' associations put pressure on their national governments to work together in achieving certain demands, such as acquiring subsidies within the framework of EC regional policies, the regulation of specific sectors, or the preservation of elements of their own national systems. Thus, national sector-specific and general coalitions seem be just as important for achieving the organization's interests as an internationalization of bargaining with a definite opposition of interests between employers' associations and trade unions.

The central problem is balancing different national interests on the European level. The emergence of neo-corporatist interest intermediation, similar to the social contracts of the late 1960s and 1970s at nation-state level, proves unrealistic for various reasons:

1   The nation-states will not disappear with advancing integration but will continue to play a central role parallel to supranational institutions, especially in the policy fields relevant in our context. A supranational social welfare state and a 'European' government, a necessary partner in political bargaining, will not appear in the foreseeable future. Such an actor would be necessary, however, to offer social policy compensations for concessions made by trade unions. Present compensations made by the Commission can not provide a substitute

because they are of a different nature and no explicit offer for trade unions.

2   As to the employers' associations, their negative attitude hinders the organization of trilateral political exchanges. UNICE prefers the status quo of purely national responsibility of member associations and of non-decisions at the European level over the creation of a European system of collective bargaining.

3   Finally, trade unions are not able to form transnational, general interest organizations necessary for 'Euro-corporatism'. They are too nationalistic in their policies, organizationally too divided, and politically too weak to carry out trilateral agreements achieved in EC-level negotiations, neither internally vis-a-vis their members nor externally.

Further development of an established 'transnational pluralism' within the framework of a European minimal state without completely developed democratic institutions is thus more likely than the creation of a transnational, corporatist system of interest formation and intermediation (Streeck and Schmitter 1991, Streeck 1992). The failure of the first attempts at a tripartite structure, such as the Permanent Committee on Employment Questions and some tripartite conferences in the 1970s, was indicative of this. At least for the foreseeable future it is unrealistic to assume that the three corporate actors will be willing to engage in trilateral exchanges. Trade unions have nothing to offer, employers' organizations are better off if they manage to maintain the status quo, threats and supports by the non-existing European 'state' are not possible.

Despite the problems mentioned here, a return to the established national paths of a fundamental consent is not possible, because the actual dovetailing of national economies has already advanced too far. As the point of no return in the integration process was reached long ago, all the Member States' relevant trade unions support the Single Market project, although its realization contains serious risks for them. It would weaken their institutional and political power base at the national level, without offering sufficient compensation at the supranational level. German trade unions have given not only much clearer support to the Single Market project, but also came out much earlier with their support (Streeck 1991: 322).

Employee participation at the plant level by statutory regulation

At the decentralized level, there is the problem of setting up supranational representation of interest with specific rights. Company decisionmaking structures and processes have been and will be fundamentally changed by cross-border developments in the Single Market, especially by a wave of company mergers, takeovers and fusions. By contrast, codified law of employees' representation ends *ex definitione* at the country's border: moreover, these national laws could be eroded by increasing internationalization of strategic business units ('divisionalization') and by centralization of important decisions at the top of the company. For this reason, parallel structures of transnational representation of interests are necessary, not to replace or make superfluous their national *pendants*, but to supplement them. Up to now, international cooperation of national representatives has been difficult, both legally and in practice.

The solution cannot lie in making one of the quite different European models of interest representation into a reference model and exporting it Europe-wide, as was discussed in relation to the German system in the early 1970s. The idea of transplanting comparably extensive German co-determination rights (*Mitbestimmungsrechte*) would have as little chance of achieving agreement within the EC as would the middle way, which would entail a rolling back of employees' rights, especially in Germany. Such a step would be neither sensible nor possible because of historical features and institutional differences. Corporate actors' interests in the different countries can hardly be harmonized. Moreover, the national legal systems are quite different in respect to form of regulation, customs and practice, extent, intensity and areas of participation (Krieger 1991: 20-34, Jaeger 1991: 59-95).

There is no question of complete alignment, in the sense of the transplantation of one national system to other countries. Rather, an institutionalization of minimum regulations which allows for a certain dependability, calculation and stability of action is needed. Given the multiplicity of models, the object is not worker participation in a specific national context. Rather the object is improved employee participation through hearings, consultation, information and cooperation as a general principle to increase 'social' productivity.

Various earlier legislative initiatives to regulate what was long known to be a problem failed in their purpose, especially the Fifth Directive of 1972 and the Draft of the Vredeling Directives of 1980 (revised in 1983). Employers' associations unanimously rejected this draft. In 1986 it was decided not to pursue it further.

After a prolonged and controversial discussion, the Commission finally presented its proposal for a directive on 'the establishment of European committees or procedures in Community-scale undertakings and Community-scale groups of undertakings for the purposes of informing and consulting employees' in December 1990. Purely national companies, and the participation rights which apply to them, remained untouched.

In 'Community-scale undertakings' with at least 1,000 employees within the Community and at least two companies in different Member States with at least 150 employees each European Works Councils (EWC) are to be set up. These EWC, which should consist of at least three and at most thirty workers' representatives and should meet at least once a year, should 'be informed and consulted by the central management of the undertaking or controlling undertaking about any management proposals likely to have serious consequences for the interests of the employees of the undertaking'. This prompt informing and consulting should include investment perspectives and plans to reduce or increase the labour force. More extensive provisions of participation rights and methods which lie beyond the directives' minimal standards are, according to the subsidiarity principle, matters for negotiation at the establishment or company level. Thus the Directive tries to combine legally and contractually introduced elements of participation whereas on the national level such rights are defined either by legal enactment or by contractual agreement. This combination could lead to qualitatively different forms of participation within the same frame of reference and not to some sort of 'harmonization'.

Arguing along the lines of the German Works Constitution Act (*Betriebs-verfassungsgesetz*) there be no multinational Company or Group Works Councils (*Gesamt-/Konzernbetriebsrat*) with participation rights in social, personnel and economic matters, but only a Economic Committee (*Wirt-schaftsausschuß*) with merely consultative and information rights but no joint decision making or veto rights. The final decision remains, in any case, 'with the management of the company or its decisionmaking bodies'. The partner in the processes of information and consultation is not, as in for example the Vredeling directive, local management, but rather that at the headquarters.

The EWCs are to be autonomous, independent of national interest representation, and separate from these existing bodies. They are to have quite flexible structures, but not solid 'European' substructures. They consist of only the interest representatives in the respective countries. Using the above cited criteria, the directive applies to a minority of approximately fourteen million employees. EC-wide it applies to more than 1,200 multinational companies, in Germany to more than 250. In comparison to earlier initiatives, we observe a development from substantive to procedural forms of regulation, which legally and economically guarantee Community-wide forms of cooperation between representatives of both sides. Proposed are indirect representative forms of participation, not the direct representative forms which have been demanded to a greater or lesser extent in the controversial discussions on flexible production and lean production.

On the national level the social partners had given quite different assessments of the draft. The reactions by the German peak organizations are quite typical of others (Niedenhoff 1991: 6-21):

1   Business and employers' associations fear friction between national works councils and the EWC, because of different responsibilities and 'negative influences on decisions planned by the enterprise level'. Both reject the draft directive as being 'inconsistent with the basic principles of the German works constitution' and favour non-binding recommendations instead of binding directives. (BDA 1991: 11, see also Niedenhoff 1992: 71-83)

2   Trade unions view proposed binding legal regulation as 'a step in the right direction', but criticize the high threshold in terms of number of employees, and demand more tasks and responsibilities for the EWC to give it an equal role in negotiations. Information should be produced 'in a written form, complete, and so punctual that the proposals and considerations of the employees can be taken into consideration' (DGB-Bundesvorstand 1991a and 1991b). Invitation of experts and trade union representatives in meetings should be possible when neccessary. Subcommittees should be set up and arbitration procedures agreed upon. The ETUC shares this criticism and also demands improvements. (Hans-Böckler-Stiftung 1991: 11, Deppe 1992: 209)

For some time, the future of the draft directive was uncertain because of Great Britain's blockade in the Council. This led to its temporary failure at the end of 1991 and it looked as if the draft would never make it to the statute book. Only the majority voting introduced by the Maastricht Treaty ended the political stalemate: The eleven, without the UK, were now able to pass a slightly changed version of the draft. But this does by no means mean that all problems have been solved because various new obstacles will arise during implementation. The directive is a necessary, not a sufficient, prerequisite for efficient forms of employee representation.

Employee participation at the company level by contractual agreement

EC institutions have delayed some proposals which have been on the political agenda since the 1970s (Northrup et al. 1988: 526). UNICE offered long and fierce resistance to EWC and leading national organizations supported this strategy in spite of their own positive experience with various forms of participation. Therefore, different national peak and sectoral unions took initiatives on the supranational level, as a form of 'double strategy'. They tried to compensate for participation deficits and for increasing information disadvantages, and tried to exploit existing divergences in national interests. Usually, works councils agreed at first among themselves on points of order which formed the basis for cooperation. After practical recognition by management, which often sought to hinder EC-directives and overtake employees' initiatives, the agreement in the narrower sense was reached.

However, only a few MNCs with strong labour representation have voluntarily agreed to institute various EWC models with mere information and consultation rights. Since the second half of the 1980s, a few MNCs with headquarters in France have accepted cross-border workers' representation and thus taken on a model role (among others Thompson-Brandt, Bull, BSN, Elf-Aquitaine, Nestlé) (Buda 1991, Deppe 1992: 101-73). Volkswagen was the first German MNC with a 'European Company Works Council', in existence since 1990 and officially recognized since the beginning of 1992 (Schulten 1992). With the exception of the UK, the situation is more balanced between the larger Member States in the 1990s than it was in the 1980s (Streeck and Vitols 1993).

Existing knowledge about the practical work of these EWCs can be summed up as follows:

> Meetings are typically held yearly. In all cases the companies meet the costs of the meeting including travel, accommodation and paid time-off for employees representatives. Trade unions operating within the companies generally have the right to determine employee representation at meetings. In most cases that nature of the arrangement is informational rather than consultative. (Hall 1992: 4)

Information passed on by management is limited to company-wide questions and excludes purely national issues. Consultation in the relatively small councils with generally fewer than thirty members is rare, real negotiation does not take place. The representatives of both sides have assessed the practical work quite positively for the representation of their interests. Often 'external' trade union representatives are members of these councils, which, following the French pattern, consist of representatives of employers and employees. While management is satisfied with existing regulations and does not want to see any changes, employee representatives would like to see the agreements more strictly formalized, their rights extended and the work more effectively organized (Gold and Hall 1992).

To overstate it a little, such EWCs are only bodies:

263

1   For permanent contact between the interest representatives from various countries.

2   For mutual information exchange of one's own intentions and management plans, among others regarding working hours, other employment conditions, and cross-border investment strategies.

3   For attempting to harmonize quite different employee interests in various locations.

Because of their lack of rights and competencies, such EWCs are hardly an effective means of realizing interests vis-à-vis management. Practical problems exist, among others, in the lack of language ability. The EWCs are only a forerunner, a precedent for legal regulation. These voluntarily agreed upon, purely informative and consultative councils certainly do not make legally binding, and therefore unitary and general regulations unnecessary: They are a necessary though not sufficient prerequisite for a directive on EWCs.

The significant disadvantage of an imbalanced mixture of the regulatory instruments 'law' and 'contract' remains, even if voluntary EWCs win greater acceptance and their number increases (Handelsblatt 6.8.1992). The reason is that more plant and company employee representatives try, through setting up such committees, to gain wide ranging experience and to achieve a certain de facto cooperation, in spite of management's principally limited preparedness to agree. Application for possible financing of preparatory conferences from EC-funds, which has become possible, has been helpful in this respect. The related 'grants for transnational meeting of employee representatives' has been greatly increased in the early 1990s.

In numbers: Towards the mid 1990s there are agreements in less than thirty companies, fifteen to twenty further agreements are being prepared. These exceptions can, however, be explained by specific parameters which make a slower extension appear more likely:

> The state ownership and socialist management of a number of the leading French examples constitute a clear political factor in these places. The prior existence of legislation providing for national group-level representative bodies in France and Germany may also have been the springboard for the extension of such arrangements to the European level. (Hall et al. 1992: 6)

The experience of various countries with different regulatory mechanisms shows that purely contractual, and thus reversible, agreements are not able to replace adequately legal, and thus binding, guarantees. We know from international comparison of labour relations (Ferner and Hyman 1992, Hyman and Ferner 1994) that purely voluntary contractual strategies are too unwieldy to provide effective nation-wide, general coverage, compared to more strictly legal ones. The piecemeal strategy implicit in all voluntary systems absorbs too much personnel and time and overtaxes the national representatives' limited capabilities for action, as initiatives must be promoted anew in every company. It also creates the additional problem of a 'plant syndicalism or plant egoism' which prevents the necessary cooperative division of labour between interest representatives within a 'dual' system of labour relations. Trade unions are in a better position with legal regulation, as their limited resources need not be used for case to case negotiation of participation rights in a process of *do ut des*.

Arguing from the point of the potential strategies, the 'state' must become active as third corporate actor. It has to create the necessary conditions for voluntary agreements through supranational re-regulatory measures and by legally binding parameters. In the lengthy process of the development of European labour relations, the EWCs could serve as a crystallization point for cooperation, as against more centralized elements of the bargaining systems. All the more so as plant-level institutions have gained in importance relative to their counterparts at the sectoral level, given the tendency towards decentralization in all countries (Sisson 1991: 153). Further tendencies toward decentralization are probable as a consequence of developments within the EC. As long as EWCs do not function everywhere, the necessary, but always precarious connection between establishment and firm employee representation cannot succeed.

Even the existence of EWCs in all MNCs would not solve all problems of employee representation. Within an EWC, rather heterogeneous, both national and site-specific, possibly conflicting, member interests exist. They need to be aggregated and mediated to make effective representation possible. Even with non-ideological, pragmatic attitudes towards management, strategies of 'trustful cooperation' would be difficult to establish because of the lack of experience with 'cooperative' labour relations. The relation of the EWCs and 'their' various national works councils would have to be newly defined within the parameters of a presently nonexistent, transnational system of interest representation.

Participation at the company level

In Germany employee participation refers to both *establishment* and company participation, i.e. the Works Constitution Act (*Betriebsverfassungsgesetz*) and the various Co-determination Acts (*Mitbestimmungsgesetze*) as the legal framework for mutually agreed upon regulation. At the upper level we

265

assume implicitly a two-body model with separate bodies for management and control of the company - and not a one-body model for executive and supervising functions as exists in most other countries (monistic vs. dualistic system).

However, in the context of the Single Market, participation at the plant level is more in discussion than that at the company level. The latter exists only in a limited number of countries, such as Germany, Denmark, France, Holland, Luxembourg (European Trade Union Institute 1990: 12, Gold and Hall 1990: 15). Therefore, only these countries favour the creation of a two level transnational system of employee representation. However, various, more conflict-oriented national trade unions are not particularly interested in such 'social partnership' regulation. Thus, the differences of opinion within the EC over participation at the company level are even greater than those over participation at the plant level. Generally there exists, with the exception of the UK, a clear north-south divide.

Various older initiatives to 'harmonize' national regulations of employee representation failed, such as the draft directive of the Societas Europaea (SE), fifth directive and tenth directive. The Commission therefore introduced in 1989 and in a modified form in 1991 a number of participation models, partly as a by-product of a draft directive for a new 'European Joint Stock Company' (Societas Europaea or SE) (Di Marco 1991). They were intended to supplement, not to replace existing national regulations. These models could be applied in monistic as well as in dualistic systems and thus would leave open the choice between alternatives considered to be equivalent:

1   In a supervisory board separate from management employees nominate a third to a half of the members (German-Dutch model).

2   Management informs the employees' representatives quarterly, who sit in a separate SE body, about business prospects and foreseeable developments (French-Belgian model).

3   An agreement on participation rights is not established legally, but rather by collective bargaining between management and employees' representatives (Italian and Swedish model).

The Commission, following the cafeteria principle and not, as before, the unitary principle of standardization, thus created a range of choice, 'a menu of worker participation options' (Addison and Siebert 1991: 604), in that they proposed that each country could choose one model as binding for itself. SE's with headquarters in Germany would then have to provide participation of the German model. This compromise-supporting solution would, on the one hand, create a very flexible model with competing minimum regulations. On the other hand, it would probably complicate rather than simplify or harmonize company and labour law.

These proposals have been the target of fierce criticism by the trade unions, who fear a 'participation flight' to countries with weaker employees' rights. The European Parliament criticized the proposals as well and pushed through substantive improvements, by which the choice of a model required the approval of the works council. The Economic and Social Committee made some proposals aimed at achieving a balance in level and intensity of participation, above all in models two and three (Wendeling-Schröder 1991: 418).

> Despite its optional nature, the European Company Statute has been strongly opposed by certain Member State governments and employer's organizations, not least because they see it as a stalking horse for other, more far-reaching Community instruments on worker participation. (Hall 1991: 27)

As at the plant level, only very few voluntary regulations on participation at the company level could be agreed upon.

The draft directive for SE once again failed to pass the Council in late 1992, with the representatives of the FRG and Great Britain expressing different opinions. While the German government disputed the equivalence of the models, the British government voted against any legislative intervention. Because of conflicting interests, it is likely that participation regulation might be totally excluded from further political treatment of SE draft directives.

For Germany, the country with perhaps the most advanced regulation in this regard, the situation arose where there was plant level workers' participation, but none at the company level. This scenario is not very attractive, neither for trade unions nor for works councils having operated in a 'dual' system of interest representation for many years.

European collective bargaining at the sectoral level

All developed industrial nations experience trends toward internationalization, flexibilization, deregulation, and decentralization in their labour relations (Keller 1993: 329-72). National bargaining systems are adapting more or less successfully to changing economic and technical conditions. European unification will also, at least in the long run, encourage a certain internationalization of the social partners and their nationally aligned and divided policies, through a liberalization of all national markets and above all the EMU. This applies not only for regulation of participation rights on various levels, but also for internationally coordinated collective bargaining (Lecher 1991a: 194-201) including mediation procedures and strike rights. The controversy over the establishment of EWCs started much earlier than the discussion about a European system of collective bargaining, which has received less attention.

Difficulties arise, on the one hand, from differences between Member States repeatedly emphasized in the literature:

1 The level of legalization (*Verrechtlichung*) varies enormously. For example, there are no binding collective contracts in the UK. The significance of the regulatory instruments 'law' and 'contract' varies from country to country and with the object of regulation.

2 Collective bargaining takes place at different levels (plant, company, sector, nation). The relation between plant and company interest representation is, legally and in practice, quite differently structured in monistic and dualistic systems.

3 Regulatory standards and the extent of regulation are also clearly different on various levels.

On the other hand, difficulties arise from economic, legal and organizational problems of establishing a European system of labour relations.

1 As already mentioned, the European peak organizations ETUC and UNICE are hardly suitable as bargaining partners: In some larger countries, national peak organizations - mainly DGB and TUC - are not competent in this area, and thus would not be so at the EC level. Moreover, European peak organizations would be unlikely to receive a general mandate to conclude intersectoral agreements from their national member organizations (Däubler 1992: 334). Finally, the interest heterogeneity in intersectoral organizations is almost by definition even greater than at the sectoral level. Therefore it is rather likely that the European peak organizations will be less involved in collective bargaining than in negotiations within the Social Dialogue along the principles set out in the Maastricht Treaty. In this context they represent general, encompassing interests regarding labour, social and industrial policy. Such a division of competencies and tasks is quite controversial with the ETUC's membership. The ETUC and especially its French members tend towards centralization, while German, Austrian and North European trade unions want more competencies at the sectoral level (Kreimer 1992: 43). Furthermore, peak organizations take on different

tasks of policy coordination and support. They integrate on the horizontal instead of on the vertical axis.

2   Authority to set strategic norms would therefore most likely lie with the representative organizations at the sectoral level, that is with the European Industrial Committees (EIC) and with business or employers' associations. Who the counterparts of unions are is not clear in all cases as UNICE has no organizations at the industry-level. First efforts to 'form a European collective bargaining system' have been started by the European Metalworkers' Association. Similar initiatives have been taken in some other industries, such as the chemical, banking and food industry, but hardly in the majority.

Further development in this direction requires, however, that the internal and external legitimacy of these organizations be strengthened. They have to become autonomous partners for collective bargaining and power has to be transferred from national organizations, which up to now have protected their complete bargaining autonomy. Collective bargaining in MNCs must be distinguished from other forms of supranational collective bargaining, as it should be comparatively easier to organize (Keller 1994).

However, European sectoral unions would have serious intraorganizational problems of opinion formation and coordination, given the heterogeneity of interest regarding ends and means. These would doubtless be even greater than the difficulties of national organizations with interest aggregation and intermediation. To carry this scenario a step further, given the need for intraorganizational democracy, sectoral unions would have to form internationally balanced bargaining committees for taking on coordination tasks. These European committees or their leaders would have to secure a bargaining mandate. The application of this transnational mandate would have to be controlled by national constituencies and, if necessary, strike ballots and strike measures would have to be organized to back up Community-wide collective agreements.

3   The literature has mostly dealt with problems of the formation of bargaining institutions and policies. However, enforcing or controlling their execution at national and more decentralized levels are of equal importance. Implementation of EC-wide contracts would be very difficult because various national representatives and institutions lack the power to implement effectively. Successful implementation assumes a willingness for constructive dialogue on both sides of the bargaining table, even regarding contested issues.

Moreover, legal problems might arise with the implementation of such agreements as they have no direct binding effect. Member States are not required to make the agreements binding, nor are the organizations able to make commitments binding on their members. The Protocol on Social Policy of the Maastricht Treaty only requires in art. 4 par. 2: 'Agreements concluded at Community level shall be implemented either in accordance with the procedures and practices specific to management and labour and the Member States or ... at the joint request of the signatory parties, by a Council decision on a proposal from the Commission.' Both alternatives are equally vague and indeterminate (Keller 1994).

4   Also unsolved is the question, important above all for countries with low density ratios such as Italy or Ireland, of an EC-wide generally binding procedure, i.e. a declaration of the validity of contracts beyond the circle of membership of the social partners. The same applies to regulation of conflict resolution through mediation procedures, agreements and obligations to avoid industrial action during negotiations.

5   The currently non-existent framework would have to include the possibility of cross-border mobilization and industrial action, including the right to strike. The question of cross-border union strike rights - a necessary prerequisite for an actual ability to strike - remains as unsolved as that of employers' lockout rights, which are regulated differently in various Member States.

6   It is unlikely that the Community will, in the foreseeable future, create the statutory prerequisites necessary for the conclusion of transnational collective agreements, which have been completely absent up to now. The legal instruments for backing up such contracts are explicitly absent in Community law and remain totally in national competence. As regards the 'freedom of coalition and free collective bargaining', the Action Programme for the realization of the Social Charter emphasizes only the role of the Social Dialogue, without saying anything about cross-border rights of coalition and collective bargaining. Neither does it define fundamental social rights. The same is true for the Maastricht Treaty.

7   Last but not least, the scope is limited to integrative bargaining and excludes the distributive type (Walton and McKersie 1991). Relative chances of success exist only with those bargaining objects which offer bilateral and transnational advantages. Community-wide framework agreements are only possible for certain 'qualitative' matters, such as

safety at work, holidays, internal and external flexibility, working hours, work organization, training and further training, and equal opportunity for men and women. Details of 'quantitative' matters remain to be regulated at the national or sectoral level. Generally it is true that, 'the choice of themes and objects for European collective bargaining should be considered very carefully. Any attempt at setting up a catalogue would be abstract, premature and unproductive'. (European Trade Union Institute 1992: 50).

Differences in wages stemming from large differences in productivity will continue to exist and will prevent the conclusion of EC-wide collective agreements on 'quantitative' matters. A general rise in wages is not possible, as this would end specific advantages of location, especially for the southern Member States. A levelling down of wages would meet resistance of employees and their organizations in the northern, high wage countries.

General, broad cross-border agreements at the Community level are thus unlikely for the mid and long term, as long as current differences in interests, institutions, economic performance and productivity levels continue to exist (Silvia 1991: 7641).

There is not yet much potential for integration of national labour relations into a European system. New European institutions which are preconditions and supports for such a development are at best in their early formative stages. Existing national institutions will only slowly grow closer together. There is a somewhat more realistic prospect for the development of a transnational system of interest representation in MNCs (Lecher 1991b).

Complete 'homogenization' of different national patterns within the framework of a 'European Bargaining Union' has not been possible in the past and is not likely to be so in the future. This might also not be desirable given the tendencies for maintaining national diversity. However, a certain convergence would be necessary for the realization of the social dimension of European integration.

European collective agreements could only be framework agreements formulating minimal unitary standards which could be further elaborated upon in additional agreements at lower levels. They could in no way replace or substitute for national agreements, but only supplement them. Their broad arrangements would need to be adapted and reformulated according to the specific conditions at the national, industry and factory level. Such processes of adaption could be another source of conflict and disagreement.

271

Prospects

The political results of the Single Market project are fairly limited. National and transnational corporate actors have not been able - or not even willing - to create a social dimension to the Single Market. There is an enormous gap between the significant economic and political structural changes and the lack of social cohesion. Advances in the policy areas dealt with here - essential parts of any social dimension - can hardly be seen. Also, the development of a European social welfare state is as absent from the political agenda as is a system of European labour relations (Lange 1992: 256). Partial intervention in isolated issues, such as health and safety, equal rights for men and women, and migrant workers, is no substitute for a coherent system.

The Maastricht Treaty extends the concept of Social Dialogue (Art. 118b EECT). The social partners are encouraged to meet not only at the national, but also at the sectoral level, to 'lead to relations based on agreement'. Political authorities will recognize the precedence of bilateral contracts over legal provisions in that they surrender their right of initiative and do not unilaterally intervene in this sphere of government-free self regulation.

With these improved possibilities for independent production of 'quasi-guideline proposals', the social partners' autonomy and options for action, as well as their influence on the legislative process have been extended. At the same time the Commission's and Council's social policy responsibilities have been reduced. Concomitantly, pressure has increased on the social partners to take the initiative instead of waiting for the Commission, and to reach agreements in order to overcome the general stalemate in their policy areas. However, considering the interest heterogeneity on both sides, it will be difficult for the social partners to formulate common strategies for accomplishing such tasks in the foreseeable future.

The already existent gap between advancing economic integration and a still largely absent social dimension could certainly grow (Jacobi 1992b: 773). In order to prevent this, it is necessary to realize the social dimension with substantial and procedural labour standards. This cannot take as much time as earlier developments at the national level took. 'Decisions currently being taken and the institutions resulting from such decisions will impose their stamp at the European level of industrial relations for a long time to come'. (Jensen et al. 1992: 6).

If standards are not developed quickly, the consequences could be a legitimacy deficit for the Community. There are already clear signals in this direction indicated by the referenda on the 'Treaty of European Unity' in Denmark, France and the UK. Furthermore, political stability could be endangered, leading to a loss of 'social' productivity so urgently needed in highly competitive global markets.

Note

1   The author wants to thank Wolfgang Lecher (WSI of the German trade
     union DGB, Düsseldorf), George Strauss (IIR, UC Berkeley), the
     participants of the Political Economy Seminar at UC Berkeley and of the
     SASE Conference in New York City in 1993 for many useful comments
     on earlier drafts of his paper.

References

Addison, John T., and W. Stanley Siebert (1991), 'The social charta of the
     European Community: Evolution and controversies', *Industrial and Labor
     Relations Review*, vol. 44.
Armingeon, Klaus (1991), 'Die doppelte Herausforderung der europäischen
     Gewerkschaften', *Gewerkschaftliche Monatshefte*, vol. 42.
BDA (1991), *Jahresbericht 1991*, Cologne.
Blank, Michael, and Margit Köppen (1991), 'Europäischer Binnenmarkt', in
     Kittner, Michael (ed.), *Gewerkschaftsjahrbuch 1991. Daten-Fakten-
     Analysen*, Cologne.
Buda, Dirk (1991), *Auf dem Weg zum europäischen Betriebsrat*, Friedrich
     Ebert Stiftung, Reihe Eurokolleg 6.
Däubler, Wolfgang (1991), 'Die soziale Dimension des Binnenmarktes -
     Realität oder Propagandafigur?', in Däubler, Wolfgang, and Wolfgang
     Lecher (eds), *Die Gewerkschaften in den 12 EG-Ländern. Europäische
     Integration und Gewerkschaftsbewegung*, Cologne.
Däubler, Wolfgang (1992), 'Europäische Tarifverträge nach Maastricht',
     Europäische Zeitschrift für Wirtschaftsrecht, vol. 3.
Däubler, Wolfgang, and Wolfgang Lecher (eds) (1991), *Die Gewerkschaften
     in den 12 EG-Ländern. Europäische Integration und Gewerkschaftsbe-
     wegung*, Cologne.
Deppe, Frank (ed.) (1992), *Euro-Betriebsräte. Internationale Mitbestimmung
     - Konsequenzen für Unternehmen und Gewerkschaften*, Wiesbaden.
Deppe, Frank, and Klaus-Peter Weiner (eds) (1991), *Binnenmarkt '92. Zur
     Entwicklung der Arbeitsbeziehungen in Europa*, Hamburg.
DGB-Bundesvorstand (1991a), *Stellungnahme des Deutschen Gewerk-
     schaftsbundes zur Anhörung des Ausschusses für Arbeit und Sozialordnung
     des Deutschen Bundestages am 6.November 1991 zu dem Vorschlag für
     eine Richtlinie des Rates über die Einsetzung Europäischer Betriebsräte zur
     Information und Konsultation der Arbeitnehmer in gemeinschaftsweit
     operierenden Unternehmen und Unternehmensgruppen*, Ms. Düsseldorf.

DGB-Bundesvorstand (1991b), *Ergänzende Stellungnahme des DGB zu dem Vorschlag für eine Richtlinie des Rates über die Einsetzung Europäischer Betriebsräte zur Information und Konsulation der Arbeitnehmer in gemeinschaftsweit operierenen Unternehmen und Unternehmensgruppen, zugleich Erwiderung zu der Arbeitgeber-Stellungnahme zum Richtlinien-Entwurf der EG-Kommission vom März 1991*, Ms. Düsseldorf.

Di Marco, Guiseppe (1991), 'Zum Stand des europäischen Gesellschaftsrechts - Angleichung des nationalen Rechts und Schaffung neuer europäischer Rechtsformen', *Schmalenbachs Zeitschrift für betriebswirtschaftliche Forschung*, special issue 29.

EIRR (1991a), 'European industry committees - a register', *European Industrial Relations Review*, no. 211.

EIRR (1991b), 'Collective bargaining, trade unions and employers' organisations in Europe', *European Industrial Relations Review*, EIRR Report Number Seven, London.

EIRR (1992a), 'Social policy and the Maastricht summit - confusion reigns', *European Industrial Relations Review*, no. 216.

EIRR (1992b), 'The social dialogue - Euro-bargaining in the making?', *European Industrial Relations Review*, no. 220.

European Trade Union Institute (ed.) (1990), *Arbeitnehmervertretung und Arbeitnehmerrechte in den Unternehmen Westeuropas*, Brussels.

European Trade Union Institute (ed.) (1992), *Die europäischen Dimensionen der Kollektivvertragsverhandlungen nach Maastricht*, Brussels.

Ferner, Anthony, and Richard Hyman (eds) (1992), *Industrial relations in the new Europe*, Oxford and Cambridge.

Gold, Michael, and Mark Hall (1990), *Gesetzliche Regelung und Praxis der Arbeitnehmerbeteiligung in der Europäischen Gemeinschaft*, Working Paper no. WP/90/41/DE, European Foundation for the Improvement of Living and Working Conditions, Dublin.

Gold, Michael, and Mark Hall (1992), *Report on European-level information and consultation in multinational companies - An evaluation of practice*, Dublin.

Hall, Mark (1991), *Industrial relations regulation at European level*, Ms. Industrial Relations Research Unit, University of Warwick.

Hall, Mark (1992), *Legislating for employee participation: A case study of the European works council directive*, Warwick Papers in Industrial Relations no. 39, Warwick.

Hall, Mark, Paul Marginson, and Keith Sisson (1992), *The European works council: Setting the research agenda*, Warwick Papers in Industrial Relations no. 41, Warwick.

Hans-Böckler-Stiftung (ed.) (1991), *Europäische Betriebsräte. Ein Beitrag zum sozialen Europa*, Düsseldorf.

Hyman, Richard (1991), 'The new kakania - a rejoinder to O. Jacobi's theses', in Sadowski, Dieter, and Otto Jacobi (eds), *Employers' associations in Europe: Policy and organisation*, Baden-Baden.

Hyman, Richard, and Anthony Ferner (eds) (1994), *New frontiers in European industrial relations*, Oxford.

Jacobi, Otto (1991a), 'Trade unions and the single European market - remarks on a certain disorientation', in Sadowski, Dieter, and Otto Jacobi (eds), *Employers' associations in Europe: Policy and organisation*, Baden-Baden.

Jacobi, Otto (1992a), *Soziale Demokratie als gewerkschaftliche Perspektive in Europa*, Ms., European Observatory of Industrial Relations, Frankfurt.

Jacobi, Otto (1992b), 'Industrielle Demokratie und intermediäre Organisationen in Europa', *WSI-Mitteilungen*, vol. 45.

Jaeger, Rolf (1991), 'Arbeitnehmervertretung und Arbeitnehmerrechte in den Unternehmen Westeuropas', in Hans-Böckler-Stiftung (ed.), *Europäische Betriebsräte. Ein Beitrag zum sozialen Europa*, Düsseldorf.

Jensen, Carsten S., Jorgen St. Madsen, and Jesper Due (1992), *Internationalisation of the European trade union movement, the EC single market and the Maastricht treaty - patterns of union power and influence*, paper presented at the Ninth World Congress of the IIRA, Sydney.

Keller, Berndt (1993), *Einführung in die Arbeitspolitik. Arbeitsbeziehungen und Arbeitsmarkt in sozialwissenschaftlicher Perspektive*, 3rd edition, Munich and Vienna.

Keller, Berndt (1994), *Perspektiven europäischer Kollektivverhandlungen - vor und nach Maastricht*, Ms., Konstanz.

Kreile, Michael (1991), 'European market integration, institutional competition, and employers' interests', in Sadowski, Dieter, and Otto Jacobi (eds), *Employers' associations in Europe: Policy and organisation*, Baden-Baden.

Kreimer, Johannes (1992), 'Konferenz der gewerkschaftlichen Tarifpolitiker in Luxemburg. Europäische Tarifverhandlungen?', *Forumarbeit* vol. 7.

Krieger, Hubert (1991), 'Mitbestimmung in Europa', in Hans-Böckler-Stiftung (ed.), *Europäische Betriebsräte. Ein Beitrag zum sozialen Europa*, Düsseldorf.

Lange, Peter (1992), 'The politics of the social dimension', in Sbragia, Alberta M. (ed.), *Euro-politics. Institutions and policymaking in the 'new' European community*, Washington, D.C.

Lecher, Wolfgang (1991a), 'Konturen europäischer Tarifpolitik', *WSI-Mitteilungen*, vol. 44.

Lecher, Wolfgang (1991b), 'Arbeitsbeziehungen und Tarifpolitik in Europa', *Gewerkschaftliche Monatshefte*, vol. 42.

Lodge, Juliet (1990), 'Social Europe', *Journal of European integration*, vol. 13.

Mosley, Hugh G. (1990), 'The social dimension of European integration', *International Labour Review*, no. 129.

Niedenhoff, Horst-Udo (1991), 'Europäischer Betriebsrat. Eine Übersicht über den aktuellen Stand der Diskussion', *Gewerkschaftsreport*, vol. 25.

Niedenhoff, Horst-Udo (1992), 'Euro-Betriebsräte aus der Sicht des Instituts der deutschen Wirtschaft', in Deppe, Frank (ed.), *Euro-Betriebsräte. Internationale Mitbestimmung - Konsequenzen für Unternehmen und Gewerkschaften*, Wiesbaden.

Northrup, Herbert R., Duncan C. Campbell, and Betty J. Slowinski (1988), 'Multinational union-management consultation in Europe: Resurgence in the 1980s?', *International Labour Review*, no. 127.

Platzer, Hans-Wolfgang (1991), 'Eine neue Rolle für den Europäischen Gewerkschaftsbund', *Gewerkschaftliche Monatshefte*, vol. 42.

Platzer, Hans-Wolfgang (1992), *Struktur und Politik der Euro-Akteure EGB und UNICE*, Ms., Fulda.

Rath, Fritz (1991), 'Strukturelle Koordination gewerkschaftlicher Europapolitik', in Däubler, Wolfgang, and Wolfgang Lecher (eds), *Die Gewerkschaften in den 12 EG-Ländern. Europäische Integration und Gewerkschaftsbewegung*, Cologne.

Schulten, Th. (1992), *Internationalismus von unten: europäische Betriebsräte in transnationalen Konzernen*, Marburg.

Silvia, Stephan J. (1991), 'The social charta of the European Community: A defeat for European labor', *Industrial and Labor Relations Review*, vol. 44.

Sisson, Keith (1991), 'Employers' organisations and industrial relations: The significance of the strategies of large companies', in Sadowski, Dieter, and Otto Jacobi (eds), *Employers' associations in Europe: Policy and organisation*, Baden-Baden.

Sisson, Keith, Jeremy Waddington, and Colin Whitston (1992), *The structure of capital in the European community: The size of companies and the implications for industrial relations*, Warwick Papers in Industrial Relations no. 38, Warwick.

Streeck, Wolfgang (1991), 'More uncertainties: German unions facing 1992', *Industrial Relations*, vol. 30.

Streeck, Wolfgang (1992), 'From national corporatism to transnational pluralism: European interest politics and the single market', in Treu, Tiziano, (ed.), *Participation in public policy-making: The role of trade unions and employers' associations*, Berlin and New York.

Streeck, Wolfgang, and Philippe C. Schmitter (1991), 'From national corporatism to transnational pluralism: Organized interests in the single European market', *Politics and Society*, vol. 19.

Streeck, Wolfgang, and Sigurd Vitols (1993), *European works councils: Between statutory enactment and voluntary adoption*, WZB Discussion Paper FS I 93-312, Berlin.

Teague, Paul (1989), 'Constitution or regime? The social dimension to the 1992 project', *British Journal of Industrial Relations*, vol. 27.

Tyszkiewicz, Zygmunt (1991), 'UNICE: The voice of European business and industry in Brussels - A programmatic self-presentation', in Sadowski, Dieter, and Otto Jacobi (eds), *Employers' associations in Europe: Policy and organisation*, Baden-Baden.

Ullmann, Hans, Ulrich Walwei, and Heinz Werner (1990), 'Etappen und Probleme der Vollendung des Europäischen Binnenmarktes', in Buttler, Friedrich, Ulrich Walwei, and Heinz Werner (eds), *Arbeits- und Sozialraum im Europäischen Binnenmarkt*, Nürnberg.

Walton, Richard, and Robert B. McKersie (1991), *A behavioral theory of labor negotiations. An analysis of a social interaction system*, 2nd ed. Ithaca.

Wendeling-Schröder, Ulrike (1991), 'Mitbestimmung auf Unternehmensebene und gesamtwirtschaftliche Mitbestimmung', in Kittner, Michael (ed.), *Gewerkschaftsjahrbuch 1991. Daten, Fakten, Analysen*, Cologne.

12 'Leaders' and 'laggards' in European clean air policy[1]

Adrienne Heritier

EU
Q28
Q25
F02

Summary

Policy patterns in the Member States of the European Union are under challenge. The ongoing transformation, however, is not a one way process of influence exerted by supranational institutions, but a process of interaction between Member States and European institutions. Member States seek to shape European policymaking according to their interests and institutional traditions. At the same time they have to adapt their institutions to European legislation once the latter has been enacted.

In the field of environmental policy established patterns of statehood such as policy strategies, policy instruments, administrative practices and regulatory cultures have changed in Germany, Great Britain and France. The pressure to change resulted from a 'regulatory competition' among leading Member States. Especially Germany and Great Britain - each in turn - in cooperation with European institutions have successfully incorporated their administrative traditions and policy instruments into Community legislation and environmental regulation. Member States seek to influence European legislation and to impose their own institutional patterns on European policymaking because they wish to avoid costs of institutional adaptation and want to establish a level playfield for their own industry in European markets. The Commission as the major policy initiator, in turn, is interested in receiving policy proposals from Member States because it depends on the regulatory expertise of the latter and altogether seeks to expand regulatory activities to enhance its own position. From the 'regulatory competition' and the question 'who wins out' follow varying degrees of institutional adaptations which are required from Member States.

Introduction

To an ever increasing extent domestic policymaking in environmental affairs is made within the European Community. The reasons underlying this process are twofold. Firstly, since problems of atmospheric pollution transgress national boundaries, they cannot efficiently be dealt within the territorial boundaries of one state. Secondly, since the regulation of emissions into air has immediate impacts on the competitive situation of the regulated industries in an integrated market, harmonization is a prime concern especially of the high-level regulation countries. Although the exigencies of Community policymaking seem self-evident and plausible, the actual process underlying Europeanization, in all its stages from problem definition, agenda setting, to policy formulation on the supranational level, not to mention implementation on the Member State level, is a highly complicated process. It is a process of partial convergence and learning, of negotiation, pressuring, stalling and, ultimately, of mostly incremental change.

The questions to be discussed here in the context of the 'internationalization' of domestic politics and policies are the following: What are the specific patterns linking national and Community policymaking in clean air regulation? Why and under what conditions is atmospheric pollution considered to be a policy problem that calls for public intervention? How do problem perceptions of atmospheric pollution diverge or converge among Member States? How do these problem-views affect the practical solutions proposed and under which circumstances do they become European legislation?

The two countries under investigation (FR Germany, Great Britain) have alternated between acting as 'leaders' and 'laggards' in different periods of the development of Community environmental legislation. The FR Germany played the role of a 'leader' in conjunction with the Commission in shaping Community legislation aimed at reducing industrial and power plant emissions between 1980 and 1988. In the same period the behaviour of Great Britain may be characterized as the one of a 'laggard', resisting external pressure to reduce pollution into the atmosphere. In recent years, however, a significant conversion of the respective roles played by the FR Germany and Great Britain has taken place in important fields of Community environmental regulation: Germany becoming a partial 'laggard' resisting European policy innovations when it comes to changing administrative and industrial decision procedures. The United Kingdom, by contrast, set, in full accordance with the Commission and quite successfully in some domains, the tone and abandoned the more passive and resistant role it took in the early 1980s. How can these different behaviours of the Member States in interaction with the Commission be explained?

Variables and analytical approach

The typical behaviour of a 'leader' or pace-setter and a 'laggard' are conceived of as the dependent variables to be explained. Obviously, a complex bundle of factors are responsible for the development of specific problem-views and policy-options in the two countries and their respective attempts to bring them to bear on policy formulation in the Community. In order to grasp the complexity of independent variables for analytic purposes we distinguish between external context variables, nation-specific variables, and network structures and processes in the countries under investigation. All the external context variables are considered to be of potential relevance for the country-specific policy networks and the interaction of Member State actors with Community actors.

The group of external context variables comprises:

1 International treaties.

2 Environmental 'events' (environmental catastrophes as Tschernobyl, Seveso) or newly perceived problems (*'Waldsterben'*).

3 New scientific evidence.

4 World-wide economic recessions or growth phases.

5 Technological or general problem approach innovation and their model function (Japan, United States).

6 World-wide international ecologic-technological competition.

Simultaneously, some nation-specific context variables come to bear on the processes and structures in national policy networks and thereby also on the interactions of Member State actors with Community actors. Nation-specific context variables considered are the:

1 Geographic situation.

2 Patterns of settlement, density of population.

3 National recession or boom.

4 Budget situation.

5 Structure and ownership in the energy sector; nuclear programme.

6   Salient national policy developments (privatization, centralization in Britain or unification in Germany) which are independent of environmental policy.

The framework of policy network analysis is used to explain the different patterns of Member State and Community policy interlinking. Policy network analysis (Windhoff-Héritier 1993a) helps to draw together different strands of theoretical explanation:

1   A model of rational actors exchanging resources (material and immaterial) engaging in strategic interaction and bargaining in view of a theme (Mayntz 1993).

2   An institutionalist approach stressing the importance of institutional limits to this process of rational resource exchange by setting legal barriers and institutional rules and defining the regulatory tradition in the policy field.

3   A symbolic-interactionist approach emphasizing the role of social rules and cultural traditions as well as the diffusion of new ideas in defining policy problems and their 'solution'.

4   Policy analysis pointing to the fact that network processes also depend on the specific problem nature to be dealt with and the circumstance that policies change as they go through different stages, that is problem definition, agenda setting, policy formulation, implementation, evaluation etc.

Accordingly, the specific patterns of behaviour of 'leaders' are to be explained in terms of network processes influenced by external and nation-specific context variables. Institutional features of the network, processes of exchange and bargaining between powerful actors, the dominant policy approach as well as the opportunities and restrictions linked to the policy-specific problems need to be considered. The impact of nation-specific context variables on network structures and processes explain why Member States pursue distinct policies. Besides national policy networks, the supranational network also has to be integrated into the analysis. Its actors and institutional structure influence problem definition and policy formulation in a specific way.

   Given the above conceptual and theoretical considerations, four hypotheses are formulated to explain why the Member States under investigation deal with European regulation in this field in a specific way:

1   Each Member State seeks to impose its own regulatory style and regulatory philosophy on the other Member States in order to reduce the costs of legal adaptation to European legislation.

2   At the same time each Member State seeks to present the national industry with a certain regulatory stability because the absolute costs of environmental investments are less important than the stability and predictability of those costs.

3   High-regulating Member States seek to establish the same level of regulatory strictness on the European level in order not to jeopardize the competitive situation of their own industries.

4   Governmental actors in Member States with high regulatory standards are interested in raising standards on the European level to their own because lower European standards reduce the bargaining power in dealing with industry in the national network. Member States with a highly developed environmental technology industry are interested in enacting European legislation which requires Member States to use such technology to reduce emission into atmosphere to widen their markets.

The distinctive roles of Member States in European policymaking

The leadership of FR Germany (1982-1988): emission-orientation and best available technology

The factors conducive to the FR Germany becoming a 'pace-setter' in emission regulation for industrial and power plants in the European arena are a combination of international pressure, environmental events and internal political and social pressure. These influences eventually translated into a new national regulation (The Power Plant Regulation 1982). Subsequently, it was only rational for Germany to attempt to carry this legislation to the European level in order to prevent imported long-range transboundary damage and competitive disadvantages of German industry. Hence, in the case of Germany, national policy innovation preceded policy innovation in Europe.

External influences played an important role in bringing about the change in domestic policy, to the extent that the FR Germany was under pressure, especially from the Scandinavian countries, to take measures to combat industrial emissions, particularly SO2 and NOx from coal-fired and industrial plants. This pressure was reinforced by voluntary international

282

treaties. Until 1982, this international pressure produced no positive response and Germany was not willing to reduce SO2 emissions under the 1979 Geneva Convention on Long-Range Transboundary Air Pollution. However, in 1982 it made a 'U-turn', joining the thirty per cent Club and acquiescing to reduce its SO2 emissions by thirty per cent by the year 1993 (as compared to 1980). How did this change in policymaking come about?

It is a general insight from the study of the two cases that international pressure and voluntary agreements per se do not trigger domestic policy changes. Rather, internal problem perception and political pressure must join the international pressure in order to bring about the changes. Put differently: international pressure has to correspond to interests of key national actors. This change of interest positions and a new dynamics in the German policy network were set off by an external event (which came to be an internal event): Acid rain and its perceived impact on forest dieback (*Waldsterben*) and the growing awareness that the damage to forests was not limited to Scandinavia. The forest dieback was viewed as a threat 'for German economy and culture' (Boehmer-Christiansen and Skea 1991: 6).

In the course of the international network processes which evolved around the *Waldsterben* controversy, it became clear that the German problem perception of air pollution and the practical approach linked to it diverged from the problem perception of other European countries, particularly the British one. This divergence is to this day at the heart of controversies about adequate European intervention measures (Interview, European Commission, DG XI, March 1993). Put briefly, forest dieback as a result of acidification of rain was perceived to be a problem calling for policy measures in the Federal Republic although there was no valid scientific evidence linking forest damages to air pollution. It is the typically German policy approach that precautionary environmental policy measures should be taken - in the absence of scientific certainty - that allow for technology-forcing measures. Whereas the presence of emitted materials which call for precaution (*Vorsorge*) is considered to be an adequate basis for policy measures in the Federal Republic, in the United Kingdom a harmful effect must be identified before action is taken (Boehmer-Christiansen and Skea 1991: 15).

Corresponding to its problem view, the typical German regulatory style in environmenmental policy is emission- and technology-oriented rather than air quality oriented. It is based on detailed state regulation and intervention. This exacerbates the divergences in problem perception and problem approach between different countries of the Community. Of course, nation-specific features such as the geographical situation and the industrial structure, which make Germany a heavy exporter and importer of pollutants as well as the fact that Germany is a very densely populated country, explain to some extent why this specific problem approach is predominant (Interview VdTÜV - Essen, February 1993). By contrast, Britain as an island and a heavy pollutant exporter tends to favour ambient air quality standards.

But how did the event of forest deterioration set into motion a new dynamics in the national policy network which, in turn, prompted action in the European arena? The enactment of a comprehensive Air Quality Protection Act (*Bundesimmissionsschutzgesetz - BImschG - 1974*) in the social-liberal reform era defined environmental protection - besides it being a responsibility of the *Länder* - as a federal task. The *BImSchG* enabled the Federal Government to issue regulations and administrative directives (Weidner 1989: 16) to reduce pollution. The Länder governments under the old *Technische Anweisung Luft (TA Luft)*, an administrative directive for air pollution control, however, were still able to set their own emission standards which led to varying requirements for industry in the different *Länder*. This in turn invited the new environmental organizations to challenge the lower standards in the administrative courts, in which 'the students of 1968 had meanwhile become the judges' (Müller 1984: 136) in order to obtain an overall tightening of standards on the *Länder* level. Even industry, especially the regional power industries, complained about an unequal interpretation of the 'state-of-the-art of technology' by the regional authorities under the *TA Luft* and called for a uniform Federal emission standard (Boehmer-Christiansen and Skea 1991: 171-2). However, agreement on the level of the standard could not be reached because economic considerations in the Cabinet clearly outweighed environmental concerns (Müller 1986, Weidner 1989).

At that point, international developments provided the issue of acid rain with additional political salience, and thereby advanced the national policy process. In preparation for the United Nations Economic Committee for Europe (UNECE) on Long Range Trans-boundary Air Pollution (LRTAP), a federal agency for environmental protection (the *Umweltbundesamt*) held a hearing on forest damage and the long-range transport of SO2. Simultaneously, in a public hearing on air pollution control draft revisions to both the *BImSCHG* and the *TA Luft* were discussed. Additionally, world-wide technological competition accelerated the process. The awareness grew in Germany that the state-of-the-art environmental technology (Fuel Gas Desulphurization Technique) had made considerable progress, particularly in Japan. Consequently, German industry cautiously accepted technology-forcing national regulation to strengthen its own position in the world-wide competition in this sector (Boehmer-Christiansen and Skea 1991: 188).

The policy process was further advanced by the appearance of a new political actor in the federal arena: the Green Party. The Greens, unwittingly, joined forces with unequal partners in supporting anti-acid rain policy: the Christian Socialist Union (CSU) in Bavaria who (especially given that Bavaria produced little SO2) were defending Bavaria's large forested areas, and with the Liberal Democrats (FDP) who felt threatened by the electoral victories of the Green Party and were looking for new popular issues. The CSU saw in the issue of fighting acid rain an opportunity to blame the governing SPD-FDP coalition for its tall-chimney policy to disperse emissions, and particularly, North-Rhine Westphalia and the Saarland, the main coal mining regions and traditional SPD fiefdoms, for excessive air pollution (Boehmer-Christiansen and Skea 1991: 191). The institutional factors of federalism and party competition, therefore, were important elements of policy innovation in the domestic network. Also, divergence in the approaches taken by regional authorities invited the Federal government to step in and become active in environmental regulation. This was all the more true since the Federal government has few powers in implementation of clean air policy, hence had an incentive to put issues on the agenda which justified federal initiatives (Boehmer-Christiansen and Skea 1991: 103).

Federal politicians also saw the possibility of a trade-off of political benefits between nuclear energy policy and the emission abatement issue. During the (Pershing) nuclear missile crisis of 1981, the crumbling social-liberal coalition perceived the debate about the 'Waldsterben' as a popular policy theme and an opportunity to take the heat out of the rising grassroots opposition against nuclear policy. In order to diffuse political opposition against the missile programme and nuclear energy in general, Germany made its U-turn on the international arena and committed itself to join the 'thirty per cent Club' for SO2 abatement in 1982. While up to this point '... the FRG and the UK arm-inarm had resisted international progress in this field, Germany - to the great disappointment of the British - completely reversed its position' (Interview, European Environmental Bureau, Brussels, March 1993). As we have seen, internal political dynamics were at the root of this change of policy. Inadvertently, a heterogenous coalition of the Liberal Party, Green Party, and the Christian Socialist Party became the prime force behind the development of the German Large Combustion Plant Regulation of 1982 (Boehmer-Christiansen and Skea 1991: 192, Weidner 1989).

Once the policy change had been made in favour of more stringent pollution abatement, and the Large Combustion Plant Regulation 1982 had been enacted, it was only a logical step for German politics to push European legislation along similar lines on the European level. Before its downfall in 1982, the social-liberal coalition had developed a rather progressive environmental protection programme - similar to what the Greens had called for - requiring that the ministry in charge begin an initiative at the intergovernmental level (OECD, UNECE, EC) to make German emission and product standards the guidelines for international environmental policy. The role of pace-setter was defined. These initiatives to pressure for more stringent European emission standards in the Community was supported by the Confederation of German Industry (BDI) and the trade unions which abandoned their opposition to stricter emission control. It became a strategy of German politics to 'sell' the *Bundesimmissions-schutzgesetz*, its regulations and its problem-solving approach whenever possible:

> *Reden, reden, überzeugen* ... We try to 'sell' our regulatory style and the virtues of the *Bundesimmissionsschutzgesetz* on all occasions, in all walks of life: at international conferences, workshops, study tours abroad. For the more European legislation reflects our national regulatory style, the emission-oriented, technology-forcing approach, the less trouble we have in translating it into national legislation. (Interview *Umweltbundesamt*, Dec. 1992).

The more stable the regulatory requirements for German industry, the less competitive disadvantages arise for German industry, and - last but not least - the better the products of the advanced German environmental technology industry can be sold (Interview EU Commission, DG XI, March 1993; Interview CITEPA Paris, March 1993). Also, the German environmental bureaucracy is not put on the defensive vis-à-vis industry due to lower European standards. As will be shown, this strategy and these considerations are not unique to Germany, but typical for all high-regulating Member States in dealing with the Community agenda.

The United Kingdom as a 'laggard' in emission control

British air pollution policy in the 1980s offered a stark contrast to German policies. It tried to resist European initiatives to promote a more stringent policy. While the Germans had tailored a national solution first, and then sought to put it on the European agenda, the United Kingdom successfully fended off the demands of SO2 abatement from the international community and Scandinavia in general and the European Community in particular. 'The British played in Brussels like a very successful soccer team with eleven goal-keepers' (quoted after Boehmer-Christiansen and Skea 1991: 250). However, in 1989 the UK put forward very comprehensive environmental legislation which complied with the European Large Plant Combustion Directive, and even included innovative elements such as integrated pollution control covering air, water and soil, public access to authorization processes and self-regulation by enterprises. This brought decisive changes in British environmental policy. With the new Environmental Protection Act of 1990, Britain not only complied with European legislation of the 1980s, but also anticipated European legislation yet to come and put itself into a position of setting the pace in specific areas of European environmental policy. This behaviour reflects a typical pattern of policy agenda-setting in the interaction of the European Community and Member States: the anticipation of future European policies tends to shape the agenda setting of Member States in areas affecting an integrated market to an ever increasing extent. This has a further consequence: the multiplication of national regulations in order to impose one's own rules onto the European level.

What factors explain this amazing turn-about in British clean air policy? Why did Britain resist so long despite facing the same international pressure - initiated by the Scandinavian countries - that was applied to the Federal Republic of Germany? Although Britain had signed the Geneva Convention on LRTAP in 1979, it sought to prevent the inclusion of any specific commitments to stabilize or reduce SO2 emissions. When Britain acquiesced to the SO2 and Dust Particles Directive of the European Community in 1980 which lays down ambient (immission-oriented) air quality standards as opposed to emission standards, it did so only because it obtained a package deal. After deploying massive resistance against the directive, it finally consented under the condition that the Commission would withdraw a planned directive on heavy fuel from the agenda (Haigh 1989: 215ff.)

Specific national features are helpful in explaining the strategies of resistance deployed by Britain in the European arena. Given its geographical situation (and the relative scarcity of forested areas) Britain - unlike Germany - does not itself experience the impacts of transboundary long range air pollution from another country, but rather is itself a heavy exporter of SO2 and NOx to Scandinavian countries. That is, there was no perception of an immediate problem in the UK at that time.

Another factor explaining British resistance to abatement of atmospheric pollution is the structure and ownership of the energy industry in Britain. The Central Electricity Generating Board as a state-owned enterprise was responsible for the bulk of Britain's SO2 emissions. Not surprisingly, the CEGB resisted the political actors trying to push pollution abatement on the national agenda.

The CEGB (and the National Coal Board) in alliance with the Department of Energy was a key actor in fending off the German initiated European requirements to reduce SO2 emissions. CEGB's ever-repeated

287

argument was that the causal link between SO2 emissions and environmental damage had not been established on the basis of sound scientific evidence (Interview DoE, Jan. 1993) and that the technology of fuel gas desulphurization (FGD) suggested by Germany was too expensive (Boehmer-Christiansen and Skea 1991: 209) and not very efficient (Interview former member of CEGB, Sept. 1993). CEGB emphasized that a strict retrofitting of existing plant and equipment of new plants with FGD would have jeopardized the overall objective of Government to cut back public borrowing. Due to its close links to CEGB the Department of Energy was able to build up a strong position in conflicts with the Department of Environment. Also, the Department of Trade and Industry, the main channel of influence for the Confederation of British Industry, strongly opposed acid emission controls in the early 1980s (Boehmer-Christiansen and Skea 1991: 213, 111-2). By contrast, the administration responsible for controlling industrial emissions, the former Alkali Inspectorate, had a relatively weak position since it had been integrated into the Health and Safety Executive with its strong links to industry (Boehmer-Christiansen and Skea 1991: 160) and for this reason was not very assertive.

Also, important national policy developments, which were pursued by the Conservative government, conflicted with stricter emission control and regulation of industrial plants and explain British resistance (Interview DoE, Nov. 1992). By means of privatization and deregulation and the reduction of public expenditures the government sought and seeks 'to roll back the frontiers of the state' (Interview National Association Metropolitan Authorities, Jan. 1993) and did not want to increase statutory emission control in industry.

Since in Britain the acidification of forests, water bodies, and soil, was not regarded as a pressing problem, there was no strong public opinion pointing out the consequences of industrial and power plant emissions. To the extent that there was an environmental movement, it was - at that time - more concerned with the countryside and wildlife. Furthermore, given the institutional structure of the British political system - specifically its electoral law with the winner-takes-all principle and the resulting two-party systems - access to the political arena is more difficult for new parties such as the Green party. Also, because Britain is a unitary system which was even further centralized under the Thatcher government, there are few political arenas in which environmental political organizations can engage in political controversies and negotiations. Thus, environmental groups in Britain are more concerned with creating general support for the environment, thereby gradually altering the context of policymaking and the political cultures:

They have changed the climate for other forces to have more room for maneuvering than they would otherwise have had. What they have been doing is successfully colonizing the (political and administrative) mainstream ... You don't have the kind of aggressive action that you get in Germany and France. (Interview DoE, Jan. 1993).

The conflict of Britain with its European partners and the Commission has to be seen against the background of these policy network features and specific national features and developments. Once the issue of SO2 emission control had been forced upon the European agenda by the Germans, the ensuing consultation and bargaining processes revealed that there was a strong divergence in definition and perception of the problem of air pollution. The British apply the harmful effect notion of pollution which requires valid scientific results regarding the damage caused by SO2 and NOx emissions to soil, water bodies and forests (Interview DoE, Jan. 1993). By contrast, German politicians considered the mere presence of pollutants in the atmosphere reason for precautionary action.

The British not only had reservations about the German means of defining the problem. They also felt uncomfortable about the - again typically German - emission-oriented problem-solving approach which was linked with detailed statutory regulation. This German approach contrasted with the British air-quality oriented style of regulation based on consensual bargaining between inspector and industrialist under the principle of 'Best Practicable Means' (Interview Royal Commission for Environmental Pollution, Sept. 1992). 'It's a very British thing to think that actually legislating makes things worse' (Interview AMA, Jan. 1993).

When the Commission submitted a draft of a Large Combustion Plant Directive and the Scandinavian countries called for a more stringent protocol to the LRTAP Convention requiring signatories to reduce SO2 emissions by thirty per cent, Britain found itself under double international pressure. This pressure from 'outside' was underlined by new pressure from 'inside', as environmental groups stepped up their campaign characterizing Britain as 'the dirty man of Europe'. At this point, the internal development in Britain accelerated. Interestingly enough, ideas for an innovative policy of air pollution abatement had been elaborated by the Royal Commission for Environmental Pollution in a report as early as 1976. The report called for integrated pollution control, greater accountability and transparency of the British administrative authorization process and integration of administrative powers into one administrative body. However, neither the Labour nor the Conservative government had responded to the report until 1982 (Interview Royal Commission, Sept. 1992). The ideas had been 'shelved' until under the pressure of the European Community and the domestic environmental movement, they were integrated into the Environmental Protection Act of 1990. In addition to the environmental movement, there were forces in the Conservative party (Bow Group - the 'wet' wing - and the Conservative think tank 'Center for Policy Studies') which called for stricter industrial emission controls to expropriate the Green issues. So did forces in the Labour party, although there was still considerable concern about the implications for the British coal with its high sulphur content (Boehmer-Christiansen and Skea 1991: 213). The parties of the center (the social-democrats and liberals, today's liberal-democrats) argued most strongly for higher standards of environmental protection (Interview DoE, Jan. 1993). Further, a report of the House of Lords' Committee on the European Communities recommended the retrofitting of Fluid Gas Desulphurizaton to two UK power stations (Boehmer-Christiansen and Skea 1991: 211). Very critical of the government's policy was a House of Commons Committee of the Environment report (Interview House of Commons, Jan. 1993). This committee had engaged in a process of international policy learning. After visiting research centers in Scandinavia and Germany and being confronted with impressive scientific evidence of acidification, the report expressed great concern over UK policy positions on acid rain, deplored the increasing international isolation of Britain, and recommended a complete reversal of British clean air policy (Boehmer-Christiansen and Skea 1991: 212). Surprisingly to all, Margaret Thatcher held a much publicized speech for the Royal Society in 1988 in which she pointed out the dangers of global warming and the impacts of acid rain. Additionally, the electoral success of the Green Party in the 1989 European election surprised the party in power (Interview DoE, Jan. 1993).

Obviously, the British discussion of environmental policy had changed in the second half of the 1980s. Under the impact of Community negotiations on the LCP Directive, new scientific evidence, and under pressure from within, the British finally passed their Environmental Protection Act of 1990 under a new minister of the Environment, Chris Patton.

The negotiations in the European arena should be observed simultaneously. Britain had supported the Framework Directive for Large Industrial Plants in 1984, the first response of the Community to the discussion on forest dieback and acid emissions. The Framework Directive itself does not specify emission limits for any particular class of plant, but lays out the circumstances under which certain types of industrial plants may operate after prior authorization and which plants and substances would be subject to controls. Although the UK was critical of setting emission standards, it voted in favour of the Framework Directive. However, it insisted on an important concession. Decisions on emission limits would require unanimity rather than a qualified majority so that the UK retained a veto power. Also Britain added the NEEC ('not entailing excessive costs') part into the principle which was to be applied in authorization procedures, i.e. Best Available Technology (BATNEEC). The Community thus paid a high price for Britain's support of the Framework Directive in that the directive lost some of its 'bite' by the reintroduction of the unanimity principle in all standard setting (Interview HMIP, Sept. 1991).

The LCP Directive which was simultaneously negotiated with the above directive met with opposition from Britain which argued that the Commission's first draft favoured economic interests of the strictly regulated German industry and neglected interests of other Member States, such as late-industrializing countries like Spain and Ireland. Of course, every country sought to project its own national energy development into the Directive. 'The negotiations were worse than horse-trading' (Interview Commission Brussels, DG XI, March 1993). While the UK was quite isolated in the negotiations of the LCP Directive and the Framework Directive from 1984 to 1986, with Spain joining the European Community it gained an ally in its resistance. However, the sheer length of negotiations (over five years), and the fact that Britain itself held the presidency in the Council of Ministers in 1986 increased its willingness to find constructive solutions. Also, there was more scientific evidence with respect to the acidification process (Interview DoE, Jan. 1993) Finally, the privatization of the electricity industry favoured the acquiescence of Britain to the Large Combustion Power Plant, since it ended the strong position of the state-owned Central Electricity Generating Board. Arguably, only private electricity companies could provide for the level of 28 billion pounds to update technology. The governnment would not have been able to do so (Interview European Commission, DG XI, March 1993). In that sense, privatization has allowed Britain to go ahead and meet the requirements of those directives (European Commission, March 1993). In 1988 finally, under the German presidency, an agreement was reached in the Council requiring SO2 and NOx reduction on a staggered basis to reach emission limits fixed by the Council. Limit values were set for new plants, and a 'national bubble' of total emission for existing plants.

The UK as a 'leader' 1990 - 1994: the transparency of decision processes and self-regulation of operators

For all its resistance to the European agenda in industrial pollution abatement in the early and mid-1980s, Britain's preoccupation with the directives triggered new environmental legislation (the Clean Air Act) in Britain which seriously transformed environmental policy for the first time since 1974. Responding to existing European legislation and in anticipation of future European legislative activities, Britain enacted a very comprehensive act, the Environmental Protection Act of 1990 covering all fields of environmental policy. Under the EPA all processes are subject to an authorization process. Local authorities are responsible for small and medium-polluting plants and HMIP is responsible for larger plants which are subject to Integrated Pollution Control and have to choose a Best Environmental Option. All authorization processes and monitoring data gathered by companies are open to Access to Information to the public.

Thus, EPA introduces elements which were not realized on the European level yet, such as Integrated Pollution Control (IPC) and an extensive public access to authorization procedures. In the words of one official,

> EPA ... enables government to absorb EC legislation more easily and/or get ahead with national legislation and set their own standards in a way which would be more impervious and set Britain ahead of EC legislation (integrated pollution control). The argument from government ministers throughout the act was that IPC was setting the standard, that we are ahead, that everybody else was welcome to follow, and that, as a matter of fact, good old Britain had done it again. (Interview AMA, Jan. 1993)

In short, at the end of the 1980s Britain used European legislation as a leverage point or policy opportunity to rationalize and modernize its own national legislation in this field and to change its role in European policy-making.

In enacting EPA, Britain, to some extent, changed its regulatory style from an air-quality orientation to an emission-orientation which is defined by centrally issued, statutory guidelines prescribing the use of the best available technology, not entailing excessive costs (BATNEEC) and Best Environmental Options across the different media of air, water and soil at the source (Interview Commission, DG XI, March 1993). By setting statutory emission standards for specific procedures and plants a higher degree of transparency was introduced into administrative decision processes. This meant a departure from the old 'chumminess between inspectors and industrialists' (Interview DoE, Nov. 1992) and the consensual bargaining processes under Best Practicable Means.

At the same time, quite contrary to the British tradition of a secretive state, the act provides extensive possibilities for the public to inform itself on the authorization process and the monitoring data of the operator. To be sure this development has been favoured by Thatcher's policy of consumerism stressing individuals' rights to high quality public services (citizen charter).

Interestingly, EPA - to some extent - also runs counter to the general policy development of centralization in the relationship between central government and local authorities. Under EPA local authorities are, for the first time, given formal control and the right of ex ante authorization over a wide range of medium-polluting plants (Interview DoE, Jan. 1993; Interview Corporation of London, Local authority of Bexley, Sept. 1991, Institute of Local Environmental Health Officers, Dec. 1991). 'EPA did confirm the local authorities' role ... And that is not insignificant in a climate where local authorities were not regarded as partners of central government.' (Interview AMA, Jan. 1993) In the British context, more than in other Member States, the definition of subsidiarity is very controversial, because it is embedded in the struggle between central government and local authorities which has been going on for the past 10 years. While the national government understands subsidiarity in terms of 'getting Brussels from its back' (Interview AMA, Jan. 1993), local authorities would like to define it in terms of more discretion and more autonomy for local authorities. Therefore, in order to enlarge their discretion and get more support for environmental activities, local authorities increasingly address Brussels and the European Court (most grievance complaints come from Britain - Interview Commission, DG XI, March 1992; Butt 1994) and seek to establish a direct network-link between local authorities associations and Brussels.

> There is tremendous detail knowledge (on environmental affairs) on the local level, but there is no mechanism to connect them into the policymaking process. Therefore, in order to influence European legislation the professional organizations of local authorities joined the European Environmental Bureau ... to get some possibilities to influence European policymaking. (Interview DoE, Jan. 1993; Interview Local Authorities Management Board, Luton, Jan. 1993; Interview AMA, Jan. 1993).

The Commission in Brussels (DG XI) did not confirm that such initiatives have been addressed to the Commission, emphasizing that it would hesitate to invite this explicitly (Interview European Commission, DG XI, March 1992). However, there is no denying, as will be shown, that the Commission in recent years has pursued a strategy of favouring pressure from below in order to guarantee implementation of Community legislation.

Hand in hand with the new legislation there has been a partial transformation of Britain's position in European policymaking. The British deliberately changed their attitude by 180 per cent. It's not that they gave up their in principal skeptical attitude toward quick innovations. They still want to know 'what will be the costs, what will be the benefits' (European Commission, DG XI, March 1993). What is new is that the British now try to define the problems to be dealt with at an early stage, seek to put issues which are congenial to their policy approach and their interests on

293

the European agenda, such as in the cases of integrated pollution control, access to information and eco-auditing (Interview DoE, Jan. 1993; Interview Commission, DG XI, March 1992, Sept. 1992). The strategy employed is as follows: knowledge is gathered by independent experts at an early stage before a directive is put forward by the Commission as a pre-draft. Once the objectives of the Commission have become clearer, the conclusions of the expert panel are available and Britain can take some influence on the discussion (Interview DoE, Jan. 1993). Another mode of taking influence on the discussion is to approach the Commission with the proposal for a specific directive. The Commission with a relatively small staff welcomes expert support of Member States with some experience in specific fields to cooperate in the drafting process in the working groups. Cases in point are the planned Volatile Organic Compounds, a planned Benzene guideline or the shaping of the Ground Ozone Directive. 'The structure and approach of that directive is strongly influenced by what we have been starting to do in the UK, in turn, we had to change our procedure only in a few details' (Interview DoE, Jan. 1993).

Another common way to bringing a Member State's influence to bear in the policymaking process of the Commission is by seconding personnel from national environmental bureaucracies to Brussels for up to three years. When the Commission has decided to prepare a directive in a specific field, it solicits the Member States to second personnel with special knowledge. Thus, a British expert civil servant from the Department of the Environment who worked on British legislation on Integrated Pollution Control was seconded to the Commission to draft the European draft on Integrated Pollution Control (Interview European Commission, DG XI, March 1993).

The rationality underlying the present British initiatives is the same that motivated the Germans to seek to transfer the principles of their Large Combustion Plant Regulation of 1982 to the European level. If important elements of a Member State's legislation are adopted at the European level, the costs in adapting its own legislation to the directives are smaller and the regulatory environment for national industry is more stable. Furthermore, competitive disadvantages for a Member State's industry due to national regulations may be diminished. Thus, the application for a full-scale integrated pollution control authorization required in the UK implies competitive disadvantages for British industry, because it takes so long to make a bid anticipating all environmental impacts for a specific product or procedure (Interview pharmaceutical firm, Jan. 1993). Hence, not surprisingly, Britain ardently supported the predraft of an Integrated Pollution Control Directive of the Commission.

After some hesitation, the UK also welcomed the Access to Information Directive of the Community because it is in full accordance with the strategy of free access to authorization procedures which had been introduced under the new EPA. The political leadership under Environment minister Chris Patton, supported this Directive strongly. 'Traditionally Britain was quite secretive. So that was quite a change' (Interview European Commission, DG XI, March 1993).

Similarly, the British supported the Eco-Auditing Regulation on the European agenda. The Commission used the eco-management standard, which has been developed by the British Standard Institution, as a basis for the regulation (Interview BSI, Jan. 1993; European Commission, DG XI, March 1993). Although the latter was a Commission initiative, 'once it was out, Britain was very interested' (Interview European Commission, DG XI, March 1993).

Clearly, in the past four years Great Britain has more positively influenced the European agenda, initiating and supporting new European legislation, whereas in the first half of the 1980s it tended to block decisionmaking. However, upon closer consideration, British policy-making develops along two different lines. Innovations in changing administrative and industrial decision procedures are supported. However, more reticence is shown when it comes to rendering emission standards more stringent because Britain still partly adheres to its tradition of ambient air quality regulation. Thus, Britain demonstrates a divided role in terms of policy leadership on the European level. This became clear in the conflict which arose particularly with Germany in the debate on integrated pollution control and eco-auditing.

Reversed roles: FR Germany as a 'laggard' in creating a new transparency, integrated pollution control, and operators' self-regulation

Unlike with SO2 and NOx reductions in recent years the Federal Republic of Germany has tried to slow down European environmental policy development as far as procedural reforms are concerned. In cases in which it could not prevent such issues from being put on the agenda, it implemented them only half-heartedly. The issues concerned are typically related to decisionmaking procedures in administration and in industry. The German strategy shows an opposite pattern to that of Britain. As one German official said with regard to British policies in Brussels: 'They recommend some of their own solutions, some fads, like public access. But if you look more closely, it's nothing which truly helps to improve air quality' (Interview Environmental Agency Berlin, Nov. 1992).

The Germans have strong reservations concerning the procedural innovations aimed at by the Environmental Impact Assessment Directive, the Access to Information Directive, the Eco-Auditing Regulation as well as by Eco-Labeling.

Germany will implement the Access to Information Directive with as much enthusiasm as the Environmental Impact Assessment Directive, that is, they do only what is absolutely inevitable ... Even we, as a federal agency, have difficulty getting information from the regional inspectorates (*Gewerbeaufsichtsämter*) and *Länder* authorities if we want to have exact information about the emission data of a specific plant. (Interview *Umweltbundesamt*, Nov. 1992).

Accordingly, the Commission found 'Germany was very reluctant in the case of Access to Information Directive' (European Commission, DG XI, March 1993). However, insofar as the directive has been complied with, the decrees issued by the German *Länder* to implement it have rendered administrative procedures more transparent. This holds for relations between public authorities as well (Interview BUND, March 1993) and is most clearly felt by the factory inspectorates.

Industry sees, however, Germany as 'the victim' of its former pace-setter role. Persuaded that Germany is still 'ahead of the pack' as far as industrial investment in atmospheric pollution control is concerned, German industry did not pay enough attention to procedures: 'We did not take them seriously' (Interview DIHT, March 1993). Thus, industry did not expect the Environmental Impact Assessment to become European law. But '... all of a sudden it was there, after five or six years of negotiations' (Interview DIHT, March 1993). When in 1987, Klaus Töpfer entered office as Minister of the Environment he focussed on EIA to gain political profile. Now that the EIA legislation is in force, its relation to existing German legislation, such as the *TA Luft*, is sometimes unclear or contradictory. Thus the question has been raised whether an operator still is entitled to have a specific procedure authorized if single emission standards are complied with as has been the case under the *BImschG*. Such questions reflect the uncertainty created by the imposition of new decisionmaking procedures by the Community which are perceived to be alien to the German legal system.

Similarly, Germany was the only state that did not accept the Eco-Auditing Regulation. This regulation recommends the evaluation of an enterprise's environmental activities by an external 'verifier'. The results of the verification are handed over to the responsible inspectorate. The UK puts the issue high on the agenda under its presidency of the Council, and Germany considered this as an attempt to by-pass the regular control of public authorities in order to replace it by an entirely voluntary report system run by industry. By contrast the German control system is considered to be '... much stricter. Eco-auditing, the voluntary system does not fit within our system' (Interview DIHT, March 1993). Interestingly enough, the position of the German government and German industry is shared by German environmental organizations. They prefer clear standards and mandatory regulations because these can be criticized and challenged more easily than 'soft standards', such as eco-auditing (Interview European Environmental Bureau, March 1993).

Thus, when it comes to changing decision procedures in enterprises and administrations, the German attitude has been reserved or rather negative. However, in formulating stricter emission standards or requiring the use of more demanding technology, Germany is still seeking to lead European policymaking. In drafting an Integrated Pollution Control Directive, the old differences in problem solving approaches between some Member States and Germany reemerged. German industry and the German government favour the application of an emission-oriented approach based on best-available technology as opposed to an air quality-oriented approach. The latter is being supported by most of European industry (Interview BDI, March 1993) and the Commission. German industry, however, would like to see the same regulations extended to other states. By writing specific technological requirements into European legislation, this policy also offers opportunities for the creation of new markets for the highly developed German environmental technology industry. However, high costs may be incurred for industries in the other Member States. 'Many trade associations see the danger that a pure technological approach may be used by a few smart vendors to sell their new solutions by writing them into the authorization requirements, thereby creating their own markets' (Interview European Commission, DG XI, March 1993; Interview Ministère de l'Environnement, Paris, March 1993). German authorities favour strict emission standards based on best available technology because lower European standards would put them at a disadvantage in negotiating with German industry (Interview Department of Environment, Bonn, July 1993). Also air quality standards allow for the 'filling up of the environment' as long as the overall measured ambient air values are below the level set by air quality standards (Interview Steel Industry, March 1993; Interview European Commission, German expert, DG XI, March 1993).

In the view of other Member States, Germany is also trying to write its (planned) strict domestic regulations into the European pre-draft for a Volatile Organic Compounds Directive. In four out of ten sectors of industry for which regulations are being drafted, the drafting is seen to have been strongly influenced by Germany.

> ... On sait très bien qui est l'éminente grise de la Commission, l'Allemagne ... Dans cette directive il y a dix secteurs d'activités différents dont six étaient objets d'études préalables pour choisir les meilleures techniques disponibles à coûts économiques acceptables.

297

Dans les autres quatre secteurs qui n'ont pas fait l'objet d'étude, les réglementations se sont inspirées des réglementations allemandes. Pour des raisons historiques que je ne connais pas il y a une liaison historique entre ce bureau d'études allemand et la DG XI ... On dit que les réglementations proposées par les Allemands ne peuvent être respectées qu'en utilisant les techniques allemandes. C'est un genre d'information qu'on ne peut avoir que quand on suit une directive de très, très près ... Les Allemands ont eu l'intelligence et la sagesse de considérer l'environnement comme étant une arme économique, pour eux c'est un marché comme un autre (Interview CITEPA, Paris, March 1993)[2].

Germany also pursued an active policy in the drafting of the Hazardous Waste Incineration Directive. This draft is emission-oriented and based on authorizations which will only be granted if the best available technology is used. The proposed directive is a particularly stringent one. It is no coincidence that the drafter comes from a German authorizing body which has a reputation for strictness (Interview European Commission, DG XI, March 1993). According to the directive Member States should report their yearly authorizations and the results of monitored emission reductions to the Commission. The latter summarizes the national reports, adds information, and hands them back to Member States to transmit them to their inspectorates. 'There has been vehement protest against this last passage by all Member States' (Interview European Commission, DG XI, March 1993), arguably because it makes implementation procedures by Member States more transparent.

The emergent pattern shows that Germany pursues a two-fold objective in European policymaking: firstly, resisting procedural changes and secondly, by contrast, pushing for inclusion of the principle of best available technology along with emission-orientation based on strict standards. The motives for resistance lie primarily in the implications for the German legal system and administrative practices, and in the unwillingness of industry and authorities to reveal information on the emissions of individual plants. However, Germany is still seeking to drive European policymaking in pushing for the use of BAT. This can be mainly attributed to two facts: for one, it has an important environmental technologies industry with a world-wide market share of twenty-one per cent (SZ, p. 28, 10-19-1994) profiting from strict standards. Secondly, industry is afraid that the administrative culture of BAT of the German inspectorates would put their industry at a disadvantage if more lenient standards of environmental quality would be applied in other Member States.

The relative success of a Member State in imposing its policy approach on the European level depends on the cooperation with European institutions, especially the Commission. In the period under investigation Germany and Great Britain, respectively, fitted in better with the problem perspective of the Commission at different points in time. At the beginning of the 1980s, air quality standards were fixed by European bodies to provide for a minimum standard for all Member States. Implementation, though, turned out to be less than perfect, and it became evident that it was difficult to make Member States comply along these lines. Therefore, in a second phase a change in problem approach occurred. Emissions into the atmosphere were regulated and to be controlled by using the best available technology not entailing excessive costs. This made implementation easier to control at the individual source. However, it became evident that approach was insufficient to promote technical progress. For if harmonization of technical standards has been achieved, there is no economic incentive for further innovation.

As a consequence, currently the Commission tends again to use environmental quality standards. The Commission has, however, added an important new element of leverage to give air quality standards 'a bite'. This leverage is public opinion, the practice is 'regulation by publication' (Majone 1994) or 'whistle blowing'. Member States are under the obligation to observe standards in the new directives, but the mode in which these limits are reached is up to the Member States under the subsidiarity principle. At the same time it is required, though, that if a Member State exceeds the limits set and measured under a planned new monitoring directive, the public will be extensively informed (Interview European Commission, DG XI, March 1993). And if the public in Western Europe is informed about the exceeding of limit values, it is expected that this in turn will mobilize pressure from below (Interview Air Paris, Paris, March 1993). Almost all new directives in this field include this element of public access to environmental information.

In summary, therefore, once the Germans had put into place a system of emission-oriented intervention based on BAT, they successfully sought to change it in cooperation with the Commission which wanted more effective implementation of Community legislation in this field. The latter approach, however, displeased the British who only consented to the new approach after a long resistance. Once they had accepted it, though, they proceeded to a quite significant modification of their regulatory style, and in doing so, went several steps further than the Community legislation of that time in order to become themselves pace-setters. In introducing possibilities of public access and integrated pollution control as well as elements of

299

self-regulation by industry, Britain now is in full accordance with the Commission which seeks to stress the subsdiarity principle by leaving Member States discretion in reaching air quality standards, mobilizing the public during implementation, stressing self-regulation by firms and cooperating directly with individual firms. Conversely, the Germans are, as the evidence has shown, much more reluctant to accept the wisdom of this new approach of the Commission which has been supported and pushed by the British.

Conclusions

Having explained why Germany and Britain play a role of 'leader' or 'laggard' in colluding with the Commission at different points in time in different areas of environmental regulation, the question emerges: What are the implications for the convergence or divergence of policymaking in Europe? Is there at least a partial change and - as a result convergence - in patterns of policymaking in Germany and in Britain? With the new Environmental Protection Act the UK changed its policy style from an air-quality to an emission-orientation, departed to some extent from its tradition of consensual bargaining and abandoned its tradition of secrecy in policy implementation. Germany, by contrast, some years later had to accept new elements of a combination of air-quality orientation and public access to administrative and industrial decision processes heretofore unknown to German administrative and industrial practice. To the extent that each country has complied with the two different types of European regulation, the UK more so than Germany, policymaking in Germany and Britain has converged.

However, important differences in policy preferences persist. Britain still dislikes detailed and strict emission standards. Even though its policies have become more emission-oriented, Britain still prefers to give general 'guidelines' to industry and to use procedural rules, rather than prescribing strict and detailed emission standards, and, therefore, supports European policy initiatives pursuing those targets. It favours those procedural changes that fit in with its tradition of voluntariness and implementation through negotiation, as is demonstrated by its support for the voluntary self-regulating system of Eco-Auditing and Eco-Labels ('market reputations should guide entrepreneurial policy, rather than mandatory standards').

Germany - by contrast - still prefers strict, detailed and compulsory norms, based on 'best available technology' which are technology-enforcing and seeks to push new European legislation into this direction. However, it rejects cumbersome voluntary information procedures and voluntary arrangements as Eco-auditing (which they fear will not work or will be implemented differently in different countries). Germany is also still the staunchest defender of an emission-oriented approach, whereas the regulation of air-quality is favoured by most of European industry.

The changes towards convergence are first of all due to independent factors, present in both countries - albeit in different degrees. Both countries experience common problem contingencies:

1 The increasing seriousness of the pollution problem, leading to a convergence of problem perceptions.

2 More and more convincing scientific evidence that there is a relation between air pollution and acidification.

3 Increasing public awareness of the problem, resulting in more political pressure by environmental groups. Due to differences in electoral laws, the federative structure, this pressure manifests itself in Germany first of all outside of the dominant parties (Green Party). In Britain it manifests itself within the dominant parties (Bow Group, Center for Policy Studies).

The changes towards convergence are, however, also due to the interrelatedness of countries, the competitiveness of their industries, the negative external effects of pollution problems and their environmental policies:

1 The internationalization of the air pollution problem produces pressure from foreign governments who suffer from the consequences and from international treaties designed to reduce the problem.

2 Political and legal international integration has brought about a form of policy competition. Countries try to stay ahead of EU-regulations and regulatory intentions in their national policies. Especially the high-regulating countries try to assume a leadership role in order to save on costs of transforming national legislation to bring it in line with EU-legislation, and, of course, in order not to endanger the competitive position of their industries. They try to function as pace setters by taking first the initiative for national regulations, then taking initiatives for EU-regulations. This role may also be facilitated by anticipating Commission regulations and accumulating national expertise at an early point in time in order to influence the drafting process.

3 Community regulation is also used as an argument and legitimation by agencies responsible for the environment to convince resisting

301

industrial interests and the departments that represent them to accept rationalization and modernization of national legislation. For if industry does not accept national policy innovations now, it may be worse off in the future with more stringent EU-regulations.

4   Increased international economic competition also plays a role in producing policy convergence. Governments fear that national regulations place national industries at a competitive disadvantage. Hence, they are motivated to force their norms and standards on supranational regulation. This could lead to convergence at a high level of regulation.

5   International policy learning (such as the trip of British public servants to Scandinavia to discuss research results on acidification) and fear of international isolation may lead to regulatory convergence.

At the same time policy differences persist, because of differences in geography, industrial structure, political institutions, administrative structure and legal traditions:

1   Geographic and geopolitical conditions and industrial structure determine whether a country is a net exporter of pollution or not and thereby influence the perception of the problem.

2   With respect to the industrial structure it is important whether there is a environmental technology industry or not, since there is a tendency to push for technology-based environmental solution if there is an important environmental industry in a country.

3   The institutional political structure determines the access of environmental groups and issues and industrial interests to the political arena and produces differences in responsiveness to changing concerns among the public.

4   The administrative structure and traditions influence the access of environmental and other interest groups to administrative decisionmaking.

5   The existing national legal systems which prefer either voluntary self-regulation (see the concept of common law as a form of societal self-regulation rather than state regulation imposed from above) or detailed mandatory regulations (German legalistic tradition) tends to produce a persistence of policy patterns.

302

6   Politics in terms of party competition 'matters' insofar as it produces - under the distinct institutional setting in Britain and Germany - distinct patterns of policy innovations. In the UK a policy change occurred through the change in party government on the central level leading among other things to an opening up of administrative procedure and industrial decision processes, stressing the rights of the individual (citizen charter, consumerism) as a concomitant of 'rolling back the state'. In Germany, by contrast, policy innovations were triggered by the interaction of party competition in a federalist state as well as administrative court decisions on the *Länder* level.

Notes

1. The paper is based on an empirical research project financed by the German Science Foundation 'The transformation of national policy patterns under the impact of European Community policies in the field of clean air policy' ($SO2$, NOx, dust particles from stationary sources) (Héritier, Mingers, Knill, and Becka 1993).

2. Translated: 'It is very well known who the 'grey eminence' of the Commission is, Germany ... In this directive there are ten different sectors of activity, of which six have been studied to choose the best available techniques at economically acceptable costs. For the other four sectors, which have not been the object of study, the regulations have been inspired by the German regulations. For reasons which are unknown to me, there is a historical connection between this German bureau of research and the DG XI... It is said that reglementations proposed by the Germans are only accepted if they use German techniques. Such information one can only get if one follows the directive from very, very close ... The Germans have had the intelligence and the wisdom to view the environment as an economic weapon. For them this is just a market like any other'. (Interview CITEPA, Paris March 1993, translated by B.U.)

References

Boehmer-Christiansen, Sonja, and Jim Skea (1991), *Acid Politics: Environmental and Energy Policies in Britain and Germany*, Belhaven, London.
Butt Philip, Alan (1994), *Implementing the Rules of The European Single Market: Social and Environmental Regulations Compared*, unpublished manuscript.

Haigh, Nigel (1989), *EEC Environmental Policy and Britain*, Longman, Harlow.

Héritier, Adrienne, Susanne Mingers, Christoph Knill, and Martina Becka (1993), *Die Veränderung von Staatlichkeit in Europa. Ein regulativer Wettbewerb: Deutschland, Großbritannien, Frankreich*, Leske + Budrich, Leverkusen.

Jaenicke, Martin (1994), oral communication.

Majone, Giandomenico (1989), 'Regulating Europe: Problems and Prospects' in Ellwein, Thomas, Joachim Jens Hesse, Renate Mayntz, and Fritz W. Scharpf (eds), *Jahrbuch zur Staats- und Verwaltungswissenschaft*, vol. 3, Nomos, Baden-Baden.

Mayntz, Renate (1993), 'Policy-Netzwerke und die Logik von Verhandlungssystemen' in Héritier, Adrienne (ed.), *Policy-Analyse. Kritik und Neuorientierung, Politische Vierteljahresschrift Sonderheft* no. 24.

Müller, Edda (1984), 'Umweltpolitik der sozial-liberalen Koalition', *ZfU*, vol. 2.

Müller, Edda (1986), *Innenwelt der Umweltpolitik: Sozial-liberale Umweltpolitik. (Ohn)macht durch Organisation?*, Westdeutscher Verlag, Opladen.

Weidner, Helmut (1989), 'Die Umweltpolitik der konservativ-liberalen Regierung. Eine vorläufige Bilanz', *Aus Politik und Zeitgeschichte*, vol. 39, no. 2.

Windhoff-Héritier, Adrienne (1993a), 'Wohlfahrtsstaatliche Intervention im internationalen Vergleich Deutschland-Großbritannien', *Leviathan*, no.1.

Windhoff-Héritier, Adrienne (1993b), 'Policy Network Analysis. A Tool for Comparative Political Research' in Keman, Hans (ed.) *Comparative Politics. New Directions in Theory and Method*, VU University Press, Amsterdam.

Abbreviations

AMA	Association of Metropolitan Authorities
BAT	Best Available Technology
BATNEEC	Best Available Technology Not Entailing Excessive Costs
BDI	Bundesverband der Deutschen Industrie
BImSchG	Bundesimmissionsschutzgesetz
BSI	British Standard Institution
BUND	Bund für Umwelt und Naturschutz Deutschland
CEGB	Central Electricity Generating Board
CITEPA	Centre Interprofessionnel Technique d'Etudes de la Pollution Atmosphérique
DG XI	Directorat Général XI
DIHT	Deutscher Industrie- und Handelstag
DoE	Department of Environment
EIA	Environmental Impact Assessment
EPA	Environment Protection Act
FGD	Flue Gas Desulphurization
HMIP	Her Majesty's Inspectorate of Pollution
LAMB	Local Authorities Management Board
LCP	Large Combustion Plant Directive
LRTAP	Long Range Trans-Boundary Air Pollution
RCEP	Royal Commission for Environmental Pollution
TA Luft	Technische Anleitung Luft
UNECE	United Nations Economic Committee for Europe
VCI	Verband der Chemischen Industrie
VdTÜV	Verband der Technischen Überwachungsvereine

13 Environmental policy in the European Union: The struggle between Court, Commission and Council

R. Daniel Kelemen

Summary

This paper probes the question of whether European integration is likely to produce convergence in EU Member States' environmental regulations, and, if so, what level of protection convergence will move toward. The paper first shows how the scope and level of protection of EU environmental regulations has been shaped by the struggle between pro-integration Community institutions (in particular the Court of Justice) and recalcitrant Member States in the Council. Next, the paper shows how the Commission's monitoring and enforcement problems hurt the prospects for convergence. The major findings suggest that convergence will progress slowly: There is pressure on laggard Member States to raise their standards, but the Commission's monitoring problems, the resurgence of the principle of subsidiarity, and the exemptions granted to laggard states in the Maastricht Treaty will all allow recalcitrant Member States to put up a long resistance.

Introduction

There is considerable debate over the impact of European integration on the environmental policies of Member States. Many environmentalists from states with high standards fear that their hard-won environmental protection measures may be struck down as non-tariff barriers to trade. Similarly, they fear that their own governments may revoke existing environmental legislation in an effort to lower production costs and prevent industrial flight to less regulated Member States. They suspect that any Community-wide convergence in environmental policy will come at a low common denominator. By contrast, others would emphasize that the development of

Community-wide environmental standards has put pressure on states with low standards to improve their environmental protection regimes. From this perspective, it appears that integration will produce convergence by pulling the lower standard states closer to the level of those with high standards. Finally, a more skeptical view suggests that little convergence will actually occur; high standard states will be allowed to maintain their standards and low standard states will fail to implement any Community measures. This paper attempts to determine which of these views lies closer to the truth.

The paper proceeds in four sections. First, I briefly identify the central actors in Community environmental policymaking and describe their interests. Second, I analyze how the struggle between Member States and Community institutions (in particular the European Court of Justice) has affected convergence of Community environmental policy. In this section I compare the utility of neofunctionalist and intergovernmental theories in explaining the development of Community environmental policy. Third, I assess how the Community's past, present and potential future capacity for monitoring and enforcing environmental legislation affects convergence. Fourth, I draw together the findings from my analyses and offer hypotheses about the likely future trends in European environmental legislation.

Actors in the environmental arena

The Member States

There is great variance in the development of environmental regulatory frameworks and political salience of environmental issues among Member States. Member States can be broken down into three general categories (Bird and Veiga-Pestana 1993). The first category includes Member States such as the Netherlands, Germany, Denmark, and since their recent accession, Sweden, Finland and Austria. All of these states have extensive regulatory regimes and a high levels of political commitment to environmental protection. The second category includes Belgium, France, Ireland, Italy, Luxembourg and the UK. These states have less stringent environmental standards than those in group one, and, in some cases, have less coordinated administrative and enforcement structures. The third group includes Spain, Portugal and Greece. These states have weak environmental standards, notoriously weak enforcement structures and lower levels of political commitment to environmental protection than the more developed northern countries. Much of the environmental regulation in these states consists of measures adopted to comply with Community directives.

Member States basic positions regarding Community environmental policy can be summarized quickly. States with higher regulatory standards view laxer standards in other states as industrial subsidies that serve to keep production costs low. They fear 'social dumping', i.e. the flight of domestic industries to states with less costly regulatory frameworks. Therefore, they hope that convergence will lead to stricter regulations in low standard states. On the other hand, states with lower standards resent states with higher standards using environmental protection concerns as a justification for blocking certain imports. They suspect that often such explanations may be guises for protectionist motives, and hope that Community legislation will end such barriers. Moreover, they often complain that their industries can not afford to meet higher environmental standards and demand side payments to defray the costs of new legislation. Member States differ not only differ over the level of protection, but also over the appropriate means to achieve environmental protection objectives. As Héritier shows in her chapter in this volume, Member States want to see their regulatory style adopted at the Community level, since this reduces their costs of complying with Community legislation.

The categorization made above is a good general guide, but will fail to explain Member States' positions in many specific instances. For instance, high regulation states may take anti-environmental positions on some issues. The German opposition to calls for a Community speed limit (which promotes fuel conservation) is a good example.

The Community institutions

The Commission, the European Parliament and the European Court of Justice all prefer extensive Community environmental legislation. Their preference for Community-wide standards is easily understood. First, harmonization removes non-tariff barriers to trade and facilitates the completion of the internal market. Second, the extension of Community competence in this area gives more power to Community decision makers. Finally, given the public concern for environmental issues, Community officials see environmental regulation as a means to create a 'friendlier' EU, and dispel the impression that the EU is only oriented to the desires of big business. (See Eichener's chapter in this volume for more discussion of the Commission's interest in high-level regulation.) The roles these institutions have played in the development of Community legislation will be discussed in detail in section II.

In addition to these primary Community institutions, a new institution dedicated explicitly to Community environmental policy was established recently: the European Environment Agency. The politics behind this agency, and the role it may (or may not) play in solving the Commission's implementation problems is discussed in sections III and IV.

A description of Community institutions cannot ignore the 'comitologie', the complex web of expert committees that advise the Commission. The subheadings in this section indicate that I have tried to divide Member States, the Community institutions and interest groups. However, in the case of the comitologie all of these groups overlap. Interest groups and Member States have representatives on the committees which advise the Commission. Algieri and Rometsch show that the number of committees populated mostly by representatives of Member States has been growing rapidly while the number of committees to which representatives of interest groups belong has stagnated (Algieri and Rometsch 1994). They attribute this pattern to the fact that Member States have taken a greater interest in the technical details of Community legislation while interest groups have turned to more informal means of lobbying to influence Community policy. Also as Héritier mentions in her contribution to this volume, Member States can influence policy formation in the Commission by seconding expert personnel to the Commission to assist in the development of legislation. Member States have an interest in doing so, because they avoid costs of adjustment if their national regulations are adopted at the Community level.

Interest groups

At the Community level, just as at the domestic level, interest groups play a crucial role in shaping legislation. The general categories of interest groups concerned with environmental regulation are business interests on the one hand, and environmental or consumer interests on the other hand. The specific groups involved in policymaking vary depending on the issue; however, some general patterns can be identified.

Environmental interests are drastically underrepresented at the European level. National and subnational environmental interest organizations lack the resources to become directly involved in the drafting of Community legislation. At best they can influence Community legislation indirectly by pressuring their national governments to look out for environmental interests in Brussels. Environmental interest groups are represented by one umbrella organization, the European Environmental Bureau (EEB). The EEB receives support from the Commission (Grant 1992: 42); however, it still has very limited staff and resources (Krämer 1992: 125). In addition to the EEB only a few international environmental organizations such as the World Wildlife Fund, the Friends of the Earth, and Greenpeace have offices in Brussels. They too have extremely limited staff and resources. In 1992, Ludwig Krämer, the head legal advisor to the Commission's Directorate General on Environmental Protection, estimated that there were less than fifteen people working for environmental groups monitoring Community activities in Brussels. This clearly leaves environmental interests in a weak position, and as Krämer put it, Community officials are, 'much more inclined to discuss new concepts, plans or solutions with those persons who do have time, money and expertise'. (Krämer 1992: 125) The EEB and the other environmental organizations are excluded from the committees of experts which help the Commission develop policies and set technical standards. (ibid.: 126 and Mazey and Richardson 1993: 18-9) Mazey and Richardson note that an *ad hoc* consultative group to the Commission on chlorofluorocarbons (CFCs) included representatives of the chemical industry, and refrigerator, foam-rubber, plastics, and aerosol manufacturers and users, but included no representatives of environmental organizations (Mazey and Richardson 1992: 18-9). In his 1992 book, Krämer noted, 'there does not seem to be any representative of any national, European or international environmental organization in any advisory commission existing within the Commission' (Krämer: 126). Environmental groups do appear to be gaining more representation; the EEB was represented on seven Commission working groups in 1993 (EEB 1993 Activity Report). Environmental interests can overcome their disadvantages in the policy process to some extent through their strong ties with the EP which has been a consistent advocate of high environmental standards. They use the EP as a forum in which to influence Community agenda-setting. However, it should be emphasized that the EP is not immune to lobbying from industrial interests. To the extent that the EP gains an increased role in Community policymaking, industrial interests will surely focus more of their time and resources on it. The influence such groups gain as a result will make the EP a less reliable ally for public interest organizations.

Business interests of course have far better representation in Brussels than their environmental counterparts. They influence Community policy makers through a variety of channels. First they can work through Europe-an-level business associations, often referred to as 'Euro-groups'. These groups are regularly included in Community policymaking through a variety of advisory committees. There has been a sharp increase in the number of such organizations since the passage of the SEA; there are well above five-hundred (Schmitter and Streeck 1991: 52, and Mazey and Richardson 1993: 6). Euro-groups range from peak associations, to sectoral and subsectoral associations, to product-level associations. Membership in some Euro-groups is restricted to national associations, while others allow firms to be direct Members. Euro-groups are generally have only modest resources at their disposal; typically far less than the national associations which they encompass (Grant 1993: 31, Schmitter and Streeck 1991). Euro-groups often have difficulty reconciling the conflicting interests of their members. National associations and large firms (especially multinatio-nals) dissatisfied with such Euro-groups often lobby the Commission

310

directly (Sargent 1993, Grant 1993). Large firms often establish government relations offices, 'corporate embassies', in Brussels to monitor and influence Community legislation. Firms also hire professional lobbyists to influence Community legislation on their behalf. In addition to these efforts at direct Community-level representation, firms and associations can influence policymaking indirectly by pressuring their national government to defend their position in the Council. These multiple channels indicate that, as Schmitter and Streeck (1991) argued, a pluralist system of interest representation is taking shape at the Community level.

Business interests are generally against environmental regulation. There first preference is for the use of the principle of 'mutual recognition' by which products legally manufactured and sold in one Member State should be freely admitted to the markets of all other Member States (Schmitter and Streeck 1991: 59). Mutual recognition increases pressure for deregulation by disallowing states from barring imports which do not meet their standards. This gives states an incentive to engage in a 'race-to-the-bottom'; repealing costly regulations which hurt the competitiveness of domestic industries. In their chapters in this volume, Héritier and Eichener find that this process did not in fact occur. Regardless, mutual recognition is not always an option. As will be discussed in detail below, the treaties and subsequent ECJ case law allow Member States to block imports on environmental grounds under certain conditions. Where mutual recognition is impossible, business' interests diverge. Export oriented industries and prefer harmonized standards as they would rather have to meet with one standard, than with twelve (or now fifteen) disparate ones. Similarly, firms from states with high levels of regulation will favor harmonization at a high standard of protection, which forces firms in less regulated states to face the same costs as them. Firms from less regulated states which do most of their business domestically will oppose any harmonization which imposes increased costs on them.

One specific area of industry deserves mention in the context of environmental legislation: environmental technologies industry. This industry is an exception to the general rule in that it profits from the extension of environmental regulations. German firms dominate this industry, and they certainly benefit from exports to states forced to meet with new environmental measures (Levy 1993; Maddox 1994).

The development of Community environmental policy

Whether, and if so how, Member States' environmental policies will converge depends on the interactions between Member States and Community institutions. Two theoretical frameworks predominate in analyses of

311

these interactions: neofunctionalism and intergovernmentalism. The central disagreement between the two theories is over whether the Member States or the Community institutions control the pace of integration.

Neofunctionalism emphasizes the role of supra- and subnational actors, and the importance of functional and political 'spillover' in the integration process (Haas 1958). Neofunctionalists explain how self-interested Community institutions (the Commission, the European Court of Justice and the European Parliament) push for the gradual extension of Community competencies to new fields, such as environmental policy. The Community institutions conceal their activism to a degree by making their activities seem like technical necessities. Thus they emphasize that Community environmental regulations are necessary to avoid distortions to competition in the internal market (neofunctionalists term this process 'functional spillover'). Community policymaking attracts the attention of firms and interest associations which become increasingly involved in the policymaking process.

In particular, I will emphasize a variant of neofunctional analysis which emphasizes the role of the ECJ in the integration process (Burley and Mattli 1993, Weiler 1991). According to this perspective, the ECJ is able to promote an integrationist agenda within the sheltered legal domain. As long as the Court can mask its activist agenda by presenting its decisions as objective interpretations of the law, political forces are hesitant to interfere. Thus ECJ decisions extend Community competencies following a functional 'logic of the law'. National courts have come to accept ECJ jurisdiction in a number of areas through an incremental process following this 'logic of the law'. Accepting an ECJ precedent leads to a shift in expectations which makes the next ECJ decision seem a logical next step following the internal logic of the law.

The intergovernmental perspective takes a fundamentally different view of Community institutions (Moravcsik 1991; Garrett 1992, 1993, 1995a). Community institutions such as the ECJ are not autonomous actors which push forward the pace of integration, rather they are tools in the hands of the Member States. For instance, Member States use the Court to monitor compliance with the treaties and to mitigate their incomplete contracting problems (i.e. their inability to apply treaty rules to unanticipated issues.) This view extends beyond orthodox realism by admitting that supranational Community institutions play an important role and by taking into account the changing interests of states. However, it is still realist in its assertion that powerful Member States ultimately control the pace of integration. Any movement towards integration is a result of interstate bargaining (which may include issue linkage and side payments), and reflects the interests of the most powerful states in the Community.

312

Given the preferences of Community institutions (discussed in section I) it is clear that if the neofunctionalist view is correct then Community environmental policy will lead environmental policies of the Member States to converge at a high level of protection. On the other hand, if the intergovernmental perspective lies closer to the truth, then we would expect less convergence of regulations and convergence only at a low common denominator. The truth, as is so often the case, lies somewhere in between. The account that follows will show that although the ECJ was able to use its leeway in interpreting the 'incomplete contract' (the treaty) to promote an integrationist agenda, the Member States were able to restrain the ECJ when they rewrote the contract (in the treaty revisions). In section III, I will also show how lax enforcement served as another means by which states could resist regulatory convergence.

I begin this section by looking at the ECJ's decisions regarding environmental regulation under the Treaty of Rome. Second, I analyze the revisions made by the Member States in the Single European Act and the developments in ECJ case law under the SEA. Third, I look at the Member States' reactions, evidenced in the revisions in the Treaty on European Union (Maastricht) and developments in case law since Maastricht. Finally, I summarize and highlight the theoretical implications of these events.

Environmental protection and the Treaty of Rome

The 1957 Treaty of Rome was signed at a time when environmental policy was of little, if any, concern to the peoples and leaders of Europe. The Treaty included no mention of environmental policy. By the late 1960s, however, environmental issues had become politically salient in many Member States, and the Community responded by beginning to issue environmental directives (the first came in 1967). Community environmental policymaking took-off in 1972, a year which witnessed both the United Nations' Conference on the Human Environment in Stockholm (in June) and the Paris Summit of the EEC Heads of State (in October). This timing proved fortuitous for environmental policy. The Stockholm Summit increased the political salience of environmental issues just months before the Heads of State tried to revive the integration movement at the Paris Summit.(Weiler 1991: 2445-48) The Heads of State channelled some of their integrationist energies into dealing with the environmental concerns raised at the Stockholm Summit. They called on the Commission to draw up a plan of action on the environment and to establish a Directorate for environment.

Joseph Weiler suggests that the momentum generated by the Paris Summit was channelled to ancillary issues such as environmental policy because the Member States were unable to cooperate on issues more basic to the Community such as industrial policy (Weiler 1991: 2449). This helps explain why the Community's active promotion of environmental legislation contrasts with the general stagnation of European integration during the early 1970s and mid-1980s. During this period the Commission issued 120 Directives and Regulations on the environment (Vogel 1993: 116). The Community institutions had another incentive to promote such legislation. It helped enhance their legitimacy in the eyes of a public ever more concerned with environmental issues.

ECJ case law played an important role in establishing the legal basis for Community environmental policy, since the Treaty of Rome made no mention of the subject. The Community adopted environmental legislation under Articles 100 and 235 of the Treaty. Under Article 100 the Community can adopt legislation that promotes the completion of the Common Market. The Community used this article as the basis for harmonizing environmental regulations that impacted commercial activities. Clearly, this required a broad interpretation of the article and rested on shaky legal ground. Only when a 1980 ECJ decision (Case 91/79 and 92/79) firmly recognized Article 100 as an appropriate legal basis for environmental legislation was the interpretation secured. (Bird and Veiga-Pestana 1993: 234)

Some environmental measures fell even outside the range of Article 100, as they did not directly effect the functioning of the common market (Wurzel 1993: 182). These measures took Article 235 as their basis. Article 235 is an 'implied powers' clause. It allows the Community to adopt measures not explicitly stated in the Treaty when such measures are necessary to attain one of the Community's objectives. Of course, it had to be established that environmental protection was one of these unstated goals. The ECJ established just that in its ruling on Case 240/83. (Bird and Veiga-Pestana 1993: 233 and Kraemer 1990: 3, 54)

Where were the Member States during this period of judicial activism and regulatory expansion? They were quietly in control. The Luxembourg compromise, which had governed Community decision making since 1966, required that Community legislation win unanimous approval in the Council. Because Member States could be assured that any Community measure would need to meet with their approval, they were willing to allow for Community legislation in new areas, such as environmental policy. Thus, Joseph Weiler explains, there was an equilibrium in which states allowed for a wide range of legislation, so long as it remained under their control (Weiler 1991: 2430, also see Dehousse 1992: 390)

Revision of the Treaty The 1987 Single European Act (SEA), which amended the Treaty of Rome, was the source of the renewed drive toward European integration and completion of the internal market. The SEA called for the elimination of many nontariff barriers to trade (such as those produced by differences in national regulations). The SEA called for harmonization of many regulatory standards by 1992, and declared that those standards which could not be harmonized by that time would be subject to the principle of mutual recognition. The Member States realized that to produce this slew of regulations decision making in the Council would have to be streamlined through procedural reform (Moravscsik 1991: 20). To this end they introduced a new cooperation procedure under Article 100a. In another section, the SEA introduced Title VII on the Environment (Articles 130r-t). Ostensibly, this title served to strengthen the legal basis of Community environmental measures and represented a step forward for environmental concerns in the Community. However, I will argue that the creation of Title VII on the environment is better understood as an effort by the Member States to avoid allowing environmental provisions to be taken under the qualified majority voting procedures they were introducing in Article 100a of the SEA.

The new 'cooperation' procedure pertains to measures aimed at the establishment and functioning of the internal market and calls for qualified majority voting in the Council and increased involvement of the Commission and the EP (see Garrett 1995b for a detailed summary of the procedure). In the cooperation procedure, the Commission gains agenda setting power in that it alone can make proposals, which the Council can amend only by unanimity. The procedure also gives the EP the power, acting by an absolute majority, to amend proposals at a 'second reading'. If the Commission approves these amendments then the Council may accept them by qualified majority, but needs unanimity to reject or modify them. These procedures clearly add to the agenda setting power of the Commission and the amendment making power of the EP. They can now make proposals and amendments that lie as close as possible to their interests, so long as they will receive the support of a qualified majority of the Member States in the Council.

While the Member States wanted the cooperation procedure to facilitate liberalization, they did not want it to apply to environmental legislation. Allowing for qualified majority voting on environmental measures would have led to harmonization at a level above that desired by some Member States. Moreover, given that the EP had been a consistent advocate of higher community environmental standards, the increased involvement of the EP under the cooperation procedure was clearly against the interests of some Member States. Therefore, the Council wanted to relegate environmental policymaking to Title VII on the environment, where unanimity in the Council would be required to adopt legislation.

This view is supported by the fact that the Council acted to ensure that the procedural article of Title VII, Article 130s, would require unanimity voting. In the Commission's original proposal for Article 130s, it called for qualified majority voting (Krämer 1991: 88; Wurzel 1993: 183). However, the Council revised this article so that environmental provisions would require unanimity voting, unless the Council agreed unanimously to take certain decisions by qualified majority voting. (Art. 130s(2)) Even in this latter case, the input of the EP would be limited to simple consultation, denying the EP the amendment making power afforded it under the cooperation procedure.

The SEA also adds new 'escape clauses' that reaffirm the right, which was originally articulated in Article 36 of the Treaty of Rome, of states to maintain standards stricter than those of the Community. Such provisions were included to appease Member States with high levels of regulation who feared that their national standards would be replaced by lower Community standards. In the new title on the environment, Article 130t allows states to maintain or introduce more stringent regulations than those taken by the Community, as long as such measures do not constitute a disguised restriction of trade. Interestingly, the original Commission proposal did not contain an 'escape clause' like Article 130t. This is understandable given the Commission's preference for harmonization and that Community legislation loses significance if high standard Member States ignore them and maintain their national standards (Kraemer 1991: 93). Similarly, Article 100a(4) allows such an escape clause for environmental harmonization measures relating to the functioning of the internal market. In addition, it allows for a 'fast-track' complaint procedure whereby the Commission, or any Member State can protest directly to the ECJ regarding a measure it suspects to be a disguised trade restriction. These two Articles parallel Article 36 of the Treaty of Rome in that they allow states to take measures for purposes of environmental protection, even where such measures impede intracommunity trade. They go beyond Article 36 by clearly establishing that states can take more stringent measures even where Community legislation exists. The Commission would have preferred not to include such escape clauses. In fact, the initial Commission proposal for Title VII did not contain an escape clause such as Article 130t (Krämer 1991: 93). However, such provisions were necessary to gain the support of states with high standards.

The SEA also introduced a number of seemingly pro-environment revisions. First and foremost, by including Title VII on the environment the SEA established the constitutional basis of EC environmental policy.

Article 130r established the specific objectives of and principles behind Community environmental policy. Paragraph two of the Article adds that, 'Environmental protection requirements shall be a component of the Community's other policies'. In addition, Article 100a(3) of the SEA stated that Community measures taken to harmonize Member State laws concerning environmental protection in order to promote the internal market must 'take as a base a high level of protection'.

The notion that these revisions were major victories for the environmental camp is dubious. First, given that ECJ case law had already established that environmental protection was an area of Community competence, establishing a constitutional basis for environmental measures, while welcomed, was not necessary. Weiler notes this phenomenon and says that in areas where jurisdiction was already clearly asserted such treaty revisions did nothing more than 'reinvent the wheel' (Weiler 1991: 2434-35). Second, the demand in Article 100a that Community legislation be based on a high level of protection should also be viewed with suspicion. The EP had called for harmonization at the 'highest' level of protection, i.e. the level of regulation of the most stringent Member State. This demand was rejected by the Council, which instead called for a 'high' level of protection (Wurzel 1993: 184). Just what 'high' means is unclear, making it difficult to challenge Community directives for not being 'high' enough. Moreover, it is worth noting that while Article 100a(3) says that the Commission's original proposal for a harmonization measure must take as a basis a high level of protection, the article says nothing about environmental protection considerations in the measure that the Council finally adopts. Thus, if the Council acts unanimously and amends the proposal the measure produced as a result might have a lower level of protection than that originally called for by the Commission.

In summary, Title VII addressed three primary concerns. First, it addressed the concerns of low standard states by calling for a continued use of unanimity voting. This seemed to maintain the pre-SEA equilibrium: expansive Community jurisdiction coupled with veto rights for all Member States. Second, it addressed the concerns of highly regulated states by ensuring that they could maintain standards higher than the Community's. Third, it addressed environmental concerns, albeit in a superficial manner. Title VII gave SEA a 'green' face by proclaiming environmental protection as a Community goal and by introducing the principles which were to guide Community environmental policy.

ECJ case law under the SEA Two ECJ decisions regarding environmental issues under the SEA impacted the prospects for convergence. The first decision addressed the conflict between free trade and national regulations. It established the ECJ's pro-environment interpretation of Articles 30 and

36. The second decision undermined the Council's plan for relegating environmental issues to Title VII on the environment.

The first case (Case 302/86) (see Proceedings of the Court of Justice of the European Communities, no. 19, 1988: 5-6), commonly known as the 'Danish bottles case', pitted the Commission, supported by the UK, against Denmark. The Commission challenged the legality of a Danish bottle recycling law which required producers to market beer and soft drinks in pre-approved bottles compatible with the Danish bottle recycling system, or, in the case of non-approved bottles, to establish a deposit and return system. The Commission claimed that these provisions violated Article 30's free movement of goods requirements in that they discriminated against producers in other Member States by making it harder for their bottles to access the Danish market. Denmark claimed that its measures were justified under Article 36 due to environmental protection concerns.

The ECJ upheld most of Denmark's recycling law. It did strike down one restriction in the Danish had placed on the quantity of beer and soft drinks a producer could market in non-approved containers. However, in upholding the rest of the recycling law, the ECJ established firmly for the first time that environmental protection concerns could justify a barrier to intracommunity trade. While restrictions on trade with a more direct barring on human health had been upheld previously, this decision marked the first time that an environmental provision with less direct relevance to human health was upheld (Vogel 1993: 128). This decision showed that the ECJ would not allow convergence of to be achieved by repealing legitimate environmental regulations, where no Community legislation existed. It remained to be seen how the ECJ would rule in cases where national regulations conflicted with existing Community standards. Along with its decision the ECJ set out a list of conditions which such environmental barriers to trade must meet: they must not serve as disguised protectionism, must not discriminate against foreign goods or producers (nondiscrimination) and may only impede trade as much as is necessary to achieve the environmental objective in question (proportionality).

The second case regarded the appropriate legal basis for a Community Directive (89/428/EEC) regulating waste from the titanium dioxide industry (Case 300/89). The case pitted the Commission, supported by the European Parliament, against the Council. The Commission had originally proposed the Directive under Art. 100a, which provided for the use of the cooperation procedure. The Commission argued that the Directive was intended to promote the establishment and functioning of the internal market by harmonizing regulation, and should have Article 100a as its legal basis. The Council, however, rejected this legal basis and chose instead to adopt the measure under Article 130s, which allowed for merely unanimity voting. The Council argued that this legal basis was appropriate because

318

the directive concerned environmental protection.

The ECJ ruled in favor of the Commission. In its decision the ECJ emphasized that, '...a Community measure could not be covered by Article 130s merely because it also pursues environmental objectives'; but rather that, 'the main intent of the Directive should be the determinant of the legal basis chosen'. (see Proceedings of the Court of Justice no. 12 1991: 9-10) The Court deemed that the main intent of the Directive in question was to improve competitive conditions in the titanium dioxide industry, making Article 100a the appropriate legal basis.

This decision was important and controversial because, as one legal scholar noted, 'The Treaty does not contain any criterion for making a clear distinction between Articles 130s and 100a.' (Krämer: 41; also see Vandermeersch 1987: 418). The choice of legal basis had become a matter of contention between Community institutions; the Council on one side, and the Commission and the Parliament on the other (Bird and Veiga-Pestana 1993: 236). Thus this decision sent a message to the Council; it would not easily be able to relegate environmental measures to Article 130s where a least common denominator bargain could be reached.

The ECJ's decisions under SEA weighed most heavily on low standard states. First, these states had lost their individual veto over Commission proposals when the ECJ allowed legislation to be taken under the cooperation procedure in Article 100a. Second, the precedent set in the Danish bottles case told these states that states with high standards would be able to keep out their imports on environmental grounds. Many Member States were displeased with these decisions but were unwilling to disregard them, because they valued the Community legal system as a tool to help monitor compliance with the Treaty and to help solve their incomplete contracting problems (Garrett 1992, 1995a). The Member States waited for their next opportunity to restrain the ECJ's judicial activism on environmental matters. The opportunity came when the Member States prepared to further amend the Treaty of Rome with the 1992 Treaty on European Union.

Environmental protection and the Maastricht Treaty

Revision of the Treaty In the Maastricht Treaty the Member States defended themselves against the Court's judicial activism both by providing for 'escape mechanisms' for states with low standards and by demanding unanimity in the Council in certain areas of environmental policymaking. Both sets of provisions impede regulatory convergence. In an effort to appease environmental interests and critics in the EP, the Council also made some ostensibly pro-environmental changes in decision making procedures. However, I will show below that these procedural changes are actually likely to restrict convergence of policy and make policies which

319

are harmonized take lower levels of protection.

Maastricht introduces an important change regarding states with low standards. Under the new Article 130s(5) the Council is allowed to grant, 'temporary derogations' from a Community environmental measure if the measure involves costs, 'deemed disproportionate for the public authorities of a Member State'. Thus the Community can 'temporarily' excuse Member States with low environmental standards from meeting burdensome Community regulations. The meaning of 'temporary' is ambiguous, but it is worth noting that Spain and Portugal received ten year, 'temporary' derogations in implementing some provisions of Directive 88/609 on large combustion plants (Verhoeve 1992: 23).

With this revision, holes in the 'floor' of Community regulation are added to the holes that already existed in its 'ceiling'. Article 130s(5) gives lower standard states the same right that higher standard states already had (under Article 130t). They too can maintain national standards even when Community standards already exist. Thus the low standard states have established a new equilibrium: as the ECJ had taken away their veto power, they demanded an 'opt-out' of Community regulations via temporary derogations. In addition to this opt-out, low standard states won a promise from the Community that they would receive financial assistance from the Cohesion fund for implementing Community measures (Article 130s(5)).

Maastricht also introduced some procedural changes which, ostensibly, support the convergence of environmental regulations at a high level of protection. Maastricht extends the use of the cooperation procedure to environmental regulations taken under Article 130s. As good as this provision may sound to those who favor strict Community standards, it was really nothing new. After all, the ECJ had already established (in Case 300/89) that environmental measures could be taken under the cooperation procedure under Article 100a. Nearly all environmental directives in recent years had been based on Article 100a (Vogel 1993: 122). More significantly, the Council designated specific areas of environmental policy (in Article 130s(2)) which would be subject to unanimity voting in the Council instead of to the cooperation procedure. The areas subject to unanimity were: proposals relating to fiscal measures, town and country planning, land use, management of water resources and choice of energy sources. The unanimity requirements in these areas are presented as merely exceptions to the general use of the cooperation procedure. However, these 'exceptions' cover a number of prominent environmental issues. Given that at least some of the measures taken in these areas (and very likely nearly all of them) were subject to the cooperation procedure under the SEA, Maastricht's call for unanimity in these areas seems regressive from an environmental perspective. The area of energy policy is a notable exception. A

320

declaration annexed to Article 130 of the SEA had provided that energy policy should remain in control of the individual member states and not be subject to Community legislation. Thus, allowing energy policy to be addressed by the Community, albeit only by unanimity in the Council, is a step forward from an environmental perspective. In its position paper on the Maastricht Treaty, the EP warns that the exclusion of these areas from the cooperation procedure, 'could weaken the Community's involvement in the whole field of 'resource management'. (European Parliament 1992: 85).By establishing in the Treaty that these vital areas will be addressed by unanimity, the Council has safeguarded them.

The procedural changes do not end with Article 130s; important changes were also made to Article 100a. One might assume that most environmental legislation under Maastricht would be taken under Article 100a, as was the case under the SEA. In this case, all the procedural changes made in Article 130s would be pointless! However, this is not likely to be the case, because given the procedural changes made in Article 100a, the Commission now prefers to use Article 130s for environmental legislation.

Article 100a of Maastricht employs a new decision making procedure, the codecision procedure (described in Article 189b) to adopt measures promoting the completion of the internal market. This procedure aims, at least ostensibly, to redress the 'democracy deficit' in the Community by empowering the EP. It provides for a conciliation committee, made up of an equal number of representatives from the EP and the Council, to negotiate compromises between the two bodies in case of disagreement at the initial stage of policy development. Secondly, the procedure gives the EP the power to veto Council proposals by an absolute majority if negotiations in the conciliation committee fail to produce acceptable legislation.

While it empowers the EP to some extent, the codecision procedure clearly decreases the role to the Commission. The negotiations that occur in the codecision procedure's conciliation committee are between the EP and the Council. They exclude the Commission, affording it less influence on policymaking (Garrett 1995b: 24-7; and Verhoeve et al. 1992: 27, 30). Moreover, the codecision procedure reduces the Commission's agenda setting power. Under the cooperation procedure, amendments made by the EP and approved by the Commission are submitted as a package deal to the Council, which can then accept them by a qualified majority or reject them by unanimity. Codecision, by contrast, requires each individual amendment to win the support of a qualified majority in the Council. This transfers agenda setting power back to the Council and weakens the bargaining position of both the Commission and the EP. The EP is compensated for this loss by the new veto powers codecision affords it and by its increased status in the early stages of negotiations (via the conciliation committees). The Commission, on the other hand, is excluded from the negotiation process, loses agenda setting power and wins no new powers under codecision.

Given a choice between the cooperation and codecision procedures, the Commission will likely opt for cooperation, in which it wields more influence. Thus the Commission's choice of procedure now conflicts with that of the EP, whereas under SEA they had been united in favor of the cooperation procedure. While the EP may prefer that measures be taken under codecision, the Commission has the power to select the legal basis for a provision. A recent ECJ decision suggests that the Court will overrule attempts by the EP to challenge the Commission's choice of legal basis (Case 187/93, discussed below).

ECJ case law under Maastricht Earlier decisions (such as the Danish bottles case) showed the Court's willingness to let national environmental regulations stand in the way of trade where no Community standards existed. Two recent cases indicate that the ECJ is now trying to prevent Member States from maintaining stricter national standards in areas where the Community has already issued standards. Clearly, this position would promote convergence by restricting the upward escape mechanisms provided in Article 100a(4) and Article 130t.

In the first case (Case 41/93), France complained that the Commission should not have upheld German rules concerning the prohibition of pentachlorophenol(PCP), a toxic chemical (see Proceedings of the Court of Justice of the European Communities, 17 May 1994: 10-3). The German rules put more stringent restrictions on PCP than did an already existing Community directive on PCP. Germany, later supported by the Commission, based its stricter measure on Article 100a(4) which allows Member States to maintain stricter national measures for the protection of human health and the environment even where harmonization has occurred, so long as they are notified to and approved by the Commission.

The ECJ sided with France, determining that the Commission had not clearly established that the German measure was justified on environmental or health grounds, and not simply a disguised restriction on trade between Member States. With this decision, the ECJ has set a high threshold for national measures to meet in order to be justified under Article 100a(4). The Commission would need convincing evidence that stricter national standards were justified and did not constitute arbitrary discrimination.

The ECJ issued a similar decision a few months later in Case 294/92. (Proceedings of the Court of Justice of the European Communities, 20 Sept., 1994: 2-4). In this case, the Commission challenged an Italian requirement that imports of all plants susceptible to fire blight *(Erwinia amylovara)* be authorized in advance, before entering Italy. The Commission argued that this rule contradicted a Council Directive (Directive 77/93 amended by 88/572 and 89/439) designed to promote intra-Community trade in plants and to organize health inspections for plants, and contradicted Article 30 of the Treaty of Rome. The Community directive had called for inspections to occur in the state exporting the traded plant, and had limited inspections by importing States to selected border inspections. Italy admitted that its requirement of advanced authorization obstructed trade, but defended it on environmental grounds under Article 36. (Readers should appreciate the irony of Italy fighting for higher environmental standards!) The ECJ ruled that where harmonization measures had already been taken under Article 100 which, 'ensure the protection of animal and human health and establish Community procedures to check that they were observed, recourse to Article 36 was no longer justified...' (Proceedings of the Court of Justice of the European Communities, 20 Sept. 1994: 2-3, emphasis mine.)By disallowing a Member State from maintaining higher standards where Community standards exist, this ruling ignores Article 100a(4). The ruling seems to establish the important precedent that where the Court deems that harmonization measures which sufficiently protect the environment have been taken, Member States may no longer take more stringent measures under Article 36. This decision seems to go even further than the previous one (in case 41/93) in restricting Member States' rights to maintain stricter standards. These decisions suggest that the ECJ is trying to put a ceiling on environmental protection, and prevent Member States from superseding Community regulations.

Theoretical implications

The process depicted above is one of conflict between Community institutions and Member States. They have come into conflict over both how much harmonization should occur and what level of protection harmonized measures should provide. ECJ case law supported the expansion of Community competence on environmental matters (as neofunctionalists would expect), while the Member States responded in the treaty revisions by either curtailing future expansion or rolling back past developments (as intergovernmentalists would expect). This pattern suggests that neither the supranational actors, nor the national governments were firmly in control. Rather, they engaged in a tug-of-war, the Court pulling Community policy in one direction and the Council then attempting to pull it back. Van Waarden (1994) anticipated the potential for the Member States to restrain the ECJ in this manner. He compares the impact of the ECJ's promotion of regulatory centralization with that of the American Supreme Court. He finds that the EU Member States will more easily resist their 'Supreme Court' than have the American states, because, 'it is much easier to change the European "Constitution", the various Treaties, than the American one.

By simply agreeing on another Treaty, the European Council of Member States can change the European polity again'. (van Waarden 1994: 254) The lesson here is that while the ECJ's victories are real, they are tenuous; the Member States are not powerless to resist.

The implementation deficit

Understanding the forces that shape Community environmental policy provides only half of the answer to the question (posed at the beginning of this essay) of whether Member State's policies will converge. The presence of Community legislation will only lead to substantive convergence if the legislation is actually implemented. However, the Commission lacks the administrative capacity to monitor and enforce the many environmental directives and regulations it issues. For all the negative rhetoric about the burgeoning 'Eurocracy', the Commission has an incredibly small staff considering the range and significance of the policies it handles. The Commission therefore relies on the Member States to implement Community environmental legislation (Article 130r(4)).

Moral hazard and transaction costs

Implementation of Commission directives is plagued by moral hazard problems (see Milgrom and Roberts 1992 for a discussion of moral hazard). With the Commission relying on Member States to implement Community policy, information asymmetries are highly problematic. The Commission lacks the monitoring capacity to evaluate whether states are complying. It relies primarily on Member States to report on their own enforcement. This situation gives Member States the incentive to conceal their failure to implement policies.

The Commission has an alternative way of detecting compliance failures: complaints from individuals or organizations. Recognizing that it had monitoring problems, the Commission instituted a complaint procedure to encourage individuals or organizations to report violations of Community law. While this alternative improves the Commissions' monitoring capacity in an indirect way, it is crippled by high transaction costs. When the Commission receives complaints, which it does hundreds of times annually in recent years, it initiates formal investigation procedures. Eventually, if the Commission finds evidence of the violation, it can bring a case against the violating Member State in the ECJ. However, an average of fifty months passes between the arrival of a complaint and a ruling from the ECJ. In cases where a Member State is accused of not enforcing a policy, there may be little the Commission can do while the case is pending. If the case involves a challenge to the legality of a specific project the Court has the right, upon request of the Commission, to issue an injunction. However, this has not been the practice. Instead devastating projects have often continued while the ECJ considered the case, sometimes coming to completion before the ECJ issues a ruling. Moreover, this mechanism is unsatisfactory in that the number of complaints received relates more to the level of public awareness than to the actual number of violations ('The Dirty Dozen' *The Economist* July 20, 1991; 'The High Costs of a Cleaner Europe' *Financial Times* November 3, 1992).

The variations in domestic regulatory regimes (discussed above in section I) were often reflected in differences in enforcement of Community regulations. Wealthy states, in particular Denmark, Germany and the Netherlands, tended to enforce regulations more so than their poorer Southern neighbors, Italy, Spain, Portugal and Greece. While enforcing states may have been angered by those that shirked, they lacked proof of their negligence. The Commission had no comprehensive data on states' enforcement of laws, and therefore could not substantiate claims that certain states were lax enforcers ('The High Cost...' *Financial Times* November 3, 1992). The only information the Commission could obtain was whether Member States had transposed Commission directives into national law. For instance, recently Denmark and UK had incorporated eighty per cent of the Single Market directives while Italy had only incorporated thirty per cent. (Mazey and Richardson 1993: 20) This, however, told them nothing about enforcement. A recent article quoted the current environment commissioner Ioannis Paleokrassas saying, 'in the absence of statistics we cannot say anything' about the degree of enforcement ('Can Europe Compete?' *Financial Times* March 3, 1994). The Commission had its suspicions, but only the Member States themselves knew their degree of enforcement.

To mitigate this information asymmetry and to reduce the transaction costs associated with ECJ enforcement, the Commission proposed the establishment of the European Environment Agency (EEA) in 1990 (Council Regulation 1210/90). The Commission called for an EEA with enforcement powers that could conduct inspections throughout the Community to ensure that Member States were implementing Community legislation.

Interstate bargaining

The EEA was forged under the pressure of the conflicting interests of the Member States. The establishment of the EEA required the backing of all the Member States. Their interests regarding the EEA varied along the lines described in section I; the same states which wanted high standards tended to favor creating a strong EEA with enforcement powers. For instance German and Dutch officials favored the creation of an agency with the power to issue regulations and enforce them. (Interview with William Reilly, former EPA administrator; also 'Can Europe Compete?' *Financial Times* March 3, 1994). States with interests as divergent as Germany and Britain had to come to some kind of compromise. States, such as Britain and Spain, which opposed the creation of a strong EEA had to be included in the design of the agency. They eviscerated the original Commission proposal and produced a watered down version EEA.

Mindful of the costs of environmental regulation and of its sovereignty, Britain strongly opposed granting the EEA the authority to conduct inspections (Interview with EEA Taskforce Official: May 1994). In the lowest common denominator world of interstate bargaining, British concerns prevailed. The EEA will collect data through already existing information services of Member States. Together these information services will comprise the 'European environment information and observation network'. This information gathering system is intended to provide the Commission and the Member States with objective, scientific knowledge requisite to draft effective environmental policies. Clearly though, the incentives to misrepresent information that have long characterized Community environmental policy remain. Lacking the authorization to conduct its own inspections, the EEA will be unable to ensure the validity of data. The European information and observation network which the EEA is to coordinate will consist of existing national information sources, both public and private. These sources are to report to a 'national focal point' to be named by each Member State which will in turn report to the EEA. In addition the EEA will contract private institutions, referred to as 'Topic Centres' to conduct research on salient issues. As will be discussed below, the variety of sources from which the EEA collects data may in some ways make up for its lack of an independent inspectorate (Interviews with EEA officials: May 1994).

The struggle surrounding the EEA is by no means over. After being held up for four years during a battle over the location of various Community institutions, the EEA was recently established in Copenhagen. While the EEA's current mandate is limited, there remains the possibility that its role will grow. The potential for an increased EEA role, along with the general prospects for Community environmental policy are discussed in the following section.

Conclusions

Finally, I can return to my original question, 'Will integration produce convergence of Member States' environmental regulations and, if so, at what level of protection?' The trends identified above suggest that convergence will progress slowly. There has certainly been an upward pressure on the regulatory regimes of laggard states. However, the weakness of the Community's implementation monitoring and enforcement mechanisms, plus the opportunity for temporary derogations from Community policies granted under Maastricht will allow recalcitrant Member States to put up a long resistance to regulatory convergence.

First I can address the fears held by some environmentalist in high standard states that their national regulations will be repealed. Community institutions will certainly not lead a drive for widespread deregulation. Maastricht and ECJ case law support the right of high standard states to maintain their national standards. However, recent ECJ decisions suggest that now that it now favors restricting Member States from taking higher standards where Community standards already exist (See Cases 41/93 and 294/92 above; also see Shapiro 1992: 133-4 for an earlier prediction of this). Member States may still be able to take higher standards, but they will have to be prepared to make a convincing case before the ECJ that their measures do not violate the 'non-discrimination' and 'proportionality' principles; i.e. they must prove that the measures are not disguised trade restrictions and that they are the least trade disruptive means of achieving the environmental objective. Thus it appears that the ECJ is trying to put a cap on national legislation; promoting convergence by not letting Member States go beyond existing Community standards.

The Commission will continue trying to improve its monitoring capacity, which would of course promote convergence. Extending the EEA's powers to include direct monitoring of the implementation of Community legislation is, however, unlikely (Interview with EEA Taskforce Official May 1994). Weak institutions like the EEA can help create the conditions for stronger rule making later, once political winds have shifted.(Levy, Keohane and Haas 1993; Levy 1993a) Even the weak EEA can help develop networks of experts from different Member States that build scientific consensus on environmental problems and diffuse knowledge quickly. The EEA may increase domestic capacity to monitor pollution. The weak institution may also mobilize subnational actors, such as environment ministries, research centers and environmental organizations, to bring pressure to bare on their states. The fact that the EEA has already begun to circumvent Member States by going directly to private research centers as part of its information gathering plan offers initial support of these hypotheses (Interviews with EEA officials: May 1994).

Other improvements in enforcement are likely to come as a result of increased involvement of environmental associations in reporting violations of Community law. Community Directive 90/313 on the freedom of access to information on the environment will facilitate this process by making it easier for environmental associations or individual citizens to access information on the state of the environment (Krämer 1992: 290-309).

In the absence of effective enforcement mechanisms, the Commission appears to be moving toward an approach to environmental regulation based on voluntary self-regulation by industry and on market mechanisms. Two recent Community regulations are indicative of this approach. The most recent Community Environmental Action Programme signals a shift to this approach calling for more dialogue with industry, for more voluntary 'self-regulation' and for the use of more market mechanisms in regulation (Hildebrandt and Schmidt 1994; Hey and Brendle 1994; also see van Waarden 1994). Recent directives which reflect this approach include the Eco-Audit directive, the Eco-labelling scheme, and the failed carbon tax. The Eco-Audit regulation (1836/93) calls for voluntary participation by commercial enterprises in a system of eco-audits conducted by independent 'environmental verifiers'. The logic of the Eco-audit regulation is as follows: companies will have more incentive to comply with Community environmental policy and to institute their own environmental programmes if they know that these efforts will be recognized by the public. To provide for such recognition, Member States will certify independent, objective, expert 'environmental verifiers' who will conduct eco-audits in participating firms and publish the results of the audit to inform the public of the firms' compliance (or non-compliance) with Community policy. Firms that 'pass' the audit will receive a certificate noting this that is to be recognized Community-wide. The eco-audit system requires Member States to certify the 'verifiers'. This will likely lead to divergence in the quality and stringency of audits as laggard states make more lax requirements for certification (Hey and Brendle 1994: 22).

The Eco-label Regulation (880/92) is another recent market based regulation. It introduces a common symbol or 'eco-label' to be awarded to products which meet certain ecological standards. This market mechanism was intended to give producers the incentive to manufacture environmentally friendly products and to increase the power of consumers to make their purchasing selections based on environmental criteria. The process of determining which products should receive Eco-labels has generated a fascinating interest group battle. A committee with representatives of the twelve Member States was established to decide about the criteria for receiving an eco-label. Industrial, trade, labour, consumer and environmental interests advise the committee through a 'Consultative Forum'. To date very few eco-labels have been issued due to the extreme conflict between Member States and between interest groups over standard setting (Hey and Brendle 1994: 24). The Eco-label regulation is reflective of the general trend toward private standard setting in Community policymaking. The Commission has chosen to delegate, either through expert committees or private standardization organizations such as the *Comité Européen de Normalization* (CEN), the tasks of establishing technical standards. These standard setting organizations are dominated by representatives of industry, who have the expert knowledge necessary to write standards. Thus the Commission is relying on industry to regulate itself, or to form 'private interest governments' (Streeck and Schmitter 1984).

Despite the potential for some improvement of Commission monitoring of traditional regulations, and for the increased use of new market mechanisms, monitoring and implementation problems will continue to inhibit conversion of environmental policies in Member States. The increasing prominence of the subsidiarity principle in the debate over Community environmental policy will also restrict convergence.

Subsidiarity requires that action be taken at the Community level only when this would be more effective than action taken at the level of the individual Member States. This principle was written into Title VII on the Environment in the SEA (Article 130r(4)). However, it did not prevent the Community from extending its competencies into some areas that by most accounts do not satisfy the subsidiarity criteria (e.g. drinking water legislation). In the preparations of the Maastricht treaty the subsidiarity principle again became salient. Whereas in the SEA subsidiarity was only mentioned in reference to environmental policy, in Maastricht subsidiarity was extended to all areas of Community policymaking. Article 3b of Maastricht provides for the general use of the subsidiarity principle (and replaces Article 130r(4) of the SEA). The definition of subsidiarity in Maastricht is left vague. The definition became the subject of debate at a European Council summit in Edinburgh in December 1992. During the summit, the British called for the repealing of seventy-one pieces of Community legislation, including 27 laws or proposals relating to the Environment which it claimed violated subsidiarity (Interview with Rt. Hon. Shirley Williams, former British MP, 1994). A stricter application of subsidiarity could lead to the repeal of numerous Community regulations, and to continued divergence in environmental policy.

Unable to force convergence on recalcitrant firms and states, Community institutions are attempting to work with them and around them. Community institutions will work with firms and Member State officials when possible, and seek alternative sources of information regarding compliance when necessary. The Commission will undoubtedly get better at catching violators, working through the EEA and receiving more complaints from environmental organizations. Ironically, Member States may even become more willing to 'turn themselves in.' They will readily tell the Commission that they cannot comply with a regulation and announce that they need a temporary derogation and financial assistance from the Cohesion Fund in order to do so. The Commission's *modus operandi* of relying on unfunded

329

mandates will increasingly be challenged. High regulation Member States will have to make transfer payments to laggard states via the Cohesion fund to finance costly regulations. Upward convergence will come at a price, and even then it will come slowly, as laggard states take their time catching up.

References

Algieri, Franco, and Dietrich Rometsch (1994), 'Europäische Kommission und organisierte Interessen' in Eichener, Volker, and Helmut Voelzkow (eds), *Europäische Integration als Rahmen für Verbandliche Interessenvermittlung*, Metropolis Verlag, Marburg.

Bird, Ian and Miguel Veiga-Pestana (1993), 'European Community environmental policy and law' in Folsom, Ralph, Ralph Lake and Ved Nanda (eds), *European Law After 1992*, KLuwer, Deventer.

Burley, Anne-Marie, and Walter Mattli (1993), 'Europe before the Court', *International Organization*, vol. 47 (Winter).

Dehousse, Renaud (1992), 'Integration versus regulation? On the dynamics of regulation in the European Community', *Journal of Common Market Studies*, vol. 30 (December).

European Parliament (1992), *Maastricht: The Treaty on European Union, The Position of the European Parliament*, Office for Official Publications of the EC, Luxemburg.

Garrett, Geoffrey (1992), 'International cooperation and institutional choice: the European Community's internal market', *International Organization*, vol. 46 (Spring).

Garrett, Geoffrey (1993), 'The politics of Maastricht', *Economics and Politics*, vol. 5 (July).

Garrett, Geoffrey (1995a), 'The politics of legal integration in the European Union', *International Organization*, vol. 49 (Winter).

Garrett, Geoffrey (1995b), 'From the Luxembourg Compromise to codecision: Decisionmaking in the European Union' Forthcoming Electoral Studies.

Grant, Wyn (1993), 'Pressure groups and the European Community: An overview' in Mazey, Sonia, and Jeremy Richardson (eds), *Lobbying in the EC*, Oxford University Press, Oxford and New York.

Haas, Ernst (1958), *The Uniting of Europe*, Steven & Sons, London.

Haas, Peter, Robert Keohane, and Marc Levy (1993), *Institutions for the Earth*, MIT Press, Cambridge.

Hey, Christian, and Uwe Brindle (1994), *Towards a New Renaissance: a New Development Model*, European Environmental Bureau, Brussels.

Hildebrandt Eckart, and Eberhard Schmidt (1994), 'Industrielle Beziehungen und Umweltschutzpolitik in der EU' in Eichener, Volker, and Helmut Voelzkow (eds), *Europäische Integration als Rahmen für Verbandliche Interessenvermittlung*, Metropolis Verlag, Marburg.

Levy, Marc (1993), 'European acid rain: The power of tote-board diplomacy' in Haas, Peter, Robert Keohane, and Marc Levy (eds), *Institutions for the Earth*, MIT Press, Cambridge.

Kelemen, R. Daniel (1995), 'Supranational activism and state response: the politics of European environmental policy', unpublished paper, Stanford University: Department of Political Science.

Krämer, Ludwig (1991), *EEC Treaty and Environmental Protection*, Sweet and Maxwell, London.

Krämer, Ludwig (1992), *Focus on European Environmental Law*, Sweet and Maxwell, London.

Mazey, Sonia, and Jeremy Richardson (eds) (1993), *Lobbying in the EC*, Oxford University Press, Oxford and New York.

Milgrom, Paul, and John Roberts (1992), *Economics, Organization & Management*, Prentice Hall, Englewood Cliffs.

Moravcsik, Andrew (1991), 'Negotiating the Single European Act: National interests and conventional statecraft in the European Community', *International Organization*, vol. 45 (Winter).

Sargent, Jane A (1993), 'The corporate benefits of lobbying' in Mazey, Sonia, and Jeremy Richardson (eds) *Lobbying in the EC*, Oxford University Press, Oxford and New York.

Schmitter, Philippe, and Wolfgang Streeck (1991), 'Organized interests and the Europe of 1992' in Ornstein, Norman, and Mark Perlman, (eds), *Political Power and Social Change*, AEI Press, Washington.

Shapiro, Martin (1992), 'The European Court of Justice' in Sbragia, Alberta M. (ed.), *Euro-Politics*, Brookings Institution, Washington.

Streeck, Wolfgang and Philippe C. Schmitter (1984), *Private Interest Government: Beyond Market and State*, Sage, Beverly Hills.

Vandermeersch, Dick (1987), 'The Single European Act and the environmental policy of the EEC', *European Law Review*, December.

Vogel, David (1993), 'The Making of EC environmental policy' in Andersen, Svein, and Kjell Eliassen (eds), *Making Policy in Europe*, Sage, London.

Waarden, Frans van (1994), 'Is European law a threat to associational governance?' in Eichener, Volker, and Helmut Voelzkow (eds) *Europäische Integration als Rahmen für Verbandliche Interessenvermittlung*, Metropolis Verlag, Marburg.

Weiler, Joseph (1991), 'The transformation of Europe', *Yale Law Journal*, no. 100 (June).

Wurzel, Rüdiger (1993), 'Environmental policy' in Lodge, Juliet (ed), *The European Community and the Challenge of the Future*, St. Martin's Press, New York.

$333 - 72$

14   Persistence of national policy styles: A study of their institutional foundations

UK
France
Germany
Netherlands
USA
D73
L51

Frans van Waarden

D 78

Summary

Conflicts over the formulation and implementation of regulations within the European Union reflect differences in national regulatory styles. The paper sets out with describing the most salient characteristics of the dominant regulatory styles of the British, French, German, Dutch, and US public administrations, based on an analysis of comparative policy studies. Subsequently, it is argued that these styles are strongly rooted in state institutions of these nations. By way of example, some major elements of their legal and administrative institutions are discussed and compared. Given this institutional embeddedness, regulatory styles will be rather resistent to change, even under the pressures of internationalization. The existence of such differences could have considerable consequences for equal implementation of EU-policies in the different Member States.

Uniformity and diversity in European integration

The opposition of the British to the EC 'Charter on the Social Rights of Employees', to the directives that are intended to implement it, and to the social paragraph of the Maastricht treaty, goes deeper than mere island-isolationism and Thatcher-style conservatism. The British dislike of legal regulation of working conditions, working time, or mass lay-offs is not just a fad and fancy of the Tories, but is rooted in a more fundamental and more widely spread aversion against solving societal problems through state interference, detailed regulation, injunctions, prohibitions and sanctions. Even the Labour opposition harbors largely similar sentiments, notwithstanding its support for the Social Charter.

333

As such this opposition is but one manifestation of a principal problem of European integration: Supranational regulation is likely to clash headlong with the variety of national traditions of regulation, with national preferences of problem definition and problem solving, with different conceptions of social order and state intervention. It is insufficiently understood that the resistance of nation-states to central EC measures is often more than just political, that it can be an indication of underlying differences in styles of regulation. A preference for activist interventionist policies does not just reflect a political dominance of the left, and a predilection for a more passive attitude of the state neither a dominance of the right. French conservatives can be staunchly supportive of an active role of the state, while the British Labour Party is at times also wary of too much state regulation of labour relations. Such differences are also reflected in the various models of European integration espoused by different European politicians. There is a Thatcher-model of European integration and a Delors-model. These differences are however more than just conceptions of different individuals or of different political ideologies, of a conservative politician versus a socialist one. All this is true, yes. But there is more to it. The different integration models reflect also different conceptions of social order, of the legitimate role of the state, etc. dominant in the countries where these politicians come from.

It is the purpose of this paper first to delineate and operationalize the concept of regulatory style. Subsequently, I will try to identify the typical regulatory styles, dominant in different democratic-capitalist countries. Thirdly, I will argue that these national regulatory styles are firmly rooted in nationally specific legal, political and administrative institutions and cultures. This foundation in a variety of state institutions should make regulatory styles resistant to change, and hence, from this perspective one would expect differences in regulatory styles to persist, possibly even under the impact of economic and political internationalization.

The concept of regulatory or policy style

The concept of regulatory or policy style refers to the routine choice behavior or 'standard operating procedures' which policymakers tend to develop in the policy process. Any individual develops routines in order to reduce the complexities of (social) life, in order not to be overburdened by the need to make endless conscious choices. Policymakers are burdened by additional complexities, resulting from lack of time and information, ambiguity of policy preferences, incomplete understanding of causal relationships, and other constraints which limit rationality. Given the uncertainties, created by such problems and constraints, task definitions and problem solutions which have proven to draw at least minimally acceptable responses from the environment

334

in the past, tend to become repeated over and over again. Members learn from past experiences and they will communicate and popularize these experiences to colleagues and newcomers in their organization. Thus organizations learn and in the process generate and store conventions of action, more or less predictable responses to challenges from the environment, internally recognized rules of the game. Subsequently, the main task of policymakers becomes less to make 'rational choices' than to identify the appropriate rules, i.e. the rules that govern a specific combination of roles and choice situation, the so-called 'logic of appropriateness' (March and Olsen 1989). These rules get modified often only after they have become manifestly dysfunctional. Any change is likely to be incremental, as organization members will tend to cling as much as possible to the familiar, using the tried solutions, if not as a whole at least in part, for as long as possible.

Several types of policy styles have been proposed in the literature. Lindblom's (1959) famous article on 'muddling through' can be seen as the introduction of an incremental, as opposed to a rational-synoptic policy approach. Hayward's (1974) distinction of radical-heroic and incremental-humdrum approaches is a modification thereof, as is Wilson's (1973) differentiation between policy innovation and policy adaptation. More recently, typologies have been proposed by Richardson, Gustafsson and Jordan (1982), who coined the concept of 'policy style', and by Feick and Jann (1988).

Elaborating on these typologies, I propose to distinguish a three main dimensions of regulatory styles, the answers to the 'what', 'how', and 'who' questions of the policy process:

a   What is the substance, content, or the 'intensity' of the policy interven-
     tion? i.e. the *routine intervention modus*.

b   How do policies come about? How do they get formulated and imple-
     mented? i.e. the *routine procedures*

c   Who is involved in these processes of policy formulation and implemen-
     tation? Or: What do *routinely created policy networks* look like?

Elsewhere I have distinguished a number of subdimensions of regulatory styles under these headings. For the purposes of this paper I will limit myself to the following types of regulatory styles:

1   *Liberal-pluralist versus étatist versus corporatist styles.* Liberal-pluralist
     styles comprise a preference for 'market' solutions to policy problems
     and use market-like structured associational systems (open network
     boundaries, many network members, flexibility, lobbyism and limited

335

involvement of interest associations in public policy). Etatism implies a preference for 'state' solutions to policy problems, i.e. a dominant role of the state in policymaking and in network structures. Corporatism represents a preference for 'associational' solutions to policy problems, that is, self-regulation by civil society and/or delegation of public policy to interest associations, and framework regulation facilitating this. The network structures are characterized by relatively small size, closed boundaries, privileged access, representational monopolies, and stability over time.

2   *Active versus reactive styles.* Active styles are intensive, radical, and sometimes innovative. Reactive ones are less intensive and radical.

3   *Comprehensive versus fragmented or incremental styles.* Comprehensive or synoptic policies are either integrated over time (long term and stable policies) and 'space' (integrated with other policy measures) or make at least attempts to this end or profess an ambition to be so. That is, policies are usually part of larger plans. In fragmented or incremental styles they are not.

4   *Adversarial versus consensual versus paternalistic styles.* Adversarial styles rely on coercion and imposition, consensual ones on consultation, persuasion and negotiation. Paternalism is a variety of the second form: there may be consultation and cooperation, but arbitrarily, at the discretion of administrators who assume a superior, hierarchic or even haughty position vis-à-vis the subjects of regulation, typical for étatism.

5   *Legalistic versus pragmatic styles.* Legalistic styles are characterized by formalism, detailed regulation, rigid rule application, active prosecution, centralization and low discretion for lower administrators, while pragmatic styles are informal, flexible, and with an importance of means (e.g. considerations of practicality) in relation to ends, both in policy formulation and policy implementation.

6   *Formal versus informal network relations* between state agencies and organizations of civil society.

On the question whether intervention modi, routine procedures, and policy networks systematically differ between countries there is disagreement in the literature. On the one extreme there are those who emphasize the universal nature of styles of regulation. Wilensky (1976) argued that the intensity of state intervention (welfare states) was related to economic development, and that eventually all nations would pass through similar phases. Ehrmann (1968,

336

orig. 1961: 259) considered the need for closer cooperation between the public administration and organized interests a functional necessity for any developed state bureaucracy.

On the other extreme there are authors who maintain that styles differ so much within nations, i.e. between individual state agencies and policy sectors, that it is impossible to speak of national styles. James Wilson (1989) has argued that the Foreign Service has a different culture and policy style than the Forest Service, the Secret Service a different one from the Postal Services. Others found differences between policy sectors and considered these more important than differences between nations (Sturm 1987: 427, Jann 1983, Von Beyme 1990, Feick and Jann 1988. The mesocorporatist literature also has cast doubts on the appropriateness of characterizing nations by a single type of state - industry relations (Keeler 1987, Atkinson and Coleman 1989).

Such studies may qualify characterizations of national styles and state - industry relations, they do not invalidate them. Sectoral patterns do differ within and across nations. However, there are enough indications for significant differences between nations too. As Lehmbruch (1989) has argued, referring to a study of Keeler (1987):

Keeler demonstrates that the largest farmers' union always had a higher membership density than all labour unions taken together (in France, Britain, Germany, Italy and the US), but that the cross-national rank-order of membership density is identical for organized agriculture on the one hand, organized labour on the other. He interprets these observations as indicating a 'corporatist' imperative in agriculture ... But the data seem to indicate that the tendency of the state to seek such collaboration varies also - and independently from sectoral characteristics - across nations.

Others have supported this thesis by distinguishing national styles (Richardson 1982, Heidenheimer, Heclo, and Adams 1983, Katzenstein 1985, and those authors who rank-ordered countries on scales of corporatism, such as Lehmbruch 1982 and 1984, Cameron 1984, Lehner 1985, Calmfors and Driffill 1988).

National styles

In this paper I will attempt to distinguish national regulatory styles. By now, there are enough comparative studies on policy analysis and state - industry relations to base such characterizations on. Such studies are among others Ashford and Heaton 1982, Asimov 1983, Badaracco 1985, Brickman, Jasanoff and Ilgen 1985, Chick 1990, Derthick and Quirk 1985, Döhler 1990, Duchene and Shepherd 1987, Dunlop 1980, Dyson and Wilks 1983, Hall 1986, Hancher 1990, Hayward 1972, 1975 and 1983, Hirst and Zeitlin 1989, Katzenstein 1987, Kelman 1981, Lundqvist 1980, Nef 1962, Peacock 1985, Premfors 1980, Richardson 1982, Schneider 1985 and 1988, Süllow 1982, Vogel 1986, 1987 and 1992, Wilks and Wright 1987, Graham Wilson 1985 and 1985a, James Wilson 1980 and 1989, Windhoff-Héritier 1989, van de Wijngaart 1991, and Zysman 1983. In the following, the various country styles will be discussed along the six main types distinguished above.

Liberal-pluralism, étatism, and corporatism

The distinction between liberal-pluralism, étatism and corporatism is a commonly made one, étatism being typical for France, liberal-pluralism for Britain and the US, and corporatism for Germany and some of the smaller European countries, such as the Netherlands, Austria, and Sweden (e.g. Katzenstein 1985). Less well-known is how these different conceptions of social order are elaborated and reflected in legislation in specific policy areas. In another paper (Van Waarden 1994) I have demonstrated how these types of state intervention are apparent in the state regulation of labour relations. Let me just summarize the findings.

France is typified by far reaching state regulation of the substance of working conditions, vocational training, conditions for union recognition, collective negotiations, and compulsory conflict mediation. There is a preference for policy solutions through state regulation. Interest associations play a minor role. Unions are weak in terms of membership, density ratio, and finance, and they are divided along ideological and other lines. Hence they are not taken very serious by their interlocutors, such as employers and state agencies.

In England, state abstention, voluntariness, and informality reign in the central areas of negotiations, strikes and union rights. The right to strike is practically unlimited, collective wage agreements cannot be enforced in state courts and cannot be declared generally binding, unions and their shop stewards do not want any state support, mediation and arbitration are possible but not compulsory, and with vocational training the state is much less involved than elsewhere. 'There is, perhaps, no major country in the world in which the law has played a less significant role in the shaping of the labour relations than in Great Britain' wrote Kahn-Freund (1967: 44). The state leaves room for the 'market' as the main principle of allocation and coordination and provides at most a legal framework for private organizations such as firms and interest associations. American policymakers have also a preference for 'market' solutions to policy problems. Moreover, in both countries there are many and many different trade unions and employers' associations, with overlapping memberships and competing for members and

338

for influence with interlocutors. The associational systems are hence fragmented and pluralist in character.

In Germany and in the Netherlands there is like in France also a conception of active state involvement in civil society, but here the state uses organizations of civil society itself, such as interest associations, as intermediaries and 'assistants' in policy formulation and implementation. Therefore, the state actively supports the emergence and existence of interest associations and their mutual agreements. It leaves room for, and sustains, interest associations as important principles of allocation and coordination in society. Thus unions and employers' associations have a legally guaranteed autonomy, but their structure and functioning is regulated in detail in law. There are limitations to the right to strike and formal conditions for the recognition of interest associations and their mutual contracts. Much regulation of labour and labour relations takes place at the initiative of interest associations and acquires first the form of private contracts. They can however be subsequently transformed into statutory regulations by declaring them generally binding. Furthermore, interest associations play an important role in the formulation and implementation of public policy, e.g. in the areas of labour market and vocational training. They have substantial resources (membership, density ratios, finance, access to interlocutors) and are relatively comprehensively organized. Competition between associations is practically absent in Germany and in the Netherlands less than in Britain or France.

Active and reactive policies

Obviously, an étatist policy style implies and active style, as exemplified by France. One is also tempted to link liberal with reactive styles. This would however be a mistake, as a comparison of the US and Britain shows. British policymakers tend indeed to follow a reactive approach. American authorities however have, notwithstanding their liberal-pluralist orientation, an inclination for activist policies. This indicates that the typologies of étatism-liberalism-corporatism and active-reactive should be distinguished as relatively independent ones. US state agencies may have a preference for market solutions. However, when the state interferes it does so intensely. There is a belief in the American culture that problems are there to be solved. That law can and should be used to shape the direction of society and to solve social ills, whether it be criminality, racial discrimination and inequality, or environmental pollution. American regulations tend to be strict and detailed. Authorities intervene intensely in the society and the economy. Businessmen are confronted with strict, high, and detailed rules regarding competitive practices, product safety and liability, or environmental effects. Decades before the introduction of unleaded gasoline in Europe, Americans were

339

pumping it already. By setting high and strict standards US administrators try to be technology forcing.

Germany and the Netherlands fit somewhere in between the activist countries France and the US and the reactive country Britain. The states in these nations have relatively high ambitions of regulating and steering their societies. They have assumed responsibility for a multitude of policy goals, including a well-ordered and stable economy and a just income distribution. As a result, these nations are among the most developed welfare states. In the Netherlands, the public sector, including transfer payments, account for almost sixty per cent of GDP. However, their corporatist orientation makes them delegate policy formulation or implementation to private organizations and/or wait for initiatives from the private sector. This implies also that the intensity of state regulation, the degree in which it constrains and directs business action, is probably less than in the activist countries. However, this may be compensated for by stricter and more intense regulation of economic sectors by associational self-regulation. More often, state regulation is framework regulation, allowing for and facilitating self-regulation.

Comprehensiveness versus fragmentation

The policy analysis literature may have, since the famous article of Lindblom (1959), sufficiently discredited the view that policymaking can be rationally planned, synoptic, or comprehensive. Most policymaking has to be done under conditions of bounded rationality, ambiguity of goals, incomplete understanding of causal relationships, etc. and will tend to be of an incremental nature. Nevertheless, many policymakers will at least try to rationally design their policies, even if they do not always succeed in realizing rational policies. This ambition to integrate individual policies into more comprehensive plans, as well as the capacity to do so, will differ between countries.

France's activist policies are usually given the form of rather comprehensive plans, as is generally known. The planning ambition is present, more than in other societies. Furthermore, the organizational preconditions for realization of such plans are better than in other nations. The centralization of political power in the state bureaucracy, the latter's status and influence in society, and the long terms of office of politicians, in particular the president, facilitate integration and long term consistency of policies.

By contrast, the US may often pursue activist policies, but they are usually less integrated in comprehensive plans. The concept of planning has certainly much less legitimacy than in France. Furthermore, the extreme fragmentation of political power, the relatively low status of government bureaucrats and their high turnover, the short term policy orientation of American politicians, the lack of party discipline, resulting in log-rolling and pork barrel, all frustrate any attempts at more comprehensive and stable policies. US policies are typically fragmented and short-lived.

The other countries fit somewhere in between these extremes. Britain shares with the US a belief that planning is synonymous with socialism, which gives the concept low legitimacy among the bureaucracy. The belief in the wisdom of stepwise, incremental policies is even stronger than in the US and fits with the legal system and general political culture. On the other hand, the political institutions allow for greater integration and stability over time. Such institutions are the centralization of political power in this union-state, the parliamentary system and the voting rules which provides for one party dominating the executive and the legislative, party discipline and the authority of the prime minister, and, perhaps most importantly, the lifetime career civil service, its status and image of neutrality, and the regular circulation of top civil servants over the ministries.

In the Netherlands, planning is more legitimate and a clear ambition of the executive, as also expressed in the presence of several influential state agencies for geographic, for economic, and for social-cultural planning. Furthermore, the country has a centralized polity and a professional bureaucracy with a relatively high status in society and politics. However, institutional factors which frustrate policy integration are consociationalism and coalition governments, requiring often extended and complicated policy negotiations, and the segmentation of the executive in relatively independent ministries. Holland has nothing like the British, German or French integrated civil service. Each department has its own hiring and training policies and there is no circulation of personnel between ministries. Germany shares with Holland a certain planning ambition, which is reinforced by German legalism and perfectionism. The integration and status of the national bureaucracy facilitates its realization. However, federalism results in complicated forms of vertical 'Politikverflechtung' which may complicate policy integration and frustrate stability over time.

Legalism versus pragmatism

American public authorities tend to 'go by the books' (Cf. also Bardach and Kagan 1982 and Wilson 1989). They implement regulations rather formally and inflexible, and are unwilling to take account of specific circumstances of individual firms. They frequently give orders and injunctions and do not hesitate to impose fines. Great value is attached to universal rule application to all citizens or organizations alike. By contrast, British civil servants are flexible in rule formulation and application. They are much more open to negotiations with business over the observation of the rules. Transgressions on one issue may be overlooked in exchange for strict observation of other standards. There is usually more understanding for the technical and financial

341

problems of firms in meeting strict air or water emission standards. Rules may be temporarily suspended, and exemptions or deferral granted. Good intentions count.

Kelman (1981) compared American and Swedish factory inspectors and Wilson (1985) did the same for British and American regulation of health and safety at work. They found American inspectors to be much more formal, easier given to citations and fines, and less willing to listen to arguments of employers why they could not abide by the rules. Swedish and British inspectors see themselves much more as advisers and educators than as policemen. They tend to give advance notice to the employer so as to allow him to show his best, advice him on how to improve conditions, rarely impose fines, are willing to listen to the problems he may have with the rules, are flexible in allowing him time to bring the situation in line with the rules, and try to promote cooperation between the local trade union representatives and the employer as a way of providing a more localized and hence more permanent control system. The inspectors have a much greater discretionary authority. The rules to which the Swedish agencies bind their inspectors are contained in a six-page booklet, whereas American factory inspectors are provided with a sizable manual which prescribes in great detail the procedures they have to follow in dealing with employers.

German authorities are more like American ones. They also attach importance to universal and equal rule application. Civil servants have relatively little discretionary authority in negotiating with business over the observation of the rules. Most of them are trained lawyers or had to pass legal exams. This gives them a legalist orientation to policymaking. But unlike their American counterparts, the system as a whole does allow for more flexibility than in the US, because of the involvement of private interest associations in policy formulation and implementation. Although they do find themselves confronted with statutory constraints and obligations, the absence of a civil servant status gives them more leeway. Furthermore, the peculiarities of German federalism, requiring often the collaboration of authorities on the federal, state, and even county or municipal level in the implementation of a single measure, does also create more room for negotiation, even if only within the state organization.

Dutch policymakers combine corporatist (as in Germany) with pragmatic (as in Britain) and lenient policies. They follow often policies of 'gedogen', of permitting, tolerating a lesser evil in order to fight a greater evil. Soft drugs are tolerated and regulated, in order to fight hard drug abuse more effectively. Formal cartels are tolerated and registered, in the expectation that inevitable informal (and more harmful) collusion between firms may be less necessary. The Dutch policy of the lesser evil is related to corporatism. It has favored self-regulation in cartels and trade associations. In order to have an interlocutor and partner in regulating and fighting abuses, the authorities have even actively encouraged relevant industries to organize. Thus there are official business' associations of brothels and of 'coffee shops' which trade soft drugs. Such associations try to control and prevent excrescences, which could threaten their hard-won recognition or could precipitate state intervention. Thus the Coffeeshop Association forbids and tries to control the sale of hard drugs in the coffee shops.

Adversarialism, consensualism, and paternalism

The strictness of policymaking of US authorities influences their relation to their clientele. Rather than avoiding conflict they seem to look for it. Hence their relation to private business has also been called an adversarial one (a.o. Chandler 1980, Fritschler and Ross 1980, Marcus 1984). American authorities are relatively less interested in listening to and involving collective interest representatives of the regulated. They dislike being dependent on particularistic interests for information and feel less need to legitimize their policies since they are less interested in consensus building.

The flexible and pragmatic style of British authorities makes them look for cooperation and consultation with the subjects to be regulated. Officials tend to rely more on persuasion than on coercion in implementing policies. Their style is a consensual one. In their search for consensus and conciliation, they are keen on building and maintaining close contact and cooperation with representatives of the to-be-regulated. They listen to their problems, work on building trust relations, involve them in and make them co-responsible for implementation, and by convincing them of the reasonability of the policy goals and means try to acquire voluntary compliance. In time, cooperation with interest groups has become routinized and 'a mere form of courtesy and good manners' (Ehrmann 1968: 259). American authorities on the other hand see it as a good democratic practice to keep special interests at arms' length.

The Netherlands also combines pragmatism with consensualism. The country shares with Britain an inclination to involve societal interests in the formulation and implementation of public policy. Policymakers search for compromise and consensus, whether through consultations, negotiations or cooperation. Dutch consensual administrative culture is even institutionalized in its language. The Dutch word for policy, *beleid*, means not only 'course of action' but also prudence, discretion, tact, and is related to the word *overleg* which means both deliberation, judgement, forethought, consideration ánd consultation, concertation, to take council together.

Legalism can however also go together with consensualism, as the German case shows. This indicates that legalism-pragmatism and adversarialism-consensualism are different and relatively independent policy dimensions. Dyson (1982) and Katzenstein (1987) saw as typical for the German administration a search for consensus, but if necessary, and probably more

343

than in Britain and the Netherlands, do administrators resort to force in the case of enduring conflicts over policy solutions. Then, matters are decided either authoritatively (through decisions of higher levels) or formally through the courts. The legalism of German law and administration requires this.

The French authorities have their own version of adversarialism. They are much less enthusiastic about involving private interests in public policy, as they fear that the particularism of these interests will threaten the 'national interest' for whom they themselves stand guard. Their attitude towards such particularistic interests has been characterized by a certain contempt, haughtiness, superiority, and paternalism. As Hayward wrote, in France

> paternalistic government officials have generally regarded the private sector as composed at best of 'partners' and at worst of satellites ... The relationship between the public authorities and business is conceived primarily in hierarchical and unilateral terms, with government bodies exercising regulatory tutelage over their private sector clientele. (Hayward 1975: 119)

Formal versus informal network relations

American authorities are not only formal in the substance and form of their regulations, but also in their contacts with organized interests. In sofar as American public authorities make themselves accessible to organized interests, they apply the same universalistic criteria they also use in their interaction with individual firms. They are careful not to give privileged access to specific groups, for fear of being accused of favoritism and bias. To ensure such universalism, relations with interest representatives are formalized. Procedures at public hearings and lobbying activities are strictly regulated. Hence every interest group has more or less equal access and the number of participants in policy networks is in principle unlimited. That is, the boundaries of such networks are extremely open and fluid.

British state agencies, by comparison, are not only informal in their regulatory style, but also in their relations to organized interests. They are rather selective in with whom they deal and give privileged access to those interests of most strategic importance to policy implementation. Particularism rather than universalism is the norm. As a result, the policy networks they create, have only a limited number of participants and have relatively closed boundaries.

Part of this informality is the acceptance of secrecy. In Britain, both the membership of the networks and the internal processes are shrouded in secrecy, just as the general policy process, a secrecy which seems to be perfectly legitimate among bureaucrats, the interests concerned and the general public alike. Such a secrecy would be unthinkable in the US.

For decades, the British quietly have accepted a level of governmental secrecy that would have led to rebellion in the United States. It is inconceivable that the United States would ever adopt an Official Secrets Act comparable in scope and severity to that which long has been on the books in Great Britain. (James Q. Wilson 1989: 301).

Dutch administrators combine pragmatism (as in Britain) with formalism in relations to organized interests (unlike Britain and in common with the US). Interlocutors of state agencies are mostly interest organizations, whereas British civil servants also like to deal with individual leading businessmen or firms. Such interest associations are often formally recognized and have been given formal access to the state, such as a statutory right to be consulted before policy decisions are made, or the legal right to a number of seats in an advisory committee to the government. At the interface between state agencies and interest associations, a great number of bi-, tri- or multipartite semi-state agencies have been created. Relations within the networks are intense, multiplex and relatively symmetric - unions e.g. are at many levels and sectors involved.

German state - industry relations are also formalized, among others in legislation framing the rights and responsibilities of private associations. However, it seems that formalism in these relations is somewhat less than in the Netherlands, as Germany lacks the Dutch necessity to treat associations from different societal pillars (catholics, protestants, socialists) equally, an essential ingredient of Dutch pillarization and consociationalism. For this reason, Dutch corporatism is probably more formal than the Austrian or German variety.

Although Dutch and German state - industry relations do not share the informalism found in Britain, they do share the British tendency to provide privileged access to selected associations. Monopoly recognition is also not uncommon. However, because the Dutch and German associational systems are much more integrated than the British pluralist one, privileged access poses less problems. There are less associations which are excluded. Actually, the provision of state privileges to certain associations has encouraged mergers and affiliations between associations, up to the point of the formation of comprehensive peak associations. As a result, Dutch and German policy networks have relatively closed boundaries.

In line with French paternalism in policy networks is the informality of these relations. In sofar as interest associations are consulted at all by civil servants, this happens on an ad hoc and arbitrary manner. It is up to the discretion of the civil servants. Interest associations are not formally recognized and have no formally guaranteed access to the state. More in general, the sovereignty and status, which public administrators have as representatives of the French état, give them substantial leeway in implementing public policy towards societal clientele. This informality in relations between state and civil society stands in marked contrast to the formality which reigns within the French public administration (Crozier 1964).

Institutional foundations of policy styles

The differences in the characteristics of the national regulatory styles of the American, British, French, German, and Dutch public administrations are of course relative, relative to the other nations. If one would study policies in only any one of these nations, one might perhaps not so readily identify national regulatory styles as I have done here. It is often only from a comparative perspective, that one can identify such national traits, and than always only relative to some other nations. The US is more formal in its state - industry relations, when seen in contrast to Britain or France.

Furthermore, these national characterizations do not mean that elements of other styles are not found in each country. There are always exceptions to the rule. Furthermore, styles may also be different between policy fields and economic sectors. Styles may also differ between policy formulating and policy implementation agencies or between top-levels of the bureaucracy and the street-level bureaucrats. Nevertheless, some general traits will be more dominant in one nation than in another. The styles identified as national ones are more common, more widespread and/or more dominant.

That nations have their own styles is no accident nor incident. They are so widely spread across policy fields and relatively stable over time because they reflect different conceptions of the state, of its position, authority and tasks vis-à-vis civil society. In étatist France, the state is much stronger differentiated out of civil society that in liberal Britain. The French state is clearly placed outside and above society, has the responsibility for maintaining social order, and the legitimacy and authority to intervene in society to this end. These state conceptions are first of all fixed in culture - both the general political culture and the administrative culture of state agencies - and in institutions of the state: the legal system, the polity, the organizational structure of the state bureaucracy, and the characteristics of civil servants. Secondly, such state conceptions are also sustained in the institutions and culture of civil society, in the organizational strength and in the values and attitudes of private interest associations. Culture and institutions reinforce and support each other, thus contributing to the stability of these conceptions of the state. It is impossible to deal with all of these at length in the context of an article. Hence, a few state institutions have been selected to demonstrate the institutional foundations of national intervention styles.

First of all, law, as its importance is often underrated by social scientists. However, it is one of the most central state institutions and among the clearest expressions of state - society relations. Most other state institutions, such as the polity and the bureaucracy, acquire their form through law. Hence it can not be overlooked by anyone interested in institutional analysis of the state.

Conceptions of the state in legal systems

The conceptions of tasks and authority of the state have first of all been precipitated and subsequently maintained in the various legal systems. An in this connection useful typology of legal systems is that of Damaska (1986), as he links legal systems with different conceptions of state authority and state tasks. Damaska distinguishes two dimensions of legal systems, a structural one, and a functional one. On the *structural* dimension he distinguishes between hierarchically and horizontally ('coordinate') organized systems, which each are representative of an analogical 'ideal' of state authority. On the *functional* dimension he differentiates between legal systems which are in the first place instrument for 'policy implementation' - for activist states designing policies to structure and steer society according to their ideals and goals - and legal systems which are a mere instrument for the 'resolution of conflicts' arising in civil society - representing a more reactive state role. The latter distinction relates to the often made distinction between adversarial and inquisitorial legal systems. In conflict settlement, the legal process takes the form of a contest between two private parties, with the state intermediating and adjudicating as a neutral third party. In policy implementation the legal process is structured like an inquest, with judges presiding not as neutral third parties, but as state officials serving the policy goals of the state, by investigating transgressions of the law and reaching a verdict. The combination of the structural and functional dimensions produces the two-by-two table 14.1. The various types are ideal types and are not in all their elements found in any one real country. Nevertheless, some countries come close to certain ideal types, and these are indicated in the table.

Table 14.1
Typology of legal systems according to Damaska, 1986

	Function of the Legal System	
	Policy Implementation - Inquest Procedure - Activist State	*Conflict Settlement* - Contest Procedure - Reactive State
Hierarchic Authority	Church of Rome French and Prussian criminal justice USSR, Maoist China	Continental Civil Procedure
Structure of **Legal Officialdom**		
Coordinate Authority	Activist Justice in the USA	English Common Law

The English 'common law' system has stood model for the ideal type of a coordinately structured system with conflict resolution as its principal function, within a reactive state intervention style. Typical for a 'coordinate' system is the absence of hierarchy between different judges and courts, a preference for lay-functionaries and a greater importance of substantial norms as compared to formal norms.

The absence of hierarchy within the legal system reflects a limited superiority of the state over civil society. The British state is insufficiently differentiated out of society. It is still closely tied to that society. That is apparent from the legal system, both from its rule-system and its functionaries. Both are directly 'derived' from civil society. Typical for the common law system is the absence of codified law, of abstract rules which could pertain to a wide variety of legal cases, abstract rules formulated and 'made' by people, by a state authority placed over society and imposed from above upon that society. English law is to be found in the precedents given by earlier and concrete court decisions, which have been minutely recorded over the past centuries. These court decisions are not considered to have been 'made' by judges, but are regarded as manifestations of law that has always existed in society, from 'time immemorial' on. It is, and always has been, in the conventions and customs between people. The task of the judge is only to discover this law and to make it relevant for social action and social conflicts. Geldart (1991) uses the metaphor of the discovery of America by Columbus. America existed from 'time immemorial' on. We know it however only because Columbus discovered it. The task of judges of the common law is a similar one: to discover something that existed already, not to create something. Specific norms are expression of the legal 'essence' in society and are to be found in individual court decisions and the jurisprudence they form together. Thus, in English law, unwritten codes of practice emerged bottom-up in society and gradually have become integrated into a body of valid law. Collective wage agreements could be considered as just one form of such customs and contracts which materialized in civil society. Since all judges 'discover' law that already exists, there cannot really be a hierarchy between judges. One judge cannot invalidate 'discoveries' of another. Hence appeals procedures are limited and there are only a few levels in the judicial system.

As said, no system completely covers the ideal type. Over past two centuries, statute law, enacted by Parliament, has become increasingly important in England and has partly replaced the common law. However, statutes have neither been codified, and are interpreted by the judges according to common law principles. Furthermore, one could argue that in the British state conception, Parliament is a representation of civil society, and not an organization of the state. Hence statute law could still be considered as emanating out of civil society.

Not only the rules, but also the legal functionaries stem largely from civil society in the English legal system. Many are amateurs (Eddey 1987). The jury has been called the cornerstone of the English legal system. The accused are allowed to defend themselves and do not have to let themselves be represented by a lawyer. The 'Magistrates', the judges who preside and decide over simple cases, are unpaid volunteers, respectable members of the local society, without any legal training. The training of other judges and lawyers (solicitors and barristers) takes place still largely in practice and during age-old rituals such as the 'dinners' in the 'Inns of Court', during which, according to the tradition, the established members of the profession initiate the newcomers. Furthermore, unlike in continental Europe, judges do not get a special training. They are recruited from among experienced barristers (and these in turn again from among solicitors). That is, judges are not in the first place seen as representatives of the state, socialized through a state education, but are considered as coming from civil society, from among lawyers which represent citizens in court. The influence of amateurs in the system implies that technical and formal criteria are less important that in continental European legal systems, and that substantial criteria of justice are more important. For that reason also, procedures in court are less formalized, especially in the 'Magistrates' Courts.

According to the ideal type of Damaska, English law serves a state which assumes a passive, reactive, derived role. Its primary *function* is to settle conflicts in civil society, when society cannot solve these conflicts itself. The legal form is that of the contest, as opposed to the inquest. State officials, i.e. judges, preside as neutral third parties over a dispute between two private parties. The judges and the law channel and regulate the conflict rendering process and in the end they decide which party has made the more convincing case. In the ideal model, the state has no interests of its own, has no ideals or goals towards which societal development should be steered. Hence, there is no function of law in implementation of such steering policies. In sofar as law is used for policy implementation, it should be 'yielding law'. It should yield, give priority, to regulations of civil society itself. Private contracts, market solutions, and self-regulation by societal associations take priority. Only if civil society cannot regulate itself, is there a place for state regulation. Initiatives for such intervention should come from private citizens, as the state is assumed to have no interests of its own. Policy implementation should preferably take place without the use of law, that is, through informal, rather than formal regulations. Given the priority of civil society, voluntariness of state regulations is important. Rules should not be imposed, made compulsory, take the form of injunctions and prohibitions, and backed up by rigorously applied sanctions. Policy instruments such as consultation, persuasion, informal agreements, and private contracts have priority. Bans and commands are acceptable only as ultimate means.

Liberalist values of state abstinence and preference for societal solutions and voluntariness are hence not just preoccupations of conservative-liberal political parties; they are basic ingredients of the age-old English legal system. It is a system which gives precedence to civil society. The state is still incompletely differentiated out of it. Rules and functionaries emanate from civil society, private contracts and societal self-regulation take priority, initiatives for regulation are to come from individuals and associations of civil society. Hence, state representatives will seek the cooperation of representatives of civil society, will value consensus and compromise, and this will be facilitated by the legitimacy of informal procedures.

There are several historical reasons for the survival of a legal system which reflects an incomplete differentiation of the state out of society. The comparatively easy internal communication over the sea allowed for an early centralization of political power, for early state formation. However, the relatively secure borders of the island-nation made it less dependent on unlimited centralized power which controlled a standing army, capable of defending the country against foreign threats. Early state formation meant under such conditions also incomplete state formation. The British Kings have never felt the need to codify and in the process redefine local customs, as continental monarchs did to break the power of local feudal lords and to extend their authority into the periphery of their realm. The island location and colonial empire facilitated subsequently early industrialization, which could, in the absence of foreign industrial competition, be successfully guided by the market. This enhanced the trust in state abstinence, markets, free trade and contracting, freedom of firms and associations, and voluntariness further. The first forms of state intervention to correct externalities of unfettered capitalism took place in an era in which laissez-faire ideology was the dominant ideology, with the result that present-day socio-economic policy still bears this historical imprint.

Countries with other historical experiences have developed different legal systems. France and Prussia were countries with greater problems of internal communication and central control, less secure borders, and had a less adaptive nobility. This contributed to the eventual development of the Ständestaat into absolutist monarchy. The monarchs used and redefined the law in their attempts to break the strength of competing powers such as the feudal lords, and to centralize and extend their control over the whole territory of their realm. In the process, a new legal system was created, which exhibited the properties of what Damaska called a legal system, reflecting a hierarchic ideal of state authority: a hierarchy between state and society and between different levels of courts, a preference for professional functionaries, and a greater importance of formal instead of substantial norms.

Originally, Continental European countries also had a case law system. As in England, law was present in and emerged from society. It existed out of a great variety of distinct local 'coutumes' and conventions, as apparent from concrete case decisions. Codification implied that the more abstract principles, underlying these individual cases, were identified, formulated and collected in codexes. In the process of abstraction, law was often redefined to suit the interests of the monarch, striving for a centralization of power and location of state sovereignty in himself. Thus 'natural law', present in society, came to be replaced by man-made law, made by the monarch and his legal advisers. Rather than emerging 'bottom-up' out of society, it came to be imposed 'top-down' upon society. Thus legal changes facilitated and secured a differentiation of state out of society. This was enhanced as the codifiers used ancient Roman law as a source of inspiration, which makes a more explicit distinction between public and private law, between relations among private citizens and relations between citizens and the state. The codifiers needed Roman law also as a new source of legitimacy for the law, to back up the legitimacy and sovereignty of the absolutist monarch who became the new source of law, rather than society and christianity.

To identify and formulate abstract codified law, the monarch needed specially trained advisers. Both the formulation and the application of law

351

came to be regarded as an eminently technical, professional pursuit. Although of course recruited from civil society, the professional officials became detached from society by their special legal training. In addition, this specific socialization served also to make them identify with and represent the state and its interests. The technical training of these officials made for an increasing importance of formal and procedural norms over substantial ones. Thus both rules and officials no longer emanated from society, but were shaped in a separate entity, placed over society, the state apparatus, and imposed from above upon society. In line with the hierarchic relation between state and civil society, the internal structure of the judiciary became also hierarchic.

In addition, law acquired a major function in an activist state tradition, especially in France. Early on, French state authorities came to identify specific interests of the state. The mercantilism of Colbert implied that the economy, part of civil society, was to serve the interests of the state in acquiring income and international standing and power. Later on, the French revolution and the Enlightenment introduced other notions of the ideal society, which the state was to realize. Law was to play a major role as instrument of these policy goals. Such a policy implementation function of the law was facilitated by the fact that the legal process on the Continent - under the influence of the Church of Rome - had of old assumed the form of an inquest, as opposed to a contest. The inquest does not assume a neutral role for judges as state officials. Instead, the judge is to serve the state interests. He investigates transgressions of the law by citizens and comes to a verdict of the basis of his own, actively sought, findings, instead of judging from a neutral perspective and assuming a passive role in a conflict, fought out before him between private parties. The early activist role of the judge in adjudicating, anticipated an activist role of the state. Thus French étatism, a legitimacy of state authority and state interventionism, is expressed and bolstered in its legal system. It is expressed in the differentiation of the state out of civil society, the state as the legitimate source of law, the distinction between public and private law, the authority of technical professionals, the internal hierarchical structure of the judiciary, and the inquest as the typical process form.

American law combines a coordinate or horizontal structure with a policy implementation function. This reflects its historical roots in the English common law, overlaid by continental influences and the relics of its specific process of state formation. The English common law is still largely valid in the US and has certainly strengthened the liberal-pluralist tradition in the US. It functions as an important bridge between the two main liberal-pluralist nations. Furthermore, British traditions have also influenced the structure of the legal officialdom. The jury-system - fixed in the Bill of Rights to the Constitution - exemplifies the importance of laymen. The state official, the judge, presides as a more or less neutral third party between the contestants.

Furthermore, the court system is rather horizontally structured, with overlapping jurisdictions and no clear hierarchy between lower courts. This coordinate structure is actually enhanced by federalism, which gives the US court system its multilayered character. However, there is a central authority, the Supreme Court, which has more central authority that the Law Lords in Britain. This greater authority of the Supreme Court is in part a product of federalism, as federalism requires an agency to resolve conflicts over competence between different state levels.

The specific genesis of the US state has produced a hybrid principle as to the source of law. On the one hand the legal system subscribes to the old common law principle that law has existed from 'time immemorial' and that it is only to be discovered, rather than made by judicial officials. As in Britain, this 'eternal' law has authority over the state, rather than it being the product of that state. On the other hand, the US also considers law man-made - and hence changeable and a possible instrument for social change - more precisely, made by the state. And, paradoxically, in order to control that state. With, again a paradox, the result that the courts have become a major part of state authority, much more so than in Britain. The US-state emerged out of a revolt against a centralizing state, Tudor England. The American revolutionaries wanted to prevent the emergence of a central power in the US, similar to that against which they revolted. Therefore they created a constitution, a set of rules, man-made, and consciously designed to constrain state power, with instruments which built in the well-known checks and balances, such as federalism and the separation of powers. Whereas in France and Prussia, state-made law, codified law, emerged out of an attempt of a centralizing power to support and enhance its authority, the American process of state formation shows the opposite: state-made law in order to constrain that very state.

The experience of having designed their own state has enhanced the belief in the prospect of explicit and conscious social design, in the possibility of solving social problems through intentional action. That is the basis of the strong legal activism in the US. Perhaps nowhere else has legal engineering become so popular. More than in other countries do Americans belief that social ills (e.g. criminality, discrimination) can be cured by law, by regulation. Essential element of the ideal American society is the capitalist market economy. Thus the law was used as an instrument for the political goal of industrialization and economic growth. The instrumental nature is apparent from its opportunistic use. When necessary, judges and legislatures bent and modified the common law, e.g. to limit property rights to allow for the building of railroads in the 19th century, and thus to foster economic growth (Hall 1989). At other times, the common law was strictly interpreted, purportedly for the same end. Thus many early social regulations, such as child labour laws and the New Deal, were declared unconstitutional by the

353

Supreme Court with reference to the common law limitations on state intervention in the market (Solo 1974: 65-90). An instrumental vision on law is now reflected in the severity of its criminal law (capital punishment), the attempts to fight alcoholism and drug abuse by law, that is, in its activist policies. Furthermore, it may be also discerned behind the importance of coercion in its regulatory style, in the impatience in implementation, and the inability to allow time for the creation of consensus and legitimacy, which could facilitate compliance with regulation.

By contrast, the British are extremely careful to bend the law, so that it can serve as an instrument of social change. Continuity and predictability are considered very important, and decisions of judges centuries ago are still valid. Obviously, such an inflexible use of law has created frequently problems, as where the predictability of the law required the upholding of former decisions, but moral justice required adaptation to new circumstances. This tension has been solved by the gradual emergence of what is practically a second system of law. The common law has become overlaid by the system of 'equity', with its own rules and officials. Whenever the maintenance of the common law produced obvious injustices, these could be corrected under 'equity'. This double system has enhanced the 'coordinate', fragmented, pluralist character of english law.

Presence or absence of judicial review

US and German legalism and formalism in their regulatory styles is related to the presence of judicial review and extensive administrative law in these countries. Judicial review is the ability of the courts to overturn or declare statutes enacted by parliament, or administrative decisions of the executive, unconstitutional. The US and Germany have constitutional courts who can do so. It is absent in Britain, where the principle of the supremacy of parliament dominates. A weak intermediary form is found in e.g. France and the Netherlands. Here the courts cannot invalidate laws of parliament, but there is a ex-ante review of legal drafts by the *Conseil d'Etat* (France) or the *Raad van State* (Netherlands).

The US has kept the principle of the 'rule of natural law' from medieval times, except that they have replaced natural law by (man-made) constitutional law. They did this at a time when the British were replacing the supremacy of law by the supremacy of parliament, and apparently this fear of British centralization of power and arbitrary government - under which the North-American colonies suffered - made the Americans stick to the supremacy of law, in order to limit state powers. Judicial review was hence part of the system of checks and balances in the American polity. Although the principle was established with the constitution, it took many years to evolve into its present importance. A number of fundamental decisions of the Supreme Court gradually affirmed and extended its authority vis-à-vis Congress and the Executive. In addition, Congress used the principle to subject executive agencies to control. To this end, judicial review of agency rulemaking was included in more and more statutes. The 1946 Administrative Procedures Act provided a general statutory framework. Later on Congress mandated it explicitly in the statutes establishing the various regulatory agencies.

The principle became so important, not only because the possibility was provided, but also because it was vigorously used, thanks to the litigious and activist tradition in US politics.

> The US has long had a tradition of civic activism. Compared to their counterparts in other capitalist democracies, Americans are more likely to believe that they have both the ability and the opportunity to affect government decisions. ... The ability of the public-interest movement to use the courts to affect regulatory policy was in turn made possible by three important changes in administrative law. The first was a significant expansion of the doctrine of standing - the grounds upon which an aggrieved party could demand the right to have its grievances heard in the federal courts. The second was the increased willingness of the courts to broaden the grounds on which they were willing to overturn agency decisions. The third involved the legal recognition of the right of private citizens to participate in the decisions of administrative agencies. (Vogel 1989: 95, 108-9).

Judicial review is important because it provides interest associations with multiple channels for access to the government. If they do not like the regulations of a specific state agency, they have an alternative to go to. They can appeal the law or the administrative decision. This makes the Supreme Court an important actor in state - business relations. Interest groups have less of an incentive to try to reach a compromise with the regulatory agency or to defer to its authority. Thus state - industry relations can evolve into the formal and adversarial ones they are.

> Implementation can be informal and flexible only if the interests involved have an incentive to accept the agency's actions, and they will have that incentive only if they do not think they can get a better deal elsewhere - in court, the press, Congress, or the streets. (James Q. Wilson 1989: 300).

Furthermore, multiple access points to the government foster fragmentation of policy networks, thus contributing to pluralism. In countries where the road to the courts is absent, interest associations are more condemned to reach an understanding with the regulatory agencies. Furthermore, with less points of access there is less 'berthing' place for interest associations, compelling them to cooperate or even form more comprehensive peak associations.

Judicial review is also important, because the possibility of judicial control of administrative decisions will make civil servants more careful in their clientele relations. They will try to 'stick to the books', keep records of considerations and decisions, and prevent any contacts to particularistic interests which could cause suspicion. If the rule of law does not already limit their discretionary authority, they will try to limit it themselves.

> It makes sense then for the bureaucracy to take a tough line: Insist that everything be on the public record, insist that everything be done 'by the book', insist that 'everybody be treated the same', and insist that the full force of the law fall on every violator. (James Q. Wilson 1989: 300)

Thus this external control forces administrators to be more formal in their relations to organized interests and to keep them at bay when this could create problems. The extensive judicial review in the US is hence in part responsible for the formalism and legalism of American administrators, as well as the pluralist structure of interest associations and the adversarial nature of state-industry relations.

Although Germany also has a system of judicial review, these effects are mainly restricted to formalism and legalism. There is less adversarialism and pluralism. The extensive system of judicial and administrative review in Germany and the existence of specialized courts for social welfare and labour matters have enhanced a legalism and rule orientation in the administration, which was already present because of the influence of legal positivism on 'Beamtenrecht' and on the structure of the administration. The courts'

> presence encourages the cautious legalistic approach to administration so characteristic of the German bureaucracy. Knowing that their mistakes may quickly find them in some court, makes civil servants more concerned about the legal correctness of their actions and less concerned about the political implications of such actions. (Conradt 1989: 177)

The cautiousness is enhanced by the fact that in Germany civil servants are not anonymous as in Britain, but visible and responsible for decisions of their sections. This fosters incrementalism in policy.

> Sections tend to concentrate on limited short run projects that will in effect yield only minor modifications in an already existing policy. Risky projects will be avoided in part because they exceed a sections limited capacity but also because their failure can be easily attributed to specific individuals. (Conradt 1989: 177)

In Germany, legalism has contributed to corporatism and consensualism, rather than to adversarialism in state - industry relations. This is first of all because of the rich historical tradition of close cooperation between the state and organized interests, institutionalized in many semi-state agencies such as the Chambers of Industry and of Artisans. Given this environment, public administrators seem to have chosen also for another strategy of risk aversion: delegation to private organizations - as long as politicians and the courts agree. Risk aversion implies however also that the reliability of the private partners should be ensured and that their authority be circumscribed. Hence the importance of legal framing of unions and employers' associations, and even more, an active involvement of the German state with the structure of interest associations has enhanced their comprehensiveness (Czada 1990).

The importance of legalist principles in law for the regulatory styles of administrators becomes also apparent in a comparison between Germany and the Netherlands. German legalism forces the public prosecutors to bring all cases that come to their attention to court. By contrast, the less legalism orientation of Dutch law is reflected in its so called 'opportunity principle'. Dutch public prosecutors have some discretion to decide whether it is 'opportune' to prosecute a case or to drop it. Collectively that can even develop policies on specific issues, e.g. not to prosecute trade in soft drugs on certain locations or certain abortion or euthanasia cases. This legal provision is both a reflection of, and has allowed for, the pragmatic, negotiating, and tolerant elements in Dutch regulatory style.

The public administration

The differences in state conceptions behind the various regulatory styles are also reflected in the structure and culture of the public administration. In Britain, not only the representatives of the judicial state power are recruited and still tied to civil society; the same holds for the representatives of the executive state power, the civil servants. As in the legal system, there is a predilection for amateurs and for informal procedures. The English civil service prefers generally educated and intelligent amateurs, which are recruited at an early age and subsequently transferred regularly, in order to prevent them from becoming specialist in any one policy area or to become 'captured' by a specific clientele. There is no real state education, where they get socialized in any norms and values of the state. They should be civilized gentlemen, groomed in the fine educational institutions of society, the independent universities of Oxford and Cambridge. That is, as lawyers, civil servants are coming from civil society, and are supposed to 'serve' that society rather than some abstract state, as the word 'civil servant' indicates. This indicates the weak differentiation of the British state out of its civil society. The policy of rotation of officials within the civil service has

357

enhanced the image of neutrality of British civil servants, which in turn explains the large discretionary authority they have and the possibility of practicing secrecy. Administrative law, that is, legal control over the civil service and possibilities of citizens to appeal decisions of the administration, is comparatively underdeveloped. This is related to the flexibility and the preference for informal over formal procedures within the administration as well as in its relations to societal interests (Hennessy 1990). Finally, staff rotation has also allowed for greater policy integration.

By contrast, French representatives of the executive state power are not amateurs, recruited directly from society. They are given special training in state operated elite schools, created specifically for the civil service, such as the *Ecole Normale d'Administration*, de *Ecole Polytechnique*, and the *Ecole des Mines*. Originally, many had a technical training as engineers. Later on, other disciplines have become important such as economics, law and social science. These schools do not only transmit knowledge, but also norms and values pertaining to 'serving the interests of the state', and the entry to the elite *Grand Corps*, brotherhoods which reinforce the socialization in public norms and which give their members an elite self-image.

German civil servants fit somewhere in between. They are supposed to have legal training and have to pass several entrance exams which test this legal knowledge. On the one hand, this training is a bit more general than French civil servants get; on the other hand it is also a form of training into the values and norms of the state. Furthermore, it gives them also a preference for formal procedures and - given German legal positivism - for legalistic use of and interpretations of the law. This fits with detailed legal framing of the structure and authority of private interest associations which are allowed to share in the sovereignty of the state by participating in the implementation of public policy.

Dutch civil servants are neither amateurs nor exclusively lawyers, and are neither trained in elite schools. As a result, Dutch administrators lack the strong identification with the state, as in France, but also with civil society, as in Britain, or with legalism, as in Germany. They usually have an academic training, but in a variety of disciplines: law, economics, engineering, and particularly social sciences. Each ministry recruits its own personnel and has a preference for a certain discipline. Lawyers in the Justice Department, economists in the Department of Trade, political scientists in the Interior Ministry and social scientists in a variety of welfare state Ministries. One result of this is a close relation between state bureaucrats and university academics (the more so as cabinet ministers are often recruited from among university professors). This is an important factor behind the planning orientation in policymaking. However, because there is no central civil service, there is practically no rotation between departments, a factor which has enhanced fragmentation in policies.

The French, British, German, and Dutch public administrations all have a relative high status in society - compared to e.g. the American public administration - and are conscious of it. In part, this is related to their selective recruitment - giving them a sense of belonging to the select few - and to their well-endowed material position and security. In part it is also because over time they have acquired an image of reliability, neutrality, impartiality and stability. Almond and Verba found in their famous study of political culture that Germans had more confidence in their bureaucracy and courts than in other branches of government (1963: 189 ff.). The German administration is old and has been a factor of stability during frequent and radical political changes. The Prussian administration has been a model of efficiency, dedication and incorruptibility, giving it a legitimation on the basis of performance. Likewise, the French administration, also old and dating back to the times of Louis XIV, Richelieu and Napoleon, has provided for stability and continuity during the many constitutional changes, the alternating republics, monarchies and empires, which the French have had during the last two centuries.

This relatively high status allows them a certain freedom in developing their own regulatory style. But it has gone in different directions in the various societies. Because of their different socialization patterns, state bureaucrats harbor different role perceptions, and that influences their relation with civil society.

In Britain, high status allows for discretionary authority and for informality, privileged access, and secrecy in state industry relations. In France, the selective recruitment and socialization in special elite state schools, combined with the respect for *l'Etat* in general French political culture, gives the French administration a specially strong sense of having to serve the public interest and to protect it against particularistic threats. The famous study of Aberbach, Putnam and Rockman (1981) on role models of bureaucrats and politicians provides further support for this. They distinguished a variety of role models. One of them was that of 'trustee' of the interests of the state. Seventy-seven per cent of French top civil servants emphasized this role, as against only fifty-eight per cent in Britain and fourty-eight per cent in Germany. This high self-esteem and distrust of particularism is reflected in their attitude towards private interests. This attitude has been characterized by a certain contempt, haughtiness and superiority. Thus French étatism, activism, and haughtiness vis-à-vis special interests is also rooted in role models and recruitment and socialization patterns in the administration.

Among German (and British and Dutch) top civil servants different role models were dominant. They saw themselves more as 'brokers', 'who focus on mediating or resolving conflicts of interest and political conflict'. Fifty-two per cent of all interviewed German civil servants stressed this role, as against only fourty-four per cent in France (Aberbach et al 1981: 97). (The same

359

study also confirmed the legalism of German administrators. They were top scorers on a legalist role interpretation (sixty-one per cent). In Britain (twenty-one per cent) and France (ten per cent) this aspect was unimportant.)

The relatively high status of German and Dutch administrators has allowed them to maintain close contacts with organized interests, to delegate policymaking to them, and to maintain consensual relations, without immediately being suspected of bias and corruption.

> Societies that have had among the most positive conceptions of the public bureaucracy - Germany, the Netherlands, and the Scandinavian countries - have been much more successful in accommodating the role of pressure groups into policy making than have political systems that have a less exalted conception of their civil servants. In fact, a relative positive evaluation of the civil service may be required to allow the civil servants latitude in dealing with the pressure groups and in making accommodations to their commands. (Peters 1989: 156)

Graham Wilson wrote:

> A teacher whose authority is assured may be able to adopt a more friendly and relaxed approach than a teacher whose authority seems highly uncertain. (1985: 159)

And James Q. Wilson added:

> In Europe, regulators tend to have a more secure base of authority than they do here. Thus, left-leaning 'antibusiness' regimes abroad actually may have friendlier and more accommodative relationships with business than do conservative, 'probusiness' regimes in this country. (1989: 301)

The contrast is especially striking in comparison with the US, where low legitimacy of the state bureaucracy makes that close cooperation between state agencies and private interests is easily seen as 'corruption' or 'capture' (Bernstein 1955, McConnell 1966, Mitnick 1980). One might add that where administrators have a more open attitude towards industry, the latter might see them less as natural adversaries. Hence it will be more likely to consult, cooperate and get involved in corporatist arrangements. In general: a more positive public attitude towards the civil service reduces mutually the cultural if not structural separation between state and society and that allows for closer cooperation.

Embeddedness and persistence

Policy styles and policy networks of the public administration are firmly rooted in nationally specific legal, political and administrative institutions. Here, by way of example, differences in legal systems and in administrative structures have been discussed to underline this thesis. Most of these institutions are somehow interrelated and strengthen one another. In particular, there is a mutual sustainment between culture and institutions. Culture is precipitated and embedded in legal and administrative institutions and the latter in turn buttress these cultural values, making them so enduring.

American liberal-pluralism, activism, fragmentation, legalism, adversarialism, and formalism are the product of the supremacy of natural law, judicial review, a litigious legal culture, fragmentation of state powers, federalism, a powerful Congress but weak parties (primaries and lack of party discipline), the late development of an executive administration, fragmentation (independent agencies) and politicization of the civil service, high external and low internal mobility within the administration, limited discretionary powers of civil servants, a culture of individualism and particularism, a fragmented system of interest associations, dominance of business values but also a distrust of big-business, fear of big-government and low status and legitimacy of the state, and a disinclination for economic intervention, notwithstanding an instrumental vision on law.

British liberalism, reactivism, pragmatism, consensualism and informalism are related to the common law tradition, the absence of judicial review, weak separation of state functions, concentration of political sovereignty in parliament, a first-past-the-post voting system, relatively strong parties, strong majority party governments, high internal and low external mobility within the administration (lifetime employment), the preference for generalists in the civil service, a self-image of civil servants as interest intermediators, a ban on political activity of civil servants, relatively great public trust in the administration, a tradition of secrecy, extensive discretionary authority for civil servants, and a relatively well, albeit somewhat informally organized civil society.

French étatism, activism, paternalism, contempt for interest associations, and informality in state - industry relations are linked to the roman law system, the limited possibilities for legal review of administrative decisions, the weakness of parliament and the concentration of power in the executive, monocratic decisionmaking, a relatively specialist public administration, organization of the civil service in elite corps with their special training systems, corps spirit, exalted self-image, and possibilities for mobility both within and outside the administration, a weakly organized civil society, and a historically problematic relation between church and state.

Dutch corporatism, activism, fragmentation, pragmatism, consensualism and formalism in state - industry relations are related to the roman law tradition, the absence of judicial review, a separation of state functions but concentration of political power in the executive, proportional representation in voting, coalition governments, a central political position of christian democracy, collegiate decisionmaking in politics and administration, a somewhat fragmented public administration, low internal as well as external mobility within the administration, a relatively high status of civil servants, a historical tradition of delegation and privatization of state tasks, and a well-organized and pillarized civil society. Some of these principles date still back to the polity of the Dutch Republic, others were the product of later centralization of political power.

German corporatism, legalism, consensualism and formalism are associated with German legal positivism, judicial and administrative review, federalism and vertical 'Politikverflechtung', strong party discipline, the relative importance of christian democracy, low external and low internal mobility of civil servants, a high status of the state bureaucracy whose structure has been rather formalized, a historically well-organized civil society and a tradition of delegating state tasks.

National regulatory styles are hence solidly embedded in various institutions of state and civil society. These institutions have been the outcome of long term historical processes and often date back to the original phases of state formation in these countries. Given this strong rootedness, these institutions are not easily changed and with them national regulatory styles.

The impact of internationalization

Will economic internationalization be strong enough to force these institutions and regulatory styles to change? To make them converge? Will the pressure from unlimited and unregulated international competition force countries to equalize competitive positions and conditions? Will social dumping force legislation to its lowest common denominator?

It is doubtful whether the danger of social dumping will be really so great. Many aspects go into the make-up of national competitive positions. Corporatist countries like Germany may have relative high costs of wages, social security, and regulatory protection of labour. However, they have also generally more peaceful labour relations, good training systems, a productive workforce, and less strong business cycle fluctuations. Highly regulated corporatist countries score certainly not low in the World Competitiveness Reports of the World Economic Forum. Less regulated, more market oriented countries may compete with lower wages, weaker unions, and less regulatory protections. Hence, economic internationalization perse does not have to

362

reduce such institutional differences. The small European countries like the Netherlands, Sweden, Switzerland and Austria have already for a long time been exposed to international competition. They export between fourty and fifty-five per cent of their GNP. Nevertheless, this exposure has not destroyed their corporatist institutions. On the contrary, it has been argued that these corporatist institutions were necessary, or at least, helpful, in weathering international competition (Katzenstein 1985). It seems hence unlikely that economic internationalization will reduce the diversity of regulatory styles and institutions. The market pressure to equalize will remain limited.

Another question is political unification, as takes place within the EU, and perhaps later also in the GATT or WTO. Will national forms of regulation not come into conflict with EU-measures of regulatory harmonization? Is not the chance of them being invalidated and outlawed substantial? Is this already not taking place? Indeed, European integration is bringing considerable change to many Member States. First of all in institutions. Thus Britain and the Netherlands experience for the first time in history judicial review - from the European Court of Justice. Furthermore, national governments are confronted with a veritable flood of supranational regulations from the European Commission. Already now, seventy per cent of all legislation passed by the Dutch parliament concerns the implementation of EU-directives in national law. In the process of formulating these regulations and directives of the Commission, civil servants of Member States are involved and get to meet their colleagues in Brussels and from other Member States. These intense international contacts will enhance mutual learning and imitation between nations. All these structural changes could indeed affect national regulatory styles. Furthermore, EU-initiatives impinge also directly on national policy preferences. Cartels, so far tolerated by a pragmatic Dutch policy style, are being persecuted by the EU-Executive and Judicial powers. Dutch tolerant drugs policy is coming under attack from neighboring states in the context of the Schengen treaty. Price control as under the Austrian *Sozialpartnerschaft* will no longer be possible. Actually, with the entry of Austria in the European Economic Space in view, the price subcommittee (*Preisunterausschuß*) of the *Paritätische Kommission*, which had to approve price increases for a large number of Austrian products sold on the domestic market, was abolished in 1993 (Schreckeneder 1994). German regulation of vocational training may become perceived as illegitimate limitation of market-entry. The resistance of Belgian unions against incorporation may be incompatible with a European charter for firms and unions, etc.

However, the resistance to the eradication of national forms of regulation will be great, considering how strongly rooted there are in national state-institutions. British resistance to the still very vaguely formulated Social Charter is only a harbinger of greater difficulties to come - and is more than just a Tory hang-up.

Furthermore, the substance of regulations may prove to be easier subject to harmonization than the form and style by - and the networks in - which they are formulated and implemented. Political integration in the EU-suprastate is more likely to produce a convergence of regulations than a convergence of regulatory styles. Countries may agree on standardization and harmonization of substantive regulations and policies. It will be much more difficult to attune political culture and political institutions. Could the very different legal systems of France and Britain ever be integrated? And could British and French politicians and administrators ever agree on the same qualification requirements for civil servants? Free movement of people within the EC does not yet bring exchange of politicians and administrators who could thus infuse each others' ideologies, attitudes and styles across borders, towards a common European style. It is not foreseeable that a German will campaign for office in France - if only because of the cultural and language differences. Neither is it foreseeable that a British administrator will assume a top civil service position in France - if only because of the differences in legal regimes in which they have to be trained, and the differences in qualification requirements.

Although the different nations may be confronted with similar economic and political developments, their different institutions and regulatory styles will cause them to react differently to these common contingencies. This could even produce further divergence, rather than convergence. In the US new issues and interests will enlarge and open up policy networks (Cf. Heclo 1978) and will increase fragmentation further. As the number of alternative channels for influencing public policy increases, interest groups will be even less likely to defer to authoritative decisions and will, within the prevailing litigious legal culture, resort still more to the courts, enhancing adversarialism. In the Netherlands, new issues and interests tend to become gradually integrated in and by the established corporatist networks. External threats to consensualism and corporatism from newcoming outside interests, such as the environmental movement, have been averted by cooptation of the movement-elites - in a long-standing tradition of what one could call repressive tolerance.

Even in the capacity for change there are differences between countries. Thus the extremely open legal, political and administrative institutions of the US seem to be much more susceptible to modification than the more closed British ones. Indeed, US-state institutions have undergone quite significant changes in the 1960s and 1970s in reaction to the emergence of 'public interest' organizations and to their accusations of 'capture' of the administration by particularistic business interests, accusations such groups derived from earlier social-scientific literature (Vogel 1987 and 1989). Furthermore, the erratic political development of France over the last two centuries, with e.g. regular changes in the power balance between the legislature and the executive or in the voting system, does seem to make this country easier prone to institutional change. For one, because quite a few state-institutions are not as solidly embedded in political an popular culture as in countries which experienced a more gradual and legitimate political development, such as Britain and the Netherlands.

Consequences of persistent style differences

These persistent differences in regulatory styles could have significant consequences. Policy networks around rule formulation could form at the EC-level and indeed they have. Those who have studied them observed by the way that the system of interest associations at the EC-level shows much greater likeness to US pluralism than to European corporatism (Schmitter and Streeck 1994). However, policy networks around policy implementation at EC-level will be difficult to imagine, as long as implementation of EC-regulations - whether or not they replace national ones - is left to the national public administrations. And so it will have to be, as central administrators in Brussels cannot possibly implement their own rules all over Europe. They will remain dependent on regional and local civil servants, and these will be imbued with national administrative culture and regulatory styles.

Given the differences in style of implementation, it is likely that central EC-regulations will be implemented differently in various Member States, as long as implementation remains the domain of the Member States. In some countries the administrators will involve interest associations - or even delegate implementation to them - in others they will not or less. In some implementation will be done centrally and through imposition, in others locally, and through negotiations with the clientele, through a process of give and take. As they have each done in their own way so often before. Different styles of implementation may imply also different degrees. Thus the distance between the 'law-in-the-books' and the 'law-in-action' may remain greater in some countries than in others.

Implementation of EC-fisheries policy e.g. has in the Netherlands traditionally been done in a typically corporatist fashion: by involving the statutory fishermens' associations. It turned out recently that this implied much less strict implementation. Dutch fishermen could in practice take much more fish from the North Sea than their quotas allowed.

The Dutch government did not only for years leave the organizations of the field their way, but it has even tacitly tolerated cooperation of these organizations to transgressions of the fish quota policy. ... This passive - and sometimes even active - policy of tolerance has legitimated the ineffective policy enforcement by the fisheries organizations. (Vervaele, Ruimschotel, and Widdershoven 1990: 162).

A scandal over this forced the Dutch minister of agriculture and fisheries to resign by the way. When the government subsequently was forced by the EU to increase its control, it could no longer rely on self-regulation by the industry as this had lost its legitimacy.

Vogel (1992) referred to differences in enforcement of food safety standards.

> National and local governments vary in both their ability and willingness to enforce safety standards for food and beverages. If inspection is not uniform throughout the Community, consumers are likely to be increasingly exposed to hazards from food produced in nations with less effective public controls. ... The EC's 1989 directive on the official control of foodstuffs while emphasizing the need for 'harmonization and approximation of different national food control systems', allowed member states to continue to maintain their own inspection systems. Moreover, the Food Inspection Directive made no attempt to harmonize either the frequency of inspections or the fines to be imposed when a violation is found. As a result, national practices and policies continue to diverge widely; some nations have perfunctory inspection systems, while others have quite comprehensive ones. Their administration also varies significantly. For example, in Britain, food inspection is the responsibility of local authorities and individual inspectors enjoy substantial autonomy. By contrast, Germany has a system of centrally employed inspectors who follow a strict inspection programme. The inspection system of these two nations have no more in common than they had prior to the creation of the EC. ... The Commission has encouraged representatives of national food inspection systems to meet together on a regular basis. But these meetings have accomplished relatively little - in part because of language barriers. (Vogel 1992: 49, 52, 53-4)

Such differences in actual policy implementation may imply that the costs of regulation may not be distributed equally among Member States, creating differences in competitive conditions for their national industries. Differences in styles of implementation under a shared regulatory regime could hence produce new forms of social and economic inequality across nations. Such inequalities in implementation have already been identified by legal scholars (Vervaele 1994). However, they do not seem to be aware that behind such differences may be more than just administrative overload, sloppiness, fraud, opposition, or even sabotage by interests affected. Such implementation differences may have structural roots in national regulatory styles and the institutions behind them.

References

Aberbach, S.D., R.D. Putnam, and B.A. Rockman (1981), *Bureaucrats and Politicians in Western Democracies*, Harvard University Press, Cambridge and London.

Almond, Gabriel A., and Sidney Verba (1963), *The Civic Culture*, Princeton University Press, Princeton.

Ashford, N., and G. Heaton (1982), *Environmental Regulation of the Automobile*, Center for Policy Alternatives, MIT, Cambridge.

Asimov, M. (1983), 'Delegated legislation: The United States and the United Kingdom', *Oxford Journal of Legal Studies*, vol. 3, no. 2.

Atkinson, Michael M., and William D. Coleman (1989), 'Strong states and weak states: Sectoral policy networks in advanced capitalist economies', *British Journal of Political Science*, vol. 19.

Badaracco, Joseph L. (1985), *Loading the Dice. A Five-Country Study of Vinyl Chloride Regulation*, Harvard Business School Press, Cambridge.

Bardach, Eugene, and Robert A. Kagan (1982), *Going by the Book*, Temple University Press, Philadelphia.

Bernstein, Marver H. (1955), *Regulating Business by Independent Commission*, Greenwood Press, Westport, Conn.

Beyme, Klaus von (1990), 'Politikfeldanalyse in der Bundesrepublik Deutschland', in Beyme, Klaus von, and Manfred G. Schmidt (eds), *Politik in der Bundesrepublik Deutschland*, Opladen.

Brickman, Ronald, Sheila Jasanoff, and Thomas Ilgen (1985), *Controlling Chemicals: The Politics of Regulation in Europe and the United States*, Cornell University Press, Ithaca.

Calmfors, L., and J. Driffill (1988), 'Bargaining structure, corporatism and macroeconomic performance', *Economic Policy*, vol. 6.

Cameron, David (1984), 'Social democracy, corporatism, labour quiescence, and the representation of economic interest in advanced capitalist society', in Goldthorpe, John (ed.), *Order and Conflict in Contemporary Capitalism*, Clarendon Press, Oxford.

Chandler, Alfred D. (1980), 'Government versus business: An American phenomenon', in Dunlop, John T. (ed.), *Business and Public Policy*, Harvard University Press, Cambridge.

Chick, Martin (ed.) (1990), *Governments, Industries and Markets: Aspects of Government-Industry Relations in the UK, Japan, West Germany and the USA since 1945*, Edward Elgar, Aldershot.

Conradt, David P. (1989), *The German Polity*, Longman, New York and London.

Crouch, Colin (1986), 'Sharing public space: states and organised interests in Western Europe', in Hall, John A (ed.) *States in History*, Oxford.

Crozier, Michel (1964), *The Bureaucratic Phenomenon*, University of Chicago Press, Chicago.

Czada (1990), 'Brückenköpfe in der Gesellschaft. Der Anteil des Staates an der Organisation ökonomischer und sozialer Interessen', in Hartwich, Hans-Hermann, and Gorttrik Wewer (eds), *Regieren in der Bundesrepublik II*, Leske & Budrich, Opladen.

Damaska, Mirjan R. (1986), *The Faces of Justice and State Authority. A Comparative Approach to the Legal Process*, Yale University Press, New Haven and London.

Derthick, Martha, and Paul J. Quirk (1985), *The Politics of Deregulation*, The Brookings Institution, Washington D.C.

Döhler, Marian (1990), *Gesundheitspolitik nach der 'Wende'. Policy-Netzwerke und ordnungspolitischer Strategiewechsel in Großbritannien, den USA und der Bundesrepublik Deutschland*, Sigma Bohn, Berlin.

Duchene, Francois, and Geoffrey Shepherd (eds) (1987), *Managing Industrial Change in Western Europe*, Pinter, London.

Dunlop, John T. (ed.) (1980), *Business and Public Policy*, Harvard University Press, Cambridge and London.

Dyson, Kenneth (1980), *The State Tradition in Western Europe. A Study of an Idea and Institution*, Oxford.

Dyson, Kenneth (1982), West Germany: The search for a rationalist consensus' in Richardson, Jeremy (ed.), *Policy Styles in Western Europe*, Allen & Unwin, London.

Dyson, Kenneth, and Stephen Wilks (eds) (1983), *Industrial Crisis: A Comparative Study of the State and Industry*, Basil Blackwell, Oxford.

Eddey, Keith (1987), *The English Legal System*, Sweet und Maxwell, London.

Ehrmann, Henry W. (1968, orig. 1961), 'Interest groups and the bureaucracy in western democracies', in Bendix, Reinhard (ed.), *State and Society. A Reader in Comparative Political Sociology*.

Feick, Jürgen, and Werner Jann (1988), 'Nations matter - Vom Eklektizismus zur Integration in der vergleichenden Politikforschung', in Schmidt, Manfred O. (ed.), *Staatstätigkeit*, PVS-Sonderheft, Westdeutscher Verlag, Opladen.

Friedman, Lawrence M. (1985), *Total Justice*, Russell Sage, New York.

Friedman, Lawrence M., and Harry N. Scheiber (eds) (1988), *American Law and the Constitutional Order. Historical Perspectives*, Harvard University Press, Cambridge.

Fritschler, A. Lee, and Bernard H. Ross (1980), *Business Regulation and Government Decision-Making*, Winthrop, Cambridge.

Geldart, William (1991), *Introduction to English Law*, edited by D.C.M. Yardley, Oxford University Press, Oxford and New York.

Hall, Kermit L. (1989), *The Magic Mirror. Law in American History*, Oxford University Press, New York and Oxford.

Hall, Peter A. (1986), *Governing the Economy: the Politics of State Intervention in Britain and France*, Polity Press, Cambridge.

Hancher, Leigh (1990), *Regulating for Competitition: Government, Law and the Pharmaceutical Industry in the United Kingdom and France*, Clarendon Press, Oxford.

Hayward, Jack E.S. (1972), 'State intervention in France: the changing style of government industry relations', *Political Studies*, vol. 20.

Hayward, Jack E.S. (1974), 'National aptitudes for planning in Britain, France and Italy', *Government and Opposition*, vol. 9, no. 4.

Hayward, Jack E.S. (1975), 'Employers' associations and the state in France and Britain', in Warnecke, Steven J., and Ezra N. Suleiman (eds), *Industrial Policies in Western Europe*, Praeger, New York.

Hayward, Jack E.S. (1983), *Governing France: The One and Indivisible Republic*, Norton, New York.

Heclo, Hugh (1978), 'Issue networks and the executive establishment', in King, Alan (ed.), *The New American Political System*, Washington D.C.

Heidenheimer, A.J., H. Heclo, and C.T. Adams (1983), *Comparative Public Policy. The Politics of Social Choice in Europe and America*, London and Basinstoke.

Hennessy, Peter (1990), *Whitehall*, Harper Collins, Glasgow.

Hirst, Paul, and Jonathan Zeitlin (1989), *Reversing Industrial Decline? Industriel Structure and Policy in Britain and Her Competitors*, Berg, Oxford.

Huntington, Samuel P. (1968), 'Political modernization: America versus Europe', in Bendix, Reinhard (ed.), *State and Society. A Reader in Comparative Political Sociology*.

Jann, Werner (1983), *Staatliche Programme und Verwaltungskultur. Die Bekämpfung des Drogenmißbrauchs und der Jugendarbeitslosigkeit in Schweden, Großbritannien und der Bundesrepublik Deutschland im Vergleich*, Westdeutscher Verlag, Opladen.

Kahn-Freund, Otto (1967), 'Legal framework', in Flanders, Allan, and Hugh A. Clegg (eds), *The System of Industrial Relations in Great Britain*, Blackwell, Oxford.

Katzenstein, Peter J. (1985), *Small States in World Markets. Industrial Policy in Europe*, Cornell University Press, Ithaca.

Katzenstein, Peter J. (1987), *Policy and Politics in West Germany. The Growth of a Semisovereign State*, Philadelphia.

Keeler, John (1987), *The Politics of Neocorporatism in France*, Oxford University Press, Oxford.

Kelman, Steven (1981), *Regulating America, Regulating Sweden: A Comparative Study of Occupational Safety and Health Policy*, MIT-Press, Cambridge.

Lehmbruch, Gerhard (1982), 'Neo-corporatism in comparative perspective', in Lehmbruch, Gerhard, and Philippe C. Schmitter (eds), *Patterns of Corporatist Policy-Making*, Sage, London.

Lehmbruch, Gerhard (1984), 'Concertation and the structure of corporatist networks', in Goldthorpe, John (ed.), *Order and Conflict in Contemporary Capitalism*, Clarendon Press, Oxford.

Lehmbruch, Gerhard (1987), 'Administrative Interessenvermittlung', in Adrienne Windhoff-Heritier (ed.), *Verwaltung und ihre Umwelt. Festschrift für Thomas Ellwein*, Westdeutscher Verlag, Opladen.

Lehmbruch, Gerhard (1989), 'Networks of bureaucracies and organized interests: cross-sectoral and cross-national approaches toward an analytical model', paper presented at the Conference 'Government and Organized Interest' of the IPSA Research Committee 'Structure and Organization of Government', Zürich, September 27-30.

Lehner, Franz (1985), 'The political economy of distributive conflict', in Castles, Francis, Franz Lehner, and Manfred Schmidt (eds), *Managing Mixed Economies*, De Gruyter, Berlin and New York.

Lindblom, Charles E. (1959), 'The Science of "Muddling Through"', *Public Administration Review*, vol. 19.

Lundqvist, L. (1980), *The Hare and the Tortoise: Clean Air Policies in the United States and Sweden*, Ann Arbor.

March, James, and Johan Olsen (1989), *Rediscovering Institutions. The Organizational Basis of Politics*, Macmillan, London.

Marcus, Alfred A. (1984), *The Adversary Economy. Business Responses to Changing Government Requirements*, Quorum Books, Westport, Conn.

McConnell, Grant (1966), *Private Power and American Democracy*, Knopf, New York.

Mitnick, Barry (1980), *The Political Economy of Regulation*, Columbia University Press, New York.

Nef, John U. (1962), *Industry and Government in France and England*, Cornell University Press, Ithaca.

Peacock, Alan (1985), *The Regulation Game - How British and West German Companies Bargain with Government*, Oxford.

Peters, B. Guy (1989), *The Politics of Bureaucracy*, Longman, New York and London.

Premfors, R. (1980), *The Politics of Higher Education. France, Sweden, United Kingdom*, Stockholm.

Richardson, J. J., and N. S. J. Watts (1985), 'National policy styles and the environment; Britain and West Germany compared', *WZB-Discussion Paper*, Berlin.

Richardson, Jeremy (ed.) (1982), *Policy Styles in Western Europe*, Allen & Unwin, London.

Richardson, Jeremy, Gunnel Gustafsson, and Grant Jordan (1982), 'The concept of policy style', in Richardson, Jeremy (ed.), *Policy Styles in Western Europe*, Allen & Unwin, London.

Schneider, Volker (1985), 'Corporatist and pluralist patterns of policy-making for chemicals control: A comparison between West Germany and the USA', in Cawson, Alan (ed.), *Organized Interests and the State - Studies in Mesocorporatism*, Sage, London.

Schneider, Volker (1988), *Politiknetzwerke der Chemikalienkontrolle*, Berlin.

Schreckeneder, Bertha (1994), *Die Lohnpolitik des Östenreichische Gewerkschaftsbundes*, Masters Theis of the Wirtschaftsuniversität Vienna.

Solo, Robert A. (1974), *The Political Authority and the Market System*, South-western, Cincinnati.

Streeck, Wolfgang, and Philippe Schmitter (1994), 'From national corporatism to transnational pluralism: organized interests in the Single European Market', in Eichener, Volker, and Helmut Voelzkow (eds), *Europäische Integration und verbandliche Interessenvermittlung*, Metropolis Verlag, Marburg.

Sturm, Roland (1987), 'Verwaltungskultur', in Berg-Schlosser, D., and J. Schissler (eds), *Politische Kultur in Deutschland*, PVS-Sonderheft 18, Westdeutscher Verlag, Opladen.

Süllow, B. (1982), *Korporative Repräsentation der Gewerkschaften. Zur institutionellen Verbandsbeteiligung in öffentlichen Gremien*, Frankfurt an Main.

Vervaele, J.A.E., D. Ruimschotel, and R.J.G.M. Widdershoven (1990), *Rechtshandhaving bij visquotering. Een evaluatieve studie naar rechtshandhaving van nationale en Europese regelgeving*, NISER, Utrecht.

Vervaele, John (1994), *Handen en tanden van het gemeenschapsrecht*, inaugural lecture, Utrecht University.

Vogel, David (1986), *National Styles of Regulation. Environmental Policy in Great Britain and the United States*, Cornell University Press, Ithaca and London.

Vogel, David (1987), 'Government-industry relations in the United States: an overview', in Wilks, Stephen, and Maurice Wright (eds), *Comparative Government-Industry Relations. Western Europe, the United States, and Japan*, Clarendon Press, Oxford.

371

Vogel, David (1989), *Fluctuating Fortunes. The Political Power of Business in America*, Basic Books, New York.

Vogel, David (1992), 'Protective regulation and protectionism in the European Community: THe creation of a Common Market for food and beverages', *Minda da Ginzburg Center for European Studies, Harvard University Working Paper*, no. 37, Cambridge.

Waarden, Frans van (1994), 'Government intervention in industrial relations', in Ruijsseveldt, Joris van, and Jacques van Hoof (eds), *Comnparative Industrial and Employment Relations*, Sage, London.

Wijngaart, G.F. van de (1991), *Competing Perspectives on Drug Use: the Dutch Experience*, Swets & Zeitlinger, Amsterdam.

Wilensky, Harold (1976), *The New Corporatism. Centralization and the Welfare State*, London.

Wilks, Stephen, and Maurice Wright (eds) (1987), *Comparative Government-Iindustry Relations. Western Europe, the United States, and Japan*, Clarendon Press, Oxford.

Wilson, Graham K. (1985a), *Business and Politics. A Comparative Introduction*, Macmillan, Houndsmill and London.

Wilson, Graham K. (1985b), *The Politics of Safety and Health*, Clarendon Press, Oxford.

Wilson, James Q. (1973), *Political Organizations*, Basic Books, New York.

Wilson, James Q. (ed.) (1980), *The Politics of Regulation*, Basic Books, New York.

Wilson, James Q. (1989), *Bureaucracy. What Government Agencies do and why they do it*, Basic Books, New York.

Windhoff-Héritier, Adrienne (1989), *Verwaltungen im Widerstreit mit Klientelinteressen*, Deutscher Universitäts Verlag, Opladen.

Wright, Maurice (1991), 'The comparative analysis of industrial policies: policy networks and sectoral governance structures in Britain and France', *Staatswissenschaften und Staatspraxis*, vol. 4.

Zysman, John (1983), *Government, Markets and Growth: Financial Systems and the Politics of Industrial Change*, Martin Robertson, Oxford.

About the authors

Wieger E. Bakker (1958) is Assistant Professor in Public Policy at the Centre for Policy and Management of Utrecht University. He studied sociology and public administration science in Utrecht. His research focusses on the transformation of welfare state structures and the role of public policy, especially with respect to education. He has published on policy instruments and intervention strategies in public policy.

Christian Bellak (1964) is Lecturer of Economics at the University of Economics and Business Administration, Vienna. He was recently Visiting Research Fellow at the Helsinki School of Economics and the University of Reading (UK). Main research interests are foreign direct investment and multinational enterprises, industrial Policy and especially small nations' industrial Policies. He published articles in diverse international books and journals. Recently he published: 'Foreign direct investment from small states and integration - A survey of theory and empirical evidence from Austria', in Seev Hirsch and Lars Oxelheim (eds) (1994), *Outsiders' Response to the Unification of the European Community*, Copenhagen, 'FDI - Fairly Disappointing Indicator', in *Transnational Corporations*, Summer (1994).

Volker Eichener (1959) is manager of the InWIS-Institute for Housing, Real Estate, Urban and Regional Development at the Ruhr University, Bochum. He is a social scientist who spent five years from 1989 - 1993 as a research fellow at the special research centre 'New Information Technologies and Flexible Work Systems' in Bochum. He published among others *Social Dumping or Innovative Regulation?*, EUI Working Paper, Florence (1993) and (as co-editor with Helmut Voelzkow) *Europäische Integration und verbandliche Regulierung*, Metropolis, Marburg (1994).

Godfried Engbersen (1956) is Professor of Welfare States and Social Inequality at the Department of General Social Science at the University of Utrecht, the Netherlands. He studied sociology at the University of Leyden and was a succesful cabaretier. He did empirical studies on political journalism, poverty, social inequality, social welfare agencies, migration and illegal aliens in the Netherlands and has advised the Dutch government on a reorganization of social welfare agencies. He published several books, among others *Moderne armoede. Overleven op het sociale minimum* (Modern poverty. Surviving on Society's Minimum) (1987), *Publieke Bijstandsgeheimen* (public welfare secrets) (1991), and (with others) *Cultures of Unemployment. A Comparative Look on Long-term Unemployment and Urban Poverty* (1993).

Anton C. Hemerijck (1958) is Assistant Professor in Public Administration at the Erasmus University in Rotterdam. He studied economics at Tilburg University and political science at the University of Oxford and Massachusetts Institute of Technology. At Oxford he wrote his dissertation on *The Historical Contingencies of Dutch coporatism* (1993). His research interests are comparative public policy and political economy.

Adrienne Héritier is Professor of Political Science at the University of Bielefeld, Germany, and is presently also working at the Max Planck Institute for Societal Research in Cologne. For many years she was the editor of the German political science journal *Politisches Vierteljahresheft*. Her main research fields are policy analysis and European policymaking. Recently, she received the German Leibniz price for her work on comparative analysis of European environmental policy. Her publications include *Politikfeldanalyse* (1987), (with others) *Verwaltungen im Widerstreit von Klientelinteressen. Arbeitsschutz im internationalen Vergleich* (1989), (as co-editor) *Political Choice* (1990), and (with others) *Veränderung von Staatlichkeit* (1994).

R. Daniel Kelemen (1970) is a Ph.D. student in the Department of Political Science at Stanford University. His current research focusses on policy making in the European Union. His special interests are comparative politics, especially environmental politics, and international relations.

Berndt K. Keller (1946) is Professor of Public Administration at the University of Konstanz, Germany. He received his Ph.D. in 1973 and wrote his habilitation in 1981. He specialized on Social Policy and Labour Relations. His recent boooks are *Einführung in die Arbeitspolitik. Arbeitsbeziehungen und Arbeitsmarkt in sozialwissenschaftlicher Perspektive*, 3rd ed., Oldenbourg, Munic and Vienna (1993), and *Arbeitspolitik des öffentlichen Sektors*, Nomos, Baden-Baden (1993).

Edith Kitzmantel (1944) is Adjunct Director-General for the Budget at the European Commission and formerly Deputy-General in the Austrian Ministry of Finance. She holds a Ph.D. from the Vienna University of Economics and a post-graduate diploma from the Institute for Advanced Studies, Vienna. She has worked on a broad range of international and domestic policy issues, including fiscal and monetary policies, tax policy and industrial policy. Her professional career includes work as a staff member at the International Monetary Fund (3 years) and as a visiting scholar at Brookings Institution. Since 1989 she has mostly worked on issues related to Austria's entry into the EEA and EU respectively.

Erhard Moser (1958) holds a degree of economics from the University of Linz, Austria. Since 1983 he worked in the Austrian Ministry of Finance in the field of general economic policy and tax policy. In 1989 he spent a research year at the International Monetary Fund in Washington, D.C. Since 1993 he is a deputy of Austria's permanent representation in Brussels.

Hugh Mosley received his Ph.D. in political science from Duke University. He is a senior research fellow in the Labor Market and Employment Research Unit at the Science Centre Berlin (Wissenschaftszentrum Berlin), where he has works since 1986. His current research is on comparative labor market policies, especially labor market regulation and working time issues, and on European integration. He is the author of *The Arms Race: Economic and Social Consequences* (1985) and of numerous articles and reports on labor market and social policy topics.

Saskia Sassen is Professor of Urban Planning at the School of Public and International Affairs of Columbia University. She wrote *The Mobility of Labor and Capital*, Cambridge University Press (1988), *The Global City: New York, London, Tokyo*, Princeton University Press, Princeton (1991), and *Cities in a World Economy*, Sage Publications, Pine Forge, California (1994). A new book *Immigrants and Refugees: A European Dilemma?* will be published in 1995 with Fischer Verlag in Frankfurt. She has just received a grant from the Twentieth Century Fund to write a book about immigration policy in a world economy and has begun a new five year project on 'Governance and Accountability in a World Economy'.

Claus Thomasberger (1952), is Professor of Economics at the FHTW Berlin. He holds a diploma degree in sociology and in economics, and a Ph.D. from the University of Bremen. His habilitation at the Free University of Berlin was published by Mohr, Tübingen under the title *Europäische Währungsintegration und globale Währungskonkurrenz* in 1993. He was lecturer at the Università di Pavi (Italy), visiting professor at the University of Tennessee, Knoxville, at the Duke University Kurham/Berlin, and was professor at the University of Osnabrück. His main research interests are monetary economic theory, economic policy, socioeconomics and international exchange-rate regimes. He wrote several books, published in various journals and books and edited recently a book on the institutions of European monetary policy, *Europäische Geldpolitik zwischen Marktzwängen und neuen institutionellen Regelungen*, Metropolis, Marburg (1994).

Brigitte Unger (1955) is Assistant Professor of Economics at the University of Economics and Business Administration in Vienna (Austria). A Joseph Schumpeter, Erwin Schroedinger and Dr. Maria Schaumayer fellowship allowed her consecutively to spend research years at Harvard University and at Stanford University. She works interdisciplinarily with political scientists and sociologists. She specialized in institutional economics, public finance, and open macroeconomics. Among her latest publications are (with Franz Traxler) 'Governance, economic restructuring, and international competitiveness' in the *Journal of Economic Issues*, no 1, March (1994). She coedited (with Karl Althaler, Egon Matzner and Manfred Prisching) *Sozioökonomische Forschungsansätze*, Metropolis, Marburg (1995). At the moment she writes her habilitation book on 'how much room for manoeuvre is left for economic policymaking'.

Frans van Waarden (1950) is Professor of Organization and Public Policy at Utrecht University in the Netherlands. He studied sociology, history and political science at the Universities of Toronto and Leyden. Before, he taught at Leyden and Konstanz. He has published on labour relations, codetermination, history of technology, textile industry, industrial policy, collective action, business' associations, corporatism and state-industry relations. His books include (as co-author) *Fabriekslevens* (1987), *Het geheim van Twente* (1987), *Organisatiemacht van belangenverenigingen* (1989), (as co-editor) *Organizing Business for War. Industrial Policy and Corporatism during the Second World War* (1991), and (as co-author) *Cultures of Unemployment. A Comparative Look on Long-term Unemployment and Urban Poverty* (1993). He is presently working on a comparative history of government-industry relations, regulatory styles and state formation in various countries.